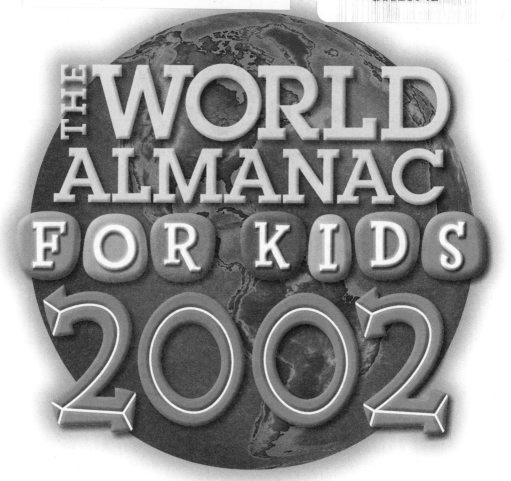

WORLD ALMANAC BOOKS
A Division of World Almanac Education Group, Inc.
A WRC Media Company

EDITOR: Elaine Israel

CURRICULUM CONSULTANT:
Jean Craven, Director of Instructional Support, Albuquerque, NM, Public Schools

CONTRIBUTORS: Lisa Feder-Feitel, Matt Friedlander, Monica M. Gallen, Inez Glucksman,
Jane Havsy, Raymond Hill, Dr. Tom Hull, Lelia Mander, Randi Metsch-Ampel,
Allen Mogol, Sean Price, Terry Simon, Curtis Slepian, Oliver Trager
Consultants: Lee T. Shapiro, Ph.D. (Astronomy), Bernadette Fiscina, M.D. (Health)

KID CONTRIBUTORS: Heidi Alder, Will Barnes, Ashley Bruggeman,
Gabriela Flores, Shelbi Jentz, Megan Ji, Sabrina Karim,
Elana Metsch-Ampel, Daniel Morizono, Bill Okoji, Greg Saffles, Brooke Wilczynski

Thanks to all the kids who wrote to us with their great ideas!

DESIGN: Bill SMITH STUDIO
Creative Director: Jay Jaffe   **Design:** Eric Hoffsten, James Liebman
Photo Research: Christie Silver   **Illustration Buying:** Paula Radding

WORLD ALMANAC BOOKS

Vice President–
Sales and Marketing
James R. Keenley

**Editorial
Director**
William McGeveran Jr.

Managing
Editor
Lori P. Wiesenfeld

Editorial Staff: Kevin Seabrooke, David M. Faris, Mette Bahde, Associate Editors;
Lloyd Sabin, Desktop Publishing Associate

WORLD ALMANAC EDUCATION GROUP
Chief Executive Officer, WRC Media Inc.: Martin E. Kenney Jr.
President: Alfred De Seta
Publisher: Ken Park
Desktop Production Manager: Elizabeth J. Lazzara
Director–Purchasing and Production/Photo Research: Edward A. Thomas
Director of Indexing Services: Marjorie B. Bank; **Index Editor:** Walter Kronenberg
Marketing Coordinator: Sarah De Vos

235 Wellesley Street
Weston, MA 02493

CONTENTS

Faces & Places
9-29

Animals
30-42

Art
43-45

Books
46-51

Buildings & Bridges
52-53

Calendars & Time
54-55

4

Signs & Symbols
200-203

Space
204-213

Sports
214-229

Transportation
230-233

Travel
234-237

United Nations
238-239

Faces & Places

BINARY STARS

Drew BARRYMORE & Tom GREEN

Are they or aren't they married? That question about movie stars Drew and Tom had their fans guessing in 2001.

Freddie PRINZE JR. & Sarah Michelle GELLAR

He may be headed for movie superstardom. Her TV series, BUFFY THE VAMPIRE SLAYER, was headed for a new network. But Freddie and Sarah Michelle had one direction in common. They were engaged and headed for the altar.

Julia ROBERTS & Benjamin BRATT

Julia Roberts, winner of the Oscar for best actress in 2001, flashes her famous smile as she attends a movie premiere with her boyfriend, actor Benjamin Bratt.

11

Oh So Popular

Destiny's CHILD

This girl group released SURVIVOR in 2001 and headlined MTV's TRL tour. Lead singer Beyoncé, 19 years old when the album hit the stores, cowrote almost all of its tracks.

From left: Kelly Rowland, Beyoncé Knowles, and Michelle Williams.

O-TOWN

Reality TV shows have been hot. One of the more unusual was MAKING THE BAND. It followed the formation of a boy band, O-Town.

Clockwise from bottom left: Ashley Parker Angel, Erik Michael Estrada, Jacob Underwood, Trevor Penick, and Dan Miller.

Britney SPEARS

Just in time for Mother's Day 2001, the nation's top pop star and her mom, Lynne Spears, wrote a book together. A MOTHER'S GIFT was published for teenage readers. Britney doesn't plan to quit her day job, though. In fact, she's writing some of the songs she'll sing on her next CD.

TV TERRIFIC

Steve IRWIN

Want to invite a slimy, scaly creature into your home? Just watch THE CROCODILE HUNTER and its human star, Steve Irwin. Here, Steve, who's from Australia, and his American wife, Terri, admire one of their pals, a nine-foot-long female alligator, at Irwin's "Australia Zoo."

Amanda BYNES

Amanda, the star of ALL THAT and THE AMANDA SHOW, won Nickelodeon's Kids' Choice Award as favorite TV actress in 2000. In her first movie, she plays costar Frankie Muniz's best friend.

Carson DALY

While attending college, Carson thought about becoming a priest. Instead, the native of Santa Monica, CA, became a radio DJ. Now he's the host of MTV LIVE.

15

TEEN POWER

Olsen twins

Teens Mary-Kate (left) and Ashley have their own Web site, magazine, books, videos, fashion dolls, TV series, and movies. They sing, too—on sing-along CDs and a Christmas album, MARY-KATE AND ASHLEY'S COOL YULE.

Frankie MUNIZ

MALCOLM IN THE MIDDLE is a series about a family that's more true-to-life than most on TV. Frankie Muniz's character, Malcolm, may be a genius, but he has problems like most real kids—and his parents aren't perfect either!

Billy GILMAN

Billy's first album ONE VOICE won him a Grammy nomination just before turning 13. Selling more than one million albums around the world hasn't changed him. He still likes to play baseball with his brother back home in Rhode Island.

IN THE MONEY

Tiger WOODS

Tiger is on a roll! He won three Majors in a row in 2000 (U.S. Open, British Open, PGA Championship). In April 2001, he won the Masters championship–his fourth Major in a row. No golfer ever did that before.

Derek JETER & Alex RODRIGUEZ

These two friends have more in common than playing shortstop (Derek for the NY Yankees, Alex for the Texas Rangers). In December 2000, Alex signed the largest sports contract in history. In February 2001, Derek signed the second largest. Derek's only 26 and already has four World Series championship rings! (This photo was taken in 2000, when Alex played for Seattle.)

Venus & Serena WILLIAMS

Venus (right) and Serena are great players alone (as of May 2001, they were ranked #2 and #7 in the world) or together—they won the 2001 Australian Open doubles title. In December 2000, Venus signed a $40 million endorsement contract with Reebok, the biggest such deal ever for a woman.

TOP OF THEIR GAMES

"ICHIRO"

Ichiro Suzuki was such a huge star in Japan that he was known by his first name alone. But most of America never heard of him until he started playing for the Seattle Mariners in 2001. At the end of May, Seattle had the best record in baseball, and Ichiro led the Majors in hits and stolen bases. He's the only player in the Majors with his first name on the back of his jersey!

Mia HAMM & Julie FOUDY

They're having a ball! Mia Hamm (left) of the Washington Freedom and Julie Foudy of the San Diego Spirit were all ready for the first season of the Women's United Soccer Association (WUSA).

Marshall FAULK

Though his team didn't repeat as Super Bowl champs, the St. Louis Rams' Marshall Faulk had a super season. He scored a record 26 touchdowns in 2000 and was named MVP of the NFL and AP Offensive Player of the Year.

Tony HAWK

On a skateboard, this high-flying legend lives up to his name. He judges and takes part in competitions, has written an autobiography, has his own video game, and owns several companies. His biggest wish is that more people would respect skateboarding as a sport.

21

NEWS MAKERS

The BUSH Family

At the 2001 inauguration, Jenna Bush looks on as her dad George W. Bush takes the presidential oath of office on a Bible held by her mom, Laura. Barbara, Jenna's twin, also attended the historic ceremony.

Hillary RODHAM CLINTON

As the first lady of the U.S., she traveled the world. Now she is Senator Clinton, Democrat, of New York. In her new role, she deals with issues that affect New Yorkers and all Americans, such as protecting the environment and improving education.

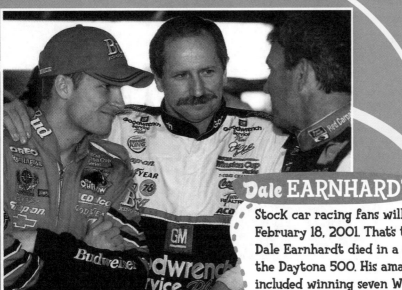

Dale EARNHARDT

Stock car racing fans will never forget February 18, 2001. That's the day driver Dale Earnhardt died in a crash during the Daytona 500. His amazing career included winning seven Winston Cup championships and being voted NASCAR's All-Time Greatest Driver. Earnhardt (center) is shown with his son Dale Earnhardt Jr. (left) and Dale Jarrett at the Daytona in 2000.

Spy Plane CREW

Suppose you're on a U.S. Navy plane that's spying on China. The plane collides with a Chinese jet, but lands on an island in the South China Sea. The Chinese hold you and the 23 other crew members for 11 days. That's what happened to Petty Officer Josef Edmunds, shown arriving back in the U.S. in April 2001, to a big welcome.

23

"B"-YOND COMPARE

George THAMPY

What would it be like to win the National Spelling Bee and come in second in the National Geographic Bee–in the same year? George of Maryland Heights, MO, did that in 2000 when he was 12 years old. One of seven children, George is home-schooled by his parents. (For more on both bees, see page 186.)

The BEATLES

On February 7, 1964, the Beatles arrived for their first appearance in the U.S. Who would have guessed that they'd have a best-selling album four decades later? BEATLES 1, a compilation of 27 hits, was released in November 2000.

From left: John Lennon, Paul McCartney, Ringo Starr, and George Harrison.

ANNIVERSARIES

IN 2002

50 YEARS AGO—1952

► Bicycle maker Schwinn introduced its top-of-the-line model, with whitewall tires, a battery-powered headlight, and tasseled handlebars.
► The Boeing YB-52 bomber, with eight engines and a 185-foot wingspan, made its first flight.
► Elizabeth II became queen of England after her father, George VI, died.
► World War II General Dwight D. Eisenhower was elected president of the United States. ►

► The United States set off the first hydrogen bomb (H bomb) at a test on a Pacific island.
► The classic children's story *Charlotte's Web*, by E. B. White, was published.
► *Mad* comic books were introduced. They eventually led to *Mad* magazine.

100 YEARS AGO—1902

► A toy store owner, Morris Michtom, put a stuffed bear in his window next to a cartoon of President Theodore Roosevelt refusing to shoot a bear. And that's how the Teddy bear was born.
► J.C. Penney announced plans to build nationwide branches of his store, known as "chain stores."
► Joseph Horn and Frank Hardart opened the first "automat" in Philadelphia. In it, diners chose food by dropping coins into slots next to glass-fronted little doors.
► Helen Keller's *The Story of My Life*, recalling her struggle to overcome being both blind and deaf, became a best-seller.
► Beatrix Potter published the *Peter Rabbit* children's stories. ►
► Sir Arthur Conan Doyle's famous story *The Hound of the Baskervilles* was published.

IN 2003

50 YEARS AGO—1953

► More than 75 million people viewed the first U.S. inauguration broadcast on TV, as Dwight D. Eisenhower was sworn in as the 34th president.
► The New York Yankees won the World Series for a record-breaking fifth straight time. They beat the Brooklyn Dodgers, four games to two.
► George Marshall earned the Nobel Peace Prize for the Marshall Plan, providing vital economic aid to war-torn Europe.
► Reaching a speed of more than 760 mph as she flew her Sabre jet, Jacqueline Cochran became the first woman to fly a plane faster than the speed of sound.
► C.A. Swanson & Sons created the first TV dinner. Sold for 98 cents, it was a frozen meal served on an aluminum tray and reheated in the oven. ►

100 YEARS AGO—1903

► Henry Ford sold his first Model A automobile for $850.
► In the first World Series, the Boston Pilgrims upset the Pittsburgh Pirates, five games to three.
► *The Wizard of Oz* opened at the Majestic Theater on Broadway in New York City.
► The United States recognized the independence of Panama, partly to get permission to build the Panama Canal.
► President Theodore Roosevelt used the new Pacific communications cable to send the first message around the world—to himself.
► *Rebecca of Sunnybrook Farm*, by Kate Douglas Wiggin, was published.
► Jack London, a former sailor, gold miner, and hobo, struck gold as a novelist with his latest adventure novel, *The Call of the Wild*.
► Orville Wright took off on a 12-second, 120-foot flight at Kitty Hawk, North Carolina, making the first successful airplane flight in history. ▼

A YEAR OF BIRTHDAYS

Which famous person has the same birthday you do? Who shares birthdays with your friends and classmates? The year of birth is given after each name.

JANUARY

1 Paul Revere, *patriot*, 1735
2 Cuba Gooding Jr., *actor*, 1968
3 Mel Gibson, *actor*, 1956
4 Louis Braille, *inventor*, 1809
5 Warrick Dunn, *football player*, 1975
6 Joey Lauren Adams, *actress*, 1971
7 Katie Couric, *TV personality*, 1957
8 Elvis Presley, *singer*, 1935
9 Richard Nixon, *37th president*, 1913
10 George Foreman, *boxer*, 1949
11 Alexander Hamilton, *statesman*, 1755
12 John Hancock, *statesman*, 1737
13 Julia Louis-Dreyfus, *actress*, 1961
14 L.L. Cool J, *rapper*, 1968
15 Rev. Martin Luther King Jr., *civil rights leader*, 1929
16 Sade, *singer*, 1959
17 Jim Carrey, *actor*, 1962
18 Kevin Costner, *actor*, 1955
19 Dolly Parton, *singer*, 1946
20 Edwin "Buzz" Aldrin, *astronaut*, 1930
21 Geena Davis, *actress*, 1957
22 Beverly Mitchell, *actress*, 1981
23 Tiffani-Amber Thiessen, *actress*, 1974
24 Mary Lou Retton, *gymnast*, 1968
25 Virginia Woolf, *writer*, 1882
26 Wayne Gretzky, *hockey player*, 1961
27 Wolfgang Amadeus Mozart, *composer*, 1756
28 Elijah Wood, *actor*, 1981
29 Oprah Winfrey, *TV personality*, 1954
30 Franklin D. Roosevelt, *32nd president*, 1882
31 Justin Timberlake, *singer*, 1981

FEBRUARY

1 Langston Hughes, *poet*, 1901
2 Christie Brinkley, *model*, 1954
3 Norman Rockwell, *artist*, 1894
4 Rosa Parks, *civil rights activist*, 1913
5 Jennifer Jason Leigh, *actress*, 1952
6 Babe Ruth, *baseball player*, 1895
7 Laura Ingalls Wilder, *author*, 1867
8 Alonzo Mourning, *basketball player*, 1970
9 Joe Pesci, *actor*, 1943
10 Greg Norman, *golfer*, 1955
11 Sheryl Crow, *singer*, 1962
12 Abraham Lincoln, *16th president*, 1809
13 Chuck Yeager, *pilot*, 1923
14 Gregory Hines, *dancer*, 1948
15 Matt Groening, *cartoonist*, 1954
16 Jerome Bettis, *football player*, 1972
17 Michael Jordan, *basketball player*, 1963
18 John Travolta, *actor*, 1954
19 Seal, *singer*, 1963
20 Brian Littrell, *singer*, 1975
21 Jennifer Love Hewitt, *actress*, 1979
22 Drew Barrymore, *actress*, 1975
23 Julio Iglesias, *singer*, 1943
24 Joe Lieberman, *U.S. senator*, 1942
25 Tea Leoni, *actress*, 1966
26 Erykah Badu, *singer*, 1971
27 Chelsea Clinton, *President Clinton's daughter*, 1980
28 Mario Andretti, *auto racer*, 1940
29 Antonio Sabato Jr., *actor*, 1972

Babe Ruth

MARCH

1 Ron Howard, *director*, 1954
2 Jon Bon Jovi, *singer*, 1962
3 Jackie Joyner-Kersee, *Olympic champion*, 1962
4 Patricia Heaton, *actress*, 1959
5 Jake Lloyd, *actor*, 1989
6 Shaquille O'Neal, *basketball player*, 1972
7 Gary Sinise, *actor*, 1955
8 Freddie Prinze Jr., *actor*, 1976
9 Bobby Fischer, *chess champion*, 1943
10 Jasmine Guy, *actress*, 1964
11 Thora Birch, *actress*, 1982
12 James Taylor, *musician*, 1948
13 William H. Macy, *actor*, 1950
14 Albert Einstein, *scientist*, 1879
15 Andrew Jackson, *7th president*, 1767
16 James Madison, *4th president*, 1751
17 Rob Lowe, *actor*, 1964
18 Queen Latifah, *rapper/actress*, 1970
19 Bruce Willis, *actor*, 1955
20 Fred "Mr. Rogers" Rogers, *TV personality*, 1928
21 Rosie O'Donnell, *TV personality*, 1962
22 Reese Witherspoon, *actress*, 1976
23 Keri Russell, *actress*, 1976
24 Peyton Manning, *football player*, 1976
25 Sarah Jessica Parker, *actress*, 1965
26 Steven Tyler, *singer*, 1948
27 Mariah Carey, *singer*, 1970
28 Julia Stiles, *actress*, 1981
29 Jennifer Capriati, *tennis player*, 1976
30 Celine Dion, *singer*, 1968
31 Ewan McGregor, *actor*, 1971

Albert Einstein

APRIL

1 Debbie Reynolds, *actress*, 1932
2 Hans Christian Andersen, *author*, 1805
3 Eddie Murphy, *actor*, 1961
4 Maya Angelou, *poet*, 1928
5 Colin Powell, *secretary of state*, 1937
6 Paul Rudd, *actor*, 1969
7 Russell Crowe, *actor*, 1954
8 Kofi Annan, *UN secretary general*, 1938
9 Juliette Binoche, *actress*, 1964
10 Haley Joel Osment, *actor*, 1988
11 Jennifer Esposito, *actress*, 1973
12 Claire Danes, *actress*, 1979
13 Rick Schroder, *actor*, 1970
14 Sarah Michelle Gellar, *actress*, 1977
15 Emma Thompson, *actress*, 1959
16 Kareem Abdul-Jabbar, *basketball player*, 1947
17 Lela Rochon, *actress*, 1966
18 Melissa Joan Hart, *actress*, 1976
19 Ashley Judd, *actress*, 1968
20 Carmen Electra, *actress*, 1973
21 Queen Elizabeth II of Great Britain, 1926
22 Jack Nicholson, *actor*, 1936
23 William Shakespeare, *playwright*, 1564
24 Barbra Streisand, *singer*, 1942
25 Tim Duncan, *basketball player*, 1976
26 I. M. Pei, *architect*, 1917
27 Ulysses S. Grant, *18th president*, 1822
28 Jay Leno, *TV personality*, 1950
29 Andre Agassi, *tennis player*, 1970
30 Kirsten Dunst, *actress*, 1982

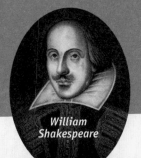

William Shakespeare

MAY

1 Tim McGraw, *musician*, 1967
2 Christine Baranski, *actress*, 1952
3 Jewel (Kilcher), *singer*, 1974
4 Lance Bass, *singer*, 1979
5 Nellie Bly, *journalist*, 1867
6 George Clooney, *actor*, 1961
7 Johannes Brahms, *composer*, 1833
8 Enrique Iglesias, *singer*, 1975
9 Billy Joel, *songwriter*, 1949
10 Bono, *singer*, 1960
11 Natasha Richardson, *actress*, 1963
12 MacKenzie Astin, *actor*, 1973
13 Harvey Keitel, *actor*, 1939
14 George Lucas, *filmmaker*, 1944
15 Madeleine Albright, *former secretary of state*, 1937
16 Pierce Brosnan, *actor*, 1953
17 Mia Hamm, *soccer player*, 1972
18 Yun-Fat Chow, *actor*, 1955
19 Pete Townshend, *musician*, 1945
20 Cher, *singer*, 1946
21 Fairuza Balk, *actress*, 1974
22 Naomi Campbell, *model*, 1970
23 Drew Carey, *actor*, 1958
24 Bob Dylan, *songwriter*, 1941
25 Mike Myers, *actor*, 1963
26 Lenny Kravitz, *musician*, 1964
27 Joseph Fiennes, *actor*, 1970
28 Jim Thorpe, *Olympic champion*, 1888
29 John F. Kennedy, *35th president*, 1917
30 Lisa Kudrow, *actress*, 1963
31 Brooke Shields, *actress*, 1965

John F. Kennedy

JUNE

1 Morgan Freeman, *actor*, 1937
2 Dana Carvey, *comedian*, 1955
3 Curtis Mayfield, *songwriter*, 1942
4 Angelina Jolie, *actress*, 1975
5 Mark Wahlberg, *actor*, 1971
6 Dalai Lama, *Tibetan spiritual leader*, 1935
7 Liam Neeson, *actor*, 1952
8 Keenen Ivory Wynans, *actor*, 1958
9 Natalie Portman, *actress*, 1981
10 Tara Lipinski, *Olympic champion*, 1982
11 Jacques Cousteau, *undersea explorer*, 1910
12 George H. W. Bush, *41st president*, 1924
13 Ashley and Mary-Kate Olsen, *actresses*, 1986
14 Steffi Graf, *tennis player*, 1969
15 Courteney Cox-Arquette, *actress*, 1964
16 Yasmine Bleeth, *actress*, 1968
17 Venus Williams, *tennis player*, 1980
18 Paul McCartney, *musician*, 1942
19 Paula Abdul, *musician*, 1963
20 John Goodman, *actor*, 1952
21 Prince William of Great Britain, 1982
22 Meryl Streep, *actress*, 1949
23 Kurt Warner, *football player*, 1971
24 Mick Fleetwood, *musician*, 1944
25 Chris Isaak, *songwriter*, 1956
26 Derek Jeter, *baseball player*, 1974
27 Tobey Maguire, *actor*, 1975
28 John Elway, *football player*, 1960
29 Theo Fleury, *hockey player*, 1968
30 Vincent D'Onofrio, *actor*, 1959

Venus Williams

JULY

1 Liv Tyler, *actress*, 1977
2 Richard Petty, *auto racer*, 1937
3 Tom Cruise, *actor*, 1962
4 Neil Simon, *playwright*, 1927
5 P. T. Barnum, *circus founder*, 1810
6 George W. Bush, *43rd president*, 1946
7 Michelle Kwan, *figure skater*, 1980
8 Kevin Bacon, *actor*, 1958
9 Tom Hanks, *actor*, 1956
10 Jessica Simpson, *singer*, 1980
11 E. B. White, *author*, 1899
12 Bill Cosby, *comedian*, 1937
13 Harrison Ford, *actor*, 1942
14 Robin Ventura, *baseball player*, 1967
15 Jesse Ventura, *governor/wrestler*, 1951
16 Barry Sanders, *football player*, 1968
17 David Hasselhoff, *actor*, 1952
18 Nelson Mandela, *anti-apartheid leader*, 1918
19 Anthony Edwards, *actor*, 1962
20 Carlos Santana, *musician*, 1947
21 Robin Williams, *actor*, 1952
22 David Spade, *actor*, 1965
23 Nomar Garciaparra, *baseball player*, 1973
24 Jennifer Lopez, *singer/actress*, 1970
25 Matt LeBlanc, *actor* 1967
26 Sandra Bullock, *actress*, 1964
27 Alex Rodriguez, *baseball player*, 1975
28 Beatrix Potter, *author*, 1866
29 Peter Jennings, *TV anchor*, 1938
30 Arnold Schwarzenegger, *actor*, 1947
31 J. K. Rowling, *author*, 1966

Nelson Mandela

AUGUST

1 Edgerrin James, *football player*, 1978
2 Edward Furlong, *actor*, 1977
3 Martha Stewart, *TV personality*, 1941
4 Jeff Gordon, *auto racer*, 1971
5 Patrick Ewing, *basketball player*, 1962
6 David Robinson, *basketball player*, 1965
7 David Duchovny, *actor*, 1960
8 Joshua "JC" Chasez, *singer*, 1976
9 Whitney Houston, *singer*, 1963
10 Antonio Banderas, *actor*, 1960
11 Hulk Hogan, *wrestler*, 1953
12 Pete Sampras, *tennis player*, 1971
13 Fidel Castro, *president of Cuba*, 1927
14 Magic Johnson, *basketball player*, 1959
15 Ben Affleck, *actor*, 1972
16 James Cameron, *director*, 1954
17 Davy Crockett, *frontiersman*, 1786
18 Robert Redford, *actor/director*, 1937
19 Matthew Perry, *actor*, 1969
20 Al Roker, *weatherman*, 1954
21 Alicia Witt, *actress*, 1975
22 Howie Dorough, *singer*, 1973
23 Kobe Bryant, *basketball player*, 1978
24 Reggie Miller, *basketball player*, 1965
25 Regis Philbin, *TV personality*, 1934
26 Macaulay Culkin, *actor*, 1980
27 Lyndon Johnson, *36th president*, 1908
28 Shania Twain, *singer*, 1965
29 Michael Jackson, *singer*, 1958
30 Cameron Diaz, *actress*, 1972
31 Hideo Nomo, *baseball player*, 1968

SEPTEMBER

1 Gloria Estefan, *singer*, 1957
2 Keanu Reeves, *actor*, 1964
3 Charlie Sheen, *actor*, 1965
4 Mike Piazza, *baseball player*, 1968
5 Jesse James, *outlaw*, 1847
6 Rosie Perez, *actress*, 1964
7 Devon Sawa, *actor*, 1978
8 Henry Thomas, *actor*, 1971
9 Macy Gray, *singer*, 1970
10 Ryan Phillippe, *actor*, 1975
11 Harry Connick Jr., *musician*, 1967
12 Joe Pantoliano, *actor*, 1954
13 Michael Johnson, *Olympic champion*, 1967
14 Sam Neill, *actor* 1947
15 Prince Harry of Great Britain, 1984
16 B. B. King, *blues musician*, 1924
17 David Souter, *Supreme Court justice*, 1939
18 Jada Pinkett Smith, *actress*, 1971
19 Trisha Yearwood, *singer*, 1964
20 Guy Lafleur, *hockey player*, 1951
21 Faith Hill, *singer*, 1967
22 Bonnie Hunt, *actress*, 1964
23 Bruce Springsteen, *singer*, 1949
24 Kevin Sorbo, *actor*, 1958
25 Will Smith, *actor*, 1968
26 Serena Williams, *tennis player*, 1981
27 Meat Loaf, *musician*, 1947
28 Gwyneth Paltrow, *actress*, 1973
29 Bryant Gumbel, *TV personality*, 1948
30 Martina Hingis, *tennis player*, 1980

OCTOBER

1 Mark McGwire, *baseball player*, 1963
2 Sting, *musician*, 1951
3 Neve Campbell, *actress*, 1972
4 Alicia Silverstone, *actress*, 1973
5 Kate Winslet, *actress*, 1975
6 Rebecca Lobo, *basketball player*, 1973
7 Toni Braxton, *singer*, 1966
8 Matt Damon, *actor*, 1970
9 John Lennon, *musician*, 1940
10 Brett Favre, *football player*, 1969
11 Luke Perry, *actor*, 1966
12 Marion Jones, *Olympic champion*, 1975
13 Paul Simon, *songwriter*, 1941
14 Usher, *singer*, 1979
15 Sarah Ferguson, *British royalty*, 1959
16 Kordell Stewart, *football player*, 1972
17 Mae Jemison, *astronaut*, 1956
18 Wynton Marsalis, *jazz musician*, 1961
19 John Lithgow, *actor*, 1945
20 Tom Petty, *musician*, 1953
21 Björk, *singer*, 1966
22 Zac Hanson, *musician*, 1985
23 Ang Lee, *director*, 1954
24 Monica, *singer*, 1980
25 Midori, *violinist*, 1971
26 Dylan McDermott, *actor*, 1962
27 Patty Sheehan, *golfer*, 1956
28 Julia Roberts, *actress*, 1967
29 Winona Ryder, *actress*, 1971
30 Nia Long, *actress*, 1971
31 Rob Schneider, *actor*, 1963

NOVEMBER

1 Jenny McCarthy, *TV personality*, 1972
2 Daniel Boone, *frontiersman*, 1734
3 Phil Simms, *football player/sportscaster*, 1956
4 Laura Bush, *first lady*, 1946
5 Bryan Adams, *singer*, 1959
6 Ethan Hawke, *actor*, 1970
7 Marie Curie, *scientist*, 1867
8 Courtney Thorne-Smith, *actress*, 1968
9 Sean "Puffy" Combs, *rapper/businessman*, 1969
10 Isaac Bruce, *football player*, 1972
11 Leonardo DiCaprio, *actor*, 1974
12 David Schwimmer, *actor*, 1966
13 Vinny Testaverde, *football player*, 1963
14 Prince Charles of Great Britain, 1948
15 Sam Waterston, *actor*, 1940
16 Oksana Baiul, *Olympic champion*, 1977
17 Danny DeVito, *actor*, 1944
18 Jason Williams, *basketball player*, 1975
19 Meg Ryan, *actress*, 1961
20 Bo Derek, *actress*, 1956
21 Ken Griffey Jr., *baseball player*, 1969
22 Jamie Lee Curtis, *actress*, 1958
23 Billy the Kid, *outlaw*, 1859
24 Scott Joplin, *composer*, 1868
25 Jenna and Barbara Bush, *president's daughters*, 1981
26 Shawn Kemp, *basketball player*, 1969
27 Jaleel White, *actor*, 1976
28 Ed Harris, *actor*, 1950
29 Madeleine L'Engle, *author*, 1918
30 Ben Stiller, *actor*, 1965

DECEMBER

1 Bette Midler, *singer/actress*, 1945
2 Britney Spears, *singer*, 1981
3 Brendan Fraser, *actor*, 1967
4 Marisa Tomei, *actress*, 1964
5 Frankie Muniz, *actor*, 1985
6 Dave Brubeck, *jazz musician*, 1920
7 Larry Bird, *basketball coach*, 1956
8 Sinead O'Connor, *singer*, 1966
9 Tom Daschle, *U.S. senator*, 1947
10 Emily Dickinson, *poet*, 1830
11 John Kerry, *U.S. senator*, 1943
12 Cathy Rigby, *gymnast/actress*, 1952
13 Wendie Malick, *actress*, 1950
14 Craig Biggio, *baseball player*, 1965
15 Don Johnson, *actor*, 1949
16 Ludwig van Beethoven, *composer*, 1770
17 Bill Pullman, *actor*, 1954
18 Steven Spielberg, *film producer*, 1947
19 Alyssa Milano, *actress*, 1972
20 Kiefer Sutherland, *actor*, 1966
21 Ray Romano, *comedian*, 1957
22 Diane Sawyer, *TV journalist*, 1945
23 Susan Lucci, *actress*, 1948
24 Ricky Martin, *singer*, 1971
25 Norm MacDonald, *actor*, 1962
26 Susan Butcher, *sled dog racer*, 1954
27 Cokie Roberts, *TV journalist*, 1943
28 Denzel Washington, *actor*, 1954
29 Ted Danson, *actor*, 1947
30 Tiger Woods, *golfer*, 1975
31 Val Kilmer, *actor*, 1959

Marie Curie

Emily Dickinson

ANIMALS

What's the biggest venomous snake? You can find the answer on page 40.

ODD BUT NATURAL

▶ You can figure out the temperature in the summer by listening to cricket chirps. Count the chirps you hear in 15 seconds, and add 39. That should give you the Fahrenheit temperature outdoors within a couple of degrees!

▶ Elephants like to be busy. To keep them from being bored, trainers at a preserve in Thailand set up the Thai Elephant Orchestra. Six elephants learned to make up their own tunes using gongs, drums, and harmonicas. After only five practice sessions, the elephants recorded their first CD. Imagine them on stage at the next Grammy ceremony. It would be big news!

▶ Polar bears on the frozen tundra in Manitoba, Canada, are thinner and have fewer cubs than they did 20 years ago. Why? The Arctic climate is slowly warming, leaving a shorter season for polar bears to hunt for seals, an important food.

▶ Koala bears eat only leaves from eucalyptus trees. Eucalyptus leaves are poison to most animals, but bacteria in koalas' stomachs break down the poisonous parts, so they can feast on these leaves without competition.

▶ The male goldfinch has bright yellow, black, and white feathers in the spring and summer during mating season. When mating season ends and winter begins, the feathers fade to a dull brown.

▶ Most sea creatures pose no threat to the great white shark. But when this shark swallows a puffer fish, the puffer inflates like a balloon, sticking its pointy spines in the shark's throat. The shark soon dies.

▶ Although it is not poisonous, the North American viceroy butterfly fools its enemies by imitating the shape and color pattern of the poisonous monarch butterfly.

▲ Koala bear

▶ When a baby gorilla loses its mother, it can become sick, hungry, and sad. Workers at a gorilla orphanage (Projet Protection des Gorilles) in the Republic of the Congo rescue and care for orphaned gorillas until the animals can live on their own. Then the workers take the gorillas back to their natural habitat.

▶ Komodo dragons, the world's biggest lizards, grow up to 10 feet long and weigh as much as 300 pounds. When they were first brought to New York in the early 1920s, they provided the inspiration for the first King Kong movie.

◀ Komodo dragon

The LARGEST and the FASTEST in the WORLD

WORLD'S LARGEST ANIMALS

LARGEST ANIMAL: blue whale (110 feet long, 209 tons)

LARGEST LAND ANIMAL: African bush elephant (13 feet high, 8 tons)

TALLEST ANIMAL: giraffe (19 feet tall)

LARGEST REPTILE: saltwater crocodile (16 feet long, 1,150 pounds)

LARGEST SNAKE: Heaviest: anaconda (27 feet, 9 inches long, 500 pounds)
Longest: reticulated python (26–32 feet long)

LONGEST FISH: whale shark (41½ feet long)

LARGEST BIRD: ostrich (9 feet tall, 345 pounds)

LARGEST INSECT: stick insect (15 inches long)

WORLD'S FASTEST ANIMALS

FASTEST ANIMAL: peregrine falcon, a bird (100–200 miles per hour)

FASTEST MARINE ANIMAL: blue whale (30 miles per hour)

FASTEST LAND ANIMAL: cheetah (70 miles per hour)

FASTEST FISH: sailfish (68 miles per hour)

FASTEST BIRD: peregrine falcon (100–200 miles per hour)

FASTEST INSECT: dragonfly (36 miles per hour)

HOW FAST DO ANIMALS RUN?

Did you know that some animals can run as fast as a car can move or that a snail would need more than 30 hours just to go one mile? If you look at this table, you will see how fast some land animals can move.

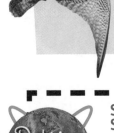

SPEEDY SPRINTERS

▶ **Lions,** one of the speediest land animals, spend about 20 hours a day resting.

▶ **Humans** at their fastest are still slower than many animals. In the 1996 Atlanta Olympics, U.S. sprinter Michael Johnson averaged 23.16 mph when he ran 200 meters in a record 19.32 seconds.

MILES PER HOUR

Cheetah	70
Antelope	60
Lion	50
Coyote	43
Hyena	40
Rabbit	35
Giraffe	32
Grizzly bear	30
Elephant	25
Wild turkey	15
Squirrel	12
Snail	0.03

How Long Do Animals Live?

Box turtle . . . . 100 years
Human . . . . 66 years
African elephant . . 35 years
Grizzly bear . . . . . . 25 years
Horse . . . . 20 years
Chimpanzee . . . . . . 20 years
Black bear . . . . 18 years
Tiger . . . . 16 years
Lion . . . . 15 years
Lobster . . . . 15 years
Cow . . . . 15 years
Rhinoceros (black) . 15 years
Moose . . . . 12 years
Cat (domestic) . . . . 12 years
Dog (domestic) . . . . 12 years
Sea lion . . . . 12 years
Giraffe . . . . 10 years
Pig . . . . 10 years
Squirrel . . . . 10 years
Deer (white-tailed) . . 8 years
Goat . . . . 8 years
Kangaroo . . . . 7 years
Chipmunk . . . . 6 years
Rabbit . . . . 5 years
Beaver . . . . 5 years
Mouse . . . . 3 years
Opossum . . . . 1 year

Most animals do not live as long as human beings do. A monkey that is 14 years old is thought to be old. A person who is 14 is still considered young. The average life span of a human being in the world today is 65 to 70 years. The average life spans of some animals are shown here. Only one of these animals lives longer than human beings.

KITS, CUBS, AND OTHER ANIMAL BABIES

ANIMAL	MALE	FEMALE	YOUNG
bear	boar	sow	cub
alligator	bull	cow	hatchling
horse	stallion	mare	foal, filly (female), colt (male)
cheetah	male	female	cub
hippopotamus, giraffe, whale	bull	cow	calf
ferrett	hob	jill	kit
fox	reynard	vixen	kit, cub, pup
gorilla	male	female	infant
duck	drake	duck	duckling
hawk	tiercel	hen	eyas
opossum	jack	jill	joey
tiger	tiger	tigress	cub

PETS AT THE TOP

TOP TEN DOG BREEDS

Here are the ten most popular U.S. dog breeds with the numbers of dogs registered by the American Kennel Club in 2000:

1. Labrador retriever — 174,841
2. Golden retriever — 66,300
3. German shepherd — 57,660
4. Dachshund — 54,773
5. Beagle — 52,026
6. Poodle — 45,868
7. Yorkshire terrier — 43,574
8. Chihuahua — 43,096
9. Boxer — 38,803
10. Shih tzu — 37,599

MOST POPULAR PETS

Here are the ten most popular pets in the U.S. today:

1. Cats
2. Dogs
3. Parakeets
4. Small rodents, such as rabbits, gerbils, and hamsters
5. Fish
6. Reptiles
7. Finches
8. Cockatiels
9. Canaries
10. Parrots

TOP TEN PET NAMES

Here's what veterinarians told the American Society for the Prevention of Cruelty to Animals (ASPCA), when asked to list the ten most popular names for pets:

1. Max
2. Sam
3. Lady
4. Bear
5. Smokey
6. Shadow
7. Kitty
8. Molly
9. Buddy
10. Brandy

All About... ODD PETS

Unusual animals are becoming more and more popular as pets. In the United States, the favorites include snakes, iguanas, geckos, pot-bellied pigs, and even tarantulas and prairie dogs. In Taiwan, orangutans became the most popular odd pet after a 1980s TV show featured a family that owned one. But many of these endangered monkeys have since been abandoned. They became too big and bossy for their owners to handle. Animal experts have this advice for people who want unusual animals as pets: Learn all about the animals before they are taken out of their natural environments. That's one way to prevent big problems.

WHAT ARE GROUPS OF ANIMALS CALLED?

The next time you describe a group of animals, try using one of the phrases below.

CATS: *chowder* or *clutter* of cats	LEOPARDS: *leap* of leopards
CHICKS: *clutch* of chicks	LIONS: *pride* of lions
CROWS: *murder* of crows	RHINOCEROSES: *crash* of rhinoceroses
DUCKS: *brace* of ducks	SEALS: *pod* of seals
ELKS: *gang* of elks	SWANS: *bevy* of swans
FOXES: *skulk* of foxes	SWINE: *drift* of swine
GEESE: *flock* or *gaggle* of geese	TOADS: *knot* of toads
GOLDFINCHES: *charm* of goldfinches	TURTLES: *bale* of turtles
HAWKS: *cast* of hawks	WHALES: *pod* of whales
KITTENS: *kindle* or *kendle* of kittens	WOLVES: *pack* of wolves

CLASSIFYING ANIMALS

The world has so many animals that scientists looked for a way to organize them into groups. A Swedish scientist named Carolus Linnaeus (1707–1778) worked out a system for classifying both animals and plants. We still use it today.

ANIMAL KINGDOM

The animal kingdom is separated into two large groups—animals with backbones, called **vertebrates**, and animals without backbones, called **invertebrates**.

These large groups are divided into smaller groups called **phyla**. And phyla are divided into even smaller groups called **classes**. The animals in each group are classified together when their bodies are similar in certain ways.

VERTEBRATES: Animals With Backbones

FISH	Swordfish, tuna, salmon, trout, halibut
AMPHIBIANS	Frogs, toads, mud puppies
REPTILES	Turtles, alligators, crocodiles, lizards
BIRDS	Sparrows, owls, turkeys, hawks
MAMMALS	Kangaroos, opossums, dogs, cats, bears, seals, rats, squirrels, rabbits, chipmunks, porcupines, horses, pigs, cows, deer, bats, whales, dolphins, monkeys, apes, humans

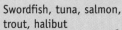

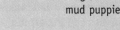

INVERTEBRATES: Animals Without Backbones

PROTOZOA	The simplest form of animals
COELENTERATES	Jellyfish, hydra, sea anemones, coral
MOLLUSKS	Clams, snails, squid, oysters
ANNELIDS	Earthworms
ARTHROPODS	
Crustaceans:	Lobsters, crayfish
Centipedes and Millipedes	
Arachnids:	Spiders, scorpions
Insects:	Butterflies, grasshoppers, bees, termites, cockroaches
ECHINODERMS	Starfish, sea urchins, sea cucumbers

Life on Earth

This time line shows how life developed on Earth and when land plants developed. The earliest animals are at the top of the chart. The most recent are at the bottom of the chart.

YEARS AGO		ANIMAL LIFE ON EARTH
4.5 BILLION		Formation of the Earth. No signs of life.
2.5 BILLION		First evidence of life in the form of bacteria and algae. All life is in water.
570–500 MILLION		Animals with shells (called trilobites) and some mollusks. Some fossils begin to form.
500–430 MILLION		Jawless fish appear, oldest known animals with backbones (vertebrates).
430–395 MILLION		Many coral reefs, jawed fishes, and scorpion-like animals. First land plants.
395–345 MILLION		Many fishes. Earliest known insect. Amphibians (animals living in water and on land) appear.
345–280 MILLION		Large insects appear. Amphibians increase in numbers. First trees appear.
280–225 MILLION		Reptiles and modern insects appear. Trilobites, many corals, and fishes become extinct.
225–195 MILLION		Dinosaurs and turtles appear. Many reptiles and insects develop further. Mammals appear.
195–135 MILLION		Many giant dinosaurs. Reptiles increase in number. First birds and crab-like animals appear.
135–65 MILLION		Dinosaurs develop further and then become extinct. Flowering plants begin to appear.
65–2.5 MILLION		Modern-day land and sea animals begin to develop, including such mammals as rhinoceroses, whales, cats, dogs, apes, seals.
2.5 MILLION–10,000		Earliest humans appear. Mastodon, mammoths, and other huge animals become extinct.
10,000–PRESENT		Modern human beings and animals.

PRECAMBRIAN · PALEOZOIC · MESOZOIC · CENOZOIC

HABITATS: Where Animals Live

The area in nature where an animal lives is called its habitat. The table below lists some large habitats and some of the animals that live in them.

HABITAT	Some Animals That Live There
Deserts (hot, dry regions)	camels, bobcats, coyotes, kangaroos, mice, Gila monsters, scorpions, rattlesnakes
Tropical Forests (warm, humid climate)	orangutans, gibbons, leopards, tamandua anteaters, tapirs, iguanas, parrots, tarantulas
Grasslands (flat, open lands)	African elephants, kangaroos, Indian rhinoceroses, giraffes, zebras, prairie dogs, ostriches, tigers
Mountains (highlands)	yaks, snow leopards, vicunas, bighorn sheep, chinchillas, pikas, eagles, mountain goats
Polar Regions (cold climate)	polar bears, musk oxen, caribou, ermines, arctic foxes, walruses, penguins, Siberian huskies
Oceans (sea water)	whales, dolphins, seals, manatees, octopuses, stingrays, coral, starfish, lobsters, many kinds of fish

FOSSILS: Clues to Ancient Animals

A fossil is the remains of an animal or plant that lived long ago. Most fossils are formed from the hard parts of an animal's body, such as bones, shells, or teeth. Some are large, like dinosaur footprints. Some are so tiny that you need a microscope to see them. Most fossils are found in rocks formed from the mud or sand that collects at the bottom of oceans, rivers, and lakes. Fossils offer scientists clues to ancient animals.

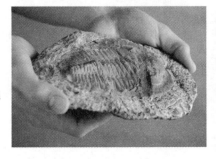

What Do Fossils Tell Us? Scientists study fossils to help them understand plant and animal life in ancient periods of the world's history. The age and structure of the rocks in which fossils are found can help scientists tell how long ago certain kinds of animals or plants lived. For example, dinosaurs lived millions of years ago, but people have known about dinosaurs only since the first dinosaur fossils were uncovered, less than 200 years ago.

Where Are Fossils Found? In eastern and southern Africa and other places, people have found fossils that are ancestors of early humans. Insects that lived millions of years ago are sometimes found preserved in amber (hardened tree sap). Fossils have also been found in ice and tar.

Did You Know?

IN 2000, SCIENTISTS DISCOVERED FIVE TYRANNOSAURUS REX SKELETONS IN EASTERN MONTANA. *This is a really big find. Only 15 others have been found in the last 100 years! When the researchers dig the bones out of the ground, they will look closely at the arms to find out if T. Rex was really more of a scavenger than a predator. A big clue is how long the arms are. Predators need long arms to struggle with their prey.*

All About... DINOSAURS

Dinosaurs lived during the Mesozoic era, from 225 to 65 million years ago. The Mesozoic era is divided into the three periods shown below.

TRIASSIC PERIOD, from 225 to 195 million years ago

▶ **First dinosaurs** appeared during the **Triassic period**. Most early dinosaurs were small, rarely longer than 15 feet.

▶ **Early meat-eating dinosaurs** were called **theropods**.

▶ **Earliest-known dinosaurs** were meat-eaters, found in Argentina: **Eoraptor** (the most primitive dinosaur, only about 40 inches long) and **Herrerasaurus**.

▶ **Early plant-eating dinosaurs** were called **prosauropods**. **Plateosaurus** and **Anchisaurus** were two early plant-eating dinosaurs.

JURASSIC PERIOD, from 195 to 135 million years ago

▶ Dinosaurs that lived during the **Jurassic period** were gigantic.

▶ Jurassic dinosaurs included the **sauropods**, giant long-necked plant-eaters, the **largest land animals** ever. **Apatosaurus** and **Brachiosaurus** (70–80 feet) and **Diplodocus** (over 80 feet) were Sauropods.

▶ **Stegosaurus** (30 feet), a large plant-eater, had sharp, bony plates along its back.

▶ **Allosaurus** and **Megalosaurus**, two giant meat-eaters, fed on large plant-eating dinosaurs like the Apatosaurus and Stegosaurus. Megalosaurus grew to 30 feet in length; Allosaurus, 30-36 feet.

CRETACEOUS PERIOD, from 135 to 65 million years ago

▶ New dinosaurs appeared during the **Cretaceous period**, but by the end of this period, all dinosaurs had died out.

▶ New plant-eaters: **Triceratops** and other horned dinosaurs, **Anatosaurus** and other duckbilled dinosaurs, **Ankylosaurus** and other armored dinosaurs.

▶ New meat-eater: **Tyrannosaurus Rex**, one of the largest and fiercest meat-eaters, growing to 20 feet high and 40 feet long.

A model of Tyrannosaurus Rex ▶

A "MICRO" DINOSAUR

The smallest fossil ever found of a grown-up dinosaur may help paleontologists prove that birds evolved from small dinosaurs. Microraptor, dug up in China, seems to have had feathers and birdlike teeth and bones. Its toes suggest that it probably perched in trees. Most important, it is only 15 inches long, about the same size as the first birds. Although this tiny dinosaur lived about 20 million years after the first bird, the researchers who found it believe that the two animals share a common ancestor.

DEADLY DINOS DISCOVERED

One hundred million years ago there lived meat-eating dinosaurs that were probably more terrifying than any that came before or after. That's what scientists believe, based on bones they dug up in Argentina in 2000. The scientists say the newly discovered dinosaurs were probably about 45 feet in length with long, sharp snouts, long skulls, and razor-sharp teeth. And they apparently traveled in packs, unlike most other dinosaurs.

ENDANGERED SPECIES

When an animal species begins to die out, the animal is said to be endangered or threatened. Throughout the world today, 1,053 species of animals are endangered or threatened. Among them are:

Mammals: 340 species

Birds: 274 species

Fish: 124 species

Reptiles: 115 species

Clams: 71 species

Insects: 43 species

Snails: 32 species

Amphibians: 27 species

Crustaceans: 21 species

Arachnids: 6 species

Some Endangered Animals

Bird: *Orange-bellied parakeet*—found only in southeastern Australia.

Fish: *Colorado pike minnow*—fighting for survival in the Colorado River near the Grand Canyon, Arizona.

Mammal: *Giant panda*—facing extinction in a small area of China

Reptile: *Galapagos tortoise*—found on the Galapagos Islands in the Pacific Ocean.

How Species Become Endangered

How do animals and plants become endangered?

Changes in Climate. Animals are endangered when the climate of their habitat (where they live) changes in a major way. For example, if an area becomes very hot and dry and a river dries up, the fish and other plant and animal life in the river will die.

Habitat Destruction. Sometimes animal habitats are destroyed when people need the land. Wetlands, for example, where many types of waterfowl, fish, and insects live, might be drained for new houses or a mall. The animals that lived there would have to find a new home or else die out.

Over-hunting. Bison or buffalo once ranged over the entire Great Plains of the United States, but they were hunted almost to extinction in the 19th century. Since then, they have been protected by laws, and their numbers are increasing.

All About... SHARKS

Sharks are one of the oldest animals on Earth; they have ruled the seas for more than 400 million years. They may be awesome predators, but they probably should fear humans more than we fear them.

Sharks can see, hear, smell, taste, and feel. They also have a sixth sense. Through tiny pores in their heads, they can pick up electrical impulses that every animal emits. This ability, combined with strength and razor sharp teeth, makes them formidable undersea competitors.

But they have one big enemy: humans. People kill 30 to 70 million sharks every year. Their fins are churned into soup that is a big favorite in some parts of Asia; the soup can sell for up to $90 a bowl in Hong Kong. Other parts are used to make health and beauty aids. Some people also hunt sharks for sport. Because sharks reproduce slowly, these killings are a serious problem, and the future of the shark is threatened in many parts of the world.

CRANES SAVED BY PLANES

There are fewer than 400 whooping cranes left in the whole world. Through a program called Operation Migration, scientists are trying to boost the crane population. The scientists use ultralight aircraft to teach young cranes how to fly south for the winter.

When wild chicks hatch, they trust and follow the first thing they see. In Operation Migration, chicks get to hear airplane engine sounds while still inside their eggshells. As soon as they hatch, they are exposed to an airplane and to a pilot wearing crane hand puppets. This way, the chicks learn to trust and follow the airplane and pilot. These become kind of substitute parents! A great movie with a similar story is *Fly Away Home*.

All About... SEA TURTLES

For sea turtles, 2000 was not a good year. More than 3,000 dead or sick sea turtles were washed ashore from the Gulf of Mexico and the Atlantic Ocean. This was the biggest number in ten years—bad news considering that all six species of sea turtles in the United States are endangered or threatened. Experts don't know exactly what caused so many turtles to become ill. But the usual suspects include pollution, boating, fishing, ocean dredging, and toxins from poisonous sea creatures.

There are other threats too. Overbuilding along beaches disturbs turtles' nesting habits. And when people drive on sand, they run over turtle nests, crushing eggs and baby turtles. Deep tire tracks sometimes block baby turtles' trek back to the sea after the females lay their eggs. And bright headlights in the dark can be enough to keep female turtles away from an otherwise good nesting site.

The United States and Mexico are working together to preserve an important nesting site along the Gulf of Mexico. The number of turtles nesting there is rising—good news for people *and* turtles.

DANGER! POISONOUS ANIMALS

What's the difference between poisonous animals and venomous animals?

Poisonous animals contain a toxin (poison) in a part of their body, like the skin, organs, or feathers. Touching or eating these animals causes sickness, pain, or death. But, these animals don't do anything to spread their poison.

Venomous animals do deliver their poison. They use body parts such as fangs, stingers, or tentacles to poison others.

DEADLY ANIMAL FACTS

▶ The largest venomous snake, the **king cobra**, uses its half-inch-long hollow fangs to inject its prey with toxin (poison) strong enough to kill an elephant. King cobras mainly eat lizards and other snakes.

▶ **Komodo dragons'** mouths are full of disease-causing bacteria. When they bite their prey, the victim gets sick and slowly dies of blood poisoning. Then the lizard returns after this has happened, to eat the body.

▶ **Assassin bugs**, a type of predatory insect, wait for just the right moment to attack other bugs. First they stab their prey with a pointy tube-like beak (called a proboscis). The poison that comes through the proboscis dissolves the bug's body into juices for the assassin to suck up.

▶ The skin, liver, and eggs of the **puffer fish** contain deadly toxins. Some chefs in Japan are trained and licensed to prepare a special treat made out of puffers. The chefs are usually able to make this dish safely. But not always. At least a few people die each year from eating it.

▶ The **blue ring octopus**, the deadliest kind of octopus, uses its arms to capture its prey. Then it bites the victim, sending in poison through its saliva.

▶ The male **duckbill platypus**, the only venomous mammal, has a venomous spur on each hind leg. He uses these spurs mainly to defend himself when fighting rivals for a mate.

▶ The skin glands of **poison dart frogs** produce a foul-smelling, bitter-tasting substance that warns away predators. A single drop can kill an animal that ignores the warning. People can get sick from touching the frog's skin. In Colombia, people have used the toxin in hunting darts (blowguns).

▶ **Pitohui birds** of Papua New Guinea are one of only two species of poisonous birds. Their feathers and skin contain a powerful toxin that makes them taste peppery and smell repulsive to predators (and humans). When a mother pitohui bird sits on her eggs, her toxin rubs onto them, helping to protect them, too.

SOME ANIMAL POISONS CAN BE HELPFUL TO HUMANS. *Researchers are working on medicines from spider venom to fight diabetes and epilepsy. Platypus venom may help scientists create pain-blocking drugs. Poison dart frog toxins may some day help people with heart problems. And the bacteria in komodo dragons' mouths may teach scientists something about building our immune systems.*

WHAT'S NEW AT THE ZOO?

Here are some of the biggest and best zoos in the country. Try visiting their Web sites if you can't visit the zoos in person.

Woodland Park Zoo

Seattle, WA • **(206) 684-4892**

WEB SITE *http://www.zoo.org*

The Woodland Park Zoo prides itself on its animal habitats. The zoo is excited about the birth of its first baby Asian elephant, named Chai, born in 2000.

The San Diego Zoo

San Diego, CA • **(619) 234-3153**

WEB SITE *http://www.sandiegozoo.org*

The San Diego Zoo first became famous for keeping animals behind moats rather than behind bars. Today, more than 4,000 animals live there in settings that look and feel like habitats in the wild. One new exhibit is the Ituri Forest, four acres that are like part of an African rainforest. The exhibit has okapis, hippos, forest buffalo, colorful birds, monkeys, lush plants, and waterfalls. Check out the Web site and take a cyber safari!

The Bronx Zoo/ Wildlife Conservation Park

Bronx, NY • **(718) 367-1010**

WEB SITE *http://www.wcs.org/home/ zoos/bronxzoo*

This is the largest city zoo in the United States. More than 6,000 animals live there mostly in realistic settings without cages. The African plains exhibit features lions and nyala (predators and prey) together, separated by a moat. In the Congo Gorilla Forest, open all year, 400 animals live on 6½ acres of what looks like African rainforest. You might enjoy touring The Bronx Zoo online.

The Shedd Aquarium

Chicago, IL • **(312) 939-2438**

WEB SITE *http://www.sheddnet.org*

The Shedd Aquarium is the world's biggest indoor aquarium. Its newest exhibit, Amazon Rising: Seasons of the River, shows the river habitat in all its stages, as it changes throughout the year. The zoo also features an underwater viewing gallery that brings you face-to-face with whales and dolphins.

Smithsonian National Zoo

Washington, D.C. • **(202) 673-4800**

WEB SITE *http://www.natzoo.si.edu*

If you are planning a trip to Washington, D.C., put the National Zoo on your list of places to visit. Two giant pandas from China arrived there in 2000. The zoo planted greenery in the pandas' enclosure to help them feel at home during the ten years they are scheduled to visit here. The pandas even have their own Web site:

http://pandas.si.edu

Did You KNOW?

THE PHILADELPHIA ZOO WAS THE FIRST ZOO IN THE UNITED STATES. *It opened on July 1, 1874. Find out more online at:*

WEB SITE *http://www.phillyzoo.org*

WHO LIVES WHERE?

Match the animals with their habitats. Draw a line from the
Animal ••••• to its ••••➤ Habitat

ANSWERS ON PAGES 317-320. FOR MORE PUZZLES GO TO
WWW.WORLDALMANACFORKIDS.COM

LAUGHS

Q What's in the middle of a jellyfish?
A A jellybutton.

Q What goes tick, tick, woof, woof?
A A watch dog.

Q How do porcupines play leapfrog?
A Very carefully.

Q Why did the parrot carry an umbrella?
A So he could be polly-unsaturated.

Q What do you call a chicken at the North Pole?
A Lost.

Q What do you call a flying monkey?
A A hot-air baboon.

ART

What do the National Gallery of Art and the Rock and Roll Hall of Fame have in common?
You can find the answer on page 44.

ART IS EVERYWHERE

The buildings in which we live, go to school, work, play, and worship may be works of art. Paintings and photographs may be works of art. So may the statues that fill museums and dot towns and cities.

Art may be true-to-life or it may be unlike anything you've ever seen. It may be funny or sad, lovely or disturbing. The way you look at art may be different from the way your friends look at it. The beauty of art is that there are endless points of view.

One Woman's Vision

Here is "Children Playing on the Beach," a painting done in 1884 by Mary Cassatt. She was an American artist who lived from 1844 to 1926. At that time, it was hard for a woman to be accepted as a painter.

Mary Cassatt painted pictures that looked real and natural. She often showed mothers and children doing ordinary things in everyday settings. Many other artists of her time painted children looking and acting like small adults, often with stiff, formal, and dark backgrounds.

Notice the natural background in this picture and the light, bright colors. And see the way we look at the children, from close up and low down, as if we are playing alongside them.

Look at the face of the child at left. You can see how hard she's working at playing. And see the way she holds her shovel and pail? It's just the way a little child handles clumsy objects.

Do you like this painting? How does it make you feel? What would you include if you were creating a picture with the same title? Cassatt often used family members and friends as models. Whom would you show in your picture?

Mary Cassatt was born in Allegheny, Pennsylvania. She was about 17 when she started studying painting. After she moved to France in 1866, Edgar Degas, a well-known artist, encouraged her work. Like him, she painted in a style called Impressionism and became interested in Japanese prints. After 1914, Cassatt's eyesight failed and she could not paint any more. But she never stopped encouraging young artists in their work.

Through Artists' Eyes

Art comes in many different forms.

PEOPLE, PLACES, AND THINGS

▶ A **landscape** is a drawing or painting of nature. A seascape shows the sea and ships. A cityscape shows city buildings, streets, and people.

▶ A **portrait** is a painting or drawing of one or more people. A self-portrait is a picture of an artist created by that artist.

▶ A **still-life** is a picture of small objects—flowers, bottles, or fruit, for example. Pictures of rooms are called **interior paintings**.

▶ Some artists create pictures using shapes, colors, or textures in ways that do not look like anything in the real world. These works are called **abstract art**.

▶ **Photography**, too, may be a form of art. Photos record both the commonplace and the exotic, and help us look at events in new ways.

▶ **Sculpture** is a three-dimensional form made from clay, stone, metal, or other material. Some sculptures have even been made from beverage cans. Sculpture may be recognizable as a person, animal, or thing. But some modern sculpture is abstract.

The Thinker, *a sculpture by Auguste Rodin* ▶

ARCHITECTURE

Architecture is the art of designing and creating buildings. The best architecture is not only beautiful to look at but comfortable to be in and convenient to use. The architecture of a place depends on the ways people there live, what they consider important, and what the weather is like. You can tell a lot about an area's past and present by looking at its architecture.

All About... I. M. PEI, AN ARCHITECT

I. M. Pei was born in China in 1917. In 1935 he moved to the United States, where he studied architecture. Since then he has designed many famous modern buildings in the United States and around the world. Several of his buildings are noted for their daring geometric shapes and large inside spaces. A few of his most famous buildings include: the Rock and Roll Hall of Fame and Museum (Cleveland, Ohio; see page 45), the Mile High Center (Denver, Colorado), the John Hancock Tower (Boston, Massachusetts), the East Building of the National Gallery of Art (Washington, D.C.), the John F. Kennedy Library (Boston), and the entrance to the Louvre Museum in Paris, France.

◀ *The John F. Kennedy Library*

A museum may not only be a place filled with art, it can be a work of art as well. For more about different kinds of museums, see the Museums chapter that starts on page 124.

THE ROCK AND ROLL HALL OF FAME AND MUSEUM

The Rock and Roll Hall of Fame and Museum is located in downtown Cleveland, Ohio. The building has three huge geometric shapes. A cylinder, a tall rectangle, and a triangle made of steel and glass seem to burst up out of the ground and over Lake Erie.

The museum, designed by I .M. Pei, was completed in 1995. Pei wanted the building to capture the same energy that rock and roll music has. Some people have said that from a certain angle, the museum looks like a turntable playing a record album.

What do you think of when you look at a picture of the museum? Does the building remind you of anything?

(For more about this museum, see page 129.)

THE NATIONAL GALLERY OF ART

Seeing great works of art in person can feel magical. How would you like to see an original painting by Rembrandt, Paul Cézanne, Vincent van Gogh, or Georgia O'Keeffe? One place to go is the National Gallery of Art in Washington, D.C. It has one of the world's largest collections of sculpture, paintings, and graphic arts masterpieces from the Middle Ages to the present. The massive collection fills two large buildings located on the National Mall, between Third and Ninth Streets at Constitution Avenue. You can also check out the Gallery's amazing Web site, which contains information on almost every artist and piece of artwork exhibited at the museum.

WEB SITE http://www.nga.gov

▲ Houses in Provence (c. 1880), *by Paul Cézanne*

BOOKS

Why does Harry Potter have lots of company in bookstores? *You can find the answer below.*

FOR FANTASY FICTION FANS

Ever since J. K. Rowling began capturing the imaginations of millions with her *Harry Potter* series, bookstores have reported a huge interest in fantasy fiction. Readers keep wanting more, and luckily, there's plenty more to be had.

The seven books of *The Chronicles of Narnia*, by C. S. Lewis, take you into an enchanted world of magic spells, talking animals, and good and evil forces. In Susan Cooper's *The Dark Is Rising* series, you can join young Will Stanton on his quest for the six magical Signs that will determine who wins the battle between the forces of Light and Dark. You'll find magic and humor in Diana Wynne Jones's many fantasy books, including *The Chronicles of Chrestomanci*, *Castle in the Air*, and *Hexwood*. And don't forget "The Lord of the Rings" novels by J. R. R. Tolkien, about the short, hairy-footed hobbits and other creatures who live in the world of Middle Earth.

Here are some other fantasy books you may enjoy:

The Book of Three, by Lloyd Alexander

Ella Enchanted, by Gail Carson Levine

Falcon's Egg, by Luli Gray

The Golden Compass, by Philip Pullman

The Moorchild, by Eloise McGraw

Redwall, by Brian Jacques

The Secret of Platform 13, by Eva Ibbotson

Tuck Everlasting, by Natalie Babbitt

Which Witch, by Eva Ibbotson

BOOK AWARDS, 2000-2001

CALDECOTT MEDAL
This is the highest honor an illustrated book can receive.
2001 WINNER: *So You Want to be President?*, by David Small

NEWBERY MEDAL
This is an award for writing. It is the highest honor for a children's book that is not a picture book.
2001 WINNER: *A Year Down Yonder*, by Richard Peck

CORETTA SCOTT KING AWARD
These are given to artists and authors whose works promote the cause of peace and world brotherhood.
2001 WINNERS:
  Author Award: *Miracle's Boys*, by Jacqueline Woodson
  Illustrator Award: *Uptown*, by Bryan Collier

the sequel to the Newbery Honor-winning *A LONG WAY FROM CHICAGO*

A Year Down Yonder
—RICHARD PECK

BEST NEW BOOKS of the Year

Among those chosen in 2001 by the American Library Association

▶ *Asteroid Impact,* by Douglas Henderson; illustrated by Toby Sherry—Travel back in time 65 million years and see what might have happened to the dinosaurs when a huge asteroid hit Earth.

▶ **The Dark Portal: Book One of the Deptford Mice Trilogy,** by Robin Jarvis—A close-knit group of mice leave their pleasant London home and enter the dark, scary underworld of the Deptford sewer system.

▶ *Gathering Blue,* by Lois Lowry—This is a story set many years from now, in a world where people are mean and greedy. Kira, an expert at embroidery, tries to preserve the history of her culture through her art.

▶ **Harry Potter and the Goblet of Fire,** by J. K. Rowling—In book four of the mega-popular series, Harry competes in the Triwizard Tournament and once again meets his enemy Voldemort.

▶ **Norman Rockwell: Storyteller With a Brush,** by Beverly Gherman—Rockwell's paintings help tell the life story of this popular American artist.

▶ *Satchel Paige,* by Lesa Cline-Ransome; illustrated by James Ransome—An entertaining biography of baseball legend Satchel Paige, the first African-American pitcher in the major leagues.

▶ **So You Want to Be President?,** by Judith St. George; illustrated by David Small—Explores the funny, everyday side of America's presidents.

▶ *The Wonderful Wizard of Oz: A Commemorative Pop-up,* by L. Frank Baum; illustrated by Robert Sabuda—Cyclones spin, balloons rise, and the Emerald City will dazzle your eyes in this pop-up version of the 100-year-old story.

All About... COMIC BOOKS

From the time comics started, kids with an extra nickel to spend would use it to buy their favorites. The first comic books were collections of comic strips from newspapers. In the 1930s, original comic books appeared. They always sold well, but by 1938 they really began flying off the shelves. That was the year Superman landed from Krypton.

Every kid (and lots of adults) loved the Man of Steel. He was soon joined by Batman, Green Lantern, and other superheroes.

In the 1940s, during World War II, kids turned to war comics with patriotic heroes like Captain America. During those grim times, funny comics, with characters like Bugs Bunny, Daffy Duck, and Archie, also became popular. By the end of the war in 1945, superheroes were fading away. Kids wanted more realistic, sometimes more violent, stories. But many adults believed comics were bad for kids, and most publishers agreed to a code that restricted what comics could show in their pages.

Some publishers closed down. It took a real marvel to come to the rescue: Marvel Comics. Marvel introduced new kinds of superheroes, such as Fantastic Four, the Incredible Hulk, Spider-Man, and the X-Men. These characters were cool. They talked and acted more like real people. But they had to battle for kids' attention with TV, and then with computers and video games. To attract new readers, publishers created ever-weirder characters, like Spawn. Drawings and stories became so realistic they began to appeal more to adults than kids.

Although Josie and the Pussycats, Sabrina the Teenage Witch, and the X-Men may have been born in comics, kids today know them mainly through movie and TV spinoffs. Still, comics remain an art form, with their own loyal fans. Don't expect to see The End any time soon.

FOR YOUR BOOKSHELF OR FROM THE LIBRARY

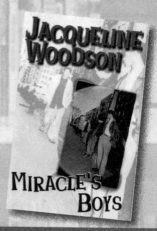

MIRACLE'S BOYS

FICTION Fiction books are stories that come out of the writer's imagination. They are not true. Some fiction books are set in a world of fantasy. Others seem incredibly real.

On this list are new books and favorites from the past. If you read and like them, recommend the books to your friends. If you want to remember which ones you've read and what you thought of them, write your comments in a small notebook.

Because of Winn-Dixie, by **Kate DiCamillo** Ten-year-old Opal befriends a big, ugly, but lovable dog who helps her heal from the loss of her mother and settle into her new home, a community of slightly weird but kind people. (One reviewer suggests having a hankie ready when you read this book.)

The Doll People, by **Ann M. Martin and Laura Goodwin** An action-packed, suspenseful story about two sets of dolls—old fashioned and modern—that come alive inside their dollhouses.

From the Mixed-Up Files of Mrs. Basil E. Frankweiler, by **E.L. Konigsburg** Claudia and her brother Jamie run away from home. They hide in the Metropolitan Museum of Art and try to solve a mystery.

Island of the Blue Dolphins, by **Scott O'Dell** After her younger brother dies, Karana lives alone on an island off the coast of California. A modern classic based on a true story.

Kit's Wilderness, by **David Almond** Kit's family moves to the old English coal-mining village where his ancestors lived, worked, and died. As he helps care for his aging grandfather, he helps his new friends triumph over the town's tragic past.

Miracle's Boys, by **Jacqueline Woodson** After their parents die, 12-year-old Lafayette and his older brothers Charlie and Tyree cope with their sadness and struggle to stay together as a family.

Orwell's Luck, by **Richard W. Jennings** A captivating tale about the magical friendship between a wounded rabbit named Orwell and the 12-year-old girl who finds him and nurses him back to health.

At the Sign of the Star, by **Katherine Sturtevant** Growing up in 17th-century London, 12-year-old Meg fears that a husband will be chosen for her and that she will have to work as a maid.

A Wrinkle in Time, by **Madeleine L'Engle** Meg Murry travels through space with her brother and friend to find her father, a scientist who disappeared while working on a secret government project.

POETRY Poems use language in new and imaginative ways, sometimes in rhyme.

In Every Grain of Sand: A Child's Book of Prayers and Praise, edited by Reeve Lindbergh An illustrated collection of poems and prayers by children of many different cultures and religions.

Night Garden: Poems from the World of Dreams, by Janet S. Wong Fifteen beautifully illustrated poems inspired by vivid dream images.

NONFICTION These books prove facts can be fascinating.

Blizzard! The Storm That Changed America, by Jim Murphy Read about the ferocious New York City snowstorm of 1888, which inspired the daily weather forecasts and emergency services we have become so accustomed to.

The Century That Was: Reflections on the Last One Hundred Years, by James Cross Giblin A collection of readable essays about the 20th century by some of the most popular children's authors, including Lois Lowry, Walter Dean Meyers, and Eve Bunting.

Darkness Over Denmark: The Danish Resistance and the Rescue of the Jews, by Ellen Levine This account, based on interviews with rescuers and survivors, tells a unique story. During World War II, the people of Denmark stood up to the Nazis and saved almost all Jewish Danes from Nazi concentration camps.

Digging For Bird-Dinosaurs: An Expedition to Madagascar, by Nic Bishop Join paleontologist Cathy Forster on a fossil dig on the island of Madagascar, where she searches for evidence that birds evolved from dinosaurs.

Michelangelo, by Diane Stanley The fascinating life story of one of the most talented artists who ever lived is told through interesting stories and computer illustrations.

No More Strangers Now: Young Voices From a New South Africa, by Tim McKee Twelve South African teens from different backgrounds share their thoughts.

REFERENCE Many reference materials are stored on CD-ROMs and are also available on the Internet.

Almanac: A one-volume book of facts and statistics.

Atlas: A collection of maps.

Dictionary: A book of words in alphabetical order. It gives meanings and spellings of and shows how words are pronounced.

Encyclopedia: A place to go for information on almost any subject.

For more on children's books, go to
WEB SITE *http://www.ala.org/booklist/v96/002.html*

HOW WE MAKE THIS BOOK

Here's the inside scoop. Every year, we put together a new edition of *The World Almanac for Kids*, with tons of new facts, all-fresh puzzles, and colorful pictures of the year's people and events.

WHAT WE NEED

▶ **IDEAS AND DATA** Ideas come to us from readers' letters and e-mails, from our Kid Contributors, and from newspapers and magazines. We get new information from the government, different organizations, books, and the World Wide Web.

▶ **HARDWORKING PEOPLE**

- **Writers and contributors** put together new features and update old ones, using the latest information. The words they produce are called *copy*.
- **Editors** plan what the writers should do and look over the copy when it is done.
- **Consultants** help decide whether the information is correct and also interesting and important for kids.
- **Artists** do drawings to go in the book.
- **Designers** plan how each page will look. They put the copy and art in place, using a program called Quark XPress.
- **Indexers** create the index in the back to make stuff easy to find.

▶ **MACHINES AND MATERIALS** Machines at a printing plant print and bind the hundreds of thousands of books. Each book uses 1½ pounds of paper.

STEPS

1 **Plan contents of book.** The main editor and other editors help plan the book. What's hot? Which people, places, and events stood out in the past year? We have a limited number of pages, so it's important to include the information that will most interest readers.

2 **Assign writing jobs and give deadlines.** The main editor assigns work to writers who are experts on the subjects they're writing about. They are given deadlines that must be met. It takes about six months each year to create a new edition of *The World Almanac for Kids*.

3 **Edit copy.** Will kids find the copy clear and interesting? Are the facts correct? Are the spelling, punctuation, and grammar OK? These are the first questions the editors must answer.

4 **Select illustrations and design pages.** Editors and designers select illustrations and photographs. The designers place the copy and art on each page.

5 **Check the proofs and make changes.** After pages are designed they are printed out on proofs. Editors look over the proofs and mark changes to be made. Some copy may be too long or short to fit, so editors may need to cut or add material. When the pages are ready, they go back to the designers.

6 **Send everything to the printer.** It's time to put together the whole book. There's one last chance to check for slip-ups. Are the *folios* (page numbers) correct? Is everything here that should be? Is the color right? When everything looks OK, a disk is sent to the printer, with electronic files that contain all the pages and art.

7 **Print and bind the book, and distribute it to bookstores.** This is the payoff time. In 2000 *The World Almanac for Kids* made the bestsellers list. We expect this to happen again. After the book is printed and bound, it is sent to bookstores all over the United States, mostly by truck.

If you were working on The World Almanac for Kids, what job would you like the most? Do you like to write? Are you an artist? Do you have a good imagination? Do you like to work with other people?

FIND THAT NAME

The last names of authors and editors listed in the box are hidden in this puzzle. An exception: The initials of one author's first and middle names are also included. The names go across, up, down, backward, and diagonally. Some of the letters are used more than once. The leftover letters spell the last name of the author of "The Lord of the Rings" novels.

T	T	T	I	B	B	A	B	E	H	O
L	J	K	R	O	W	L	I	N	G	I
B	A	U	M	K	I	E	S	I	R	B
Y	R	W	O	L	E	W	H	V	E	B
G	V	K	C	E	P	I	O	E	B	O
N	I	T	R	A	M	S	P	L	D	T
O	S	T	G	E	O	R	G	E	N	S
W	O	O	D	S	O	N	L	N	I	O
D	I	C	A	M	I	L	L	O	L	N

WORD BOX

Natalie BABBITT
L. Frank BAUM
Nic BISHOP
Kate DICAMILLO
Eva IBBOTSON
Robin JARVIS
Gail Carson LEVINE
C. S. LEWIS
Reeve LINDBERGH
Lois LOWRY
Ann M. MARTIN
Scott O'DELL
Richard PECK
J. K. ROWLING
Judith ST. GEORGE
Janet S. WONG
Jacqueline WOODSON

The leftover letters spell ___ ___ ___ ___ ___ ___ ___ ___

ANSWERS ON PAGES 317-320. FOR MORE PUZZLES GO TO WWW.WORLDALMANACFORKIDS.COM

YOUR TURN

Choose a book you'd like a friend to read. Write a brief description of the book, the way THE WORLD ALMANAC FOR KIDS describes books in this chapter. Then cut out or copy the review and give it to a friend.

Book Title _____ by _____

BUILDINGS & BRIDGES

What tall building reminds people of a giant windsurfer?
You can find the answer below.

30

TALLEST BUILDINGS IN THE WORLD

Here are the world's five tallest buildings with the year each was completed. Heights listed here stop at the top of each building and don't include antennas or other outside structures.

The World Trade Center

PETRONAS TOWERS 1 & 2, Kuala Lumpur, Malaysia (1998) **Height:** each building is 88 stories, 1,483 feet

SEARS TOWER, Chicago, Illinois (1974) **Height:** 110 stories, 1,450 feet

JIN MAO BUILDING, Shanghai, China (1998) **Height:** 88 stories, 1,381 feet

WORLD TRADE CENTER 1 (1972) **& 2** (1973), New York, New York **Height:** each building is 110 stories; Building 1, 1,368 feet; Building 2, 1,362 feet

CITIC PLAZA, Guangzhou, China (1997) **Height:** 80 stories, 1,283 feet

Did You KNOW?

► The world's tallest hotel is 1,053 feet high. It is located just off the coast of Dubai, United Arab Emirates, on the Persian Gulf. Called Burj al Arab (meaning "Tower of the Arabs"), this hotel sits on its own artificial island about 1,300 feet from shore. Its unusual design makes some people think of a giant windsurfer or a ship in full sail.

◄ *Burj al Arab*

► The Channel Tunnel, which runs under the English Channel connecting Britain and France, was finished in 1994. It is 31 miles long, the world's second-longest railroad tunnel.

LONG TUNNELS

A **tunnel** is an underground passage, dug through rock or earth or built underwater. Vehicular tunnels (on land and under water) are for cars, trucks, and the like. Some water tunnels are also for water mains, drainage, sewage, mining, and storage. Railroad tunnels are for trains and subways. Here are some of the world's longest tunnels:

TYPE OF TUNNEL	NAME	LOCATION	LENGTH
Land	Laerdal	Norway	15.3 miles
Railroad	Seikan	Japan	33.5 miles
Water	Colorado River Aqueduct	California, U.S.	92.1 miles

The SEVEN WONDERS
of the Ancient World

PYRAMIDS OF EGYPT
At Giza, Egypt, built as royal tombs from 2700 to 2500 B.C. The largest is the Great Pyramid of Khufu (or Cheops).

HANGING GARDENS OF BABYLON
Terraced gardens in Babylon (now Iraq) built by King Nebuchadnezzar II around 600 B.C. for his wife.

TEMPLE OF ARTEMIS
At Ephesus (now part of Turkey), built mostly of marble around 550 B.C. in honor of a Greek goddess, Artemis.

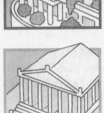

COLOSSUS OF RHODES
In the harbor on the island of Rhodes (Greece). A bronze statue of the sun god Helios, built during the 200s B.C.

STATUE OF ZEUS
At Olympia, Greece. The statue, made about 457 B.C. by the sculptor Phidias from ivory and gold, showed the king of the gods.

MAUSOLEUM OF HALICARNASSUS
(Now part of Turkey), built about 353 B.C. in honor of King Mausolus, a ruler of ancient Caria.

LIGHTHOUSE OF ALEXANDRIA, EGYPT
Built about 270 B.C. during the reign of Ptolemy II. It was probably 200 to 600 feet tall.

LONGEST BRIDGES IN THE WORLD

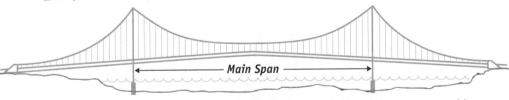

Main Span

The **span** of a bridge is the distance between its supports. The bridges below, as measured by main spans, are the world's longest suspension bridges (those that hang from cables). The longest suspension bridge in the U.S. is the Verrazano-Narrows Bridge in New York (4,260 feet).

NAME OF BRIDGE	LOCATION	MAIN SPAN
Akashi Kaikyo	Japan	6,570 feet
Storebaelt	Denmark	5,328 feet
Humber	England	4,626 feet

CALENDARS & TIME

If it is noon in Toronto, Ontario, what time is it in Sydney, Australia? You can find the answer on page 55.

CALENDARS

Calendars divide time into days, weeks, months, and years. Calendar divisions are based on movements of Earth and on the sun and the moon. A day is the average time it takes for one rotation of Earth on its axis. A year is the average time it takes for one revolution of Earth around the sun. Early calendars were based on the movements of the moon across the sky. The ancient Egyptians were probably the first to develop a calendar based on the movements of Earth around the sun.

ROMAN CALENDARS The Julian and Gregorian Calendars

The ancient Romans had a calendar with a year of 304 days. In 46 B.C., the emperor Julius Caesar decided to use a calendar based on movements of the sun. This calendar, called the **Julian calendar**, fixed the normal year at 365 days and added one day every fourth year (leap year). It also established the months of the year and the days of the week.

In A.D. 1582, the Julian calendar was revised by Pope Gregory XIII, because it was 11 minutes and 14 seconds too long. This added up to three too many days every 400 years. To fix it, he made years ending in 00 leap years only if they can be divided by 400. Thus, 2000 is a leap year, but 1900 is not. The new calendar, called the **Gregorian calendar**, is the one used today in most of the world.

OTHER CALENDARS Jewish and Islamic Calendars

Other calendars are also used. The Jewish calendar, which began almost 6,000 years ago, is the official calendar of Israel. The year 2002 is equivalent to 5762–5763 on the Jewish calendar, which starts at Rosh Hashanah. The Islamic calendar starts in A.D. 622. The year 2002 is equivalent to 1422–1423 on the Islamic calendar, which begins with the month of Muharram.

BIRTHSTONES

MONTH	BIRTHSTONE
January	Garnet
February	Amethyst
March	Aquamarine
April	Diamond
May	Emerald
June	Pearl
July	Ruby
August	Peridot
September	Sapphire
October	Opal
November	Topaz
December	Turquoise

Did You KNOW?

A SUNDIAL IS A NATURAL CLOCK. It shows the time of day by the shadow of an object on which the sun's rays fall. That object is called a gnomon. In ancient Egypt, pyramids and obelisks were gnomons! The world's largest sundial was built in Jaipur, India, in 1724. It's still standing! It covers almost one acre and has a gnomon more than 100 feet high, which is topped by an observatory.

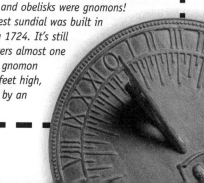

WHAT ARE TIME ZONES?

A day is 24 hours long—the time it takes Earth to complete one rotation on its axis. The system we use to tell time is called **standard time**. In standard time, Earth is divided into 24 time zones. Each zone is 15 degrees of longitude wide and runs from the North to the South Pole.

The line of longitude passing through Greenwich, England, is the starting point. It is called the **prime meridian**. In the 12th time zone (and 180th meridian) the **International Date Line** appears. When you cross the line going west, it's tomorrow. Going east, you travel backward in time and the date is one day earlier.

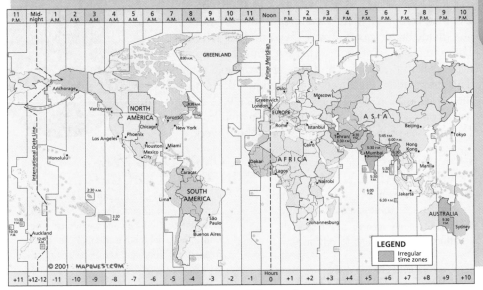

When it is 7 A.M. in Miami, Florida, it is

| 7 A.M. in Toronto, Ontario | 9 A.M. in São Paulo, Brazil | 1 P.M. in Rome, Italy | 3 P.M. in Nairobi, Kenya | 8 P.M. in Beijing, China | 9 P.M. in Tokyo, Japan | 10 P.M. in Sydney, Australia |

TIME WILL TELL

Latitude and longitude combined tell ships exactly where they are on Earth (see page 81). Many centuries ago it was fairly easy to pinpoint a ship's latitude by observing the sun and stars. But it was almost impossible to find the exact longitude. For that, sailors needed to know the time difference between their home port and their position at sea. But clocks of that period could not keep accurate time on ships. For example, a rolling sea could make the pendulum in a clock slow down or speed up, so it showed the wrong time. Or changes in temperature could make the oil in a clock thinner or thicker and cause the metal parts to expand or contract. The mistakes that resulted killed thousands of sailors in shipwrecks.

Then in 1735, an English clockmaker named John Harrison invented the first chronometer. It was a highly accurate clock that could withstand the rigors of seafaring. Once it caught on, the chronometer made finding longitude a routine chore and saved many sailors' lives.

COMPUTERS

What is artificial intelligence?
You can find the answer on page 57.

WHAT DO COMPUTERS DO?

At first, computers were used to add, subtract, multiply, and divide big numbers. Today they can do much more. For example, a pizza shop owner might use a computer to keep track of the number and type of pizzas sold each day. This information, organized and stored in a database, helps the owner order new supplies more efficiently. A student can use a computer to send e-mail, get information from the Internet (see page 61), play games, or do homework.

COMPUTERS HELP PEOPLE CREATE.

▶ People use computers to create artwork and music or to design buildings.

▶ Computers are used to create special effects for movies and television.

COMPUTERS HELP PEOPLE COMMUNICATE.

▶ Computers can be used to write letters, stories, or reports for school.

▶ Computers help create newspapers, magazines, and books.

▶ People use computers to send e-mail, sometimes across the continent or to other countries.

▶ People who cannot speak can type messages that the computer translates into speech. People who cannot type can speak into a computer that translates their speech into text.

COMPUTERS HELP PEOPLE LEARN.

▶ Programs on computers help teach school subjects.

▶ Computer programs can keep track of students' progress.

▶ Pilots and astronauts use computer flight simulators.

COMPUTERS KEEP INFORMATION ORGANIZED.

▶ Many companies and organizations keep a database with information. The FBI has a database that police departments can use to find information about criminals or stolen goods from all around the United States.

COMPUTERS ARE USED TO MANUFACTURE PRODUCTS.

▶ Engineers use special software to create detailed drawings of an object and then test it to see how to make it stronger or cheaper.

▶ Computers can control machinery used to make the new product.

COMPUTERS HELP PREDICT THE FUTURE.

▶ Companies use computer programs to help them make business decisions.

▶ Computer programs use data from satellites to help forecast weather.

COMPUTERS AREN'T JUST FOUND ON DESKS.

▶ Computers are used in automatic teller machines at the bank and with the price scanner at the supermarket checkout.

▶ Cars, VCRs, video games, calculators, and digital watches all have built-in computers.

COMPUTER TALK

artificial intelligence or AI The ability of computers and robots to imitate human intelligence by learning and making decisions.

bit The smallest unit of data.

browser A program to help get around the Internet.

bug or glitch An error in a program or in the computer.

byte An amount of data equal to 8 bits.

database A large collection of information organized so that it can be retrieved and used in different ways.

desktop publishing The use of computers for combining text and pictures to design and produce magazines, newspapers, and books.

download To transfer information from a host computer to a personal computer, often through a modem.

e-mail or electronic mail Messages sent between computers over a network.

gig or gigabyte (GB) An amount of information equal to 1,024 megabytes.

hard copy Computer output printed on paper or similar material.

home page The main page at a Web site.

Internet A worldwide system of linked computer networks.

K This stands for *kilo*, or "thousands," in Greek. It is used to represent bytes of data or memory.

laptop or notebook A portable personal computer that can run on batteries.

megabyte (MB) An amount of information equal to 1,048,516 bytes.

multimedia Software that includes pictures, video, and sound. In multimedia software, you can see pictures move and hear music and other sounds.

network A group of computers linked together so that they can share information.

password A secret code that keeps people who do not know it from using a computer or software.

program Instructions for a computer to follow.

RAM or random access memory The memory your computer uses to open programs and store your work until you save it to the hard drive or a disk. The information in RAM disappears when the computer is turned off.

ROM or read only memory ROM contains permanent instructions for the computer and cannot be changed. The information in ROM remains after the computer is turned off.

scanner A device that can transfer words and pictures from a printed page into the computer.

upload To send information from a personal computer to a host computer.

virtual reality Three-dimensional images on a screen that are viewed using special equipment (like gloves and goggles). The user feels as if he or she is part of the image and can interact with everything around.

virus A program that damages other programs and data. It gets into a computer through telephone lines or shared disks.

Web site A place on the Internet's World Wide Web where text and pictures are stored. The contents are sent to computers when the correct World Wide Web address (which begins with http:// or www.) is entered.

HOW COMPUTERS WORK

SOFTWARE

▶ **Kinds of Software** To write a story (or letter or school report) you use a type of software called a word-processing program. This program can be selected by using the **keyboard** or a **mouse**.

Other common types of software include programs for doing mathematics, keeping records, playing games, and creating pictures.

▶ **Entering Data** In a word-processing program, you can input your words by typing on the **keyboard**. The backspace and delete keys are like electronic erasers. You can also press special keys (called **function keys**) or click on certain symbols (**icons**), to center or underline words, move words and sentences around, check your spelling, print out a page, and do other tasks. When you input a command, the word-processing program tells the computer what to do.

HARDWARE

▶ **Inside the Computer** The instructions from the program you use are carried out inside the computer by the **central processing unit**, or **CPU**. The CPU is the computer's brain.

▶ **Getting the Results** The **monitor** and **printer** are the most commonly used output devices in a computer system. When you type a story, the words appear on a **monitor**, which is similar to a television screen. Your story can then be printed on paper by using a **printer**.

If you print out a story, you can mail it to a friend. But if you and your friend both have **modems**, the story can be sent from your computer directly to your friend's computer. A **modem** allows information from a computer to travel over telephone lines.

Computers perform tasks by using programs called **software**. These programs tell the computer what to do when the user enters certain information or commands. This is called **input**.

The computer then processes the information and gives the user the results **(output)**. The computer can also save, or store, the information so that it can be used again and again.

The machines that make up a computer system are kinds of **hardware**. The largest and most powerful computers are called **mainframes**. Scientists use them to perform calculations that would take years to do by hand. The computers most people are familiar with are personal computers **(PCs)**. These can be used at a desk **(desktops)**, carried around **(laptops)**, even held in your hand **(palm computers)**.

STORAGE

KEEPING DATA TO USE IT LATER A computer also stores information. You can save your work and return to it at your convenience. It is important to save often.

FLOPPY DISK

Information can be saved on a **"floppy" disk** that goes into a slot in the computer called a **disk drive.** If you use a disk to save your story, you can use the disk on another computer and your story will be there to work on. Disks today are usually stiff. Older computers used larger disks that were light and easy to bend, so people began calling them floppy disks.

ZIP DISK

Zip® disks hold much more information than floppy disks. They are used in special Zip drives. A **Jaz® disk** holds a gigabyte of information, 10 times as much as a Zip disk.

HARD DISK

Most computers have a **hard drive**. The hard drive contains a **hard disk** that is not removed. It holds much more information than zip or floppy disks. It stores your software and information you have entered into the computer.

CD-ROMs

Many computers have a CD-ROM drive. This allows you to play special disks called **CD-ROMs**, similar to music CDs. A CD-ROM can hold a huge amount of information, including pictures and sound. Almanacs, games, encyclopedias, and many other types of information and entertainment are on CD-ROMs.

DVDs

Digital Versatile Disks look like CD-ROMs, but hold about eight times more information on a single side. DVDs are currently used to store movies, encyclopedias, and other products with lots of data.

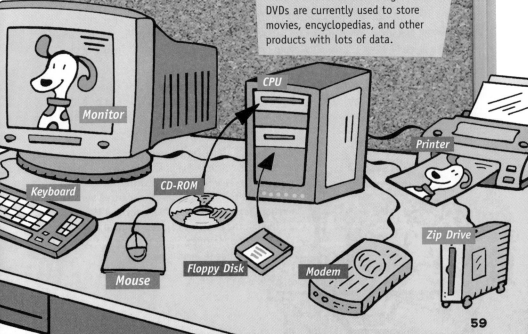

Monitor

CPU

Printer

Keyboard

CD-ROM

Zip Drive

Mouse

Floppy Disk

Modem

THE BINARY SYSTEM

For a computer to do its work, every piece of information given to it must be translated into **binary code**. You are probably used to using 10 digits, 0 through 9, when you do arithmetic. When the computer uses the binary code, it uses only two digits, 0 and 1. Think of it as sending messages to the computer by switching a light on and off.

Each 0 or 1 digit is called a bit, and most computers use a sequence of 8 bits (called a **byte**) for each piece of data. Almost all computers use the same code, called ASCII (pronounced "askey"), to stand for letters of the alphabet, number digits, punctuation, and other special characters that control the computer's operation. Below is a list of ASCII bytes for the alphabet.

A	01000001	H	01001000	O	01001111	V	01010110
B	01000010	I	01001001	P	01010000	W	01010111
C	01000011	J	01001010	Q	01010001	X	01011000
D	01000100	K	01001011	R	01010010	Y	01011001
E	01000101	L	01001100	S	01010011	Z	01011010
F	01000110	M	01001101	T	01010100		
G	01000111	N	01001110	U	01010101		

COMPUTER GAMES

Return of the Incredible Machine: Contraptions *Sierra Attractions, for Windows 95/98 and Power Mac* • It doesn't take brawn to do well in this construction game. It takes brains. The object is to build a gadget that does simple tasks, by adding blimps, mice, bowling balls, and other parts.

Nancy Drew: Message in a Haunted Mansion *Dreamcatcher/Her Interactive, for Windows* • The famous sleuth is on a case in San Francisco. Her job—and the player's job—is to solve the mystery of why "accidents" keep happening in an old mansion. There are plenty of interesting suspects and clues. This is worth investigating.

Bust-A-Move 4 *Interplay, for Windows 95/98* • To do well at these puzzle games, you need strategy and skill. In one game, you control Bob and Bud the dinosaurs. Their color bubbles must blast matching color bubbles floating down the screen. Do it before they reach the bottom—or your game goes bust. There's also a tough two-player challenge.

Backyard Baseball *Humongous Entertainment, for Windows 95/98* • Play ball! This baseball simulation features 31 Little Leaguers with distinct personalities, in addition to pint-sized versions of major-leaguers like Alex Rodriguez and Mark McGwire. Though they can hit like Jeff Bagwell and pitch like Pedro Martinez, you'll think you're playing with friends in your hometown.

THE INTERNET

What is the Internet?

The **Internet ("Net")** connects computers from around the world so people can share information. You can play games on the Net, send e-mail, shop, and find information. The **World Wide Web (www)** is a part of the Internet that lets you see information using pictures, colors, and sounds. Most people just call it the Web. Information on the Web lives on a **Web site**. To get to the Web site you want, you need to use the right **Universal Resource Locator (URL)**, or address. If you know the address, just find the place for it on the screen and type it in carefully.

If you don't know the address, hit **Search**. You may have to pick a search engine, which is like a huge index. A few popular search engines are Yahoo, Google, and Lycos. When you have the one you want, type in words that tell what you're searching for. You will get a list of sites. You can choose the site most likely to have the information you want. Some

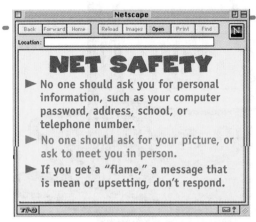

Netscape

Back | Forward | Home | Reload | Images | Open | Print | Find

Location:

NET SAFETY

► No one should ask you for personal information, such as your computer password, address, school, or telephone number.

► No one should ask for your picture, or ask to meet you in person.

► If you get a "flame," a message that is mean or upsetting, don't respond.

sites have **links**—names of other sites on the same subject.

Can you depend on information from the Internet?

Watch out when you use information from the Internet. The source may not be reliable. An official Web site produced by a company, organization, or government agency may be more reliable than a site created by a fan or someone interested in the topic you are looking up. It often may be worth checking more than one source.

SMILEYS

Smileys, or **emoticons**, are letters and symbols that look like faces when turned sideways. They tell things about yourself in messages you send. Here are a few with what they mean.

C=:-)	Chef	:-O	Shout	:-)	Smile
O:-)	Angel	;-)	Wink	:-(	Unhappy
}:->	Devil	:-b..	Drooling	:-D	Laugh

FAQ: What's a BL?

Smileys are just one quick way to express an idea or feeling on the Internet. People also use **initials** as a shorthand. For example, FAQ stands for Frequently Asked Question. And BL means Belly Laugh. Here are some other common abbreviations. For each one, can you tell the real definition from the one we made up?

❶ BBL
a. Be Back Later
b. Big Belly Laugh

❷ WB
a. Whatta Blabbermouth
b. Welcome Back

❸ WTG
a. Way To Go!
b. Why The Giggles?

❹ ROTFL
a. Rolling On The Floor Laughing
b. Read Only The First Line

❺ J/K
a. Junky Keyboard
b. Just Kidding

❻ GMTA
a. Great Minds Think Alike
b. Give Me The Answer

❼ AFK
a. Away From Keyboard
b. Awfully Funny Kid

❽ NP
a. No Parking
b. No Problem

Answers are on pages 317–320.

NEW GADGETS

Today's electronic devices not only do many different things; they are often small enough to hold in your hand or carry in your pocket. Here are some of the coolest gadgets around.

❶ Two-way radios The old fashioned walkie-talkie is making a comeback-as a pair of gadgets. Give one to a friend and you can talk on the same wavelength. Depending on the model, the range of these devices stetches from a few hundred yards to five miles. Unlike cell phones, talk is cheap with two-way radios: Once you buy the unit, your chats are free.

❷ Digital Assistant These tiny computers do dozens of tasks. A kid's version called Phusion, from VTech, includes a calculator, foreign-word translator, world clock, and calendar, as well as a built-in digital camera. The device also lets you download photos and create games based on those pictures.

❸ MP3 Player The MP3 is causing a musical revolution. These players let you transfer music from your computer or the Web into a portable device. Though these devices can be as small as a watch or pen, they pack about an hour's worth of music. More and more, MP3 players are being packaged with other electronic gadgets, such as cell phones and cameras. Some MP3 players even include tiny LCD screens. These let you download photo files, and offer video playback. That means you can watch a music video and play your favorite tunes at the same time!

❹ Video Phone Cam With this device from Ezonics, you can see your friends as you talk to them on the phone. It looks like a cell phone with a built-in camera. Plug it into a computer by cable and you can send real-time video mail of yourself-or anything else within range. You can also send a series of images that can be turned into a mini movie. The videophone cam also makes a phone list that shows snapshots of people instead of their names. You click on the photo to dial their numbers. In addition, you can create and e-mail video messages-or turn your e-mail message into a greeting card.

❺ Computer-guided Telescopes Companies like Tasco and Meade have turned home telescopes into mini observatories. With the touch of a button, these scopes automatically locate nearly 2,000 celestial objects. The location of the moon, planets, stars, planets, galaxies, and nebulae are pre-programmed in the scope's computer. How does it know where everything is? You "tell" the computer what city you're near and the time and date, and it orients itself to your position in the universe.

❻ Wireless E-mail Chat is a kid-friendly version of the hand-held wireless e-mail device. Though it isn't a computer, Chat sends or receives e-mails when you plug it into a home or pay phone jack. These e-mails are free. And Chat communicates by radio waves with other Chat machines up to one-half mile away.

❼ Video to Go Video in a Bag is a portable system that's part VCR and part built-in four inch LCD screen. Hanging from straps between the driver and passenger seats, it shows movies and displays video games.

COMPUTER PUZZLES

KEY IN THE WORDS

Each set of letters below is a computer-related term that's been scrambled. Unscramble the letters and write the answers in the correct boxes. When you do this, the letters in the shaded column will spell out the answer to this riddle: What do airports and computers have in common?

1. TINOMRO
2. YEAODRKB
3. RUSVI
4. OSUEM
5. RETTNEIN
6. NERTRIP
7. RDHA YOPC
8. WONDLDAO
9. SKID

ON SITE

On the blank lines, write in the letter of the Web site that would probably give you the best answers to the questions. Then look up the answers.

___ 1. When did Little League baseball begin?
___ 2. When did The Beatles start their first U.S. tour?
___ 3. Which U.S. president had a sign on his desk that said "The buck stops here"? What does that mean?
___ 4. What is the record low temperature in Nome, Alaska? What is the record high in Sarasota, Florida?
___ 5. What is the nickname of the astronaut who joined Neil Armstrong on the surface of the moon?

A. http://www.hq.nasa.gov/office/pao/History/apollo/apo11.html
B. http://www.weather.com/common/home/climatology.html
C. http://www.littleleague.org/history/index.htm
D. http://www.rockhall.com/hof/allinductees.asp
E. http://www.trumanlibrary.org/trivia/trivpg.htm

ENERGY

Which country uses the most energy?
You can find the answer on page 67.

ENERGY KEEPS US MOVING

You can't touch, see, smell, or taste energy, but you can observe what it does. You can feel that sunlight warms objects, and you can see that electricity lights up a light bulb, even if you can't see the heat or the electricity.

WHAT iS ENERGY? Things that you see and touch every day use some form of energy to work: your body, a bike, a basketball, a car. Energy enables things to move. Scientists define energy as the ability to do work.

WHY DO WE NEED ENERGY TO DO WORK? Scientists define **work** as a force moving an object. Scientifically speaking, throwing a ball is work, but studying for a test isn't! When you throw a ball, you use energy from the food you eat to do work on the ball. The engine in a car uses energy from gasoline to make the car move.

Are There Different Kinds of Energy?

POTENTiAL When we rest or sleep we still have the ability to move. We do not lose our energy. We simply store it for another time. Stored energy is called **potential energy**. When we get up and begin to move around, we are using stored energy.

KiNETiC As we move around and walk, our stored (potential) energy changes into **kinetic energy**, which is the energy of moving things. A parked car has potential energy. A moving car has kinetic energy. A sled stopped at the top of the hill has potential energy. As the sled goes down the hill, its potential energy changes to kinetic energy.

HOW IS ENERGY CREATED? Energy cannot be created or destroyed, but it can be changed or converted into different forms. **Heat, light,** and **electricity** are all forms of energy. Other forms of energy are **sound, chemical energy, mechanical energy,** and **nuclear energy**.

WHERE DOES ENERGY COME FROM? All of the forms of energy we use come from the energy stored in **natural resources**. Sunlight, water, wind, petroleum, coal, and natural gas are natural resources. From these resources, we get heat and electricity.

THE SUN AND ITS ENERGY

All of our energy really comes from the Sun. The Sun is a big ball of gases, made up mostly of hydrogen. Inside the Sun, hydrogen atoms join together (through a process called nuclear fusion) and become helium. During this process, large amounts of energy are released. This energy works its way to the Sun's surface, then radiates out into space in the form of waves. These waves give us heat and light. The energy from the Sun is stored in our food, which provides fuel for our bodies.

Plants absorb energy from the Sun (solar energy) and convert absorbed energy to chemical energy for storage.

Animals eat plants and gain the stored chemical energy.

Food provides the body with energy to work and play.

People eat plants and meat.

SUN POWER IN FOSSIL FUELS

The Sun also provides the energy stored in fossil fuels. Coal, petroleum, and natural gas are **fossil fuels**. Fossil fuels come from the remains of ancient plants and animals that lived millions and millions of years ago. This is what happened:

1. Hundreds of millions of years ago, before people lived on Earth, trees and other plants absorbed energy from the Sun, just as they do today.
2. Animals ate plants and smaller animals.
3. After the plants and animals died, they slowly became buried deeper and deeper underground.
4. After millions of years, they turned into coal and petroleum.

Although the buried prehistoric plants and animals changed form over time, they still contained stored energy.

When we burn fossil fuels today, the stored energy from the Sun is released in the form of heat. The heat is used to warm our homes and other buildings and produce electricity for our lights and appliances.

How Energy Reaches You

ENERGY FROM FOSSIL FUELS

Fossil fuels are a major source of energy. Your home may be heated with oil or natural gas. You may have a kitchen stove that uses natural gas. Your car needs gasoline to run. Here is how a power plant uses fossil fuel to make electricity, which is then sent by wires into homes and businesses.

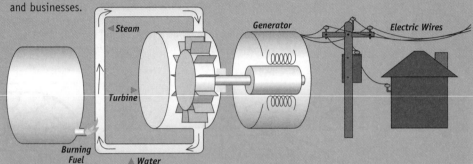

1. The **fossil fuel,** usually coal, is burned in a furnace. The **heat** from the fuel warms up water that flows through pipes. When the water boils, it becomes **steam**.

2. The steam is sent to a **turbine** (a wheel with blades). The steam pushes against the blades of the turbine and causes it to spin.

3. A shaft (a long, round bar) attached to the turbine turns a **generator**. Inside the generator, a spinning **magnet** produces **electricity** in coils nearby.

4. The electricity is sent by **wires** to homes and businesses. It can then be used for lighting and for running appliances or machines.

ENERGY FROM WATER

For centuries, people have been harnessing energy from rushing water. In a **hydroelectric plant**, water channeled through rivers or dams is used to drive machinery like a turbine. The turbine is connected to a generator, which produces electricity.

NUCLEAR ENERGY

The United States has 104 nuclear power plants. Together, they produce about one-fifth of the country's electricity. In France, 75% of the electricity comes from nuclear power. Energy experts are trying to generate more electricity without polluting the air. Nuclear reactors do not give off harmful greenhouse gases or pollute the air (thay have cooling towers that give off water vapor), but they do create radioactive waste that is difficult to dispose of safely. In 2000, the U.S. Congress funded a multimillion-dollar study of nuclear energy. It will seek ways to improve nuclear technology, nuclear safety, and the disposal of nuclear waste.

◄ Cooling towers at nuclear plant

WHO PRODUCES AND USES THE MOST ENERGY?

The United States produces about 19 percent of the world's energy—more than any other country—but it uses 25 percent of the world's energy. The table at left lists the world's ten top energy-producers and the percent of the world's production that each was responsible for in 1999. The other table lists the world's top energy-users and the percent of the world's energy use that each was responsible for.

Countries That Produce the Most Energy	
United States	19 percent
Russia	11 percent
China	8 percent
Saudi Arabia	5 percent
Canada	5 percent
Great Britain	3 percent
Iran	3 percent
Norway	3 percent
India	2 percent
Mexico	2 percent

Countries That Consume the Most Energy	
United States	25 percent
China	9 percent
Russia	7 percent
Japan	6 percent
Germany	4 percent
Canada	3 percent
India	3 percent
France	3 percent
Great Britain	3 percent
Brazil	2 percent

ENERGETIC FACTS

► About six million tons of petroleum leak or spill into the world's oceans every year.

► A typical paper mill uses about the same amount of energy as 100,000 households. Of course, this book is printed on paper.

► In one year, all of the family vehicles in the United States use enough fuel to fill a hole 40 miles deep and the length of a football field.

YOUR TURN

The United States uses up more energy than it produces. Can you think of three ways that you and your family can save energy?

1 _____

2 _____

3 _____

WILL WE HAVE ENOUGH ENERGY?

WHERE DOES OUR ENERGY COME FROM?

In 1999, most of the energy used in the United States came from fossil fuels (about 39% from petroleum, 22.9% from natural gas, and 22.5% from coal). The rest came mostly from hydropower (water power) and nuclear energy. Fossil fuels are nonrenewable sources of energy. That means the amount of fossil fuel available for use is limited and that all this fuel will get used up after many years.

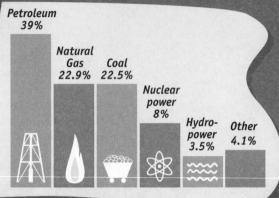

Petroleum 39%

Natural Gas 22.9%

Coal 22.5%

Nuclear power 8%

Hydro-power 3.5%

Other 4.1%

LOOKING FOR RENEWABLE RESOURCES

Scientists are trying to find more sources of energy that will reduce pollution and save some of the fossil fuels. People are using several types of **renewable resources**. Some of these forms of energy exist in an unlimited supply.

▶ **Solar power.** Solar power uses energy directly from sunlight. Solar panels can collect the sun's rays for heating. Solar cells can convert light energy directly into electricity.

▶ **Hydropower.** Water is channeled through rivers or dams to drive a turbine. The turbine is connected to a generator, which produces electricity.

▶ **The wind.** Windmills can be used to drive machinery. Today, some people are using wind turbines to generate electricity.

▶ **Biomass energy.** Biomass includes wood from trees and other plants, animal wastes, and garbage. Burning these produces heat with less pollution than fossil fuels release. Biomass energy is widely available and used in some parts of the world.

▶ **Geothermal energy.** Geothermal energy is energy that comes from the hot, molten rock inside Earth. In certain parts of the world, such as Iceland and New Zealand, people use this kind of energy for electricity and to heat buildings.

CALIFORNIA ENERGY CRUNCH

Since late 2000, California has faced severe electricity shortages. Sometimes power has been cut off in different parts of the state in what are called "rolling blackouts."

This happened partly because of a complicated new plan in which California's electric utility companies sold their power plants, then had to buy power at prices that went way up, instead of going down as had been expected.

Other states may soon have problems too, since many states need more power plants and demand for power is increasing, partly because of the use of computers and other appliances.

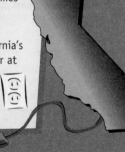

ENVIRONMENT

Why did Julia Hill live up in a redwood tree for two years?
You can find the answer on page 77.

WHAT IS THE ENVIRONMENT?

Everything that surrounds us is part of the environment. Not just living things like plants and animals, but also beaches and mountains, the air we breathe, the sunlight that provides warmth, and the water that we use in our homes, schools, and businesses.

PEOPLE AND THE ENVIRONMENT

Humans like ourselves may have lived on Earth for more than 300,000 years. For a long time people thought the Earth was so huge that it could easily absorb human wastes and pollution. And they thought that Earth's natural resources would never be used up.

In prehistoric times, people killed animals for food and built fires to cook food and keep themselves warm. They cut down trees for fuel, and their fires released pollution into the air. But there were so few people that their activities had little impact on the environment.

In modern times, the world's population has been growing very fast. In 1850 there were around a billion people in the world. In 1950 there were around 2.5 billion, and in 2001, there were more than six billion. Their activities have put a strain on the environment.

SHARING THE EARTH

We share the planet with trees, flowers, insects, fish, whales, dogs, and many other plants and animals. Each species (type) of animal or plant has its place on Earth, and each one is dependent on many others. Plants give off oxygen that animals need to breathe. Animals pollinate plants and spread their seeds. Animals eat plants and are in turn eaten by larger animals. When plants and animals die, they become part of the soil in which new plants, in their turn, take root and grow.

WATCHING OVER THE EARTH

People are becoming more aware that human activities can seriously damage the planet and the animals and plants on it. Sometimes this damage can be reversed or slowed down. But it is often permanent. On the following pages you'll learn about the damage, and about some things that can be done to help clean up and protect our planet.

You can learn more about the environment at:

WEB SITE *http://www.nwf.org/kids*

69

WHAT IS BIODIVERSITY?

Our planet, Earth, is shared by millions of species of living things. The wide variety of life on Earth, as shown by the many species, is called "biodiversity" (*bio* means "life" and diversity means "variety"). Human beings of all colors, races, and nationalities make up just one species, *Homo sapiens*.

Species, Species Everywhere
This list is just a sampling of how diverse Earth is.

SNAKES: 2,400 species
Fascinating Fact ▶ Many people fear snakes, but most snakes are harmless to humans.

FISH: 24,000 species
Fascinating Fact ▶ More than half of all known kinds of vertebrates are fish.

SPIDERS: 30,000+ species
Fascinating Fact ▶ Only six species of spiders in North America have harmful bites.

PROTOZOANS: 30,000 species
Fascinating Fact ▶ Protozoans are single-celled living beings that are an important part of the ocean food chain.

HUMAN BEINGS: 1 species
Fascinating Fact ▶ This one species holds the fate of all the other species in its hands. People can affect the environment more than any other form of living thing.

CATS: 35 species
Fascinating Fact ▶ All the breeds of pet cats make up only one species of cat. The other species include wildcats like leopards, tigers, and lions.

SOME THREATS TO BIODIVERSITY Plants and animals are harmed by pollution of the air, water, and land, and their habitats are often destroyed by deforestation. For example, in recent years, large areas of rain forests have been cleared for wood, farmland, and cattle ranches. People have become concerned that rain forests may be disappearing. Another threat is overharvesting of animals, such as fish, for food or other products. For example, the number of catfish, salmon, and trout has been falling, and some species could eventually be wiped out entirely.

PROTECTING BIODIVERSITY Efforts to reduce pollutants in air, water, and soil, to preserve rain forests, and to limit other deforestation and overharvesting help to preserve biodiversity. A few species that were once endangered now will probably survive. A few species that have been taken off the endangered species list are the bald eagle, the peregrine falcon, and the gray wolf.

THE 1300S WERE A GOOD TIME TO BE A RAT. *Because of ignorance and superstition, many people back then feared cats. Hundreds of thousands of cats were killed, so the rat population grew. This probably led to the spread of the Black Death, a sickness caused by rat fleas. One out of every four Europeans died from the disease in the 1300s.*

"ECO" WORDS

acid rain Rain, snow, hail, sleet, and fog polluted by chemicals in the air.

compost heap A pile of food scraps and yard waste that is gradually broken down by worms and tiny insects. The result looks like plain dirt. It can be used to enrich the soil.

conservation The preservation and wise use of water, forests, and other natural resources so they will not be damaged or wasted.

deforestation The cutting down of most of the trees from forested land, usually so that the land can be used for farming and housing.

ecosystem A community of living things that depend on each other, in a particular place, such as a forest or pond.

extinction disappearance of a type (species) of plant or animal from Earth. Some species become extinct because of non-human forces, but many others are becoming endangered or threatened with extinction because of the activities of people.

food chain The way each living creature depends on another living thing as a source of food. Humans eat animals. Bigger animals eat smaller animals. Smaller animals eat even smaller ones. And so on, down to the tiniest living creatures.

fossil fuel A source of energy (such as oil, gas, and coal) formed deep in the Earth from once-living matter.

global warming An increase in Earth's surface temperature due to a buildup of certain gases in the atmosphere.

greenhouse effect Warming of Earth caused by certain gases (called **greenhouse gases**) that form a blanket in the atmosphere high over Earth. Small amounts of these gases keep Earth warm so we can live here, but the larger amounts produced by factories, cars, and burning trees may hold too much heat and cause global warming.

groundwater Water in the ground that flows in the spaces between soil particles and rocks. Groundwater supplies water for wells and springs.

habitat The natural home of an animal or a plant.

ornithology The study of birds.

ozone layer A layer in the atmosphere, 15 miles above the earth, which protects our planet from the sun's harmful rays.

recycling Using something more than once, either just the way it is, or reprocessed into something else.

reforestation Planting and growing new trees where other trees have been cut down.

soil erosion The washing away or blowing away of topsoil. Trees and other plants hold the soil in place and help reduce the force of the wind. Soil erosion happens when trees and plants are cut down.

WHERE GARBAGE GOES

Most of the things around you will be replaced or thrown away someday. Skates, clothes, the toaster, furniture—they can break or wear out, or you may get tired of them. Where will they go when they are thrown out? What kinds of waste will they create, and how will it affect the environment?

LOOK AT WHAT IS NOW IN U.S. LANDFILLS

Metal
8%

Plastic
24%

Food and
Yard Waste
11%

Rubber
and Leather
6%

Other
Trash
21%

Paper
30%

WHAT HAPPENS TO THINGS WE THROW AWAY?

LANDFILLS

Most of our trash goes to places called landfills. A **LANDFILL** (or dump) is a low area of land that is filled with garbage. Most modern landfills are lined with a layer of plastic or clay to try to keep dangerous liquids from seeping into the soil and ground water supply.

THE PROBLEM WITH LANDFILLS

More than half of the states in this country are running out of places to dump their garbage. Because of the unhealthful materials many contain, landfills do not make good neighbors, and people don't want to live near them. Many landfills are located in poor neighborhoods. But where can cities dispose of their waste? How can hazardous waste — material that can poison air, land, and water — be disposed of in a safe way?

INCINERATORS

One way to get rid of trash is to burn it. Trash is burned in a furnace-like device called an incinerator. Because incinerators can get rid of almost all of the bulk of the trash, some communities would rather use incinerators than landfills.

THE PROBLEM WITH INCINERATORS

Leftover ash and smoke from burning trash may contain harmful chemicals, called pollutants, and make it hard for some people to breathe. They can harm plants, animals, and people.

Did You KNOW?

THE FRESH KILLS LANDFILL ON STATEN ISLAND, NEW YORK, WAS THE LARGEST GARBAGE DUMP IN THE WORLD. *For years, people who live nearby complained about air and water pollution caused by the massive pile of trash. They say that the fumes have made people sick. The dump closed in April 2001. Now New York City's garbage is trucked out of state.*

REDUCE, REUSE, RECYCLE

You can help reduce waste by reusing containers, batteries, and paper. You can also recycle newspaper, glass, and plastics to provide materials for making other products. At right are some of the things you can do.

WHAT IS MADE FROM RECYCLED MATERIALS?

▶ From **RECYCLED PAPER** we get newspapers, cereal boxes, wrapping paper, cardboard containers, and insulation.

▶ From **RECYCLED PLASTIC** we get soda bottles, tables, benches, bicycle racks, cameras, backpacks, carpeting, shoes, and clothes.

▶ From **RECYCLED STEEL** we get steel cans, cars, bicycles, nails, and refrigerators.

▶ From **RECYCLED GLASS** we get glass jars and tiles.

▶ From **RECYCLED RUBBER** we get bulletin boards, floor tiles, playground equipment, and speed bumps.

	To Reduce Waste	To Recycle
Paper	Use both sides of the paper. Use cloth towels instead of paper towels.	Recycle newspapers, magazines, comic books, catalogs, cardboard, and junk mail.
Plastic	Wash food containers and store leftovers in them. Reuse plastic bags.	Return soda bottles to the store. Recycle other plastics.
Glass	Keep glass bottles and jars to store other things.	Recycle glass bottles and jars.
Clothes	Give clothes to younger relatives or friends. Donate clothes to thrift shops.	Cut unwearable clothing into rags to use instead of paper towels.
Metal	Keep leftovers in storage containers instead of wrapping them in foil. Use glass or stainless steel pans instead of disposable pans.	Recycle aluminum cans and foil trays. Return wire hangers to the dry cleaner.
Food/Yard Waste	Cut the amount of food you throw out. Try saving leftovers for snacks or meals later on.	Make a compost heap using food scraps, leaves, grass clippings, and the like.
Batteries	Use rechargeable batteries for toys and games, radios, tape players, and flashlights.	Find out about your town's rules for recycling or disposing of batteries.

The Air We Breathe

All human beings and animals need air to survive. Without air we would die. Plants also need air to live. Plants use sunlight and the carbon dioxide in air to make food, and then give off oxygen.

We all breathe the air that surrounds Earth. The air is made up mainly of gases: around 78% nitrogen, 21% oxygen, and 1% carbon dioxide, water vapor, and other gases. Human beings breathe more than six quarts of air every minute. Because air is so basic to life, it is very important to keep the air clean by reducing or preventing air pollution. Today, air pollution causes health problems and may bring about **acid rain, global warming,** and a breakdown of the **ozone layer.**

Nitrogen 78%

Oxygen 21%

Carbon Dioxide, Other Gases, Water Vapor 1%

What is Air Pollution and Where Does it Come From?

Air pollution is a dirtying of the air caused by toxic chemicals or other materials. It can injure health, the enjoyment of life, or the working of ecosystems. The major sources of air pollution are cars, trucks and buses, waste incinerators, factories, and some electric power plants, especially those that burn fossil fuels, such as coal.

What is Acid Rain and Where Does it Come From?

Acid rain is polluted rain or other precipitation that results from chemicals released into the air. The main sources of these chemicals are fumes, cars' exhaust pipes, and power plants that burn coal. When these chemicals mix with moisture and other particles, they create sulfuric acid and nitric acid. Winds often carry these acids many miles before they drop down in rain, snow, and fog, or even as dry particles.

Why Worry About Air Pollution and Acid Rain?

Air pollution and acid rain can harm people, animals, and plants. Air pollution can cause our eyes to sting and can even make some people sick. It can also damage crops and trees.

A Story of Air Pollution

Several New England states blame coal-burning power plants in the Midwest for polluting the air in the Northeast. The states say that the wind carries harmful emissions from Midwestern power plants to the Northeast, causing breathing and other health problems. Northeasterners want tighter controls placed on the Midwestern plants, so they will give off fewer harmful pollutants. But Midwesterners argue that reducing emissions would require costly equipment, they cannot afford.

Think About It What are some of the sources of air pollution where you live? Think about what you and your friends could do to reduce it.

WHAT ARE WE DOING TO REDUCE AIR POLLUTION?

Many countries are trying to reduce air pollution. In the United States, cars must have a special device to remove harmful chemicals from the exhaust before it comes out of the tailpipe. Many power plants and factories have devices on their smokestacks to catch chemicals. Many people try to use less electricity, so that less coal will have to be burned to produce it. And in some places, power companies use windmills or other equipment that does not pollute the air.

GLOBAL WARMING AND THE GREENHOUSE EFFECT

Many scientists believe that gases in the air are causing Earth's climate to gradually become warmer. This is called **global warming**. The hottest year on record was 1998. The second hottest was 1997, and 1999 was the fifth hottest. The six hottest years were all in the 1990s. If the climate becomes so warm that a great deal of ice near the North and South Poles melts and more water goes into the oceans, many areas along the coasts may be flooded.

In Earth's atmosphere there are tiny amounts of gases called **greenhouse gases**. These gases let the rays of the sun pass through to the planet, but they hold in the heat that comes up from the sun-warmed Earth—in much the same way as the glass walls of a greenhouse hold in the warmth of the sun.

As cities have increased in size and population, factories and businesses have also grown. People have needed more and more electricity, cars, and other things that must be manufactured. As industries in the world have grown, more greenhouse gases have been added to the atmosphere. These increase the thickness of the greenhouse "glass," causing more heat to be trapped than in the past. This is called the **greenhouse effect.**

▼ *How the greenhouse effect happens*

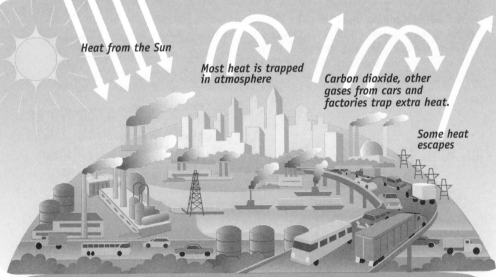

Heat from the Sun

Most heat is trapped in atmosphere

Carbon dioxide, other gases from cars and factories trap extra heat.

Some heat escapes

WILL NATIONS TRY TO STOP GLOBAL WARMING?

In 1997, representatives from more than 150 countries met in Kyoto, Japan, where they adopted a treaty on global warming. Under the treaty, the countries would reduce the emission of greenhouse gases an average of 5 percent below 1990 levels by the year 2012. However, the treaty did not go into force because industrial nations did not ratify it. The U.S. Congress and the Bush administration have opposed the treaty. Opponents of the treaty say it would be too costly for industries.

PROTECTING OUR WATER

Every living thing needs water to live. Many animals also depend on water as a home. People not only drink water, but also use it to cook, clean, cool machinery in factories, produce power, and irrigate farmland.

WHERE DO WE GET THE WATER WE USE?

Although about two thirds of the Earth's surface is water, we are able to use only a tiny fraction of it. Seawater makes up 97% of Earth's water, and 2% is frozen in glaciers and ice around the north and south poles. **Freshwater** makes up only 1% of our water, and only part of that is close enough to Earth's surface for us to use.

The water we can use comes from lakes, rivers, reservoirs, and groundwater. **Groundwater** is melted snow or rain that seeps deep below the surface of the Earth and collects in pools called aquifers.

Overall, the world has enough freshwater, but sometimes it is not available exactly where it is needed. Extreme water shortages, or **droughts**, can occur when an area gets too little rain or has very hot weather over a long period of time, causing water supplies to dry up.

HOW MUCH WATER DO WE USE?

One flush of a toilet: about 1½ gallons of water
Running the faucet for 4 minutes to wash dishes: 10 gallons
Running the dishwasher: 5–15 gallons per load
Taking a 5-minute shower: 12½ gallons
Taking a bath: 20–25 gallons

How Water is Used at Home

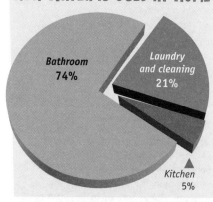

Bathroom 74%
Laundry and cleaning 21%
Kitchen 5%

WHAT IS THREATENING OUR WATER?

Water is polluted when it is not fit for its intended uses, such as drinking, swimming, watering crops, or serving as a habitat. Polluted water can cause disease and kill fish and other animals. Some major water pollutants include sewage, chemicals from factories, fertilizers and weed killers, and leakage from landfills. Water pollution is being reduced in some areas, such as Lake Erie, the Willamette River in Oregon, Boston Harbor, and the Hudson River in New York State. Companies continue to look for better ways to get rid of wastes, and many farmers are trying new ways to grow crops without using polluting fertilizers or chemicals.

Seeing the Forest and the Trees

Trees and forests are very important to the environment. In addition to holding water, trees hold the soil in place. Trees use carbon dioxide and give off oxygen, which animals and plants need for survival. And they provide homes and food for millions of types of animals.

Cutting down large numbers of trees, to use the land for something instead of a forest, is called **deforestation.** Although people often have good reasons for cutting down trees, deforestation can have serious effects. In the Amazon rain forest in South America, for example, thousands of plants and animal species are being lost before scientists can even learn about them. (For more about rain forests, see page 175.) In the Pacific Northwest, there is a conflict between logging companies that want to cut down trees for lumber and people who want to preserve the ancient forests.

Why Do We Cut Down Trees? People cut down trees for many reasons. When the population grows, people cut down trees to clear space to build houses, schools, factories, and other buildings. People may clear land to plant crops and graze livestock. Sometimes all the trees in an area are cut and sold for lumber and paper.

What Happens When Trees Are Cut Down? Cutting down trees can affect the climate. After rain falls on a forest, mist rises and new rain clouds form. When forests are cut down, this cycle is disrupted, and the area eventually grows drier, causing a change in the local climate.

If huge areas of trees are cut down, the carbon dioxide they would have used builds up in the atmosphere and contributes to the greenhouse effect. And without trees to hold the soil and absorb water, rain washes topsoil away, a process called **soil erosion.** Farming on the poorer soil that is left can be very hard.

What Are We Doing to Save Forests? In many countries trees are being planted faster than they are being cut down. Foresting companies are working on more efficient methods of replacing and growing forests. In addition, communities and individuals are helping to save forests by recycling paper.

All About... THE LADY in the TREE

For Julia "Butterfly" Hill, climbing trees is more than fun and games. It's serious business. On December 10, 1997, she climbed 180 feet up a 1,000-year-old redwood tree in northern California. She called the tree Luna. Julia stayed up there for two years! Perched on a small platform, she braved spiders, flying squirrels, bears, and stormy weather, all to bring attention to America's ancient redwood forests. Many environmentalists believe these trees are being cut down by logging companies faster than new ones can grow. Julia finally climbed down after a big logging company, the Maxxan Corporation, promised to leave Luna and the three acres of surrounding forest alone.

In November 2000, Julia and her supporters learned that someone had used a chainsaw to slash through Luna's trunk. While investigators searched for Luna's attackers, a crew of tree experts braced the damaged trunk with huge steel braces to help protect the tree from strong winds and storms.

GAMES

Which two letters earn the highest points in a Scrabble game? *You can find the answer below.*

MONOPOLY

SHARPEN YOUR SKILLS!

Some board games are based on skill. Others depend only on the throw of dice. For most, winning takes a mixture of skill and luck. Games like chess, checkers, Monopoly®, and Scrabble® are played all over the world by both kids and adults. Many board games can also be played on the computer. In fact, computers may be the toughest competitors ever.

CHECKERS is a game of skill. A form of checkers was played in ancient Egypt and Greece. It is played by two players on a board with light and dark squares. The goal is to capture all your opponent's pieces by jumping over them. To do so, you have to think ahead and take advantage of your opponent's mistakes.

DID YOU KNOW? *For over 70 years, checker champion Asa Long ranked among the top six players in the world. He captured his first title in 1922, at 18, becoming the youngest player to win a national tournament. Known as the "iron man" of the game, he triumphed again, at age 80 in 1984, and became the oldest player to win.*

MONOPOLY®, a game for two or more players, is one of the best-selling games of the 20th century. It involves both skill and luck. The skill is in making choices. Should you buy Water Works? How many houses should you put on Boardwalk? The luck is in throwing the dice and landing on the best places.

Monopoly was first sold by Parker Brothers in the 1930s. Charles P. Darrow is known as its inventor, but he actually got the idea from two earlier games, the Landlord Game, invented in 1904 by Elizabeth Magie Phillips, and a game about Atlantic City created by Charles Todd.

DID YOU KNOW? *Monopoly money is minted in every currency from the German mark to the Japanese yen. But the grand prize in the World Monopoly Championship still comes in U.S. dollars. It's $15,140—the amount of money found in each game box!*

SCRABBLE® is a crossword game for two, three, or four players, played on a board with tiles that are letters. It had its beginnings in the 1930s with a game called Criss-Cross Words, which was invented by Alfred M. Butts. To win, it helps to be a good speller, have a big vocabulary, and figure out the best places for your letters. The lucky part is picking up the letters you need.

DID YOU KNOW? *To decide the number values for each **Scrabble®** letter tile, Alfred M. Butts, the inventor, studied the front page of The New York Times. He wanted to figure out how often each of the 26 letters of the English language was used. The ones used least—Q and Z— earned the most points, 10. To make the game more challenging, Butts decided to include only four "S" tiles in each box.*

TRIBOND®, a game for two or three players or teams. The TriBond board is triangular. Each time teams correctly answer a question, they can move their three playing pieces around the three identical triangular paths. In this game, players must figure out the common bond between three clues and shout it out. The game asks such questions as "What do candidates, track stars, and pantyhose have in common?" (The answer: They all run.) A challenge feature lets players bump back an opponent's piece if they land on the same square.

More than 2 million copies have been sold in 14 countries, and TriBond is available in six languages. In 2000, on its tenth anniversary, TriBond was inducted into the Games Magazine Hall of Fame.

All About... CHESS

Chess is a game of skill for two players. The aim is to checkmate, or trap, the opponent's king. Chess was probably invented around the 6th or 7th century A.D. in India. From there it moved into Persia (now Iran); the word *chess* comes from the Persian word *shah*, which means king. Today, there are national chess contests for children, and many schools have chess clubs. For further information, contact the U.S. Chess Federation, 3054 NYS Route 9W, New Windsor, NY 12553. Phone: 845-562-8350.

WEB SITE http://www.uschess.org

THE BOARD AND THE CHESSMEN

Chess is played on a chessboard divided into 64 squares, alternately light and dark, arranged in 8 rows of 8. No matter what colors the squares and chessmen really are, they are always called white and black. White always moves first, then black and white take turns, moving only one piece at a time. Each player begins with 16 chessmen: 8 pieces (a king, a queen, 2 bishops, 2 knights, and 2 rooks) and 8 pawns. Each piece moves differently. When a chessman lands on a space taken by an opponent's piece or pawn, that piece or pawn is captured and removed from the board.

queen   rook

knight   bishop

pawn   king

When a player moves a chessman into position to capture the opponent's king, he or she says "check" and the opponent must block the move or move the king to safety. Otherwise, the king is "checkmated" and the game is over.

A TIME-LINE OF VIDEO GAMES

1962 Spacewar! comes to Planet Earth. Spacewar!, played on an early minicomputer, is the first fully interactive video game.

1974 Pong! In this pioneering home video game, players use tiny white paddles to whack a white dot—that is, a ball—back and forth across a green video screen. The first player to get the ball past the opponent's paddle 15 times wins!

1980 Pac-Man, Space Invaders, and Asteroids invade arcades.

1983 Grab that joystick and go! Super-action joysticks and steering wheels make video games feel more real.

1984 The world of video games welcomes R2-D2 from the movie *Star Wars*, and I, Robot, based on a character created by science-fiction writer Isaac Asimov.

1996 You'll never watch TV again! Instead, you'll hook up your new Nintendo 64 and play with that chubby trickster Mario for as long as your parents let you.

2000 Duck! Watch those Playstation 2 units fly out of stores!

For information about computer games, see page 60.

All About... TRADING CARDS

Are you a Pokémon player? A baseball buff? Or do boy bands make you swoon? Pick a card, any card. There's a trading card made especially for you to collect. You won't be the first—or only—one caught up in this popular pastime.

In the 1880s, baseball cards were sold in cigarette packs. Later, in 1950, the Topps Company of Brooklyn, NY, made trading cards to sell more of their newest product, Bazooka bubble gum.

A year later, the company started putting baseball players on their trading cards, and sales soon soared. Over the years, other sports stars and entertainers, from Elvis Presley to 'N Sync, have earned their own card series. Soon the cards became more popular than the gum.

In 1991, collectors complained that the gum stained the cards—so it was bye-bye bubble! Today, trading cards use high-tech tricks to appeal to collectors. Holograms and foil prisms make cards come to life. One recent series of Pokémon cards featured frame cards with an actual piece of film from a Pokémon movie!

▲ A baseball card from 1911

Trading card games, played like rummy or poker, now take place nationwide. After trading furiously with their friends, many experienced players have a deck of more than 200 cards. That adds up to big profits for cardmakers like Topps.

ROBOTICS: now you can get with the program!

How cool would it be to build and program your own robot? Now you can try it. Two companies have created products that let you create and control robots right in your own home.

The first is a kit from Lego. The robot is made from plastic blocks, programming software, a computer chip, and a system that lets you download data from a computer to your creation. What the robot does and how it reacts is controlled by programs you write. You can write a program to make the robot move across the floor—then you're off and rolling!

Sony's AIBO is no ordinary puppy. Its name says it all: it stands for Artificial Intelligence roBOt. This computerized canine contains 18 motors (four for the head, three for each leg, and two in the tail) that let it walk, sit, sleep, and beg, among other dog tricks. A remote control gives out tones that AIBO hears. These tones tell the dog to lie, sit, or stand. Ready to take it for a walk? Be patient. A walk around the block will take an hour and a half!

Need a watchdog? AIBO has a digital camera in its head that, in the future, may be programmed to send pictures from wherever it roams. A pressure sensor lets AIBO know when you pet it. Brightly lit eyes flash red when AIBO is angry and green when it's happy. You can buy software to program AIBO to do all sorts of interesting tasks, including patrolling the hallway outside your room and barking whenever your little sister or brother comes near!

Want to know more about robotics?
Visit the Tech Museum of Innovation at:
WEBSITE http://www.thetech.org

GEOGRAPHY

How old was the youngest person to climb Mt. Everest? *You can find the answer on page 85.*

LOOKING AT OUR WORLD

Did you ever travel on a spaceship? In a way, you're traveling around the Sun right now on a spaceship called Planet Earth.

THINKING GLOBAL

A **globe** is a small model of Earth. Like Earth, it is shaped like a ball or sphere. Earth isn't exactly a sphere because it gets flat at the top and bottom and bulges a little in the middle. This shape is called an oblate spheroid.

Because Earth is round, most flat maps that are centered on the equator do not show the shapes of the land masses exactly right. The shapes at the top and bottom usually look too big. For example, the island of Greenland, which is next to North America, may look bigger than Australia, though it is really much smaller.

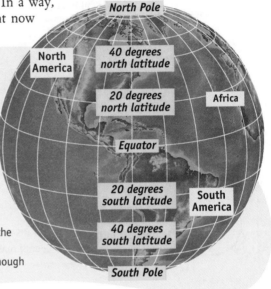

North Pole
North America
40 degrees north latitude
20 degrees north latitude
Africa
Equator
20 degrees south latitude
South America
40 degrees south latitude
South Pole

Which Hemispheres Do You Live In?

Draw an imaginary line around the middle of Earth. This is the **equator**. It splits Earth into two halves called **hemispheres**. The part north of the equator, including North America, is the **northern hemisphere**. The part south of the equator is the **southern hemisphere**.

You can also divide Earth into east and west. **North and South America** are in the **western hemisphere.** Africa, Asia, and most of Europe are in the **eastern hemisphere.**

LATITUDE AND LONGITUDE

Imaginary lines that run east and west around Earth, parallel to the equator, are called **parallels.** They tell you the **latitude** of a place, or how far it is from the equator. The equator is at 0 degrees latitude. As you go farther north or south, the latitude increases. The North Pole is at 90 degrees **north latitude.** The South Pole is at 90 degrees **south latitude.**

Imaginary lines that run north and south around the globe, from one pole to the other, are called **meridians.** They tell you the degree of **longitude**, or how far east or west a place is from an imaginary line called the **Greenwich meridian** or **prime meridian** (0 degrees). That line runs through the city of Greenwich in England.

READING A MAP

Physical maps mainly show features that are part of nature, such as rivers, mountains, oceans, and deserts. Political maps show features such as states and countries and the boundaries between them.

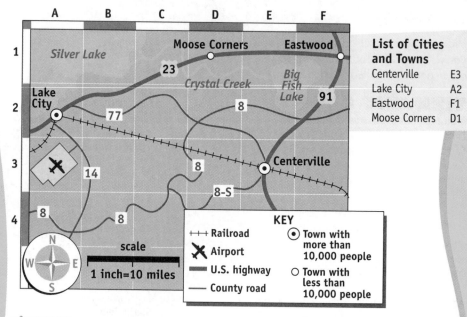

List of Cities and Towns

Centerville	E3
Lake City	A2
Eastwood	F1
Moose Corners	D1

DISTANCE Of course the distances on a map are much shorter than the distances in the real world. The **scale** shows you how to estimate the real distance. In the map above, every inch on paper stands for a real distance of 10 miles.

PICTURES Maps usually have little pictures or symbols. The map **key** tells what they mean. At the bottom of this map, you can see the symbols for towns, roads, railroad tracks, and airports. Can you tell which are the two biggest cities on the map? Can you find the airport? How would you get from the airport to Moose Corners by car?

DIRECTION Maps usually have a **compass rose** that shows you which way is north. On most maps, like this one, north is straight up. When north is up, south is down, east is right, and west is left.

FINDING PLACES To help you find places on a map, many maps have a list of places in alphabetical order, with a letter and number for each. In the map above, you can find the first city on the list, Centerville (E3), by drawing a straight line down from the letter E on top, and another line going across from the number 3 on the side. Straight lines from each letter and number on the side make a **grid.** Centerville should be near the place on the grid where the lines for E and 3 meet.

Some European and American Explorers

THE AMERICAS

AROUND 1000	**Leif Ericson,** from Iceland, explored "Vinland," which may have been the coasts of northeast Canada and New England.
1492–1504	**Christopher Columbus** (Italian) sailed four times from Spain to America and started colonies there.
1513	**Juan Ponce de León** (Spanish) explored and named Florida.
1513	**Vasco Núñez de Balboa** (Spanish) explored Panama and reached the Pacific Ocean.
1519–36	**Hernando Cortés** (Spanish) conquered Mexico, traveling as far west as Baja California.
1527–42	**Alvar Núñez Cabeza de Vaca** (Spanish) explored the southwestern United States, Brazil, and Paraguay.
1532–35	**Francisco Pizarro** (Spanish) explored the west coast of South America and conquered Peru.
1534–36	**Jacques Cartier** (French) sailed up the St. Lawrence River to the site of present-day Montreal.
1539–42	**Hernando de Soto** (Spanish) explored the southeastern United States and the lower Mississippi Valley.
1603–13	**Samuel de Champlain** (French) traced the course of the St. Lawrence River and explored the northeastern United States.
1609–10	**Henry Hudson** (English), sailing from Holland, explored the Hudson River, Hudson Bay, and Hudson Strait.
1682	**Robert Cavelier, sieur de La Salle** (French), traced the Mississippi River to its mouth in the Gulf of Mexico.
1804–06	**Meriwether Lewis** and **William Clark** (American) traveled from St. Louis along the Missouri and Columbia rivers to the Pacific Ocean and back.

ASIA AND THE PACIFIC

1271–95	**Marco Polo** (Italian) traveled through Central Asia, India, China, and Indonesia.
1519–21	**Ferdinand Magellan** (Portuguese) sailed from Spain around the tip of South America and across the Pacific Ocean to the Philippines, where he died. His expedition continued around the world.
1768–78	**James Cook** (English) charted the world's major bodies of water and explored Hawaii and Antarctica.

AFRICA

1488	**Bartolomeu Dias** (Portuguese) explored the Cape of Good Hope in southern Africa.
1497–98	**Vasco da Gama** (Portuguese) sailed farther than Dias, around the Cape of Good Hope to East Africa and India.
1849–59	**David Livingstone** (Scottish) explored Southern Africa, including the Zambezi River and Victoria Falls.

The Seven Continents

Almost two-thirds of Earth's surface is made up of water. The rest is land. Oceans are the largest areas of water. Continents are the biggest pieces of land.

	Area	Population	Highest Point	Lowest Point
North America	9,400,000 square miles	481,000,000	Mount McKinley (Alaska), 20,320 feet	Death Valley (California), 282 feet below sea level
South America	6,900,000 square miles	347,000,000	Mount Aconcagua (Argentina), 22,834 feet	Valdes Peninsula (Argentina), 131 feet below sea level
Europe	3,800,000 square miles	729,000,000	Mount Elbrus (Russia), 18,510 feet	Caspian Sea (Russia, Azerbaijan; eastern Europe and western Asia), 92 feet below sea level
Asia	17,400,000 square miles	3,688,000,000	Mount Everest (Nepal, Tibet), 29,035 feet	Dead Sea (Israel, Jordan), 1,312 feet below sea level
Africa	11,700,000 square miles	805,000,000	Mount Kilimanjaro (Tanzania), 19,340 feet	Lake Assal (Djibouti), 512 feet below sea level
Australia & Oceania	3,300,000 square miles	31,000,000	Mount Kosciusko (New South Wales), 7,310 feet	Lake Eyre (South Australia), 52 feet below sea level
Antarctica	5,400,000 square miles	Zero	Vinson Massif, 16,864 feet	Bentley Subglacial Trench, 8,327 feet below sea level

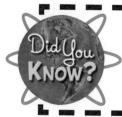
Did You Know?

THE COLDEST PART OF A MOUNTAIN IS THE TOP. Although the peak is closer to the Sun, the air there is very thin and traps less heat from the Sun's rays.

Mount Everest, the tallest mountain in the world ▼

TALLEST, LONGEST, HIGHEST, DEEPEST

Longest River: Nile, in Egypt and Sudan (4,160 miles)
Highest Waterfall: Angel Falls, in Venezuela (3,212 feet)
Tallest Mountain: Mount Everest, in Tibet and Nepal (29,035 feet)
Deepest Lake: Lake Baykal, in Asia (5,315 feet)
Biggest Lake: Caspian Sea, in Europe and Asia (143,244 square miles)
Biggest Desert: The Sahara, in Africa (3,500,000 square miles)
Biggest Island: Greenland, in the Atlantic Ocean (840,000 square miles)
Deepest Cave: Lamprechtsofen-Vogelschacht, in Salzburg, Austria (5,354 feet deep)

▲ *Sahara Desert*

AMAZING GEOGRAPHY FACTS

Most Awesome Mountain: People in Nepal call it Sagarmatha, or "goddess of the sky." Tibetans call it Chomolungma, or "mother goddess of the universe." Mt. Everest is awesome in any language. The first people to climb to the top were Sir Edmund Hillary and Tenzing Norgay on May 29, 1953. The youngest person to do it was Sambu Tamang. He reached the summit on May 5, 1973, when he was only 16! The first woman to get there was Junko Tabei, on May 16, 1975. About 4,000 people in all have tried to climb Mt. Everest. Of these, some 660 have made it, but more than 140 others have died trying.

Fishiest River: The Amazon River is gigantic. Starting high up in the Andes Mountains, it runs 4,075 miles (mostly through Brazil) to the Atlantic Ocean, where it dumps out up to 32 million gallons of water every second! That's almost one-fifth of all the fresh water sent into all the oceans by all the world's rivers. More kinds of fish live in the Amazon than in the Atlantic itself. Scientists have found over 2,400 species, including sting rays, tetras, electric eels, and 700-pound catfish. And new species are discovered every year.

Biggest Wave: On July 9, 1958, an earthquake caused the biggest wave ever recorded. It swept across Lituya Bay, along the southern coast of Alaska, and reached 1,720 feet in height! Such giant waves are called tidal waves or tsunamis.

Most Mysterious Cave: Discovered by accident in 1986, Lechuguilla Cave in Carlsbad, New Mexico, is a huge, winding, underground maze. It is 1,571 feet deep, the deepest cave in the United States. So far, explorers have mapped about 100 miles of the cave. But there's no end in sight, so no one knows exactly how long it is.

THE FOUR OCEANS

The facts about the oceans include their size and average depth.

Pacific Ocean: 64,186,300 square miles; 12,925 feet deep
Atlantic Ocean: 33,420,000 square miles; 11,730 feet deep
Indian Ocean: 28,350,500 square miles; 12,598 feet deep
Arctic Ocean: 5,105,700 square miles; 3,407 feet deep

EARTHQUAKES

Earthquakes may be so weak that they are hardly felt, or strong enough to do great damage. There are thousands of earthquakes each year, but most are too small to be noticed. About 1 in 5 can be felt, and about 1 in 500 causes damage.

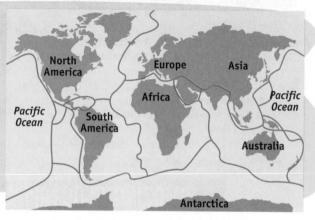

North America

Europe

Asia

Africa

Pacific Ocean

Pacific Ocean

South America

Australia

Antarctica

WHAT CAUSES EARTHQUAKES?
The Earth's outer layer, its **crust,** is divided into huge pieces called **plates** (see map). These plates, made of rock, are constantly moving— away from each other, toward each other, or past each other. A crack in Earth's crust between two plates is called a **fault.** Many earthquakes occur along faults where two plates collide as they move toward each other or grind together as they move past each other. Earthquakes along the **San Andreas Fault** in California are caused by the grinding of two plates.

MEASURING EARTHQUAKES
The Richter scale goes from 0 to more than 8. These numbers indicate the strength of an earthquake. Each number means the quake is 10 times stronger than the number below it. An earthquake measuring 6 on the scale is 10 times stronger than one measuring 5 and 100 times stronger than one measuring 4. Earthquakes that are 4 or above are considered major. (The damage and injuries caused by a quake also depend on other things, such as whether the area is heavily populated and built up.)

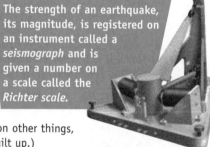

The strength of an earthquake, its magnitude, is registered on an instrument called a *seismograph* and is given a number on a scale called the *Richter scale.*

MAGNITUDE	EFFECTS
0-2	Earthquake is recorded by instruments but is not felt by people.
2-3	Earthquake is felt slightly by a few people.
3-4	People feel tremors. Hanging objects like ceiling lights swing.
4-5	Earthquake causes some damage; walls crack; dishes and windows may break.
5-6	Furniture moves; earthquake seriously damages weak buildings.
6-7	Furniture may overturn; strong buildings are damaged; walls and buildings may collapse.
7-8	Many buildings are destroyed; underground pipes break; wide cracks appear in the ground.
ABOVE 8	Total devastation, including buildings and bridges; ground wavy.

MAJOR EARTHQUAKES

The earthquakes listed here are among the largest and most destructive recorded in the past 100 years.

YEAR	LOCATION	MAGNITUDE	DEATHS
2001	India (Western)	7.9	30,000+
1999	Taiwan (Taichung)	7.6	2,474
	Greece (Athens)	5.9	143
	Turkey (western)	7.4	17,200+
	Colombia (western)	6.0	1,185+
1998	Afghanistan (northeastern)	6.9	4,700+
	Afghanistan (northeastern)	6.1	2,323
1995	Sakhalin Island (Russia)	7.5	1,989
	Japan (Kobe)	6.9	5,502
1994	United States (Los Angeles area)	6.8	61
1993	India (southern)	6.3	9,748
1990	Iran (western)	7.7	40,000+
1989	United States (San Francisco area)	7.1	62
1988	Soviet Armenia	7.0	55,000
1985	Mexico (Michoacan)	8.1	9,500
1976	China (Tangshan)	8.0	255,000
	Guatemala	7.5	23,000
1970	Peru (northern)	7.8	66,000
1960	Chile (southern)	9.5	5,000
1939	Chile (Chillan)	8.3	28,000
1934	India (Bihar-Nepal)	8.4	10,700
1927	China (Nan-Shan)	8.3	200,000
1923	Japan (Yokohama)	8.3	143,000
1920	China (Gansu)	8.6	200,000
1906	Chile (Valparaiso)	8.6	20,000
	United States (San Francisco)	8.3	503

DID YOU KNOW?

ON JANUARY 26, 2001, AN EARTHQUAKE HIT THE GUJARAT REGION OF WESTERN INDIA, turning buildings into piles of rubble. Thousands of people died. Poorly constructed buildings were partly to blame for the high death toll. Scientists had warned the government to make the buildings safer from earthquakes, but nothing was done.

ON FEBRUARY 28, 2001, A 6.8 MAGNITUDE EARTHQUAKE HIT WASHINGTON STATE. It shook buildings in Seattle and caused a crack in the Capitol Dome in Olympia. Damage was heavy in some areas, and 1 person died. Mainly because the quake was far under ground, it did less harm than it might have.

San Francisco earthquake, 1989

VOLCANOES

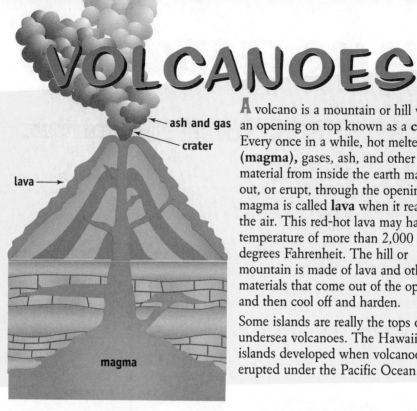

ash and gas
crater
lava
magma

A volcano is a mountain or hill with an opening on top known as a **crater.** Every once in a while, hot melted rock (**magma**), gases, ash, and other material from inside the earth may blast out, or erupt, through the opening. The magma is called **lava** when it reaches the air. This red-hot lava may have a temperature of more than 2,000 degrees Fahrenheit. The hill or mountain is made of lava and other materials that come out of the opening, and then cool off and harden.

Some islands are really the tops of undersea volcanoes. The Hawaiian islands developed when volcanoes erupted under the Pacific Ocean.

Why Do Volcanoes Erupt?

More than 500 volcanoes have erupted over the centuries. Some have erupted many times. Volcanic eruptions come from pools of magma and other materials a few miles underground. The magma comes from rock far below. After the rock melts and mixes with gases, it rises up through cracks and weak spots in the mountain.

SOME FAMOUS VOLCANIC ERUPTIONS

YEAR	VOLCANO (PLACE)	DEATHS (approximate)
79	Mount Vesuvius (Italy)	16,000
1586	Kelut (Indonesia)	10,000
1792	Mount Unzen (Japan)	14,500
1815	Tambora (Indonesia)	10,000
1883	Krakatau or Krakatoa (Indonesia)	36,000
1902	Mount Pelée (Martinique)	28,000
1980	Mount St. Helens (U.S.)	57
1982	El Chichón (Mexico)	1,880
1985	Nevado del Ruiz (Colombia)	23,000
1986	Lake Nyos (Cameroon)	1,700
1991	Mt. Pinatubo (Philippines)	800

WHERE IS THE RING OF FIRE?

The hundreds of active volcanoes found on the land near the edges of the Pacific Ocean make up what is called the *Ring of Fire.* They mark the boundary between the plates under the Pacific Ocean and the plates under the continents around the ocean. (The plates of the Earth are explained on page 86, with the help of a map.) The Ring of Fire runs all along the west coast of South and North America, from the southern tip of Chile to Alaska. It includes the San Andreas Fault in California. The ring also runs down the east coast of Asia, starting in the far north in Kamchatka and continuing down past Australia.

How many gallons of blood does your heart pump every day? *You can find the answer on page 91.*

INSIDE YOUR BODY

Your body is made up of many different parts that work together every minute of every day and night. It is more amazing than any machine or computer. Machines don't eat, run, have feelings, read and learn, or do other things that you do. Even though everyone's body looks different outside, people have the same parts inside.

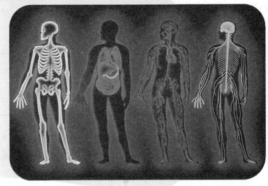

Did You KNOW?

BONES, BUDS, AND SNEEZES

► *Bones make blood. The bones in your body have three layers. Cortical (core-tick-ul) bone is the smooth hard outer layer. Inside are layers of cancellus (can-sell-us) bone, which are spongy and softer than cortical bone. Bone marrow is found inside the cancellus layer. It is thick like jelly. Bone marrow produces blood cells.*

► *Some of the taste buds on the top of your tongue die as you get older. In fact, most older people have only half as many taste buds as babies do.*

► *Most people have 12 pairs of ribs. But one out of every 20 people has at least one extra pair.*

► *Whenever you sneeze, you close your eyes. In fact, every time you sneeze you use six sets of muscles.*

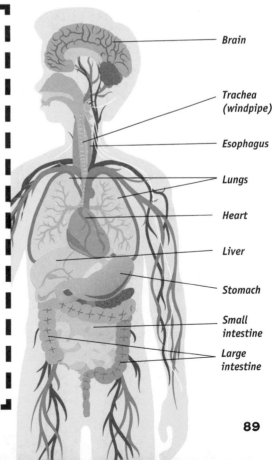

Brain

Trachea (windpipe)

Esophagus

Lungs

Heart

Liver

Stomach

Small intestine

Large intestine

WHAT THE BODY'S SYSTEMS DO

Each system of the body has its own job. Some of the systems also work together to keep you healthy and strong.

CIRCULATORY SYSTEM

In the circulatory system, the **heart** pumps **blood**, which then travels through tubes, called **arteries**, to all parts of the body. The blood carries the oxygen and food that the body needs to stay alive. **Veins** carry the blood back to the heart.

DIGESTIVE SYSTEM

The digestive system moves food through parts of the body called the **esophagus**, **stomach**, and **intestines**. As the food passes through, some of it is broken down into tiny particles called **nutrients**, which the body needs. Nutrients enter the bloodstream, which carries them to all parts of the body. The digestive system then changes the remaining food into waste that is eliminated from the body.

ENDOCRINE SYSTEM

The endocrine system includes **glands** that are needed for some body functions. There are two kinds of glands. **Exocrine** glands produce liquids such as sweat and saliva. **Endocrine** glands produce chemicals called **hormones**. Hormones control body functions, such as growth.

MUSCULAR SYSTEM

Muscles are made up of elastic fibers that help the body move. We use large muscles to walk and run, and small muscles to smile. Muscles also help protect organs.

SKELETAL SYSTEM

The skeletal system is made up of the **bones** that hold your body upright. Some bones protect organs, such as the ribs that cover the lungs.

NERVOUS SYSTEM

The nervous system enables us to think, feel, move, hear, and see. It includes the **brain**, the **spinal cord**, and **nerves** in all parts of the body. Nerves in the spinal cord carry signals back and forth between the brain and the rest of the body. The brain tells us what to do and how to respond. It has three major parts. The **cerebrum** controls thinking, speech, and vision. The **cerebellum** is responsible for physical coordination. The **brain stem** controls the respiratory, circulatory, and digestive systems.

RESPIRATORY SYSTEM

The respiratory system allows us to breathe. Air comes into the body through the nose and mouth. It goes through the **windpipe** (or **trachea**) to two tubes (called **bronchi**), which carry air to the **lungs**. Oxygen from the air is taken in by tiny blood vessels in the lungs. The blood then carries oxygen to the cells of the body.

REPRODUCTIVE SYSTEM

Through the reproductive system, adult human beings are able to create new human beings. Reproduction begins when a sperm cell from a man fertilizes an egg cell from a woman.

URINARY SYSTEM

This system, which includes the **kidneys**, cleans waste from the blood and regulates the amount of water in the body.

Surprising Facts About the Body

- Your heart is a hollow muscle about as big as your fist.

- Your heart pumps 8,000 gallons of blood a distance of 12,000 miles through your body every day.

- A meal takes as long as 15 hours to pass through your whole digestive system.

- Kidneys clean waste products out of the blood. Every minute, a quart of blood passes through your kidneys to get cleaned up.

- A newborn baby's body has 350 bones. An adult has only 206 bones. Bones grow together to make fewer, bigger bones as a person grows up.

- The body has about 100 trillion cells.

- You have 26 feet of intestines.

- It takes about 17 muscles to smile, but about 43 to frown.

- More than half of the human body is fluid.

◄ *The heart*

STAY HEALTHY WITH EXERCISE

Daily exercise makes you feel good. It helps you think better. And, believe it or not, it helps you sleep better and feel more relaxed. Once you start exercising regularly, you will feel stronger and keep improving at physical activities.

When you exercise, you breathe more deeply and get more oxygen into your lungs with each breath. Your heart pumps more oxygen-filled blood to all parts of your body with each beat. Your muscles and joints feel more flexible. Exercise also helps you to stay at a healthy weight.

Here are some types of exercise and the number of calories each burns up in one hour if you weigh about 100 pounds:

ACTIVITY CALORIES BURNED IN AN HOUR	
Jogging (5½ miles per hour)	490
Cross-country skiing	470
Running in place	430
Walking (4½ miles per hour)	290
Swimming (25 yards per minute)	180
Bike riding (6 miles per hour)	160

·· All About... DREAMS AND DREAMING ··

We spend about one-third of our lives sleeping and usually dream every night, for about one-fourth of the time we are asleep. Dreams are generally in color. The time when we do most of our dreaming is called REM, which stands for rapid eye movement. It is a busy time. Even though our eyes are closed, they are constantly moving under our eyelids. REM sleep happens three or four times during the night.

Many books have been written about the meanings of dreams. And it's possible that some dreams mean the same to everyone. But most sleep experts believe that our dreams are individual; they reflect our own thoughts and feelings.

"I had the best dream last night!" a friend may say to you. But you may not remember any of your own dreams from that night. We often forget our dreams the moment we wake up, if not before. If you remember a dream when you wake up, write it down before you think about anything else. If you keep a journal of your dreams, you may see a pattern that could help you figure out what they mean.

Every once in a while, many children (and some adults) have nightmares. These are scary or unhappy dreams. Nightmares are believed to be a way people have of dealing with normal fears and problems. Talking to an adult about your nightmares may help you feel less afraid about them.

A DREAM REPORT

Try keeping track of your dreams every day in a journal. Be patient. You may often not be able to remember anything you dreamed.

After a while, make a report on your dreams. It could answer questions such as these:

▶ Did you dream about school?

▶ Did you do things in dreams you can't do in real life?

▶ Did you have any dreams that are similar?

▶ Did you dream about your family or friends?

92

We Are What We Eat

Have you ever noticed the labels on the packages of food you and your family buy? The labels provide information people need to make healthy choices about the foods they eat. Below are some terms you may see on labels.

Nutrients Are Needed

Nutrients are the parts of food the body can use. The body needs nutrients for growth, for energy, and to repair itself when something goes wrong. Carbohydrates, fats, proteins, vitamins, minerals, and water are different kinds of nutrients found in food. **Carbohydrates** and **fats** provide energy. **Proteins** aid growth and help maintain and repair the body. **Vitamins** help the body use food, help eyesight and skin, and aid in fighting off infections. **Minerals** help build bones and teeth and aid in such functions as muscle contractions and blood clotting. **Water** helps with growth and repair of the body. It also helps the body digest food and get rid of wastes.

Calories Count

A **calorie** is a measure of how much energy we get from food. The government recommends the number of calories that should be taken in for different age groups. The number of calories recommended for children ages 8 to 10 is about 1,900 a day. For ages 11 to 14, the government recommends around 2,200 calories a day for girls and 2,400 for boys.

To maintain a **healthy weight**, it is important to balance the calories in the food you eat with the calories used by the body every day. Every activity uses up some calories. The more active you are, the more calories your body burns. If you eat more calories than your body uses, you will gain weight.

A LITTLE FAT GOES A LONG WAY

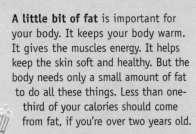

SOME LOWER-FAT FOODS:

chicken or turkey hot dog

grilled fish

baked potato

pretzels

apple

plain popcorn (with no butter)

skim milk or 1% or 2% milk

SOME FATTY FOODS:

beef or pork hot dog

fried hamburger

French fries

potato chips

donut

buttered popcorn

whole milk

A little bit of fat is important for your body. It keeps your body warm. It gives the muscles energy. It helps keep the skin soft and healthy. But the body needs only a small amount of fat to do all these things. Less than one-third of your calories should come from fat, if you're over two years old.

Cholesterol. Eating too much fat can make some people's bodies produce too much **cholesterol** (ka-LESS-ter-all). This waxy substance can build up over the years on the inside of arteries. Too much cholesterol keeps blood from flowing freely through the arteries and can cause serious health problems such as heart attacks.

To eat less fat, try eating lower-fat foods instead of fatty foods.

WHICH FOODS ARE THE RIGHT FOODS?

To stay healthy, it is important to eat the right foods and to exercise. To help people choose the right foods for good health and fitness, the U.S. government developed the food pyramid shown below. The food pyramid shows the groups of foods that everyone should eat every day.

FOOD PYRAMID: A GUIDE TO DAILY FOOD CHOICES

Milk, Yogurt, and Cheese Group • • •
2 to 3 servings
1 serving = 1 cup of milk or yogurt; or 1½ ounces of cheese

Fats, Oils, and Sweets
Use sparingly

Meat, Poultry, Fish, Dry Beans, Eggs, and Nuts Group
2 to 3 servings
1 serving = 2 to 3 ounces of cooked lean meat, fish, or poultry; ½ cup of cooked dry beans; 2 eggs; 4 tablespoons of peanut butter; or ⅔ cup of nuts

Vegetable Group • • •
3 to 5 servings
1 serving = 1 cup of raw, leafy green vegetables; ½ cup of other vegetables (cooked or chopped raw); or ¾ cup vegetable juice

Fruit Group
2 to 4 servings
1 serving = 1 medium apple, banana, or orange; ½ cup of cooked, chopped, or canned fruit; or ¾ cup of fruit juice

Bread, Cereal, Rice, and Pasta Group
6 to 11 servings
1 serving = 1 slice of bread; 1 ounce of ready-to-eat cereal; or ½ cup of cooked cereal, rice, or pasta

The foods at the bottom of the pyramid are the ones everyone needs to eat in the biggest amounts. At the top are the foods to be eaten in the smallest amounts. The number of servings needed depends on your age and body size. Younger, smaller people need fewer servings. Older, larger people need more.

SUPER SNACKS

Do you have the munchies? Try these yummy treats.

ANTS ON A LOG

You'll need: **celery stalks, peanut butter, raisins**

Wash and dry the celery. Ask an adult to cut each celery stalk into pieces about 4 or 5 inches long. Spread peanut butter inside the curved part of each celery stick. Then gently press raisins into the peanut butter. If you are allergic to peanut butter, use honey instead.

PRETZEL DIP

You'll need: **low-fat pretzels, about 1 tablespoon of honey, about 1 tablespoon of mustard**

In a small bowl, mix the honey and the mustard. Use more or less of each ingredient to make the dip taste the way you like it. Dip a pretzel in the mixture for a tasty snack.

FRUIT KABOBS

You'll need: **several different kinds of fruit such as melon, bananas, grapes, strawberries, and peaches; wooden skewers**

Wash the fruit. Have an adult help you cut it into bite-sized pieces. Push each piece of fruit onto the skewers. Make colorful kabobs by using different kinds of fruit on each skewer.

Remember: Wash your hands before touching food. Ask an adult to do any cutting with sharp knives.

BODY MAZE

This puzzle contains all the words in the Word Box. They snake through the puzzle, one following the next. The last letter of each word is the first letter of the next. The letters go up, down, backward, and forward. Start with the word **VEINS**.

R	T	E	R	I	N	T	E
A	E	H	C	E	I	T	S
R	T	R	A	S	L	I	N
A	E	H	C	K	L	N	E
V	E	M	A	I	A	D	O
N	I	O	T	N	M	R	C
S	K	E	S	E	S	I	N
T	E	L	G	R	U	A	E
A	L	U	N	V	O	R	S

WORD BOX

arteries	heart	skeletal	stomach
ears	lungs	skin	trachea
endocrine (system)	nervous (system)	small intestine	veins

ANSWERS ON PAGES 317-320. FOR MORE PUZZLES GO TO WWW.WORLDALMANACFORKIDS.COM

Drugs, Alcohol, and Tobacco:
COOL WAYS TO SAY "NO"

Drugs, alcohol, and tobacco can do serious damage to people's bodies and minds. Most kids keep away from them. But some kids have a tough time saying "no" when they are offered harmful substances. Here are some ways to say "no." They're suggested by DARE, a U.S. government program. Add your own ideas to this list.

Say "No thanks." (Say it again and again if you have to.)

Give reasons. ("I don't like cigarettes" or "I'm going to soccer practice" or "My mom would kill me.")

Change the subject or offer a better suggestion.

Walk away. (Don't argue, don't discuss it. Just leave.)

Avoid the situation. (If you are asked to a party where kids will be drinking, smoking, or using drugs, make plans to do something else instead.)

Find strength in numbers. (Do things with friends who don't use harmful substances.)

UNDERSTANDING AIDS

What Is AIDS? AIDS is a disease that is caused by a virus called HIV. AIDS attacks the body's immune system. The immune system is important because it helps the body fight off infections and diseases.

How Do Kids Get AIDS? A mother with AIDS may give it to her baby before the baby is born. Children (and adults, too) could get AIDS from blood transfusions. But this happens very seldom, because blood banks now test all donations of blood for the AIDS virus.

How Do Adults Get AIDS? Adults get AIDS in two main ways: Having sex with a person who has AIDS, or sharing a needle used for drugs with a person who has AIDS.

How Kids and Adults Don't Get AIDS. People don't get AIDS from everyday contact with infected people at school, at home, or other places. People don't get AIDS from clothes, telephones, or toilet seats, or from food prepared by someone with AIDS. Children don't get AIDS from sitting near AIDS victims or from shaking hands with them.

Is There a Cure for AIDS? There is no cure for AIDS. But researchers are working to develop a vaccine to prevent AIDS or a drug to cure it. And new treatments are beginning to increase the lifespan of many people with AIDS.

Which Caretaker Does What?

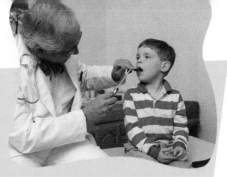

A **DENTIST** is a doctor who takes general care of your teeth.

An **ORTHODONTIST** is a doctor who straightens teeth.

A **DENTAL HYGIENIST** cleans your teeth and gums.

A **PEDIATRICIAN** is a doctor who takes care of children.

An **ORTHOPEDIST** is a doctor who fixes broken bones.

A **PHYSICAL THERAPIST** helps get your muscles to work right after an injury.

An **OPTICIAN** checks your eyesight and gets you the right eyeglasses.

THE TRUTH ABOUT COLDS

A cold is the most common illness we get. Schoolchildren often catch colds from one another—usually about five to eight colds a year. Here are some mistakes, and some facts, about colds.

FICTION: In low temperatures, you can catch a cold by going outside without a coat.

FACT: It's smart to dress warmly when it's cold out. But colds are caused by viruses, and not cold weather. Washing your hands is a good way to avoid catching many viruses.

FICTION: Some vitamins and medicines cure colds.

FACT: While some vitamins and medicines may make you feel better for a while, there is no cure for the cold. It usually lasts about one or two weeks.

FICTION: You can cure a cold by staying home.

FACT: There is no cure for the cold. Getting enough sleep, drinking juices, and eating well will help you feel better.

BE READY FOR ANY EMERGENCY

Tape a list of emergency numbers near the phone or on the refrigerator. Numbers to include are:

▶ your parents' or guardians' telephone numbers at work

▶ the telephone number of a relative or other adult who lives nearby

▶ the numbers of your family doctor, a nearby hospital, the fire department, and the police department

Emergency phone numbers can often be found inside the front cover of your local telephone book.

REMEMBER 911.

The number 911 is a special phone number for emergencies only.

When a person who needs help right away calls 911, the operator asks the caller for his or her name and address and what the emergency is. Then the operator quickly sends the police, an ambulance, and, if needed, the fire department. Dial 0 (Operator) if your town doesn't have 911, and ask the operator for help.

HOLIDAYS

What holiday in November celebrates the world's children? You can find the answer on page 99.

HOLIDAYS IN THE UNITED STATES

There are no official holidays for the whole United States. The U.S. government decides which days will be federal holidays. (These are really just for Washington, D.C.) Each state picks its own holidays, but most states celebrate the ones listed here. On these holidays, most banks and schools are closed, and so are many offices. Washington's Birthday (or Presidents' Day), Memorial Day, and Columbus Day are usually celebrated on the nearest Monday.

NEW YEAR'S DAY

Countries the world over celebrate the new year, although not always on January 1. For example, Chinese New Year falls between January 21 and February 19.

MARTIN LUTHER KING JR. DAY

Observed on the third Monday in January, this holiday marks the birth (January 15, 1929) of the African-American civil rights leader Rev. Martin Luther King Jr. In 2002, it will be celebrated on January 21.

WASHINGTON'S BIRTHDAY OR PRESIDENTS' DAY

On the third Monday in February (February 18, 2002). Americans often celebrate the births of both George Washington (born February 22, 1732) and Abraham Lincoln (born February 12, 1809).

MEMORIAL DAY OR DECORATION DAY

Memorial Day, observed on the last Monday in May (May 27, 2002), is set aside to remember all those who died while serving in the United States military.

FOURTH OF JULY OR INDEPENDENCE DAY

July 4 is the anniversary of the day in 1776 when the American colonies signed the Declaration of Independence. Kids and grownups celebrate the event with bands and parades, picnics, barbecues, and fireworks.

LABOR DAY

Labor Day, the first Monday in September, honors the workers of America. It was first celebrated in 1882. It will occur on September 2 in 2002.

COLUMBUS DAY

Celebrated on the second Monday in October, Columbus Day is the anniversary of October 12, 1492, the day when Christopher Columbus was traditionally thought to have arrived in America. Columbus Day falls on October 14 in 2002.

ELECTION DAY

Election Day, the first Tuesday after the first Monday in November (November 5 in 2002), is a holiday in some states.

VETERANS DAY

Veterans Day, November 11, honors veterans of wars. First called Armistice Day, it marked the armistice (agreement) that ended World War I. This was signed on the 11th hour of the 11th day of the 11th month of 1918.

THANKSGIVING

Thanksgiving was first observed by the Pilgrims in 1621 as a harvest festival and a day for thanks and feasting. In 1863, Abraham Lincoln revived the tradition and made Thanksgiving the fourth Thursday in November. Thanksgiving falls on November 28 in 2002.

CHRISTMAS

Christmas is both a religious holiday and a legal holiday. It is celebrated on December 25. (See p. 191.)

OTHER SPECIAL HOLIDAYS

 VALENTINE'S DAY February 14 is a day for sending cards or gifts to people you love.

 ARBOR DAY We plant trees on Arbor Day to remind us of how they protect the environment. Each state observes the day at different times in the spring.

MOTHER'S DAY AND FATHER'S DAY
Mothers are honored on the second Sunday in May. Fathers are honored on the third Sunday in June.

 HALLOWEEN In ancient Britain, Druids wore grotesque costumes on October 31 to scare off evil spirits. Today, "trick or treating" children collect candy and other sweets. Some also collect money for UNICEF, the United Nations Children's Fund.

KWANZAA This seven-day African-American festival begins on December 26. It celebrates seven virtues: unity, self-determination, collective work and responsibility, cooperative economics, purpose, creativity, and faith.

All About... UNUSUAL HOLIDAYS

What are your plans for World Kindness Day? It's on November 13 and is just one of many little-known holidays. Others include National Authors' Day (November 1), Pecan Day (March 25), Kite Day (May 13), Pay-A-Compliment Day (February 6), America's Kids Day (June 24), and International Moment of Frustration Scream Day (October 12).

 **Did You KNOW?**

MANY PEOPLE WRONGLY BELIEVE THAT THE HOLIDAY OF CINCO DE MAYO (FIFTH OF MAY) CELEBRATES MEXICO'S INDEPENDENCE IN **1810.** *The true story: Cinco de Mayo observes the victory of the Mexican army over the French army in the Battle of Puebla, Mexico, on May 5, 1862.*

HOLIDAYS around the WORLD

BASTILLE DAY On July 14, the French celebrate the fall of the Bastille, a prison in Paris, in 1789. This was the start of the French Revolution.

CARNIVAL In Brazil and some other Catholic countries, Carnival is a four-day-long celebration with parades, costumes, music, and feasts. It takes place just before Lent. In 2002, Carnival is held February 9-12.

CHINESE NEW YEAR China's biggest holiday falls between January 21 and February 19 every year. Celebrations include lively parades, fireworks, and traditional family meals.

INDEPENDENCE DAY Mexico celebrates September 16 as its national holiday.

MIDSUMMER EVE After a long, dark winter, people in Scandinavia celebrate the coming of summer and of light, usually around June 22.

UNIVERSAL CHILDREN'S DAY The United Nations has set aside November 20 to celebrate the world's children and to seek better lives for them.

If you were to suggest a new holiday, what would it be?

INVENTIONS

What is a KidKare car?
You can find the answer on page 102.

INVENTIONS CHANGE OUR LIVES

Some of the world's most important inventions were developed before history was written. These include many tools, the wheel, pottery, and the ability to make and control fire. More recent inventions help us to travel faster, communicate better, and live longer.

Inventions Take Us From One Place To Another

DATE	INVENTION	INVENTOR (COUNTRY)
1785	parachute	Jean Pierre Blanchard (France) ▶
1807	steamboat (practical)	Robert Fulton (U.S.)
1829	steam locomotive	George Stephenson (England)
1852	elevator	Elisha G. Otis (U.S.)
1885	bicycle	James Starley (England)
1885	motorcycle	Gottlieb Daimler (Germany)
1891	escalator	Jesse W. Reno (U.S.)
1892	automobile (gasoline)	Charles E. Duryea & J. Frank Duryea (U.S.)
1894	submarine	Simon Lake (U.S.)
1895	diesel engine	Rudolf Diesel (Germany)
1903	propeller airplane	Orville & Wilbur Wright (U.S.)
1939	helicopter	Igor Sikorsky (U.S.)
1939	jet airplane	Hans van Ohain (Germany)
1980	rollerblades	Scott Olson (U.S.) ▶
1983	minivan	Chrysler (U.S.)

Inventions Help Us Live Healthier and Longer Lives

YEAR	INVENTION	INVENTOR (COUNTRY)
1780	bifocal lenses for glasses	Benjamin Franklin (U.S.)
1819	stethoscope	René T.M.H. Laënnec (France)
1842	anesthesia (ether)	Crawford W. Long (U.S.)
1895	X ray	Wilhelm Roentgen (Germany)
1922	insulin	Sir Frederick G. Banting (Canada)
1929	penicillin	Alexander Fleming (Scotland)
1954	antibiotic for fungal diseases	Rachel F. Brown & Elizabeth L. Hazen (U.S.)
1955	polio vaccine	Jonas E. Salk (U.S.)
1973	CAT scanner	Godfrey N. Hounsfield (England)
1978	artificial heart	Robert K. Jarvik (U.S.)
1987	meningitis vaccine	Connaught Lab (U.S.)

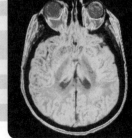

A brain scan made with a CAT scanner ▶

Inventions Help Us Communicate With One Another

YEAR	INVENTION	INVENTOR (COUNTRY)
A.D. 105	paper	Ts'ai Lun (China)
1447	movable type	Johann Gutenberg (Germany)
1795	modern pencil	Nicolas Jacques Conté (France)
1837	telegraph	Samuel F.B. Morse (U.S.)
1845	rotary printing press	Richard M. Hoe (U.S.)
1867	typewriter	Christopher L. Sholes, Carlos Glidden & Samuel W. Soulé (U.S.)
1876	telephone	Alexander G. Bell (U.S.)
1888	ballpoint pen	John Loud (U.S.)
1913	modern radio receiver	Reginald A. Fessenden (U.S.)
1937	xerography copies	Chester Carlson (U.S.)
1942	electronic computer	John V. Atanasoff & Clifford Berry (U.S.)
1944	auto sequence computer	Howard H. Aiken (U.S.)
1947	transistor	William Shockley, Walter H. Brattain, & John Bardeen (U.S.)
1955	fiber optics	Narinder S. Kapany (England)
1965	word processor	International Business Machines Corp. (U.S.)
1979	cellular telephone	Ericsson Company (Sweden)
1987	laptop computer	Sir Clive Sinclair (England) ▶
1994	digital camera	Apple Computer, Kodak (U.S.)

Inventions Make Our Lives Easier

YEAR	INVENTION	INVENTOR (COUNTRY)
1800	electric battery	Alessandro Volta (Italy)
1831	lawn mower	Edwin Budding & John Ferrabee (England)
1834	refrigeration	Jacob Perkins (England)
1846	sewing machine	Elias Howe (U.S.)
1851	cylinder (door) lock	Linus Yale (U.S.)
1879	first practical electric light bulb	Thomas A. Edison (U.S.)
1886	dishwasher	Josephine Cochran (U.S.)
1891	zipper	Whitcomb L. Judson (U.S.)
1901	washing machine	Langmuir Fisher (U.S.)
1903	windshield wipers	Mary Anderson (U.S.)
1907	vacuum cleaner	J. Murray Spangler (U.S.)
1911	air conditioning	Willis H. Carrier (U.S.)
1924	frozen packaged food	Clarence Birdseye (U.S.)
1948	Velcro	Georges de Mestral (Switzerland)
1963	pop-top can	Ermal C. Fraze (U.S.)
1969	cash machine (ATM)	Don Wetzel (U.S.)
1971	food processor	Pierre Verdon (France)
1980	Post-its	3M Company (U.S.)
1981	Polartec fabric	Malden Mills (U.S.)
2000	quiet jackhammer	Brookhaven National Laboratory (U.S.)

Inventions Entertain Us

YEAR	INVENTION	INVENTOR (COUNTRY)
1709	piano	Bartolomeo Cristofori (Italy)
1877	phonograph	Thomas A. Edison (U.S.) ▶
1877	microphone	Emile Berliner (U.S.)
1888	portable camera	George Eastman (U.S.)
1893	moving picture viewer	Thomas A. Edison (U.S.)
1894	motion picture projector	Charles F. Jenkins (U.S.)
1899	tape recorder	Valdemar Poulsen (Denmark)
1923	television*	Vladimir K. Zworykin* (U.S.)
1963	audiocassette	Phillips Corporation (Netherlands)
1963	steel tennis racquet	René Lacoste (France)
1969	videotape cassette	Sony (Japan)
1972	compact disc (CD)	RCA (U.S.)
1972	video game (Pong)	Noland Bushnell (U.S.)
1979	Walkman	Sony (Japan)

*Others who helped invent television include Philo T. Farnsworth (1926) and John Baird (1928).

Inventions Help Make Life Safer

YEAR	INVENTION	INVENTOR (COUNTRY)
1752	lightning rod	Benjamin Franklin (U.S.)
1815	safety lamp for miners	Sir Humphry Davy (England)
1863	fire extinguisher	Alanson Crane (U.S.) ▶
1923	automatic traffic signal	Garrett A. Morgan (U.S.)
1952	airbag	John Hetrick (U.S.)
1969	battery operated smoke detector	Randolph Smith & Kenneth House (U.S.)

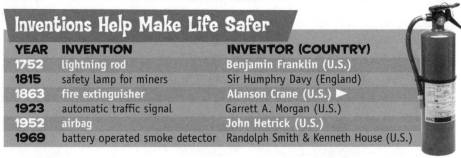

Did You Know?

BRIGHT IDEA: Thirteen-year-old Lisa Wright must have had safety on her mind when she invented the "auto-off candle," a candle that goes out by itself after 15, 30, 45, or 60 minutes, depending on how you set it beforehand.

NATIONAL INVENTORS HALL OF FAME

To learn more about inventions and the people who created them, or to make your own invention, visit

Inventure Place
National Inventors Hall of Fame
221 S. Broadway St., Akron, Ohio 44308
Phone: (330) 762-4463.
E-mail: info@invent.org
WEB SITE http://www.invent.org/book

All About...
A KID'S KIDKARE CAR

You don't have to be a grown-up to come up with big ideas! When he was eight years old, Spencer Rocco Whale created a riding toy for children in the hospital. His brightly colored KidKare cars and trucks have poles with wires attached so that children receiving medical treatments can move around during their hospital stays. In 2000, Spencer was inducted into the National Gallery for America's Young Inventors.

To learn about the National Gallery for America's Young Inventors, visit:

WEB SITE http://www.pafinc.com/nat_gal.htm

Inventions Help Us Expand Our Universe

YEAR	INVENTION	INVENTOR (COUNTRY)
1250	magnifying glass	Roger Bacon (England)
1590	2-lens microscope	Zacharias Janssen (Netherlands)
1608	telescope	Hans Lippershey (Netherlands)
1714	mercury thermometer	Gabriel D. Fahrenheit (Germany)
1926	rocket engine	Robert H. Goddard (U.S.)
1930	cyclotron (atom smasher)	Ernest O. Lawrence (U.S.)
1943	Aqua Lung	Jacques-Yves Cousteau & Emile Gagnan (France)
1977	space shuttle	NASA (U.S.) ▶

GREAT IDEAS—BY ACCIDENT!

Some of the most important inventions were inspired by accidents!

▶ Percy Spencer came up with the idea for the microwave oven one day in 1945 when he was at a lab that tested radar equipment. Scientists knew that magnetrons (the power tubes used in radar) send out microwaves. But Spencer was the first person to realize that microwaves could cook food. How did he know? As he walked past a magnetron, **a candy bar melted in his pocket!** Within a year of this accidental discovery, Spencer designed the first microwave oven.

▶ One day in 1903, Edouard Benedictus, a French chemist, dropped a glass container on the floor. He stooped down, expecting to pick up lots of small pieces of glass. Instead, he found that the **broken pieces of glass stuck together** against a thin film of liquid plastic that had been inside the flask. After this accident, Benedictus invented safety glass.

▶ An English pharmacist named John Walker tried to clean a wooden stick he had been using to mix some chemicals one day in 1826. He scraped the stick across the stone floor, and **all of a sudden the tip burst into a tiny flame.** This is how Walker invented the first friction match.

◀ MIND-BOGGLING ▶

Some inventors would be surprised if they saw how their inventions are being used today. On the blank line next to each invention, write the letter that goes with its use.

1 Traffic Signal ___
2 Electric Battery ___
3 Telephone ___
4 Telescope ___
5 Paper ___
6 Rocket Engine ___
7 Air Conditioner ___
8 Microphone ___
9 X ray ___
10 Lightning Rod ___

A. keeping sports fans comfortable in domed stadiums
B. sending a person's voice to radios and TVs around the world
C. making disposable clothing
D. letting millions of cars drive through crowded cities
E. powering devices that help the human heart
F. checking luggage for dangerous weapons
G. picking up voice and e-mail messages
H. riding satellites to find planets outside the solar system
I. making huge skyscrapers safe
J. helping cars break the sound barrier

ANSWERS ON PAGES 317-320. FOR MORE PUZZLES GO TO WWW.WORLDALMANACFORKIDS.COM

LANGUAGE

What's an e-book? A pangram? A chad?
You can find the answers below.

SHORT & SHORTER — ABBREVIATIONS and ACRONYMS

An **abbreviation** is a short form of a word or phrase used to save time or space. Here are some abbreviations:

ATM	automated teller machine
ESP	extra-sensory perception
IQ	intelligence quotient
mph	miles per hour
PS	post script
SASE	self-addressed stamped envelope

An **acronym** is a kind of abbreviation. It is a word you can pronounce, formed from the first letters, or other parts, of a group of words. These words you see every day are acronyms:

AWOL	**a**bsent **with**out **l**eave
NASA	**N**ational **A**eronautics and **S**pace **A**dministration
PIN	**P**ersonal **I**dentification **N**umber
radar	**ra**dio **d**etecting **a**nd **r**anging
sitcom	**sit**uation **com**edy
ZIP	**Z**one **I**mprovement **P**lan

NEW WORDS

The English language is always changing. New words become part of the vocabulary, while other words become outdated. Many new words come from the field of electronics and computers, from the media, even from slang.

e-book: a book in electronic format viewed on a desktop computer, laptop, or portable electronic reader. (*My mom didn't have time to go to the library, so she downloaded the e-book of* Crime and Punishment *onto her computer.*)

chad: small bits of paper or cardboard that are made when you punch holes, especially in ballots. (*In the 2000 presidential election, some chads were not clearly punched out, so those ballots did not get counted.*)

three-peat: the third championship in a row. (*Our little league championship this year gave us the first three-peat in our league's history.*)

snail mail: mail delivered by the postal system rather than by e-mail. (*I sent her a birthday card by snail mail, and it took a week to get to California.*)

half-pipe: a U-shaped ramp or runway used in snowboarding, skateboarding, or in-line skating. (*I've gotten so good at snow-boarding that I'm ready for the half-pipe.*)

Did You KNOW?

A PANGRAM IS A SENTENCE THAT CONTAINS ALL **26** LETTERS OF THE ALPHABET. Here's one that's action-packed:
The five boxing wizards jump quickly!

Challenge: Try writing a short pangram of your own.

104

PALINDROMES

A **palindrome** is a word, verse, or sentence that reads the same backward and forward. If English were a very old language, the first words ever spoken could have been a palindrome: "Madam, I'm Adam." Or maybe, "Madam in Eden, I'm Adam." The answer Adam got could have been: "Eve." Here are some other palindromes to ponder.

When your brother asks you what's for dinner, you could tell him:
Ma has a ham.

When President Theodore Roosevelt wanted to shorten the route from the Atlantic Ocean to the Pacific Ocean by creating the Panama Canal, this palindrome could have summed it up:
A man, a plan, a canal: Panama!

On election day, you might say to your dad:
Rise to vote, sir!

If your supermarket is running out of fruit, you might find:
No lemons, no melon.

When you ride in a car on a foggy day, your eyes may play tricks on you. What was that?
Was it a car or a cat I saw?

Your doctor says the best way to start your diet is to stop eating, or fast. You disagree!
Doc, note: I dissent. A fast never prevents a fatness. I diet on cod.

Can you think of some palindromes?

NEON STOCKINGS, POLO BEARS,
and More Malapropisms

Piazza Navona ▶

Pepperoni pizza ▼

A **malapropism** is a word that sounds funny because of the way it is used by mistake. It is named after Mrs. Malaprop, a character in Richard Sheridan's 18th-century play *The Rivals*. If you mean to say "optical illusion," but you say "optical delusion" it's a malapropism. Here are a few malapropisms for you to mull over. Can you spot the mistake and figure out what the speaker meant to say?

What the speaker said:

1. It was the best piazza I ever tasted.

2. I was so hungry, I gouged myself.

3. I brush my teeth in the laboratory.

4. Mom made my favorite dessert, chocolate mouse.

5. Please wash your windows. They look so dinghy!

6. This carousel will protect you from the sun.

7. My sister is a regular child progeny.

What the speaker meant:

1. **Pizza:** doughy, baked crust with tomatoes and cheese. A *piazza* is a square open place surrounded by buildings.

2. **Gorge** means to eat greedily or too much. *Gouge* means to scoop out.

3. **Lavatory:** a bathroom or restroom. A *laboratory* is where scientific experiments take place.

4. **Mousse:** rich, creamy custard of various flavors. A *mouse* is a small rodent.

5. **Dingy:** dirty or soiled. A *dinghy* is a type of boat.

6. **Parasol:** a light umbrella used to protect from the sun. A *carousel* is a musical merry-go-round.

7. **Prodigy:** a highly talented child. *Progeny* means children or offspring in general.

IN OTHER WORDS: IDIOMS

Idioms are like puzzles. Looking at the meaning of each word won't help you understand it. You have to look at the words together. "Take a stab at" solving the idioms here. In other words, try it!

BODY LANGUAGE

all thumbs: clumsy

all ears: paying attention carefully

knee-jerk reaction: an automatic response

get out of my face: stop bothering me

armed to the teeth: heavily armed

off the top of your head: using the first idea that occurs to you

pull one's leg: fool or trick someone

PLAY ON

in the groove: in top form

face the music: be realistic, face the facts

stay tuned: pay attention

play by ear: do something without planning ahead

WEATHER OR NOT

blow hot and cold: first show one feeling, then show the opposite

chill out: relax, take it easy

raining cats and dogs: raining very hard

a break in the clouds: a happy turn of events, a change for the better

once in a blue moon: rarely

BATTER UP!

out of left field: unexpected, from an unlikely source

a ballpark figure: a rough estimate

let's touch base: let's talk to each other about something

a smash hit: a big success

cruisin' into homebase: returning to your house

◄ PICTURE THIS ►

Use the picture to figure out these idioms.

1

2

3

KEEPING IN TOUCH

Did you know there's a right way to write business letters, postcards, and e-mail? Here's how to make each one letter-perfect.

Juanita Reader
123-45 Page Lane
Novell, LA 00004

January 15, 2002

Greta Ryder
c/o Words Publishing
101 Paper Street
Either, OR 90000

Dear Ms. Ryder,

I think your books are great! I am in sixth grade and I think I might be your biggest fan. I am doing a school project on my favorite author. That's you! Here's what I would like to know.

- Why did you become a writer?
- How do you get your ideas?
- Are any of your characters based on real people? Which ones?
- Do you have any advice for kids who want to be writers (like me!)?

Please write back. Maybe you could send an autographed picture, too? I am enclosing my school picture so you can see what I look like. Maybe someday, when I'm as famous as you, it will be worth something!

Sincerely yours,

Juanita Reader

Juanita Reader

Dear Gram and Grampa—

I'm having a great time in Washington, D.C. The Lincoln Memorial looks exactly as it does on the back of a penny. Today we went to the Air and Space Museum. Then we played Frisbee outside on the Mall. That's the kind of "Space and Air" I like best!

Love ya, Nick

NICK AND NANCY NEWMAN
25 SHADY LANE
NUTLEY, NJ 07110

Birthday Reminder

 Send   Compose   Send Later   **X** Delete

Date: 3 July 02 15:20:37
From: Shimmergirl@fastnet.com
Subject: It's my birthday!
To: violet13, nikkiG, jaxfax

Hi, Everyone! Just a reminder. My birthday is coming up—and guess what? I'm having a movie-and-sleepover party, and you're all invited. Let's vote on the movie we're going to see. Which of these new hits do you like best? Is it: "Very Scary Movie?" "The Nuttier Professor?" Or "Fido and Me?" E-mail me back and cast your vote! Love, SG

TOP TEN *Languages*

Would you have guessed that Mandarin, the principal language of China, is the most common spoken language in the world? You may find more surprises in the chart below, which lists languages spoken in 2000 by at least 100,000,000 native speakers (those for whom the language is their first language, or mother tongue) and some of the places where each one is spoken.

Hello!
(English)

Konnichi wa!
(Japanese)

¡Hola!
(Spanish)

LANGUAGE	WHERE SPOKEN	NATIVE SPEAKERS
Mandarin	China, Taiwan	874,000,000
Hindi	India	366,000,000
English	U.S., Canada, Britain	341,000,000
Spanish	Spain, Latin America	322,000,000
Arabic	Arabian Peninsula	207,000,000
Bengali	India, Bangladesh	207,000,000
Portuguese	Portugal, Brazil	176,000,000
Russian	Russia	167,000,000
Japanese	Japan	125,000,000
German	Germany, Austria	100,000,000

WHICH LANGUAGES ARE SPOKEN IN THE UNITED STATES?

Since the beginning of American history, immigrants have come to the United States from all over the world. They have brought their native languages with them.

¡Hola! That's how more than 17 million Americans say "hi" at home. Still, nearly 200 million Americans only speak English. The table at right lists the other most frequently spoken languages in the United States, as of the 1990 census.

LANGUAGE USED AT HOME	SPEAKERS OVER 5 YEARS OLD
❶ English only	198,601,000
❷ Spanish	17,339,000
❸ French	1,702,000
❹ German	1,547,000
❺ Italian	1,309,000
❻ Chinese	1,249,000
❼ Tagalog	843,000
❽ Polish	723,000
❾ Korean	626,000
❿ Vietnamese	507,000
⓫ Portuguese	430,000
⓬ Japanese	428,000
⓭ Greek	388,000
⓮ Arabic	355,000
⓯ Hindi, Urdu, related languages	331,000
⓰ Russian	242,000
⓱ Yiddish	213,000
⓲ Thai	206,000
⓳ Persian	202,000
⓴ French Creole	188,000

Did You Know?

THE WORD *PHONY* HAILS FROM GREAT BRITAIN. In the olden days, British swindlers used many secret code words. One such word was *fawney*, which meant a gilt, or imitation, gold ring. Criminals would sell these rings pretending they were real gold. In time, *phony*, from *fawney*, came to mean anything fake.

LANGUAGE EXPRESS

Surprise your friends and family with your knowledge of words from other languages.

ENGLISH	SPANISH	FRENCH	GERMAN	CHINESE
Monday	lunes	lundi	Montag	Xingqiyi
Tuesday	martes	mardi	Dienstag	Xingqier
Wednesday	miércoles	mercredi	Mittwoch	Xingqisan
Thursday	jueves	jeudi	Donnerstag	Xingqisi
Friday	viernes	vendredi	Freitag	Xingqiwu
Saturday	sábado	samedi	Samstag	Xingqiliu
Sunday	domingo	dimanche	Sonntag	Xingqitian
blue	azul	bleu	blau	lan
red	rojo	rouge	rot	hong
green	verde	vert	grün	lu
yellow	amarillo	jaune	gelb	huang
black	negro	noir	schwarz	hei
white	blanco	blanc	weiss	bai
one	uno	un	eins	yi
two	dos	deux	zwei	er
three	tres	trois	drei	san
four	cuatro	quatre	vier	si
five	cinco	cinq	fünf	wu
six	seis	six	sechs	liu
seven	siete	sept	sieben	qi
eight	ocho	huit	acht	ba
nine	nueve	neuf	neun	jiu
ten	diez	dix	zehn	shi
dog	perro	chien	Hund	gou
cat	gato	chat	Katze	mao
fish	pez	poisson	Fisch	yu
friend	amigo, amiga	ami, amie	Freund, Freundin	pengyou
happy birthday!	¡feliz cumpleaños!	bonne anniversaire!	Glückwunsch zum Geburtstag!	Bai shou!
hello	¡hola!	Bonjour!	Hallo!	Ni hao!
good-bye!	¡hasta luego!	au revoir!	auf Wiedersehen!	zai-jian!

BAI SHOU!

¡FELIZ CUMPLEAÑOS!

Bonne anniversaire!

Glückwunsch zum Geburtstag!

◀ PICTURE THESE ▶

Can you figure out the phrases these word puzzles represent? We've done one for you.

1 IT'S A _{WORLD}

It's a small world

2 innocent STANDER STANDER

_____

3 6 o'clock

_____

4 DANE

_____

5 Game

_____

6 M-AN

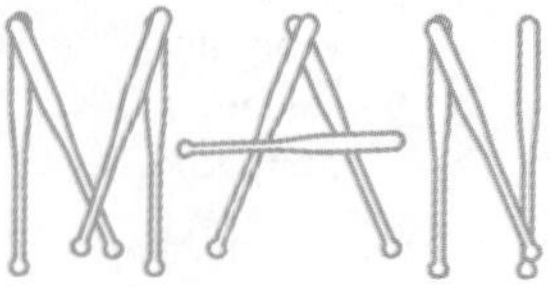

_____

7 FATHER

_____

8 RAY

_____

9 LEAGUE'S

_____

10 STRAWBERRY cake

_____

11 CHIN CHIN

_____

12 ✔ MATE

_____

13 staircase staircase staircase staircase staircase staircase staircase staircase staircase staircase

_____

14 Draw your own picture for

Sitting on top of the world

MILITARY

Which famous general used elephants to transport troops and supplies across a mountain range? *You can find the answer on page 112.*

SERIOUS BUSINESS

Soldiers risk their lives to fight for their nation or cause, often to defend the lives and freedom of others. Since the beginning of the Revolutionary War, more than 2.6 million U.S. soldiers have been killed or wounded in wars (about as many people as now live in Arkansas). Today over 2.2 million American men and women serve in four major branches of the military, the Army, Navy, Air Force, and Marines.

Having more soldiers and weapons than the other side is an important advantage in war. So is military intelligence, or gaining secret information about an enemy, as well as such factors as deception, technology, and plain old stubbornness.

Intelligence During World War II, U.S. military intelligence broke a Japanese naval code used to send secret messages by radio. Americans thus learned of a planned attack on the U.S.-held island of Midway, northwest of Hawaii. Planes from U.S. aircraft carriers were able to ambush the Japanese fleet before it got in shooting range of the island.

Deception During the Trojan War in the 12th century B.C., it is said that the Greeks built a large wooden horse, hid soldiers inside it, and left it outside Troy's main gate as a "gift." After the Trojans brought the horse inside the city, the soldiers slipped out and opened the gate so the Greek army could come in and burn the city.

Technology English forces in France used the longbow to defeat the French in the Battle of Agincourt, in 1415. Longbows, which were as tall as the archers themselves, could hurl heavy arrows 200 yards or more, or the length of two modern football fields.

Communications Communications in the 19th century were not nearly as fast as they are today. When American and British armies fought the Battle of New Orleans in January 1815, neither side knew that a peace treaty "ending" the War of 1812 had been signed in Belgium two weeks earlier!

Tactics The tactics of Confederate General Robert E. Lee led to a Southern victory in the Civil War Battle of Chancellorsville, Virginia, in May 1863. Trapped between two much larger Union forces, Lee divided his army into three parts and launched a surprise flanking attack that forced the Northerners to retreat.

Stubbornness Soldiers and civilians in the Russian city of Stalingrad (Volgograd) held off an invading German army in 1942-43. The Russians refused to surrender the city despite terrible casualties and hardships. Eventually, Russian troops launched a counterattack, and the Germans retreated.

FAMOUS FIGHTER PLANES

Navy fighter planes, based on aircraft carriers, help protect ships against enemy aircraft.

In World War II, during the 1942 Battle of Midway and throughout most of the war, the U.S. Navy's main carrier-based fighter was the Grumman F-4F Wildcat. The F-4F was a fixed-wing, propeller-driven plane.

▼ *F-14 Tomcat*

Since the mid-1970s, Navy fleets have been protected by the Wildcat's bigger "grandson," the Grumman F-14 Tomcat (featured in the 1986 movie *Top Gun*). The Tomcat is a multi-role strike fighter. This means that it also can be armed to attack ships or ground targets. The wings automatically angle forward or back during flight so they can maneuver better. The Tomcat's two jet engines can push the plane to Mach 1.88, almost twice the speed of sound.

	F-4F Wildcat	**F-14 Tomcat**
PUT IN OPERATION	1941	1973
CREW	1 (pilot)	2 (pilot and radar intercept officer)
ENGINE	14-cylinder, air-cooled	Twin turbofans with afterburners
LENGTH	28 feet, 9 inches	61 feet, 9 inches
HEIGHT	11 feet, 10 inches	16 feet
WINGSPAN	38 feet	64 feet deployed, 38 feet swept back
LOADED WEIGHT	7,952 pounds	72,900 pounds
TOP SPEED	318 miles per hour	Mach 1.88 (1,395 miles per hour)
FLIGHT CEILING	34,900 feet	Above 53,000 feet
RANGE	770 nautical miles	1,000 nautical miles
ARMAMENT	6 machine guns, up to 200 pounds of bombs	1 cannon, up to 13,000 pounds of bombs

Did You Know?

DID THEY PACK THEIR TRUNKS? *Hannibal, a general of the North African city-state of Carthage, in 218 B.C., used elephants to help transport his army across the snowy Alps mountain range from France into northern Italy and eventually march on Rome.*

MONEY

What do whales' teeth and dollar bills have in common? *You can find the answer on this page.*

HISTORY OF MONEY

Why Did People Start Using Money? People first started using money in order to trade. A farmer who had cattle might want to have salt to preserve meat or cloth to make clothing. For this farmer, a cow became a "medium of exchange"— a way of getting things the farmer did not make or grow. Cattle became a form of money. Whatever people agreed to use for trade became the earliest kinds of money.

What Objects Have Been Used as Money?

You may be surprised by some of the items that people have used every day as money. What does the form of money tell you about a society and its people?

▶ knives, rice, and spades in China around 3000 B.C.

▶ cattle and clay tablets in Babylonia around 2500 B.C.

▶ wampum (beads) and beaver fur by Native Americans of the northeast around A.D. 1500

▶ tobacco by early American colonists around 1650

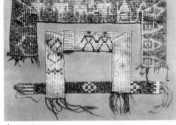

▲ *Wampum used by Native Americans*

▶ whales' teeth by the Pacific peoples on the island of Fiji, until the early 1900s

Why Did Governments Start Issuing Money? The first government to make coins that looked alike and use them as money is thought to be the Greek city-state of Lydia in the 7th century B.C. These Lydian coins were actually bean-shaped lumps made from a mixture of gold and silver.

The first government in Europe to issue paper money that looked alike was France's in the early 18th century. Governments were interested in issuing money because the money itself had value. If a government could gain control over the manufacture of money, it could increase its own wealth—often simply by making more money.

Today, money throughout the world is issued only by governments. In the United States, the Department of the Treasury and the U.S. Mint make all the paper money and coins. Nowadays, we also use checks and credit cards to pay for things we buy. These are not thought of as real money but more as "promises to pay."

THE FIRST PAPER MONEY

By the Middle Ages (about A.D. 800-1100), gold had become a popular medium for trade in Europe. But gold was heavy and difficult to carry, and the cities and the roads of Europe at that time were dangerous places to carry large amounts of gold. So merchants and goldsmiths began issuing notes promising to pay gold to the person carrying the note. These "promissory notes" were the beginning of paper money in Europe. Paper money was probably also invented in China, where the explorer Marco Polo saw it in the 1280s.

MAKING MONEY: THE U.S. MINT

What is the U.S. Mint? The U.S. Mint, founded in 1792, makes all U.S. coins. It also safeguards the Treasury Department's stored gold and silver at Fort Knox, KY. The Bureau of Engraving and Printing designs and prints all U.S. paper money. Both the U.S. Mint and the Bureau of Engraving and Printing are part of the U.S. Treasury Department and have their headquarters in Washington, D.C.

What Kinds of Coins Does the Mint Make? Branches of the the U.S. Mint in Denver and Philadelphia currently make coins for "circulation," or everday use. A tiny "D" or "P" near the year, called a mint mark, tells you which one made the coin. A Lincoln penny with no mint mark was probably made at the Philadelphia Mint, which has by tradition never marked their pennies.

Commemorative coins—made in honor of events, like the Olympics, or people, like Christopher Columbus—and other special coins and sets for collecting are usually made at the branches in San Francisco or West Point, NY, and have the mint marks "S" or "W." Commemorative coins can have values of $.50, $1.00, $5.00, or even $10.00!

Whose Portraits Are on Our Money? On the front of all U.S. paper money are portraits of presidents and other famous Americans. Presidents also appear on the most commonly used coins. From 1999 to 2008, five new quarters are being coined each year. Each quarter will feature the design of a different state on the back, with George Washington on the front. The quarters are being introduced in the same order as states entered the Union.

DENOMINATION	PORTRAIT
1¢	**Abraham Lincoln**, 16th U.S. President
5¢	**Thomas Jefferson**, 3rd U.S. President
10¢	**Franklin Delano Roosevelt**, 32nd U.S. President
25¢	**George Washington**, 1st U.S. President
$1 (bill)	**George Washington**, 1st U.S. President
$1 (coin)	**Sacagawea**, Native American woman
$2	**Thomas Jefferson**, 3rd U.S. President
$5	**Abraham Lincoln**, 16th U.S. President
$10	**Alexander Hamilton**, 1st U.S. Treasury Secretary
$20	**Andrew Jackson**, 7th U.S. President
$50	**Ulysses S. Grant**, 18th U.S. President
$100	**Benjamin Franklin**, colonial inventor and U.S. patriot

Paper Money

In 1996 the U.S. Treasury printed a new $100 bill with features to help prevent counterfeiting. A new $50 bill was printed in 1997, and a new $20 bill was issued in 1998. In 2000, new $10 and $5 bills were issued. A new $1 bill will be next.

In January 2000, the Golden Dollar coin was issued. The front of the coin shows Sacagawea, the Shoshone woman who helped Lewis and Clark explore the Louisiana Purchase. The back shows a Bald Eagle and 17 stars.

When is a dollar worth $41,395? When it's a Sacagawea coin that was struck wrong. By mistake, some of the new dollar coins had the George Washington side of the U.S. quarter stamped on them, instead of Sacagawea. Most of the mistruck coins were destroyed before they went into circulation, but the rare few that made it into the hands of the public are now worth a lot of money to collectors. One man who found a messed up dollar coin sold it for $41,395.

Read more about money at: (WEB SITE) http://www.ustreas.gov/kids **or** http://www.usmint.gov

How Much Money Is in Circulation?

As of March 31, 2000, the total amount of money in circulation in the United States came to $562,949,257,157 (about 563 billion dollars). More than 25 billion dollars was in coins, the rest in paper money. The chart below shows the number of bills of each kind in circulation.

Kind (Denomination)	Number of Bills in Circulation	Value of Money in Circulation
$1 bills	7,043,813,463	$7,043,813,463
$2 bills	604,748,958	$1,209,497,916
$5 bills	1,600,787,162	$8,003,935,810
$10 bills	1,358,201,322	$13,582,013,220
$20 bills	4,522,108,535	$90,442,170,700
$50 bills	1,061,068,146	$53,053,407,300
$100 bills	3,616,997,926	$361,699,792,600
$500 bills	286,880	$143,440,000
$1,000 bills	166,764	$166,764,000
$5,000 bills	351	$1,755,000
$10,000 bills	344	$3,440,000

WHAT ARE EXCHANGE RATES?

When one country exports goods to another, the payment from the country buying the goods must be changed into the currency of the country selling them. An exchange rate is the price of one currency in terms of another. For example, 1 U.S. dollar could buy about 7 French francs in 2001.

The chart below compares the exchange rates in 1970 and 2001 between the U.S. dollar and the currency of five of the country's biggest trading partners. The more foreign money the dollar can buy, the better the exchange rate for Americans.

WHAT A DOLLAR BOUGHT		
COUNTRY	IN 1970	IN 2001
France	5½ francs	7 francs
Germany	3⅗ marks	2 marks
Great Britain	⅖ pound	⅔ pound
Italy	623 lire	2,040 lire
Japan	358 yen	117 yen

United States   Japan

ECUADOR, GUATEMALA, AND EL SALVADOR ALL SWITCHED THEIR NATIONAL CURRENCIES TO THE U.S. DOLLAR EARLY IN 2001. Countries that use the dollar usually do so to try to help stabilize their economies and attract investment.

WHY BUDGETS ARE HELPFUL

A budget is a plan that estimates how much money a person, a business, or a government will receive during a period of time, how much money will be spent and what it will be spent on, and how much money will be left over (if any).

A Family Budget

Do you know what your family spends money on? Do you know where your family's income comes from? The chart below shows some sources of income and typical yearly expenses for a family's budget.

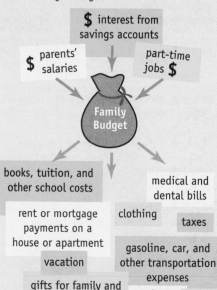

$ interest from savings accounts

$ parents' salaries

part-time jobs $

Family Budget

books, tuition, and other school costs

medical and dental bills

rent or mortgage payments on a house or apartment

clothing

taxes

vacation

gasoline, car, and other transportation expenses

gifts for family and friends or charities

savings account

food

other expenses

A Balanced Budget

A budget is **balanced** when the amount of money you receive equals the amount of money you spend. A budget is **in deficit** when the amount of money you spend is greater than the amount of money you have.

Making Your Own Budget

Imagine that you have a weekly allowance of $10. With this money you have to pay for things like snacks and magazines and also try to save up for special things. Planning a budget will help you manage your money. Here are some items you might want to put in your budget:

Possible Purchases and Cost:
Snacks: $.75 each
Collectible toy: $3.00
Book: $3.00

Savings:
For gifts: $.50–$2.00
For something special for yourself
(like a basketball, a compact disc, a computer game, or concert tickets):
$1.00 or more.

List the items you want along with their price. Add any other items that interest you—and their prices. Don't forget to add any money you want to save.

Item	Amount

Savings

Now total all your purchases and savings:

Is your budget balanced? Is the amount you plan to spend and save equal to the amount of your "income" ($10)? If not, try to reduce your planned savings or spending to make your budget balance.

THE U.S. BUDGET

The U.S. government also has a budget. It gets, and spends, lots of money.

Where Does the U.S. Government Get Money?

Here is how the U.S. government got its money in the 2000 budget year.

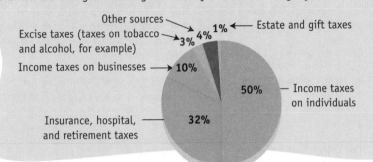

Other sources
Excise taxes (taxes on tobacco — 3% and alcohol, for example)
1% ← Estate and gift taxes
4%
Income taxes on businesses → 10%

50% — Income taxes on individuals

Insurance, hospital, — 32% and retirement taxes

Where Does the U.S. Government Spend Money?

Here is how the U.S. government spent its money in the 2000 budget year.

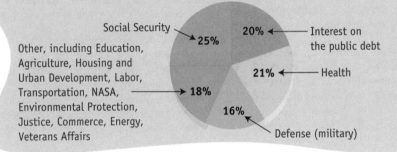

Social Security — 25%
20% ← Interest on the public debt

Other, including Education, Agriculture, Housing and Urban Development, Labor, Transportation, NASA, — 18% Environmental Protection, Justice, Commerce, Energy, Veterans Affairs

21% ← Health

16%

Defense (military)

FROM DEFICIT TO SURPLUS

Every year from 1969 to 1997 the government spent more money than it took in. This gap is called the **budget deficit**. Paying interest on such a large debt hurts the economy.

Fortunately, the budget deficit has been going down since 1993. This is partly because people and companies have been making more money and thus paying more taxes. In 1998, the U.S. began to have a **budget surplus**—it took in more than it spent. The trend is still continuing.

YEAR	$ TAKEN IN	$ SPENT	DEFICIT
1993	$1.153 trillion	$1.408 trillion	$–255 billion
1994	$1.257 trillion	$1.460 trillion	$–203 billion
1995	$1.350 trillion	$1.514 trillion	$–164 billion
1996	$1.453 trillion	$1.560 trillion	$–107 billion
1997	$1.579 trillion	$1.601 trillion	$–22 billion
1998	$1.721 trillion	$1.651 trillion	$70 billion (surplus)
1999	$1.827 trillion	$1.703 trillion	$124 billion (surplus)
2000	$2.025 trillion	$1.788 trillion	$237 billion (surplus)

MONEY TALK
AN ECONOMICS GLOSSARY

bear market a time when the prices of most stocks are falling.

bond a written promise, or IOU, to repay an amount of borrowed money on a certain date with interest paid regularly.

bull market a time when the value of most stocks goes up.

cost of living the average cost of the basic needs of life, including food, clothing, housing, medical care, and other services.

disposable income money left after paying taxes that is available for spending and saving.

Dow Jones Industrial Average an "index" measuring the prices of 30 large companies' stocks. It is used to track changes in the prices of stocks.

entrepreneur a person who starts his or her own business.

gross domestic product (GDP) all goods and services produced by a nation. The U.S. gross domestic product in 2000 was about $10,000,000,000,000 ($10 trillion)

inflation an increase in the level of prices of goods because many people want them and supplies are low.

interest money a borrower pays to borrow money. When you open a savings account, the bank borrows from you and pays you interest.

prime interest rate a key interest rate charged by banks (usually to good customers); many other rates, such as for credit cards and mortgages, are set at a certain amount "above prime."

recession a broad decline in a nation's economic output; usually defined as six months of declining GDP.

salary the payment an employer gives an employee for the work he or she performs.

stock a share in a corporation, representing partial ownership. A corporation sells shares to individuals or other companies to raise money. The shares may increase or decrease in value. When the company makes a profit, it may pay stockholders a "dividend," or part of its earnings.

stock exchange a place (or "virtual" place) where stockbrokers meet to buy and sell stocks and bonds. See "What Do You Want to Be" on the next page to find out what a stockbroker does.

taxes money that a government collects from people to pay for the programs and services it provides.

WHAT DO YOU WANT TO BE?

More than 130 million people in the United States have jobs. You see many of them every day—teachers, bus drivers, or cashiers. Many jobs exist that you may not have ever heard of or thought of: aerospace engineer or actuary, for example. Although new jobs are constantly created, some jobs become unnecessary as different ways are found to do the work.

Here are just a few of the jobs people have today. Do you think any of them will interest you when you're ready to start your career? What skills do you think you'll need?

College Professors

College teachers, who are called professors, usually have a Ph.D., or a doctoral degree, in the subject they teach. That means they studied and went to school for several years after graduating from college themselves. Professors teach classes, help students, grade students papers and tests, and do research and write about the subject they teach. To succeed, professors have to enjoy school and working with students.

COMPUTER TECHNICIANS

As more and more people own or use computers, more workers are needed to repair the machines. Computer technicians also install and replace computer equipment.

CONSERVATION SCIENTISTS

These scientists watch over public lands, such as parks, and find ways to reduce environmental damage caused by activities such as building, mining, and ranching. Conservation scientists must enjoy working outdoors. Sometimes they must also work with people who have different ideas about land use.

Graphic Designers

Graphic designers design catalogues, logos (company or product names), and Web sites. Designers must be creative and interested in art. Most use computers.

LOAN OFFICERS

When people need money to buy a house or go to college, they often borrow it from a bank. Loan officers are bank employees who decide whether or not people seeking to borrow money are likely to pay it back.

NURSES

Caring for patients and helping doctors are two of the most important responsibilities nurses have. People are living longer and scientists are finding new ways to treat and cure diseases, so nurses are needed more and more.

School Counselors

School counselors help students think about careers and what they should do to prepare for the future. Many counselors also help kids cope with family problems and other personal matters.

$ T O C K B R O K E R S $

Stockbrokers buy and sell stocks for their clients. They must know about people, businesses, and the economy. Stockbrokers must pass an exam before they can buy and sell stock.

MOVIES & TV

What kind of animal did Mel Gibson provide the voice for in a recent hit movie? *You can find the answer on page 121.*

20 MOVIE HITS (2000 and early 2001)

Bring It On (PG-13)

Cast Away (PG-13)

Charlie's Angels (PG-13)

Chicken Run (G)

Crouching Tiger, Hidden Dragon (PG-13)

Dinosaur (PG)

Disney's The Kid (PG)

Dr. Seuss' How the Grinch Stole Christmas (PG)

Josie and the Pussycats (PG-13)

A Knight's Tale (PG-13)

Mission: Impossible 2 (PG-13)

The Mummy Returns

Pearl Harbor (PG-13)

Rat (PG)

Rugrats in Paris: The Movie (G)

Shrek (PG)

Snow Day (PG)

Spy Kids (PG)

Stuart Little (PG)

X-Men (PG-13)

▲ *Eddie Murphy, John Lithgow, Cameron Diaz, and Mike Myers, who provide some of the voices in* Shrek

20 Popular KIDS' VIDEOS of 2000

The Aristocats

An Extremely Goofy Movie

The Iron Giant

Mary-Kate & Ashley: Passport to Paris

Mary-Kate & Ashley: School Dance Party

Mary-Kate & Ashley: Switching Goals

Monster Rancher: Let the Games Begin

Mulan

Muppets From Space

Pokémon: The First Movie

Pokémon: Seaside Pikachu

Pokémon: Wake Up Snorlax

The Powerpuff Girls: Bubble-Vicious

The Powerpuff Girls: Monkey See, Doggie Do

Pinocchio

The Prince of Egypt

Saludos Amigos

Scooby Doo's Greatest Mysteries

Tarzan

The Tigger Movie

SOME POPULAR MOVIES

Frankenstein (1931) Boris Karloff's scary makeup started a new era of horror movies.

King Kong (1933) Sixty years before *Jurassic Park*, King Kong, a giant ape, fought dinosaurs on a mysterious island. Captured by humans, he ended up battling civilization in New York City.

The Wizard of Oz (1939) As color was introduced into movies, Dorothy, played by Judy Garland, met a scarecrow, a tin woodsman, and a cowardly lion in the colorful land of Oz.

Gone With the Wind (1939) A massive movie set was destroyed to re-create the burning of Atlanta during the Civil War.

Jurassic Park (1993) Computer-generated dinosaurs looked and sounded very real as they thrilled audiences around the world.

Toy Story (1995) The first animated movie nominated for best screenplay written directly for the screen.

Star Wars: Episode I—The Phantom Menace (1999) The first of three prequels—movies that tell the story of what happened before *Star Wars*, *The Empire Strikes Back*, and *Return of the Jedi*.

Harry Potter and the Sorcerer's Stone (2001) The adventures of Harry, Hermione, and Ron come to the big screen in this long-awaited movie based on the writing of J. K. Rowling.

CHICKEN RUN

Chicken Run is the kind of movie that both kids and adults can really enjoy. Before making this movie, its directors, Nick Park and Peter Lord, were best known in Great Britain, where they live, as the creators of the TV show *Wallace and Gromit*.

The hero of *Chicken Run* is a rooster named Rocky (the voice of Mel Gibson). Rocky comes up with a plan for the chickens to escape from a farm. There the evil Mrs. Tweedy wants to serve them in pies.

Before making their movie, directors Park and Lord went to a real farm to study chickens. The filmmakers realized that, to make their animation work well, they had to make their chickens look a little different from real ones. Real chickens' knees and eyes would have been difficult to show. And real chickens don't have teeth. (Animated chickens do!)

Chicken Run was made with a kind of animation called "stop-motion photography." Each chicken model had to be adjusted by animators for every frame of the film. It took 18 frames for one second of film. Forty animators worked on *Chicken Run*.

In the past, directors had to wait for film to be developed before they could see if they captured the action they wanted. Now a computer records the motion, so directors can see right away what they've got. All the hard work paid off. *Chicken Run* brought lots of new fans of all ages around the world.

CARTOONS ON TV

Before the mid-1950s, before almost everyone owned a TV, going to the movies was a favorite pastime. The price of admission got you two features, a newsreel, coming attractions, and at least one cartoon. The cartoons were mainly meant to fill time between features. Yet Bugs Bunny, Mickey Mouse, and other cartoon characters became stars.

Cartoons made just for TV—rather than for the movies—became popular in the early 1960s. Among the earliest animated series was *The Flintstones*. It first aired on September 30, 1960. The last original episode was shown in 1966, but it lives on in reruns and its jazzy theme song.

Now you can watch cartoons day and night. The Cartoon Network is a cable TV channel that shows nothing but cartoons all day. *Rugrats*, a Nickelodeon cartoon about a group of mischievous babies, is a current cable hit. *Rugrats* is so popular that it's been turned into a series of full-length movies. That means cartoons have come full circle—from movie theaters to TV and back to movie theaters!

POPULAR TV SHOWS IN 2000-2001

(Source: Nielsen Media Research; as of April 29, 2001)

AGES 6-11
1. Survivor II
2. Malcolm in the Middle
3. The Simpsons
4. Wonderful World of Disney
5. Boot Camp

AGES 12-17
1. Malcolm in the Middle
2. The Simpsons
3. Temptation Island
4. Boot Camp
5. Survivor II

Popular Video Games in 2000

Pokémon Yellow—Nintendo
Pokémon Blue—Nintendo
Pokémon Red—Nintendo
Pokémon Pinball—Nintendo
Donkey Kong 64—Nintendo
Gran Turismo—Sony
Pokémon Snap—Nintendo
Super Smash Bros—Nintendo
Final Fantasy VIII—SquareEA
Driver—GT Interactive

Did You KNOW?

A MAN OF MANY VOICES, MEL BLANC WAS THE ORIGINAL VOICE OF BARNEY RUBBLE ON *THE FLINTSTONES*. *He supplied the voices for Bugs Bunny, Daffy Duck, and many other Warner Brothers cartoon characters. He also did the voice for Fred Flintstone's pet dinosaur, Dino.*

PEOPLE TO WATCH

Julia Stiles

What does it take to have a teen magazine name you one of today's hottest young stars? For Julia Stiles, success came in 1996 when she starred in *I Love You, I Love You Not* with Claire Danes, James Van Der Beek, and Jude Law. She later starred in the TV miniseries *The '60s*. Julia has also made three movies based on Shakespeare plays: *10 Things I Hate About You* (based on *The Taming of the Shrew*), *Hamlet*, and *O* (based on *Othello*). She played a ballet dancer who learns hip-hop in the 2001 movie *Save the Last Dance*.

Julia was born on March 28, 1981, in New York City. When she was 11 years old, she wrote a letter to a New York theater group asking for an audition. She not only got to try out, she got a part in a play.

Now a student at Columbia University, Julia has this advice for would-be actors: "People thinking about going into acting because they want to be famous would probably make themselves unhappy. But if you are interested in the process and you like the chance to play other people, I think that you will be happy and, more power to you!"

Daniel Radcliffe

If you've read any of the Harry Potter books—and who hasn't—you probably have your own ideas about the young wizard. What does he look like? How does he act and sound? Millions of readers have been eagerly waiting for the first Harry Potter movie.

Daniel Radcliffe was 11 years old when he was cast as Harry Potter in *Harry Potter and the Sorcerer's Stone*. Before Harry, he played young David Copperfield in a TV movie based on the book by Charles Dickens. Daniel, who was born in 1989 and lives in Great Britain, was picked over other better-known actors. J. K. Rowling, author of the Harry Potter books, liked him for the role. She said, "Having seen Dan Radcliffe's screen test, I don't think the director could have found a better Harry."

When fans see the movie, they can judge for themselves whether Daniel lives up to the Harry they imagined.

MUSEUMS

Where can you find the biggest meteorite in the U.S.?
You can find the answer on page 126.

"TEMPLES OF THE MUSES"

Museums are great places to learn new things and have fun at the same time. The word *museum* comes from a Greek word that means "temple of the Muses." The Muses were the goddesses of art and science.

The oldest museum in the U.S. is The Charleston Museum, founded in South Carolina in 1773. The U.S. now has more than 8,300 museums. Some are listed here. For others, see the Index.

KIDS' MUSEUMS

THE CHILDREN'S MUSEUM, Boston, Massachusetts. Has a full-size Japanese house, a Latino market, plus displays on Native Americans.
WEB SITE *http://www.bostonkids.org*

CHILDREN'S DISCOVERY MUSEUM OF SAN JOSE, San Jose, California. Contains a hands-on bubble-world, a post office annex with 1950s furnishings, a bank, media studio, climbing tower, miniature city, and many interesting art and science exhibits.
WEB SITE *http://www.cdm.org/aboutus.html*

CHICAGO CHILDREN'S MUSEUM, Chicago, Illinois. Hands-on exhibits let you dig for dinosaur fossils, create your own inventions, climb the rigging of a schooner, build a dam in a waterways display, sit in a real ambulance, and do artwork.
WEB SITE *http://www.chichildrensmuseum.org*

THE CHILDREN'S MUSEUM OF MAINE, Portland, Maine. Hands-on exhibits include a Star Lab and Space Shuttle, computer lab with high-speed Internet access, a bank, fire truck, grocery store, farm and animal hospital.
WEB SITE *http://www.wowpages.com/museum/generalinfo.html*

LYNN MEADOWS DISCOVERY CENTER, Gulfport, Mississippi. Here you can create your own video in a high-tech communications center, operate a crane, meet a robot, do gravity experiments in a science lab, and scramble up a huge climbing tower.
WEB SITE *http://www.lmdc.org/*

Did You KNOW?

THE YOZEUM in *Tucson, Arizona, displays more than 500 yo-yos from the collection of Donald F. Duncan, Jr. His father created the Duncan yo-yo. Once a month, museum workers teach visitors fun yo-yo tricks. Call (520) 623-7085 for more information.*

The *Official Museum Directory* lists thousands of museums. You can also check out the Association of Youth Museums on the Internet at
WEB SITE *http://www.aym.org*

MUSEUMS OF THE PERFORMING ARTS

CONTEMPORARY ARTS CENTER, New Orleans, Louisiana • Home to plays, music and dance performances, art, video, sculpture.

COUNTRY MUSIC HALL OF FAME AND MUSEUM, Nashville, Tennessee • Celebrates country music's history and stars.

DANCE ART MUSEUM OF THE AMERICAS, Santa Fe, New Mexico • A collection of costumes, books, and photos on the history of dance.

EXPERIENCE MUSIC PROJECT, Seattle, Washington • Ride through an art and musical exhibit on the story of American popular music.

SAN FRANCISCO PERFORMING ARTS LIBRARY AND MUSEUM, San Francisco, California • Among its features are objects from the theater, film, and circus, including costumes, and set designs.

ETHNIC MUSEUMS

These museums show the culture and history of different peoples.

The Latin American Art Museum, Miami, Florida • Celebrates artwork, music, poetry, and dance performances by Hispanic and Latin American artists of today.

Freer Gallery of Art and Arthur M. Sackler Gallery, Washington, D.C. • Displays art from China, Japan, India, and other Asian countries.

California African American Museum, Los Angeles, California • Displays art, books, and photographs on African-American culture.

The Heard Museum, Phoenix, Arizona • Displays art by Native Americans, primarily from the Southwestern U.S.

The Jewish Museum, New York, New York • Has exhibits covering 40 centuries of Jewish history and culture.

Museum of African American History, Detroit, Michigan • Features a large model of a slave ship, inventions by African Americans, music by black composers, and the space suit worn by the first U.S. black female astronaut.

National Museum of the American Indian, New York, New York • Has displays on the ways of life and the history of Native Americans.

ROSA PARKS MUSEUM

MONTGOMERY, ALABAMA — The Rosa Parks Library and Museum opened on the spot where Ms. Parks was arrested in 1955 for refusing to give up her seat on a public bus to a white man. Bus doors open into the museum's reception area, which has a street lamp, an old bus from the 1950s, and a sculpture of Ms. Parks sitting on a bus seat. Projections on the back wall recreate her arrest and the civil rights protests that followed. Visit the museum at 251 Montgomery Street, Montgomery, Alabama; Phone: (334) 241-8615

WEBSITE http://www.tsum.edu/museum

Odd Museums

The Cookie Jar Museum in Lemont, Illinois, is devoted to cookie jars. There are no cookies, just jars—2,000 of them!

The Nut Museum in Old Lyme, Connecticut, contains more than 100 kinds of nuts, including the largest nut in the world, a so-called double coconut that's 35 pounds.

The Barbie Hall of Fame in Palo Alto, California, claims to have every Barbie doll, outfit, and accessory ever made. It has Ken stuff, too.

There is a **Museum of Toilets, in New Delhi, India.** It has many kinds of toilets, both plain and fancy, from different times and different parts of the world.

Where Do They Belong?

These ancient treasures stir strong feelings today.

THE ELGIN MARBLES Where would you expect to find a beautiful collection of Greek gods and goddesses carved in marble? If you guessed Greece try again. In 1806, Thomas Bruce, Earl of Elgin, took more than 50 sculptures from the Parthenon, the ruins of an ancient temple in Greece. He brought them to England, where they became known as the Elgin Marbles. In 1816, he sold his treasures to the British Museum. Greece wants the sculptures back in time for the 2004 Olympics, to be held in Athens. The British have refused to return them.

THE KENNEWICK MAN In the United States there is a conflict between scientists and several Indian tribes over the remains of the Kennewick Man who lived about 9,200 years ago. Scientists want to study his bones, which make up the oldest full skeleton ever found in North America. But tribal leaders claim him as an ancestor, and say the bones should be returned to the earth. The Kennewick Man is being stored at the Burke Museum in Seattle, Washington, until a court decides his fate.

THE WILLAMETTE METEORITE The Willamette meteorite, the biggest ever found in the United States, crashed into the Earth thousands of years ago. It is believed to be the iron core of a planet that exploded billions of years ago. Since 1906, the meteorite has been on display at the American Museum of Natural History. But the American Indians said it has always been a source of healing and purifying power for them, and they wanted it back. In 2000, both sides agreed to keep it at the museum's Rose Center for Earth and Science. But Native Americans can still use it for religious, historical, and cultural purposes.

The Willamette meteorite ▶

MUSIC & DANCE

What kind of music started in the American South a century ago? *You can find the answer on page 128.*

MUSICAL INSTRUMENTS

There are many kinds of musical instruments. Instruments in an orchestra are divided into four groups, or sections: string, woodwind, brass, and percussion.

PERCUSSION INSTRUMENTS
Percussion instruments make sounds when they are struck. The most common percussion instrument is the drum. Others include cymbals, triangles, gongs, bells, and xylophone. Keyboard instruments, like the piano, are sometimes thought of as percussion instruments.

BRASSES
Brass instruments are hollow inside. They make sounds when air is blown into a mouthpiece shaped like a cup or a funnel. The trumpet, French horn, trombone, and tuba are brasses.

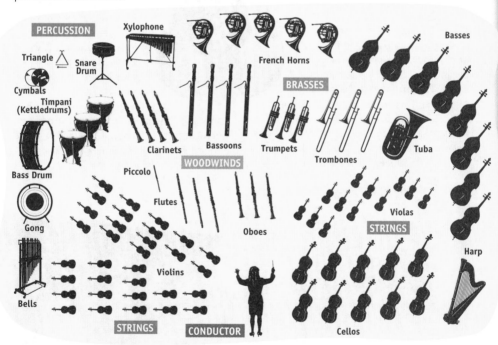

WOODWINDS
Woodwind instruments are long and round and hollow inside. They make sounds when air is blown into them through a mouth hole or a reed. The clarinet, flute, oboe, bassoon, and piccolo are woodwinds.

STRINGS
Stringed instruments make sounds when the strings are either stroked with a bow or plucked with the fingers. The violin, viola, cello, bass, and harp are used in an orchestra. The guitar, banjo, and mandolin are other stringed instruments.

127

MUSIC and MUSIC MAKERS

▶**Pop** Pop music (short for popular music) puts more emphasis on melody (tune) than does rock and has a softer beat. **Famous pop singers:** Frank Sinatra, Barbra Streisand, Whitney Houston, Madonna, Michael Jackson, Mariah Carey, Brandy, Celine Dion, Britney Spears.

▶**Rap and Hip-Hop** In rap, words are spoken or chanted at a fast pace, backed by hip-hop music that emphasizes rhythm rather than melody. Rap was created by African-Americans in inner cities. The lyrics show strong feelings and may be about anger and violence. Hip-hop includes "samples," which are pieces of music from other songs. **Famous rappers:** Coolio, LL Cool J, TLC, The Fugees, Will Smith.

▶**Jazz** Jazz has its roots in the work songs, spirituals, and folk music of African-Americans. It began in the South in the early 1900s. **Famous jazz artists:** Louis Armstrong, Fats Waller, Jelly Roll Morton, Duke Ellington, Benny Goodman, Billie Holiday, Sarah Vaughan, Ella Fitzgerald, Dizzy Gillespie, Charlie Parker, Miles Davis, John Coltrane, Thelonious Monk, Wynton Marsalis.

▶**Rock (also known as Rock 'n' Roll)** Rock music, which started in the 1950s, is based on black rhythm and blues and country music. It often uses electronic instruments and equipment. Folk rock, punk, heavy metal, and alternative music are types of rock music. **Famous rock musicians:** Elvis Presley, Bob Dylan, Chuck Berry, The Beatles, Janis Joplin, The Rolling Stones, Joni Mitchell, Bruce Springsteen, Pearl Jam, Alanis Morissette, Jewel, Kid Rock, Smash Mouth.

▶**Blues** The music called "the blues" developed from work songs and religious folk songs (spirituals) sung by African-Americans. It was introduced early in the 1900s by African-American musicians. Blues songs are usually sad. (A type of jazz is also called "the blues.") **Famous blues performers:** Ma Rainey, Bessie Smith, Billie Holiday, Buddy Guy, B. B. King, Muddy Waters, Robert Johnson, Howling Wolf, Lightnin' Hopkins.

TOP ALBUMS OF 2000

1. *No Strings Attached,* 'N Sync
2. *Supernatural,* Santana
3. *Oops...I Did it Again,* Britney Spears
4. *Human Clay,* Creed
5. *All the Way...A Decade of Song,* Celine Dion
6. *Christina Aguilera,* Christina Aguilera
7. *Millennium,* Backstreet Boys
8. *...And Then There Was X,* DMX
9. *Fly,* Dixie Chicks
10. *The Writing's on the Wall,* Destiny's Child

▼ 'N Sync

ROCK AND ROLL HALL OF FAME

The Rock and Roll Hall of Fame and Museum, located in Cleveland, Ohio, honors rock-and-roll musicians with exhibits and multi-media presentations. Musicians cannot be included until 25 years after their first record. Aerosmith, Michael Jackson, and Queen were among the performers added in 2001.

▶Country

American country music is based on Southern mountain music. Blues, jazz, and other musical styles have also influenced it. Country music became popular through the *Grand Ole Opry* radio show in Nashville, Tennessee, during the 1920s. **Famous country artists:** Hank Williams, Dolly Parton, Willie Nelson, Garth Brooks, Vince Gill, Reba McEntire, Shania Twain.

▶Classical

Often more complex than other types of music, classical music is based on European musical traditions that go back several hundred years. Common forms of classical music include the symphony, chamber music, opera, and ballet music. **Famous early classical composers:** Johann Sebastian Bach, Ludwig van Beethoven, Johannes Brahms, Franz Joseph Haydn, Wolfgang Amadeus Mozart, Franz Schubert, Peter Ilyich Tchaikovsky. **Famous modern classical composers:** Aaron Copland, Virgil Thomson, Igor Stravinsky.

▶Opera

An opera is a play whose words are sung to music. The music is played by an orchestra. The words of an opera are called the libretto, and a long song sung by one character (like a speech in a play) is called an aria. **Famous operas:** *The Barber of Seville* (Gioacchino Rossini); *Madama Butterfly* (Giacomo Puccini); *Aida* (Giuseppe Verdi); *Porgy and Bess* (George Gershwin).

▶Chamber

Chamber music is written for a small group of musicians, often only three (a trio) or four (a quartet), to play together. In chamber music, each instrument plays a separate part. A **string quartet** (music written for two violins, viola, and cello) is an example of chamber music. Other instruments, such as a piano, are sometimes part of a chamber group.

SYMPHONY

A symphony is music written for an orchestra. The sections of a symphony are called movements.

VOICE

Human voices have a range in pitch from low to high. For men, the low end is called the bass (pronounced like base), followed by baritone, and tenor. The range for women goes from contralto (the lowest) up to alto, mezzo-soprano, and soprano. The next time you listen to a singer, try to figure out his or her range.

MUSICAL NOTATION

These are some of the symbols composers use when they write music.

treble clef	𝄞	half note	𝅗𝅥
bass clef	𝄢	quarter note	♩
sharp	♯	eighth note	♪
flat	♭	sixteenth note	𝅘𝅥𝅯
natural	♮	whole rest	𝄻
whole note	𝅝	half rest	𝄼

129

DANCE

Dancers perform patterns of movement, usually to music or rhythm. Dance may be a form of art, or part of a religious ceremony. Or it may be done just for entertainment.

▶Ballet

Ballet is a kind of dance based on formal steps. The movements are often graceful and flowing. Ballets are almost always danced to music, are performed for an audience, and often tell a story. In the 15th century, ballet was part of the elaborate entertainment performed for the rulers of Europe. In the 1600s, professional dance companies existed, but without women; women's parts were danced by men wearing masks. In the 1700s dancers wore bulky costumes and shoes with high heels. Women danced in hoopskirts—and so did men! In the 1800s ballet steps and costumes began to look the way they do now. Many of the most popular ballets today date back to the middle or late 1800s.

▶Ballroom Dancing

Ballroom, or social, dancing involves dances done for fun by ordinary people. Social dancing has been around since at least the Middle Ages, when it was popular at fairs and festivals. In the 1400s social dance was part of fancy court pageants. It developed into dainty ballroom dances like the minuet and

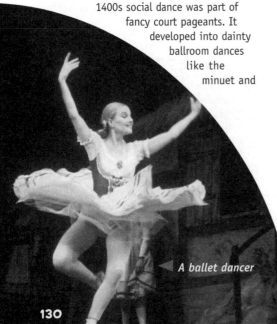

A ballet dancer

Some Famous Ballets

Swan Lake First danced in St. Petersburg, Russia, in 1895. Perhaps the most popular ballet ever, *Swan Lake* is the story of a prince and his love for a maiden who was turned into a swan by an evil magician.

The Nutcracker When this ballet was first performed in St. Petersburg in 1892, it was a flop. It has since become so popular that it is danced in many places every year at holiday time in December.

Jewels This ballet by the American choreographer George Balanchine was first performed in New York City in 1967. In *Jewels*, the dancers do not dance to a story. They explore patterns and movement of the human body.

The River This 1970 ballet by Alvin Ailey is danced to music by the jazz musician Duke Ellington. It has been described as a celebration of life.

the waltz during the 1700s. More recent new dances include the Charleston, lindy, twist, and tango, as well as disco dancing, break dancing, line dancing, and dances such as the macarena and electric slide.

▶Modern Dance

Modern dance differs from classical ballet. It is often less concerned with graceful, flowing movement and with stories. Modern dance steps are often not performed in traditional ballet. Dancers may put their bodies into awkward, angular positions and turn their backs on the audience. Many modern dances are based on ancient art, such as Greek sculpture, or on dance styles found in Africa and Asia.

▶Folk Dance

Folk dance is the term for a dance that is passed on from generation to generation and is part of the culture or way of life of people from a particular country or ethnic group. Virginia reel (American), czardas (Hungarian), jig, and the Israeli hora are some folk dances.

AMERICAN MUSICALS

American musical theater uses singing, dancing, and music to tell interesting stories in exciting ways. People come from all over the world to see musicals on Broadway, New York City's theater district. Musicals are also staged in many other places. Some musicals start as movies, or are made into movies. A few famous musicals are listed here. The date after the name of the show is the year it opened on Broadway.

Annie (1977), by Charles Strouse and Martin Charnin. Here's how Little Orphan Annie was adopted by Daddy Warbucks. One featured song: "Tomorrow." Tony Award 1977.

Beauty and the Beast (1994), by Alan Menken, Howard Ashman, and Tim Rice. First it was a story. Then it was a movie in French. Then it became an animated movie musical. Now the tale of Belle and the Beast she came to love is brought to life on a stage.

Cats (1982), by Andrew Lloyd Webber. Based on poems about all kinds of cats written by T.S. Eliot, this play closed in 2000 after a record 7,485 performances. Its best-known song was "Memory." Tony Award 1983.

A Chorus Line (1975), by Marvin Hamlisch and Edward Kleban. The story of dancers whose dream was to be on the musical stage. Tony Award 1976.

Grease (1972), by Jim Jacobs and Warren Casey. Teenagers in the 1950s sing and dance their way through high school. *Grease* was made into a movie starring John Travolta.

The Lion King (1997), by Elton John, Tim Rice, Mark Mancina, Roger Allers, and Irene Meechi. Based on the animated Disney movie, this show uses masks and puppets to tell the story of animals progressing through "The Circle of Life." Tony Award 1998.

Seussical (2000), by Lynn Ahrens and Stephen Flaherty. The magic of The Cat in the Hat, Horton, and other Dr. Seuss favorites comes to the stage.

West Side Story (1957), by Leonard Bernstein and Stephen Sondheim. This groundbreaking show used music and dance to update the story of Romeo and Juliet to the West Side of Manhattan in New York City.

IT'S MAGIC!

In movies, thrilling special effects are used all the time. We expect them. But audiences are still amazed by the magical effects in live stage shows. Like the movie, the stage version of the musical *Singin' in the Rain* had a famous scene of a character dancing in a rainstorm. It poured on stage during every performance! And, of course, there was water, water everywhere when the musical *Titanic* was on stage. That show featured an enormous ship sinking every night.

The Lion King can't use a cast of live animals on stage. So it has large puppets instead. After a while, viewers forget the animals aren't real! In the movie *Beauty and the Beast*, the Beast magically turns into a handsome prince. Audiences at the stage version are enchanted by that changeover too. How is it done? Wouldn't it spoil the fun to know? Let's just say it's a theatrical secret.

NATIONS

Where would you find a lot of people speaking Afrikaans? *You can find the answer on page 149.*

NATIONS OF THE WORLD

There are 193 nations in the world. The information for each of them goes across two pages. The left page gives the **name** and **capital** of each nation, its **location**, and its **area**. On the right page, the **population** column tells how many people lived in each country in 2000. The **currency** column shows the name of each nation's money and how much one United States dollar was worth there at the start of 2001. This column also shows which countries in Europe now use the euro, a shared currency, for some purposes. One euro was worth about 95 U.S. cents in early 2001. The **language** column gives official languages and other common languages. The last column has one **Did You Know?** for each nation.

NATION	CAPITAL	LOCATION OF NATION	AREA
Afghanistan	Kabul	Southern Asia, between Iran and Pakistan	250,000 sq. mi. (647,500 sq. km.)
Albania	Tiranë	Eastern Europe, between Greece and Yugoslavia	11,100 sq. mi. (28,750 sq. km.)
Algeria	Algiers	North Africa on the Mediterranean Sea, between Libya and Morocco	919,600 sq. mi. (2,381,740 sq. km.)
Andorra	Andorra la Vella	Europe, in the mountains between France and Spain	170 sq. mi. (450 sq. km.)
Angola	Luanda	Southern Africa on the Atlantic Ocean, north of Namibia	481,400 sq. mi. (1,246,700 sq. km.)
Antigua and Barbuda	St. John's	Islands on eastern edge of the Caribbean Sea	170 sq. mi. (440 sq. km.)
Argentina	Buenos Aires	Fills up most of the southern part of South America	1,068,300 sq. mi. (2,766,890 sq. km.)
Armenia	Yerevan	Western Asia, north of Turkey and Iran	11,500 sq. mi. (29,800 sq. km.)
Australia	Canberra	Continent south of Asia, between Indian and Pacific Oceans	2,967,910 sq. mi. (7,686,850 sq. km.)
Austria	Vienna	Central Europe, north of Italy	32,380 sq. mi. (83,860 sq. km.)
Azerbaijan	Baku	Western Asia, north of Iran	33,440 sq. mi. (86,600 sq. km.)
The Bahamas	Nassau	Islands in the Atlantic Ocean, east of Florida	5,380 sq. mi. (13,940 sq. km.)
Bahrain	Manama	In the Persian Gulf, near the coast of Qatar	240 sq. mi. (620 sq. km.)

ARCTIC OCEAN

ASIA

EUROPE

NORTH AMERICA

ATLANTIC OCEAN

PACIFIC OCEAN

AFRICA

PACIFIC OCEAN

PACIFIC OCEAN

SOUTH AMERICA

INDIAN OCEAN

AUSTRALIA

N
W — E
S

ANTARCTICA

POPULATION	CURRENCY	LANGUAGE	DID YOU KNOW?
25,888,797	$1 = 4,750 afghanis	Afghan Persian (Dari), Pashtu	Taliban Islamic fundamentalists control 90% of the country.
3,490,435	$1 = 140 leks	Albanian, Greek	One of Europe's poorest countries.
31,193,917	$1 = 72 dinars	Arabic, French, Berber Dialects	Gained independence from France in 1962 after a bloody civil war.
66,824	French franc or Spanish peseta	Catalan, French, Castilian	This tiny nation is much smaller than the state of Rhode Island.
10,145,267	$1 = 17 kwanzas	Portuguese, African dialects	Civil war has plagued diamond-rich Angola since independence in 1975.
66,464	$1 = 2²/₃ East Carribean dollars	English	Carib Indians lived on Antigua when Columbus came in 1493.
36,955,182	$1 = 1 peso	Spanish, English, Italian	Buenos Aires was the world's 10th-largest city in 2000.
3,344,336	$1 = 552 drams	Armenian	Armenia was the first nation to officially adopt Christianity (c. 300).
19,614,620	$1 = 1³/₄ Australian dollars	English, aboriginal languages	Australia's native people are known as "aborigines."
8,131,111	$1 = 14¹/₂ schillings	German	The composer Mozart was born Salzburg, Austria, in 1756.
7,748,163	$1 = 4,456 manats	Azeri, Russian, Armenian	Baku is a major center of oil refining.
294,982	Bahamas dollar Same value as U.S. dollar	English, Creole	Many international banking and finance companies are based here.
634,137	$1 = ³/₈ dinars	Arabic, English, Farsi, Urdu	Only 1% of this island nation's land supports agriculture.

NATION	CAPITAL	LOCATION OF NATION	AREA
Bangladesh	Dhaka	Southern Asia, nearly surrounded by India	56,000 sq. mi. (144,000 sq. km.)
Barbados	Bridgetown	Island in the Atlantic Ocean, north of Trinidad	170 sq. mi. (430 sq. km.)
Belarus	Minsk	Eastern Europe, east of Poland	80,200 sq. mi. (207,600 sq. km.)
Belgium	Brussels	Western Europe, on the North Sea, south of the Netherlands	11,780 sq. mi. (30,510 sq. km.)
Belize	Belmopan	Central America, south of Mexico	8,860 sq. mi. (22,960 sq. km.)
Benin	Porto-Novo	West Africa, on the Gulf of Guinea, west of Nigeria	43,480 sq. mi. (112,620 sq. km.)
Bhutan	Thimphu	Asia, in the Himalaya Mountains, between China and India	18,000 sq. mi. (46,620 sq. km.)
Bolivia	La Paz	South America, in the Andes Mountains, next to Brazil	424,160 sq. mi. (1,098,580 sq. km.)
Bosnia and Herzegovina	Sarajevo	Southern Europe, on the Balkan Peninsula, west of Yugoslavia	19,780 sq. mi. (51,230 sq. km.)
Botswana	Gaborone	Southern Africa, between South Africa and Zambia	231,800 sq. mi. (600,370 sq. km.)
Brazil	Brasília	Occupies most of the eastern part of South America	3,286,490 sq. mi. (8,511,970 sq. km.)
Brunei	Bandar Seri Begawan	On the island of Borneo, northwest of Australia in the Pacific Ocean	2,230 sq. mi. (5,770 sq. km.)
Bulgaria	Sofia	Eastern Europe, on the Balkan Peninsula, bordering the Black Sea	42,820 sq. mi. (110,910 sq. km.)
Burkina Faso	Ouagadougou	West Africa, between Mali and Ghana	105,900 sq. mi. (274,200 sq. km.)
Burundi	Bujumbura	Central Africa, northwest of Tanzania	10,750 sq. mi. (27,830 sq. km.)
Cambodia	Phnom Penh	Southeast Asia, between Vietnam and Thailand	69,900 sq. mi. (181,040 sq. km.)
Cameroon	Yaoundé	Central Africa, between Nigeria and Central African Republic	183,570 sq. mi. (475,440 sq. km.)
Canada	Ottawa	Occupies the northern part of North America, north of the United States	3,851,810 sq. mi. (9,976,140 sq. km.)
Cape Verde	Praia	Islands off the western tip of Africa	1,560 sq. mi. (4,030 sq. km.)
Central African Republic	Bangui	Central Africa, south of Chad	240,530 sq. mi. (622,980 sq. km.)

POPULATION	CURRENCY	LANGUAGE	DID YOU KNOW?
129,194,224	$1 = 54 takas	Bangla, English	This low-lying country is plagued by flooding caused by monsoons.
274,059	$1 = 2 Barbados dollars	English	English-based Barbadian traditions include cricket and left-side driving.
10,366,719	$1 = 1,180 rubles	Byelorussian, Russian	"Bela" Russian means "white" Russian, a distinct ethnic group.
10,241,506	$1 = 42½ francs	Flemish (Dutch), French, German	There are two main ethnic groups, Flemings and Walloons.
249,183	$1 = 2 Belize dollars	English, Spanish, Mayan, Garifuna	Belize is the only English-speaking nation in Central America.
6,395,919	$1 = 691 CFA francs	French, Fon, Yoruba	The Kingdom of Dahomey was a predecessor to modern-day Benin.
2,005,222	$1 = 46¾ ngultrums	Dzongkha, Tibetan	Buddhism is the official religion of this mountain kingdom.
8,152,620	$1 = 6 Bolivianos	Spanish, Quechua, Aymara	Married Bolivians can vote at age 18; single people at age 21.
3,835,777	$1 = 2 mark	Serbo-Croatian	Archduke Ferdinand's 1914 murder in Sarajevo sparked World War I.
1,576,470	$1 = 5⅓ pula	English, Setswana	The Tswana are the major ethnic group in this landlocked nation.
172,860,370	$1 = 2 real	Portuguese, Spanish, English	Brazil's economy is the biggest in South America.
336,376	$1 = 1¾ Brunei dollars	Malay, English, Chinese	This leading oil producer is in the Pacific, not the Middle East.
7,796,694	$1 = 2 leva	Bulgarian	Despite its Nazi ties in World War II, Bulgaria did not persecute Jews.
11,946,065	$1 = 691 CFA francs	French, tribal languages	Burkina Faso means "land of incorruptible men."
6,054,714	$1 = 774 francs	Kirundi, French, Swahili	Tutsi-Hutu ethnic violence killed 200,000 Burundis in the 1990s.
12,212,306	$1 = 3,835 riels	Khmer, French	The beautiful Angkor Wat temple ruins date from the 12th century.
15,421,937	$1 = 691 CFA francs	English, French	U.S. and other slave traders were very active in the Cameroon area.
31,278,097	$1 = 1½ Canadian dollars	English, French	In 1999, Canada established the Nunavut territory for native Inuits.
401,343	$1 = 117 escudos	Portuguese, Crioulo	These islands were uninhabited when discovered around 1460.
3,512,751	$1 = 691 CFA francs	French, Sangho, Arabic, Hunsa, Swahili	In the early 1960s, C.A.R. was a center of Chinese influence in Africa.

NATION	CAPITAL	LOCATION OF NATION	AREA
Chad	N'Djamena	North Africa, south of Libya	496,000 sq. mi. (1,284,000 sq. km.)
Chile	Santiago	Along the western coast of South America	292,260 sq. mi. (756,950 sq. km.)
China	Beijing	Occupies most of the mainland of eastern Asia	3,705,410 sq. mi. (9,596,960 sq. km.)
Colombia	Bogotá	Northwestern South America, southeast of Panama	439,740 sq. mi. (1,138,910 sq. km.)
Comoros	Moroni	Islands between Madagascar and the east coast of Africa	840 sq. mi. (2,170 sq. km.)
Congo, Democratic Republic of the	Kinshasa	Central Africa, north of Angola and Zambia	905,570 sq. mi. (2,345,410 sq. km.)
Congo, Republic of the	Brazzaville	Central Africa, east of Gabon	132,000 sq. mi. (342,000 sq. km.)
Costa Rica	San José	Central America, south of Nicaragua	19,700 sq. mi (51,100 sq. km.)
Côte d'Ivoire (Ivory Coast)	Yamoussoukro	West Africa, on the Gulf of Guinea, west of Ghana	124,500 sq. mi. (322,460 sq. km.)
Croatia	Zagreb	Southern Europe, south of Hungary	21,830 sq. mi. (56,540 sq. km.)
Cuba	Havana	In the Caribbean Sea, south of Florida	42,800 sq. mi. (110,860 sq. km.)
Cyprus	Nicosia	Island in the Mediterranean Sea, off the coast of Turkey	3,570 sq. mi. (9,250 sq. km.)
Czech Republic	Prague	Central Europe, south of Poland, east of Germany	30,390 sq. mi. (78,700 sq. km.)
Denmark	Copenhagen	Northern Europe, between the Baltic Sea and North Sea	16,640 sq. mi. (43,090 sq. km.)
Djibouti	Djibouti	North Africa, on the Gulf of Aden, across from Saudi Arabia	8,500 sq. mi. (22,000 sq. km.)
Dominica	Roseau	Island in the Caribbean Sea	290 sq. mi. (750 sq. km.)
Dominican Republic	Santo Domingo	On an island, along with Haiti, in the Caribbean Sea	18,810 sq. mi. (48,730 sq. km.)
East Timor	Dili	Part of an island in the South Pacific Ocean, north of Australia	5,740 sq. mi. (14,880 sq. km.)
Ecuador	Quito	South America, on the equator, bordering the Pacific Ocean	109,480 sq. mi. (283,560 sq. km.)
Egypt	Cairo	Northeastern Africa, on the Red Sea and Mediterranean Sea	386,660 sq. mi. (1,001,450 sq. km.)

POPULATION	CURRENCY	LANGUAGE	DID YOU KNOW?
8,424,504	$1 = 691 CFA francs	French, Arabic, Sara, Sango	Now partially desert, Chad was a fertile country in ancient times.
15,153,797	$1 = 518 pesos	Spanish	Chilean poets Gabriela Mistral and Pablo Neruda won Nobel Prizes.
1,261,832,482	$1 = 8¼ renminbis	Mandarin, Yue, Wu, Hakka	One of every five people in the world lives in China.
39,685,655	$1 = 2,246 pesos	Spanish	Simón Bolívar helped Colombia win freedom from Spain.
578,400	$1 = 518 francs	Arabic, French, Comorian	Comoros is made up of islands of volcanic origin.
51,964,999	$1 = 4½ Congolese francs	French	The former "Belgian" Congo lies east of Republic of the Congo.
2,830,961	$1 = 691 CFA francs	French, Lingala, Kikongo	This Congo was a colony of France before independence in 1960.
3,710,558	$1 = 318 colones	Spanish	Costa Rican President Arias won the 1987 Nobel Peace Prize.
15,980,950	$1 = 691 CFA francs	French, Dioula	Félix Houphouët-Boigny led this nation from 1960 to 1993.
4,282,216	$1 = 8 kunas	Serbo-Croatian	Croatia was part of Yugoslavia until declaring independence in 1991.
11,141,997	$1 = 1 peso	Spanish	Communist Fidel Castro has been Cuba's leader since 1959.
758,363	$1 = ⅗ pound	Greek, Turkish, English	Cyprus is divided into Greek and Turkish areas.
10,272,179	$1 = 37 koruny	Czech, Slovak	Prague largely escaped the massive destruction of World War II.
5,336,394	$1 = 7⅘ kroner	Danish, Faroese	The island of Greenland is a self-governing part of Denmark.
451,442	$1 = 175 Djibouti francs	French, Arabic, Afar, Somali	Rebels signed a peace agreement with the government in 2000.
71,540	$1 = 2⅔ EC dollars	English, French patois	Banana plantations are Dominica's economic mainstay.
8,442,533	$1 = 16⅛ pesos	Spanish	U.S. marines occupied this nation (1916–24) and intervened in 1965.
871,000	U.S. dollar	English, Portuguese, Bahasa Indonesia, Tetum	East Timorese voted for independence from Indonesia in 1999.
12,920,092	$1 = 25,000 sucres	Spanish, Quechua	The equator runs through Ecuador.
68,359,979	$1 = 3⅘ pounds	Arabic, English, French	Archaeological records of ancient Egypt date back 6,000 years.

NATION	CAPITAL	LOCATION OF NATION	AREA
El Salvador	San Salvador	Central America, southwest of Honduras	8,120 sq. mi. (21,040 sq. km.)
Equatorial Guinea	Malabo	West Africa, on the Gulf of Guinea, off the west coast of Cameroon	10,830 sq. mi. (28,050 sq. km.)
Eritrea	Asmara	Northeast Africa, north of Ethiopia	46,840 sq. mi. (121,320 sq. km.)
Estonia	Tallinn	Northern Europe, on the Baltic Sea, north of Latvia	17,460 sq. mi. (45,230 sq. km.)
Ethiopia	Addis Ababa	East Africa, east of Sudan	435,190 sq. mi. (1,127,130 sq. km.)
Fiji	Suva	Islands in the South Pacific Ocean, east of Australia	7,050 sq. mi. (18,270 sq. km.)
Finland	Helsinki	Northern Europe, between Sweden and Russia	130,130 sq. mi. (337,030 sq. km.)
France	Paris	Western Europe, between Germany and Spain	211,210 sq. mi. (547,030 sq. km.)
Gabon	Libreville	Central Africa, on the Atlantic coast, south of Cameroon	103,350 sq. mi. (267,670 sq. km.)
The Gambia	Banjul	West Africa, on the Atlantic Ocean, surrounded by Senegal	4,400 sq. mi. (11,300 sq. km.)
Georgia	Tbilisi	Western Asia, south of Russia, on the Black Sea	26,900 sq. mi. (69,700 sq. km.)
Germany	Berlin	Central Europe, northeast of France	137,800 sq. mi. (356,910 sq. km.)
Ghana	Accra	West Africa, on the southern coast	92,100 sq. mi. (238,540 sq. km.)
Great Britain (United Kingdom)	London	Off the northwest coast of Europe	94,530 sq. mi. (244,820 sq. km.)
Greece	Athens	Southern Europe, in the southern part of the Balkan Peninsula	50,940 sq. mi. (131,940 sq. km.)
Grenada	Saint George's	Island on the eastern edge of the Caribbean Sea	130 sq. mi. (340 sq. km.)
Guatemala	Guatemala City	Central America, southeast of Mexico	42,040 sq. mi. (108,890 sq. km.)
Guinea	Conakry	West Africa, on the Atlantic Ocean, north of Sierra Leone	94,930 sq. mi. (245,860 sq. km.)
Guinea-Bissau	Bissau	West Africa, on the Atlantic Ocean, south of Senegal	13,950 sq. mi. (36,120 sq. km.)
Guyana	Georgetown	South America, on the northern coast, east of Venezuela	83,000 sq. mi. (214,970 sq. km.)

POPULATION	CURRENCY	LANGUAGE	DID YOU KNOW?
6,122,515	$1 = 8¾ colones	Spanish	A 1992 treaty ended a civil war that cost an estimated 75,000 lives.
474,214	$1 = 691 CFA francs	Spanish, French, Fang, Bubi	Equatorial Guinea won independence from Spain in 1968.
4,135,933	$1 = 8 nakfa	Tigrinya, Tigre, Kunama, Afar	Eritrea won independence in 1993 from neighboring Ethiopia.
1,431,471	$1 = 16²/5 kroons	Estonian, Russian	Estonia and its Baltic neighbors split from the Soviet Union in 1991.
64,117,452	$1 = 8¼ birr	Amharic, Tigrinya, Orominga	Ethiopian Abebe Bikila won the 1960 Olympic marathon, running barefoot.
832,494	$1 = 2⅛ Fiji dollars	English, Fijian, Hindustani	Water from Fiji is now exported to the U.S.
5,167,486	$1 = 6¼ markka	Finnish, Swedish	Sauna baths are a popular activity in Finland.
59,329,691	$1 = 7 francs	French	France is the largest farming nation in Western Europe.
1,208,436	$1 = 691 CFA francs	French, Bantu dialects	Gabon is among the most prosperous Sub-Saharan nations.
1,367,124	$1 = 15²/5 dalasi	English, Mandinka, Wolof	This narrow nation lies along both banks of the lower Gambia River.
5,019,538	$1 = 2 laris	Georgian, Russian	President Shevardnadze was the Soviet Union's last foreign minister.
82,797,408	$1 = 2 marks	German	The environmentalist Green Party helps govern Germany.
19,533,560	$1 = 7,175 cedis	English, Akan, Moshi-Dagomba, Ewe, Ga	Led by Kwame Nkrumah, Ghana won independence in 1957.
59,508,382	$1 = ⅔ pound	English	Until about 6,000 B.C., Britain was part of the European continent.
10,601,527	$1 = 359 drachmas	Greek, English, French	The Olympics started in Greece; Athens will host the 2004 games.
89,312	$1 = 2¾ EC dollars	English, French patois	Grenada is the world's 2nd-largest producer of nutmeg.
12,639,939	$1 = 7⁴/5 quetzals	Spanish, Mayan languages	There are 23 Amerindian dialects spoken in Guatemala.
7,466,200	$1 = 1,855 francs	French, tribal languages	Agriculture employs 80% of Guinea's workforce.
1,285,715	$1 = 691 CFA francs	Portuguese, Crioulo	Guinea-Bissau is one of the poorest nations in the world.
697,286	$1 = 181 Guyana dollars	English, Amerindian dialects	Guyana is one of the world's most sparsely populated countries.

NATION	CAPITAL	LOCATION OF NATION	AREA
Haiti	Port-au-Prince	On an island, along with Dominican Republic, in the Caribbean Sea	10,710 sq. mi. (27,750 sq. km.)
Honduras	Tegucigalpa	Central America, between Guatemala and Nicaragua	43,280 sq. mi. (112,090 sq. km.)
Hungary	Budapest	Central Europe, north of Yugoslavia	35,920 sq. mi. (93,030 sq. km.)
Iceland	Reykjavik	Island off the coast of Europe, in the North Atlantic Ocean	40,000 sq. mi. (103,000 sq. km.)
India	New Delhi	Southern Asia, on a large peninsula on the Indian Ocean	1,269,350 sq. mi. (3,287,590 sq. km.)
Indonesia	Jakarta	Islands south of Southeast Asia, along the equator	735,350 sq. mi. (1,904,560 sq. km.)
Iran	Tehran	Southern Asia, between Iraq and Pakistan	636,000 sq. mi. (1,648,000 sq. km.)
Iraq	Baghdad	In the Middle East, between Syria and Iran	168,750 sq. mi. (437,070 sq. km.)
Ireland	Dublin	Off Europe's coast, in the Atlantic Ocean, west of Great Britain	27,140 sq. mi. (70,280 sq. km.)
Israel	Jerusalem	In the Middle East, between Jordan and the Mediterranean Sea	8,020 sq. mi. (20,770 sq. km.)
Italy	Rome	Southern Europe, jutting out into the Mediterranean Sea	116,310 sq. mi. (301,230 sq. km.)
Jamaica	Kingston	Island in the Caribbean Sea, south of Cuba	4,240 sq. mi. (10,990 sq. km.)
Japan	Tokyo	Four big islands and many small ones, off the east coast of Asia	145,880 sq. mi. (377,840 sq. km.)
Jordan	Amman	In the Middle East, south of Syria, east of Israel	34,450 sq. mi. (89,210 sq. km.)
Kazakhstan	Astana	Central Asia, south of Russia	1,049,200 sq. mi. (2,717,300 sq. km.)
Kenya	Nairobi	East Africa, on the Indian Ocean, south of Ethiopia	224,960 sq. mi. (582,650 sq. km.)
Kiribati	Tarawa	Islands in the middle of the Pacific Ocean, near the equator	280 sq. mi. (720 sq. km.)
Korea, North	Pyongyang	Eastern Asia, in the northern part of the Korean Peninsula	46,540 sq. mi. (120,540 sq. km.)
Korea, South	Seoul	Eastern Asia, south of North Korea, on the Korean Peninsula	38,020 sq. mi. (98,480 sq. km.)
Kuwait	Kuwait City	In the Middle East, on the northern end of the Persian Gulf	6,880 sq. mi. (17,820 sq. km.)

POPULATION	CURRENCY	LANGUAGE	DID YOU KNOW?
6,249,598	$1 = 21 gourdes	Haitian Creole, French	Haiti takes up the western end of the island of Hispaniola.
6,249,598	$1 = 15 lempiras	Spanish	The U.S. is Honduras's biggest trading partner.
10,138,844	$1 = 279 forints	Hungarian (Magyar)	Hungary is a little smaller than Indiana.
276,365	$1 = 84 kronor	Icelandic (Islenska)	The Icelandic language has not changed much since Viking times.
1,014,003,817	$1 = 46¾ rupees	Hindi, English	India has the 2nd-largest population in the world, after China.
224,784,210	$1 = 9,485 rupiah	Bahasa Indonesian, English, Dutch	Indonesia has 17,000 islands, but only 6,000 are inhabited.
65,619,636	$1 = 1,753 rials	Persian (Farsi), Turkic, Luri	Iran was once called Persia.
22,675,617	$1 = ⅓ dinar	Arabic, Kurdish	Iraq occupies most of historic Mesopotamia.
3,797,257	$1 = ⅘ punt	English, Gaelic	Ireland was one of the original 11 countries to adopt the euro.
5,842,454	$1 = 4⅛ new shekels	Hebrew, Arabic, English	Israel has some of the oldest-known evidence of town life.
57,634,327	$1 = 2,040 lire	Italian, German, French, Slovene	Italy has the distinction of being shaped like a boot.
2,652,689	$1 = 45⅛ Jamaican dollars	English, Jamaican, Creole	Tourism brought $1.23 billion to Jamaica in 1999.
126,549,976	$1 = 117 yen	Japanese	Japan is among the world's largest producers of steel.
4,998,564	$1 = ¾ dinar	Arabic, English	Only 1% of Jordan is forest and woodland.
16,733,227	$1 = 145 tenges	Kazakh, Russian	Kazakhstan is the 9th-largest country in land area.
30,339,770	$1 = 79 shillings	Swahili, English	Over 2 million people in Kenya are infected with HIV.
91,985	$1 = 1¾ Australian dollars	English, Gilbertese	This tiny island nation won independence in 1979.
21,687,550	$1 = 2⅕ won	Korean	North Korea is one of the few remaining Communist countries.
47,470,969	$1 = 1,263 won	Korean	President Kim Dae Jung won the 2000 Nobel Peace Prize.
1,973,572	$1 = ⅓ dinar	Arabic, English	Kuwait has the least water resources per person in the world.

NATION	CAPITAL	LOCATION OF NATION	AREA
Kyrgyzstan	Bishkek	Western Asia, between Kazakhstan and Tajikistan	76,600 sq. mi. (198,500 sq. km.)
Laos	Vientiane	Southeast Asia, between Vietnam and Thailand	91,400 sq. mi. (236,800 sq. km.)
Latvia	Riga	On the Baltic Sea, between Lithuania and Estonia	24,800 sq. mi. (64,100 sq. km.)
Lebanon	Beirut	In the Middle East, between the Mediterranean Sea and Syria	4,000 sq. mi. (10,400 sq. km.)
Lesotho	Maseru	Southern Africa, surrounded by the nation of South Africa	11,720 sq. mi. (30,350 sq. km.)
Liberia	Monrovia	Western Africa, on the Atlantic Ocean, southeast of Sierra Leone	43,000 sq. mi. (111,370 sq. km.)
Libya	Tripoli	North Africa, on the Mediterranean Sea, to the west of Egypt	679,360 sq. mi. (1,759,540 sq. km.)
Liechtenstein	Vaduz	Southern Europe, in the Alps between Austria and Switzerland	60 sq. mi. (160 sq. km.)
Lithuania	Vilnius	Northern Europe, on the Baltic Sea, east of Poland	25,200 sq. mi. (65,200 sq. km.)
Luxembourg	Luxembourg	Western Europe, between France and Germany	1,000 sq. mi. (2,590 sq. km.)
Macedonia	Skopje	Southern Europe, north of Greece	9,780 sq. mi. (25,330 sq. km.)
Madagascar	Antananarivo	Island in the Indian Ocean, off the east coast of Africa	226,660 sq. mi. (587,040 sq. km.)
Malawi	Lilongwe	Southern Africa, south of Tanzania and east of Zambia	45,750 sq. mi. (118,480 sq. km.)
Malaysia	Kuala Lumpur	Southeast tip of Asia and the north coast of the island of Borneo	127,320 sq. mi. (329,750 sq. km.)
Maldives	Male	Islands in the Indian Ocean, south of India	100 sq. mi. (260 sq. km.)
Mali	Bamako	West Africa, between Algeria and Mauritania	480,000 sq. mi. (1,240,000 sq. km.)
Malta	Valletta	Island in the Mediterranean Sea, south of Italy	120 sq. mi. (320 sq. km.)
Marshall Islands	Majuro	Chain of small islands in the middle of the Pacific Ocean	70 sq. mi. (180 sq. km.)
Mauritania	Nouakchott	West Africa, on the Atlantic Ocean, north of Senegal	398,000 sq. mi. (1,030,700 sq. km.)
Mauritius	Port Louis	Islands in the Indian Ocean, east of Madagascar	720 sq. mi. (1,860 sq. km.)

POPULATION	CURRENCY	LANGUAGE	DID YOU KNOW?
4,685,230	$1 = 48¼ soms	Kyrgyz, Russian	This Central Asian country is almost entirely mountainous.
5,497,459	$1 = 7,600 kip	Lao, French, English	The Laotians ruled a great empire in the 16th century.
2,404,926	$1 = ³/₅ lat	Lettish, Lithuanian	In 1999, Latvia elected its first female president.
3,578,036	$1 = 1,511 pounds	Arabic, French, English, Armenian	The Ottoman Turks ruled Lebanon for 400 years until World War I.
2,143,141	$1 = 7½ maloti	English, Sesotho	Lesotho is surrounded on all sides by South Africa.
3,164,156	Same as U.S. dollar	English, tribal languages	Freed American slaves founded this African country.
5,115,450	$1 = ½ dinar	Arabic, Italian, English	Most of Libya is sparsely inhabited desert.
32,204	$1 = 1³/₅ Swiss francs	German, Alemanic dialect	Liechtenstein is one of the world's smallest countries.
3,620,756	$1 = 4 litas	Lithuanian, Polish, Russian	Russians are Lithuania's largest ethnic minority.
437,389	$1 = 42½ francs	French, German	Luxembourg has the world's highest income per person.
2,041,467	$1 = 65²/₅ denar	Macedonian, Albanian	Macedonia officially withdrew from Yugoslavia in 1991.
15,506,472	$1 = 6,240 francs	Malagasy, French	This African country is the 4th-largest island in the world.
10,385,849	$1 = 80⅛ kwacha	English, Chichewa	Malawi is one of Africa's most densely populated countries.
21,793,293	$1 = 3⁴/₅ ringgits	Malay, English, Chinese dialects	A 40-year Communist rebellion was formally ended in 1989.
301,475	$1 = 11³/₄ rufiyaas	Maldivian Dhivehi, English	Nearly 2,000 islands make up this developing nation.
10,685,948	$1 = 691 CFA francs	French, Bambara	Mali is landlocked, meaning it has no outlet to the sea.
391,670	$1 = ²/₅ Maltese lira	Maltese, English	The Maltese earn more than $675 million a year from tourism.
68,126	U.S. dollar	English, Marshallese	Bikini Atoll, where the first hydrogen bomb was tested, is here.
2,667,859	$1 = 254 ouguiya	Hasaniya Arabic, Wolof, Pular	40% of Mauritania's land area is covered by sand.
1,179,368	$1 = 27⁷/₈ Mauritian rupees	English, French, Creole, Hindi	The volcanic island of Mauritius is about the size of Rhode Island.

NATION	CAPITAL	LOCATION OF NATION	AREA
Mexico	Mexico City	North America, south of the United States	761,610 sq. mi. (1,972,550 sq. km.)
Micronesia	Palikir	Islands in the western Pacific Ocean	270 sq. mi. (700 sq. km.)
Moldova	Chisinau	Eastern Europe, between Ukraine and Romania	13,000 sq. mi. (33,700 sq. km.)
Monaco	Monaco	Europe, on the Mediterranean Sea, surrounded by France	¾ of a sq. mi. (2 sq. km.)
Mongolia	Ulaanbaatar	Central Asia between Russia and China	604,000 sq. mi. (1,565,000 sq. km.)
Morocco	Rabat	Northwest Africa, on the Atlantic Ocean and Mediterranean Sea	172,410 sq. mi. (446,550 sq. km.)
Mozambique	Maputo	Southeastern Africa, on the Indian Ocean	309,500 sq. mi. (801,590 sq. km.)
Myanmar (Burma)	Yangon (Rangoon)	Southern Asia, to the east of India and Bangladesh	262,000 sq. mi. (678,500 sq. km.)
Namibia	Windhoek	Southwestern Africa, on the Atlantic Ocean, west of Botswana	318,700 sq. mi. (825,420 sq. km.)
Nauru	Yaren district	Island in the western Pacific Ocean, just below the equator	8 sq. mi. (21 sq. km.)
Nepal	Kathmandu	Asia, in the Himalaya Mountains, between China and India	54,400 sq. mi. (140,800 sq. km.)
Netherlands	Amsterdam	Northern Europe, on the North Sea, to the west of Germany	16,030 sq. mi. (41,530 sq. km.)
New Zealand	Wellington	Islands in the Pacific Ocean east of Australia	103,740 sq. mi. (268,680 sq. km.)
Nicaragua	Managua	Central America, between Honduras and Costa Rica	50,000 sq. mi. (129,490 sq. km.)
Niger	Niamey	North Africa, south of Algeria and Libya	489,000 sq. mi. (1,267,000 sq. km.)
Nigeria	Abuja	West Africa, on the southern coast between Benin and Cameroon	356,670 sq. mi. (923,770 sq. km.)
Norway	Oslo	Northern Europe, on the Scandinavian Peninsula	125,180 sq. mi. (324,220 sq. km.)
Oman	Muscat	On the Arabian Peninsula, southeast of Saudi Arabia	82,030 sq. mi. (212,460 sq. km.)
Pakistan	Islamabad	South Asia, between Iran and India	310,400 sq. mi. (803,940 sq. km.)
Palau	Koror	Islands in North Pacific Ocean, southeast of Philippines	180 sq. mi. (460 sq. km.)

POPULATION	CURRENCY	LANGUAGE	DID YOU KNOW?
100,349,766	$1 = 9³/₄ new pesos	Spanish, Mayan dialects	Mexico City is the 2nd-largest city in the world, after Tokyo, Japan.
133,144	U.S. dollar	English, Trukese, Pohnpeian, Yapese	Micronesia is made up of more than 600 islands and islets.
4,430,654	$1 = 12¹/₃ lei	Moldovan, Russian	Grapes are a major crop, and winemaking is a big industry.
31,693	$1 = 7 francs	French, English, Italian	The Monte Carlo Casino is one of the world's most famous.
2,616,383	$1 = 1,096 tugriks	Khalkha Mongolian	The Gobi Desert covers much of southern Mongolia.
30,122,350	$1 = 10¹/₂ dirhams	Arabic, Berber dialects	Casablanca is Morocco's largest city and main seaport.
19,104,696	$1 = 17,350 meticals	Portuguese, native dialects	The zebra, rhino, giraffe, lion, and elephant are native animals.
45,059,000	$1 = 6¹/₂ kyats	Burmese	More than 100 native languages are spoken in Myanmar.
1,771,327	$1 = 7¹/₂ rand	Afrikaans, English, German	Diamonds are Namibia's chief export.
11,845	$1 = 1³/₄ Australian dollars	Nauruan, English	Phosphate reserves, from bird droppings, are nearly used up.
24,702,119	$1 = 74²/₃ rupees	Nepali, many dialects	Mt. Everest, the world's highest mountain, is partly in Nepal.
15,892,237	$1 = 2¹/₃ guilders	Dutch	The tulip is the living symbol of the Netherlands.
3,819,762	$1 = 2¹/₅ NZ dollars	English, Maori	New Zealand was first to grant women full voting rights (1893).
4,812,569	$1 = 13 gold cordobas	Spanish	The eastern shore is called Costa de Mosquitos (Mosquito Coast).
10,075,511	$1 = 691 CFA francs	French, Hausa, Djerma	Niger is one of the world's top uranium-producing countries.
123,337,822	$1 = 110 nairas	English, Hausa, Yoruba, Ibo	Nigeria has the biggest population of any African country.
4,481,162	$1 = 8²/₃ kroner	Norwegian	Norway has many fjords, steep-sided narrow inlets, in its coastline.
2,533,389	$1 = ³/₈ rial Omani	Arabic	Oman has 13 males for every 10 females.
141,553,775	$1 = 59¹/₅ rupees	Urdu, English, Punjabi, Sindhi	There were cities in Pakistan 6,000 years ago.
18,766	U.S. dollar	English, Palauan	Nevada has 100 times more people than Palau.

NATION	CAPITAL	LOCATION OF NATION	AREA
Panama	Panama City	Central America, between Costa Rica and Colombia	30,200 sq. mi. (78,200 sq. km.)
Papua New Guinea	Port Moresby	Part of the island of New Guinea, north of Australia	178,700 sq. mi. (462,840 sq. km.)
Paraguay	Asunción	South America, between Argentina and Brazil	157,050 sq. mi. (406,750 sq. km.)
Peru	Lima	South America, along the Pacific coast, north of Chile	496,230 sq. mi. (1,285,220 sq. km.)
Philippines	Manila	Islands in the Pacific Ocean, off the coast of Southeast Asia	115,830 sq. mi. (300,000 sq. km.)
Poland	Warsaw	Central Europe, on the Baltic Sea, east of Germany	120,730 sq. mi. (312,680 sq. km.)
Portugal	Lisbon	Southern Europe, on the Iberian Peninsula, west of Spain	35,670 sq. mi. (92,390 sq. km.)
Qatar	Doha	Arabian Peninsula, on the Persian Gulf	4,420 sq. mi. (11,440 sq. km.)
Romania	Bucharest	Southern Europe, on the Black Sea, north of Bulgaria	91,700 sq. mi. (237,500 sq. km.)
Russia	Moscow	Stretches from Eastern Europe across northern Asia to the Pacific Ocean	6,592,800 sq. mi. (17,075,200 sq. km.)
Rwanda	Kigali	Central Africa, northwest of Tanzania	10,170 sq. mi. (26,340 sq. km.)
Saint Kitts and Nevis	Basseterre	Islands in the Caribbean Sea, near Puerto Rico	100 sq. mi. (270 sq. km.)
Saint Lucia	Castries	Island on eastern edge of the Caribbean Sea	240 sq. mi. (620 sq. km.)
Saint Vincent and the Grenadines	Kingstown	Islands on eastern edge of the Caribbean Sea, north of Grenada	130 sq. mi. (340 sq. km.)
Samoa (formerly Western Samoa)	Apia	Islands in the South Pacific Ocean	1,100 sq. mi. (2,860 sq. km.)
San Marino	San Marino	Southern Europe, surrounded by Italy	20 sq. mi. (50 sq. km.)
São Tomé and Príncipe	São Tomé	In the Gulf of Guinea, off the coast of West Africa	370 sq. mi. (960 sq. km.)
Saudi Arabia	Riyadh	Western Asia, occupying most of the Arabian Peninsula	756,990 sq. mi. (1,960,580 sq. km.)
Senegal	Dakar	West Africa, on the Atlantic Ocean, south of Mauritania	75,750 sq. mi. (196,190 sq. km.)
Seychelles	Victoria	Islands off the coast of Africa, in the Indian Ocean	180 sq. mi. (460 sq. km.)

POPULATION	CURRENCY	LANGUAGE	DID YOU KNOW?
2,808,268	Same value as U.S. dollar	Spanish, English	Christopher Columbus visited Panama in 1502.
4,926,984	$1 = 3¹/₅ kinas	English, Motu	New Guinea has human remains that are 10,000 years old.
5,585,828	$1 = 3,545 guarani	Spanish, Guarani	Jaguars, boars, tapirs, and snakes live in Paraguay.
27,012,899	$1 = 3¹/₂ new soles	Spanish, Quechua, Aymara	The Inca empire had its base in Peru's mountains.
81,159,644	$1 = 51 pesos	Pilipino, English	Japan occupied the Philippines in World War II.
38,646,023	$1 = 4 zlotys	Polish	Six million civilians were killed in Poland in World War II.
10,048,232	$1 = 211 escudos	Portuguese	Portugal's last king was driven out in 1910.
744,483	$1 = 3 ²/₃ riyals	Arabic, English	Qatar has the highest proportion of men of any nation, 66%.
22,411,121	$1 = 26,000 lei	Romanian, Hungarian	The real Dracula, Prince Vlad, lived in Romania in the 1400s.
146,001,176	$1 = 28²/₅ rubles	Russian, many others	Russia is the largest country in area and the 6th-largest in population.
7,229,129	$1 = 359 francs	French, English Kinyarwanda	The two main ethnic groups are the Tutsi and the Hutu.
38,819	$1 = 2²/₃ EC dollars	English	American statesman Alexander Hamilton was born here in 1757.
156,260	$1 = 2²/₃ EC dollars	English, French patois	Native poet Derek Walcott won the 1992 Nobel Prize for literature.
115,461	$1 = 2²/₃ EC dollars	English, French patois	Columbus landed on St. Vincent on St. Vincent's Day in 1498.
179,466	$1 = 3¹/₃ tala	English, Samoan	Five of the nation's nine islands are uninhabited.
26,937	$1 = 2,040 lire	Italian	A big source of income comes from the sale of postage stamps.
159,883	$1 = 2,391 dobras	Portuguese	The first settlers were convicts and exiled Jews.
22,023,506	$1 = 3³/₄ riyals	Arabic	Saudi Arabia is the world's leading exporter of oil.
9,987,494	$1 = 691 CFA francs	French, Wolof	Senegal's Youssou N'dour is a leader in "afrobeat" popular music.
79,326	$1 = 6¹/₃ rupees	English, French, Creole	Tourism is a major industry in the Seychelles.

NATION	CAPITAL	LOCATION OF NATION	AREA
Sierra Leone	Freetown	West Africa, on the Atlantic Ocean, south of Guinea	27,700 sq. mi. (71,740 sq. km.)
Singapore	Singapore	Mostly on one island, off the tip of Southeast Asia	250 sq. mi. (650 sq. km.)
Slovakia	Bratislava	Eastern Europe, between Poland and Hungary	18,860 sq. mi. (48,850 sq. km.)
Slovenia	Ljubljana	Eastern Europe, between Austria and Croatia	7,820 sq. mi. (20,260 sq. km.)
Solomon Islands	Honiara	Western Pacific Ocean	10,980 sq. mi. (28,450 sq. km.)
Somalia	Mogadishu	East Africa, east of Ethiopia	246,200 sq. mi. (637,660 sq. km.)
South Africa	Pretoria (admin.) Cape Town (legisl.)	At the southern tip of Africa	471,010 sq. mi. (1,219,910 sq. km.)
Spain	Madrid	Europe, south of France, on the Iberian Peninsula	194,890 sq. mi. (504,750 sq. km.)
Sri Lanka	Colombo	Island in the Indian Ocean, southeast of India	25,330 sq. mi. (65,610 sq. km.)
Sudan	Khartoum	North Africa, south of Egypt, on the Red Sea	967,500 sq. mi. (2,505,810 sq. km.)
Suriname	Paramaribo	South America, on the northern shore, east of Guyana	63,040 sq. mi. (163,270 sq. km.)
Swaziland	Mbabane	Southern Africa, almost surrounded by South Africa	6,700 sq. mi. (17,360 sq. km.)
Sweden	Stockholm	Northern Europe, on the Scandinavian Peninsula	173,730 sq. mi. (449,960 sq. km.)
Switzerland	Bern (admin.) Lausanne (judicial)	Central Europe, in the Alps, north of Italy	15,940 sq. mi. (41,290 sq. km.)
Syria	Damascus	In the Middle East, north of Jordan and west of Iraq	71,500 sq. mi. (185,180 sq. km.)
Taiwan	Taipei	Island off southeast coast of China	13,890 sq. mi. (35,980 sq. km.)
Tajikistan	Dushanbe	Asia, west of China, south of Kyrgyzstan	55,300 sq. mi. (143,100 sq. km.)
Tanzania	Dar-es-Salaam	East Africa, on the Indian Ocean, south of Kenya	364,900 sq. mi. (945,090 sq. km.)
Thailand	Bangkok	Southeast Asia, south of Laos	198,000 sq. mi. (514,000 sq. km.)
Togo	Lomé	West Africa, between Ghana and Benin	21,930 sq. mi. (56,790 sq. km.)

POPULATION	CURRENCY	LANGUAGE	DID YOU KNOW?
5,232,624	$1 = 1,899 leones	English, Mende, Temne, Krio	The UN set up a war crimes tribunal in 2000 to investigate atrocities.
4,151,720	$1 = 1¾ Singapore dollars	Chinese, Malay, Tamil, English	Singapore is a nation basically made up of a single city, Singapore.
5,407,956	$1 = 46⅛ koruny	Slovak, Hungarian	Czechoslovakia split into Slovakia and the Czech Republic in 1993.
1,927,593	$1 = 224 tolars	Slovenian, Serbo-Croatian	Slovenia broke away from Yugoslavia in 1991.
466,194	$1 = 5⅛ Solomon dollars	English, Melanesian	These include Guadalcanal, site of a key World War II battle.
7,253,137	$1 = 2,620 shillings	Somali, Arabic, Italian, English	30 U.S. soldiers died here during UN peacekeeping work (1992–94).
43,421,021	$1 = 7½ rand	Afrikaans, English, Ndebele, Sotho	Apartheid (racial separation) was the law here for nearly 50 years.
39,996,671	$1 = 175 pesetas	Castilian Spanish, Catalan, Galician	About one million people died in the 1936-39 civil war.
19,238,575	$1 = 83⅛ rupees	Sinhala, Tamil, English	Sri Lanka had the world's first elected female prime minister (1960).
35,079,814	$1 = 2,560 pounds or $1 = 256 dinars	Arabic, Nubian, Ta Bedawie	Sudan is the largest African country in area.
431,303	$1 = 981 guilders	Dutch, Sranang Tongo	In 1677, Britain "traded" Suriname to the Dutch for New York.
1,038,289	$1 = 7½ emalangeni	English, siSwati	The royal house of Swaziland has ruled for 400 years.
8,873,052	$1 = 9⅓ kronor	Swedish	Swedes have lived in this region for at least 5,000 years.
7,262,372	$1 = 1⅗ francs	German, French, Italian, Romansch	The president serves for a term of only one year.
16,305,659	$1 = 53½ pounds	Arabic, Kurdish, Armenian	Bashar al-Assad won the presidency after his father's death in 2000.
22,191,087	$1 = 32⅞ new Taiwan dollars	Mandarin Chinese, Taiwanese	Anti-Communists founded this "Republic of China" in 1949.
6,440,732	$1 = 2,200 Tajik rubles	Tajik, Russian	Government forces battled Muslim insurgents in the mid-1990s.
35,506,126	$1 = 803 shillings	Swahili, English	Tanganyika and Zanzibar joined to form Tanzania in 1964.
61,230,874	$1 = 43¼ bahts	Thai, English	Previously Siam, Thailand has been independent since 1350.
5,018,502	$1 = 691 CFA francs	French, Ewe, Kabye	About 70% of Togolese people practice traditional African religions.

NATION	CAPITAL	LOCATION OF NATION	AREA
Tonga	Nuku'alofa	Islands in the South Pacific Ocean	290 sq. mi. (750 sq. km.)
Trinidad and Tobago	Port-of-Spain	Islands off the north coast of South America	1,980 sq. mi. (5,130 sq. km.)
Tunisia	Tunis	North Africa, on the Mediterranean, between Algeria and Libya	63,170 sq. mi. (163,610 sq. km.)
Turkey	Ankara	On the southern shore of the Black Sea, partly in Europe and partly in Asia	301,380 sq. mi. (780,580 sq. km.)
Turkmenistan	Ashgabat	Western Asia, north of Afghanistan and Iran	188,500 sq. mi. (488,100 sq. km.)
Tuvalu	Funafuti Atoll	Chain of islands in the South Pacific Ocean	10 sq. mi. (26 sq. km.)
Uganda	Kampala	East Africa, south of Sudan	91,140 sq. mi. (236,040 sq. km.)
Ukraine	Kiev	Eastern Europe, south of Belarus and Russia	233,100 sq. mi. (603,700 sq. km.)
United Arab Emirates	Abu Dhabi	Arabian Peninsula, on the Persian Gulf	32,000 sq. mi. (82,880 sq. km.)
United States	Washington, D.C.	In North America; 48 of 50 states between Canada and Mexico	3,717,810 sq. mi. (9,629,090 sq. km.)
Uruguay	Montevideo	South America, on the Atlantic Ocean, south of Brazil	68,040 sq. mi. (176,220 sq. km.)
Uzbekistan	Tashkent	Central Asia, south of Kazakhstan	172,740 sq. mi. (447,400 sq. km.)
Vanuatu	Port-Vila	Islands in the South Pacific Ocean	5,700 sq. mi. (14,760 sq. km.)
Vatican City		Surrounded by the city of Rome, Italy	1/5 sq. mi. (1/2 sq. km.)
Venezuela	Caracas	On the northern coast of South America, east of Colombia	352,140 sq. mi. (912,050 sq. km.)
Vietnam	Hanoi	Southeast Asia, south of China, on the eastern coast	127,240 sq. mi. (329,560 sq. km.)
Yemen	Sanaa	Asia, on the southern coast of the Arabian Peninsula	203,850 sq. mi. (527,970 sq. km.)
Yugoslavia	Belgrade, Podgorica	Europe, on Balkan Peninsula, west of Romania and Bulgaria	39,520 sq. mi. (102,350 sq. km.)
Zambia	Lusaka	Southern Africa, east of Angola	290,580 sq. mi. (752,610 sq. km.)
Zimbabwe	Harare	Southern Africa, south of Zambia	150,800 sq. mi. (390,580 sq. km.)

POPULATION	CURRENCY	LANGUAGE	DID YOU KNOW?
102,321	$1 = 2 pa'angas	Tongan, English	Tonga's King Taufa'ahau Tupou IV has ruled since 1965.
1,175,523	$1 = 6¼ Trinidad dollars	English, Hindi, French, Spanish	Trinidad and Tobago are the southern-most Caribbean Islands.
9,593,402	$1 = 1⅜ dinar	Arabic, French	The ancient city of Carthage was located near modern-day Tunis.
65,666,677	$1 = 663,670 Turkish liras	Turkish, Kurdish, Arabic	The Ottoman Empire ruled vast areas for 400 years until World War I.
4,518,268	$1 = 5,200 manats	Turkmen, Russian, Uzbek	In 1999, parliament voted Saparmurad Niyazov president for life.
10,838	$ 1= 1¾ Australian dollars	Tuvaluan, English	Most Tuvaluan belong to the Protestant Church of Tuvalu.
23,317,560	$1 = 1,790 shillings	English, Luganda, Swahili	The tyrannical dictator Idi Amin expelled Uganda's Asians in 1972.
49,153,027	$1 = 5½ hryvina	Ukrainian, Russian	The world's worst nuclear accident occurred in Chernobyl in 1986.
2,369,153	$1 = 3⅔ dirhams	Arabic, Persian, English, Hindi	These 7 "Trucial States" were long controlled by Britain (1853–1971).
281,421,906	U.S. dollar	English, Spanish	The huge U.S. central plain is among the world's leading farm areas.
3,334,074	$1 = 11⅖ pesos	Spanish	Tiny Uruguay hosted, and won, soccer's first World Cup (1930).
24,755,519	$1 = 775 sams	Uzbek, Russian	Alexander the Great and Genghis Khan both conquered this region.
189,618	$1 = 142 vatus	French, English, Bislama	Vanuatu's top export is copra, dried coconut meat used for coconut oil.
870	$1 = 2,040 lire	Italian, Latin	The Pope rules here; it's smaller than The Mall in Washington, D.C.
23,542,649	$1 = 698 bolivares	Spanish	The Lake Maracaibo area is the center of Venezuela's oil industry.
78,773,873	$1 = 14,522 dong	Vietnamese, French, Chinese	The Mekong Valley is among the world's leading rice-growing areas.
17,479,206	$1 = 161 rials	Arabic	"Mocha" coffee takes its name from a Yemeni seaport.
10,662,087	$1 = 11⅝ new dinars	Serbo-Croatian, Albanian	Invading armies have captured Belgrade more than 30 times.
9,582,418	$1 = 4,631 kwacha	English, native languages	Zambia is one of the world's largest producers of copper.
11,342,521	$1 = 55⅛ Zimbabwe dollars	English, Shona, Sindebele	The beautiful Victoria waterfalls lie between Zimbabwe and Zambia.

NATIONS CROSSWORD

You'll find all of the answers to the crossword in this section.

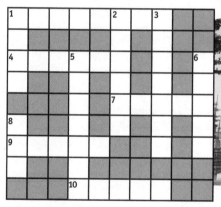

▲ Temple of Reclining Buddha, Bangkok

ACROSS

1 Bangkok is the capital of this Southeast Asian nation.

4 This nation lies on the Baltic Sea between Lithuania and Latvia.

7 Rome is this nation's capital.

9 The people who use this currency speak French.

10 This nation is an island in the Mediterranean.

DOWN

1 This currency is used in Samoa.

2 Algerians speak this language.

3 $1 will buy 7⁴/₅ kroner in this European country.

5 If you visit Hanoi, you'll be in this nation.

6 This nation in northeastern Africa is bordered by two seas.

8 Togo uses this type of franc, as do 13 other African nations.

ANSWERS ON PAGES 317-320. FOR MORE PUZZLES GO TO WWW.WORLDALMANACFORKIDS.COM

MAPS AND FLAGS OF THE NATIONS OF THE WORLD

Maps showing the continents and nations of the world appear on pages 153 through 164. Flags of the nations appear on pages 165 through 168.

A map of the United States appears on pages 268–269.

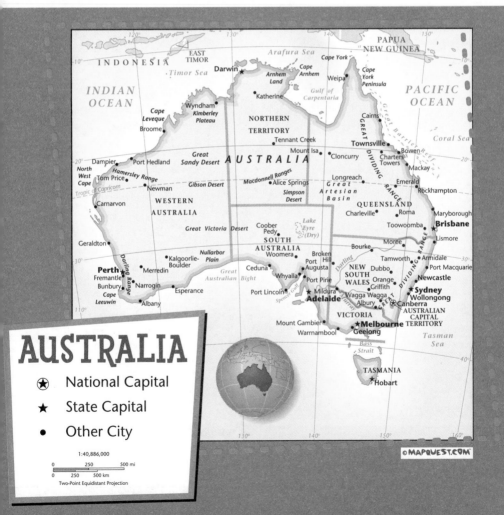

AUSTRALIA

⊛ National Capital

★ State Capital

• Other City

1:40,886,000

0   250   500 mi

0   250   500 km

Two-Point Equidistant Projection

©MAPQUEST.COM

RUSSIA

SWEDEN

NORWAY

GREAT BRITAIN

ICELAND

Spitsbergen

Greenland Sea

Denmark Strait

Cape Farewell

Tasiilaq

GREENLAND (KALAALLIT NUNAAT) (Den.)

Nuuk (Godthaab)

Labrador Sea

NEWFOUNDLAND

St. Anthony
Island of Newfoundland
Happy Valley-Goose Bay
Corner Brook
St. John's
St. Pierre & Miquelon Is. (Fr.)
Sydney
Antikosti I.
NEW P.E.I.
BRUNS.

Hebron

Schefferville
QUÉBEC
Sept-Îles
Labrador City
Chicoutimi
Chibougamau

CANADIAN SHIELD

Arctic Circle

Knud Rasmussen Land

Qaanaaq (Thule)

Nord

Cape Morris Jessup

North Pole

Arctic Ocean

Alert

Ellesmere I.

Grise Fiord

Baffin Bay

Arctic Bay

Pond Inlet

Baffin Island

Pangnirtung

Iqaluit

Davis Strait

Hudson Strait

Ungava Peninsula

Povungnituk

Belcher Is.

James Bay

ONTARIO

Mooseonee

L. Winnipeg

Queen Elizabeth Islands

Resolute

Cambridge Bay

Victoria I.

Holman

NUNAVUT

Repulse Bay

Southampton I.

Hudson Bay

Churchill

York Factory

Flin Flon

MANITOBA

Thompson

CANADA

Banks I.

Sachs Harbour

Beaufort Sea

Kugluktuk

Great Bear L.

Déline

Inuvik

Fort McPherson

Mackenzie

Point Barrow

Barrow

Kotzebue

BROOKS RANGE

Fort Yukon

Yukon

Dawson

Mayo

Carmacks

YUKON

Whitehorse

Watson Lake

NORTHWEST TERRITORIES

Ft. Simpson

Great Slave L.

Yellowknife

Fort Smith

Hay River

Uranium City

Lake Athabasca

La Loche

SASK.

La Ranche

Fort McMurray

ALBERTA

Peace River

Athabasca

Prince Albert

Saskatchewan

Saskatoon

Regina

GREAT

Point Hope

Bering Strait

Nome

Bethel

ALASKA

Mt. McKinley 6,194 m. (20,320 ft.)

ALASKA RANGE

Fairbanks

Anchorage

Valdez

Kenai

Seward

Kodiak

Mt. Logan 5,959 m (19,551 ft.)

Yakutat

Skagway

Juneau

Sitka

Gulf of Alaska

BRITISH COLUMBIA

Prince George

Jasper

Edmonton

Calgary

ROCKY

MOUNTAINS

COAST MOUNTAINS

Ketchikan

Prince Rupert

Kitimat

Queen Charlotte Is.

Williams Lake

Vancouver I.

Vancouver

Victoria

Columbia

Bering Sea

Arctic Circle

NORTH AMERICA

⊛ National Capital

★ Territorial Capital

• Other City

1:39,978,000

| 0 | 350 | 700 mi |
| 0 | 350 700 km | |

Azimuthal Equal Area Projection

©MAPQUEST.COM

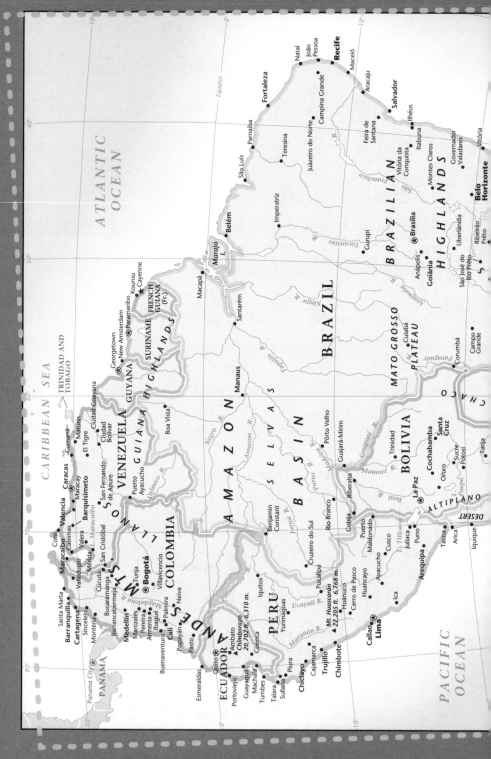

ATLANTIC OCEAN

CARIBBEAN SEA

TRINIDAD AND TOBAGO

PACIFIC OCEAN

Equator

Santa Marta
Barranquilla
Cartagena
Sincelejo
Montería

Coro
Maracaibo
Cabimas
Valledupar
Valera
Mérida
Cúcuta
Bucaramanga
Barrancabermeja

Valencia
Maracay

Caracas

Cumaná
Maturín
El Tigre
Ciudad Guayana
Ciudad Bolívar

Georgetown
New Amsterdam
Paramaribo
Cayenne
Kourou

VENEZUELA

GUYANA

SURINAME

FRENCH GUIANA (Fr.)

Barquisimeto
San Fernando de Apure
Puerto Ayacucho

COLOMBIA

Medellín
Manizales
Pereira
Armenia
Ibagué

Bogotá
Tunja
Villavicencio
Palmira
Cali
Popayán
Pasto
Neiva

GUIANA HIGHLANDS

Boa Vista

Manaus

AMAZON

SELVAS

BASIN

Macapá

Marajó L.

Belém

São Luís

Santarém

Imperatriz

Gurupi

Teresina

Parnaíba

Fortaleza

Natal
João Pessoa
Recife
Maceió
Aracaju

Campina Grande

Juàzeiro do Norte

Salvador
Ilhéus
Itabuna

Feira de Santana

Vitória da Conquista
Montes Claros
Governador Valadares
Vitória

BRAZILIAN HIGHLANDS

Belo Horizonte

BRAZIL

Brasília

Anápolis
Goiânia

São José do Rio Prêto

Uberlândia
Ribeirão Prêto

MATO GROSSO PLATEAU

Cuiabá

Campo Grande

Corumbá

BOLIVIA

Trinidad

Santa Cruz

Cochabamba

Oruro
Sucre
Potosí
Tarija

La Paz

ALTIPLANO

DESERT

Porto Velho

Guajará-Mirim

Riberalta

Cobija

Puerto Maldonado

Rio Branco

Cruzeiro do Sul

Benjamin Constant

Cusco

Juliaca
Puno
Arequipa

Tacna
Arica
Iquique

L. Titicaca

PERU

Iquitos

Yurimaguas

Pucallpa

Cerro de Pasco
Huánuco
Huancayo
Ayacucho
Ica

Lima
Callao

Mt. Huascarán 22,205 ft. 6,768 m.

Chimbote
Trujillo
Chiclayo
Cajamarca

Piura
Sullana
Talara
Tumbes
Machala

ECUADOR

Quito
Ambato
Chimborazo 20,702 ft. 6,310 m.
Cuenca
Guayaquil
Portoviejo
Esmeraldas

Buenaventura

ANDES MTS.

Panama City

PANAMA

156

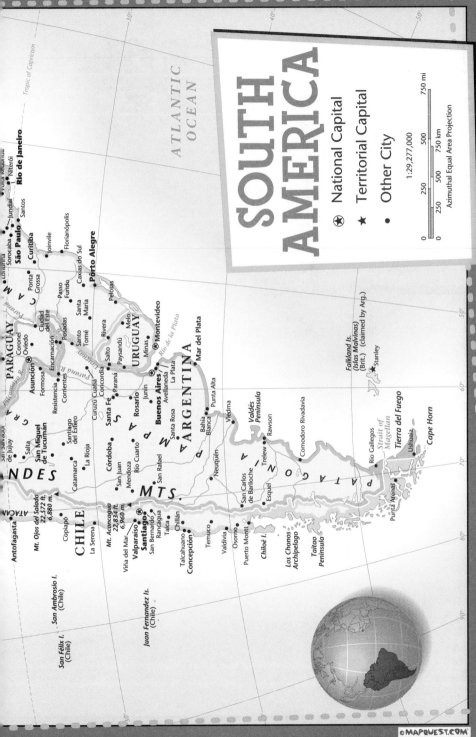

SOUTH AMERICA

⊛ National Capital
★ Territorial Capital
• Other City

1:29,277,000

| 0 | 250 | 500 | 750 mi |
| 0 | 250 | 500 | 750 km |

Azimuthal Equal Area Projection

ATLANTIC OCEAN

Tropic of Capricorn

Rio de Janeiro
Niterói
Santos
São Paulo
Sorocaba
Jundiaí
Londrina
Joinvile
Florianópolis
Curitiba
Ponta Grossa
Caxias do Sul
Porto Alegre
Passo Fundo
Santa Maria
Pelotas

PARAGUAY
Coronel Oviedo
Ciudad del Este
⊛ **Asunción**
Encarnación
Formosa
Posadas
Resistencia
Corrientes
Santo Tomé
Rivera
Salto
Melo
URUGUAY
Paysandú
Minas
Santa Fe
Paraná
Concordia
Curuzú Cuatiá
⊛ **Montevideo**
Río de la Plata
Mar del Plata
Salta
San Miguel de Tucumán
Santiago del Estero
La Rioja
Catamarca
Córdoba
San Juan
Río Cuarto
Mendoza
San Rafael
Rosario
Junín
⊛ **Buenos Aires**
La Plata
Avellaneda
Santa Rosa
Bahía Blanca
Punta Alta
ARGENTINA
Viedma
Valdés Peninsula
Rawson
Trelew
Comodoro Rivadavia
PATAGONIA
Neuquén
San Carlos de Bariloche
Esquel
Río Gallegos
Strait of Magellan
Punta Arenas
Tierra del Fuego
Ushuaia
Cape Horn

Antofagasta
Mt. Ojos del Salado 22,572 ft. 6,880 m.
San Ambrosio I. (Chile)
San Félix I. (Chile)
Copiapó
La Serena
Mt. Aconcagua 22,834 ft. 6,960 m.
CHILE
Juan Fernández Is. (Chile)
Viña del Mar.
Valparaíso
⊛ **Santiago**
San Bernardo
Rancagua
Talca
Chillán
Concepción
Talcahuano
Temuco
Valdivia
Osorno
Puerto Montt
Chiloé I.
Los Chanos Archipelago
Taitao Peninsula
San Carlos

ANDES
MTS.
ATACAMA

Falkland Is. (Islas Malvinas) (Brit.) (claimed by Arg.)
★ Stanley

©MAPQUEST.COM

EUROPE

⊛ National Capital

• Other City

1:22,107,000

| 0 | 250 | 500 mi |
| 0 | 250 | 500 km |

Azimuthal Equal Area Projection

Arctic Circle

Reykjavik • Akureyri
ICELAND

Tromsø

Bodø

Norwegian *Sea*

Faroe Is.
(Den.)

Trondheim

Sundsvall

Shetland Is.
(Brit.)

NORWAY

SWEDEN

Bergen • Oslo
Stavanger

Uppsala
Stockholm
Linköping

Orkney
Is.

Gotland

Hebrides

Aberdeen

Göteborg

Öland

Skagerrak

Kattegat

Baltic

Glasgow • Edinburgh

Jutland Århus

Belfast
GREAT BRITAIN
Newcastle

Copenhagen Helsingborg
Malmö

Dublin
IRELAND Liverpool **(UNITED KINGDOM)** Leeds
Cork Manchester Sheffield

North
Sea

DENMARK Odense

Gdańsk
Szczecin

Birmingham

Hamburg

Cardiff • Bristol
NETHERLANDS
Amsterdam

Bremen

Hannover

Elbe

Poznań

Łódź

ATLANTIC
OCEAN

Land's End
Portsmouth

London
Rotterdam

Berlin
GERMANY

Oder

English Channel
Channel Is.
(Brit.)

Antwerp
Brussels Essen
Lille Cologne
BELGIUM Bonn

Leipzig

Dresden

Wrocław

Le Havre
LUXEMBOURG
Brest

Rouen
Liège

Frankfurt

Prague
CZECH REP.

Katowice

Paris
Luxembourg

Mannheim

Brno
Ostrava

Nantes

Loire

Strasbourg

Stuttgart

Danube

SLOVAKI

Cape Finisterre

Bay
of
Biscay

Dijon

FRANCE

Munich
Bern Zürich
LIECHTENSTEIN

Linz

Vienna Bratislava

Vigo

Gijón

Geneva **SWITZERLAND**

A L P S

AUSTRIA
Graz

Budapes

HUNGAR

Porto

Bilbao

Bordeaux

Lyon

Mt. Blanc
4807 m
(15,771 ft)

Milan
Turin Verona

Ljubljana
SLOVENIA

Pécs

Zagreb

Valladolid

Toulouse

Rhône
Marseille Nice

Genoa

Venice

DINARIC

CROATIA

Po

PORTUGAL **IBERIAN**

Pico de Aneto
3404 m
(11,168 ft)

Zaragoza

PYRENEES

Toulon
ANDORRA

MONACO
Florence

APENNINES

BOSNIA &
HERZEGOVIN
SAN
MARINO.

Sarajevo

Lisbon

Badajoz

Tagus

Madrid
PENINSULA

Barcelona

Ligurian Sea

Corsica
(Fr.)

Elba

VATICAN
CITY

Rome

Split

Dubrovnik
Podgoric

Adriatic

Córdoba
Sevilla

Cádiz

SPAIN
Valencia
Granada

Majorca

Palma

Balearic Sea
Minorca

Balearic Is.
(Sp.)

Sardinia
(It.)

Naples

ITALY

Bari

Salerno

Cape
St. Vincent

Málaga

Strait of
Gibraltar

GIBRALTAR (Brit.)

Alicante

Cagliari

Tyrrhenian
Sea

Cor
Ionia
Sea

M e d i t e r r a n e a n

Palermo

MALTA

Rabat
Casablanca

Algiers

Tunis

Catania
Sicily

Mt. Etna
3323 m
(10,902 ft)

Valletta

MOROCCO

A T L A S

M O U N T A I N S
ALGERIA

TUNISIA

Sea

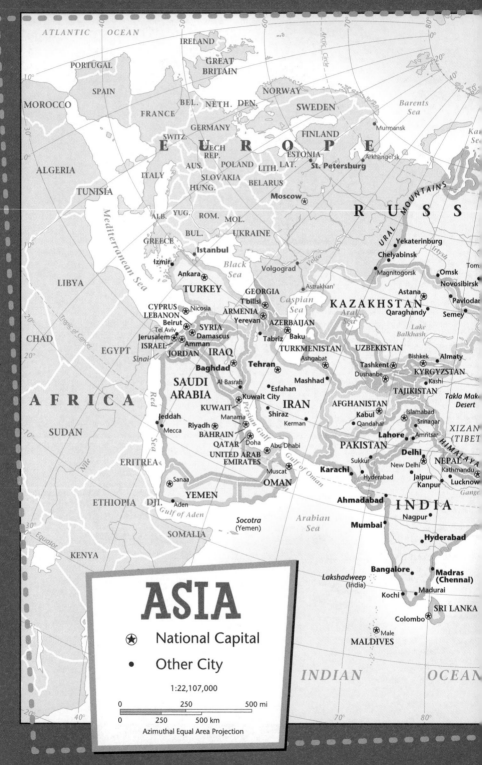

ATLANTIC OCEAN

IRELAND

PORTUGAL

GREAT
BRITAIN

SPAIN

NORWAY

MOROCCO

BEL. NETH. DEN.

FRANCE

SWEDEN

FINLAND

Barents
Sea

Murmansk

Ka..
Se..

GERMANY

SWITZ.
ECH
REP.

E U R O P E

ESTONIA

Arkhangel'sk

ALGERIA

ITALY

AUS.

POLAND

LITH. LAT.

St. Petersburg

SLOVAKIA

BELARUS

Moscow

R U S S

TUNISIA

HUNG.

URAL MOUNTAINS

ALB. YUG. ROM. MOL.

BUL.

UKRAINE

Yekaterinburg

LIBYA

GREECE

İzmir

Istanbul

Ankara

Black
Sea

Chelyabinsk

Magnitogorsk

Volgograd

Volga

Irtysh

Omsk

Tom

Astrakhan'

Novosibirsk

TURKEY

GEORGIA

T'bilisi

Caspian
Sea

KAZAKHSTAN

Astana

Pavlodar

CHAD

CYPRUS
LEBANON

Nicosia

ARMENIA

Beirut

Tel Aviv

SYRIA

Yerevan

AZERBAIJAN

Tabriz

Baku

Aral
Sea

Qaraghandy

Semey

Lake
Balkhash

Mediterranean Sea

EGYPT

Tropic of Cancer

Sinai

Jerusalem

ISRAEL

Damascus

JORDAN

Amman

IRAQ

Baghdad

TURKMENISTAN

Tehran

UZBEKISTAN

Ashgabat

Tashkent

Bishkek

Dushanbe

Almaty

KYRGYZSTAN

Kashi

A F R I C A

SAUDI
ARABIA

Al Basrah

Mashhad

Esfahan

TAJIKISTAN

Takla Mak..
Desert

SUDAN

Red
Sea

Kuwait City

KUWAIT

Jeddah

Mecca

Riyadh

Manama

BAHRAIN

IRAN

Shiraz

Kerman

AFGHANISTAN

Kabul

Qandahar

Islamabad

Srinagar

Amritsar

XIZAN
(TIBET

Lahore

HIMALAYA

ERITREA

QATAR

Doha

Abu Dhabi

UNITED ARAB
EMIRATES

Gulf of Oman

PAKISTAN

Sukkur

Delhi

New Delhi

NEPAL

Kathmandu

Nile

Muscat

Karachi

Hyderabad

Jaipur

Lucknow

Kanpur

Ganges

ETHIOPIA

DJI.

Sanaa

YEMEN

Aden

Gulf of Aden

OMAN

Ahmadabad

I N D I A

Nagpur

SOMALIA

Socotra
(Yemen)

Arabian
Sea

Mumbai

Hyderabad

KENYA

Equator

Bangalore

Lakshadweep
(India)

Madras
(Chennai)

Kochi

Madurai

SRI LANKA

Colombo

Male

MALDIVES

INDIAN

OCEAN

ASIA

★ National Capital

• Other City

1:22,107,000

0   250   500 mi

0   250   500 km

Azimuthal Equal Area Projection

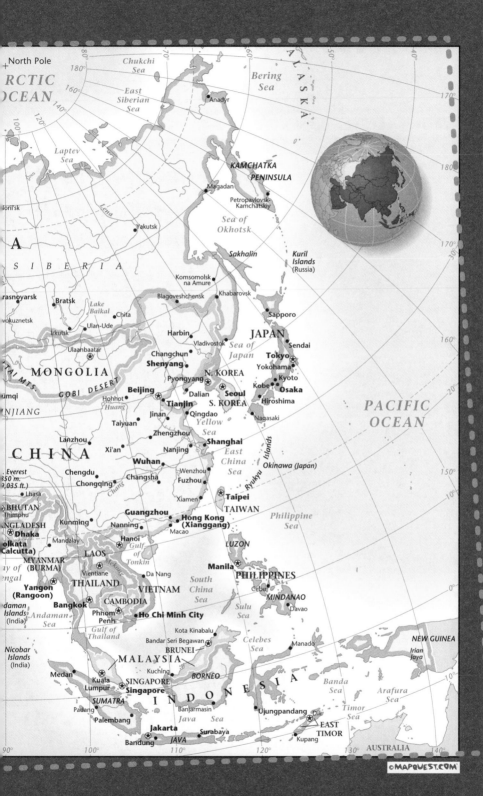

North Pole

ARCTIC
OCEAN

Chukchi
Sea

A L A S K A

Bering
Sea

East
Siberian
Sea

Anadyr

Laptev
Sea

KAMCHATKA
PENINSULA

Magadan

Petropavlovsk-
Kamchatskiy

Sea of
Okhotsk

Yakutsk

Sakhalin

Kuril
Islands
(Russia)

S I B E R I A

Komsomolsk
na Amure

Blagoveshchensk Khabarovsk

Sapporo

rasnoyarsk   Bratsk *Lake*
Baikal   Chita

Harbin

Vladivostok   *Sea of*
Japan   Sendai

JAPAN

okuznetsk
Irkutsk   Ulan-Ude   Changchun   **Tokyo**

Ulaanbaatar   **Shenyang**   Pyongyang   **N. KOREA**   Yokohama   Kyoto

MONGOLIA   Hohhot   **Beijing**   Dalian   **Seoul**   Kobe   **Osaka**

GOBI DESERT   *Huang*   **Tianjin**   **S. KOREA**   Hiroshima

umqi   Jinan   Qingdao   Nagasaki

NJIANG   Taiyuan   *Yellow*
Sea

Lanzhou   Zhengzhou   **Shanghai**   *East*
China

C H I N A   Xi'an   Nanjing   *Sea*

. Everest   **Wuhan**   Wenzhou   Okinawa (Japan)

350 m.   Chengdu   Changsha   Fuzhou

,035 ft.)   Chongqing   *Chang*

Lhasa   Xiamen   **Taipei**

BHUTAN   **TAIWAN**

Thimphu   **Guangzhou**

NGLADESH   Kunming   Nanning   **Hong Kong**
(Xianggang)   *Philippine*
Sea

Dhaka   Macao

olkata   Hanoi   *Gulf*
Calcutta)   Mandalay   *of*   *LUZON*
Tonkin

MYANMAR   **LAOS**

(BURMA)   Vientiane   Da Nang   **Manila**   **PHILIPPINES**

engal   **THAILAND**   **VIETNAM**   *South*
China   Cebu   *MINDANAO*

daman   **Yangon**   *Sea*   Davao

Islands   **(Rangoon)**

(India)   **Bangkok**   **CAMBODIA**   Phnom   *Sulu*
Penh   **Ho Chi Minh City**   *Sea*

Andaman   *Gulf of*
Sea   *Thailand*   Kota Kinabalu   *Celebes*
Sea   Manado

Nicobar   Bandar Seri Begawan   *NEW GUINEA*

Islands   **BRUNEI**   *Irian*

(India)   **MALAYSIA**   *Jaya*

Medan   Kuching   *BORNEO*   *Banda*
Sea

Kuala   **SINGAPORE**   *Arafura*

Lumpur   **Singapore**   I N D O N E S I A   *Sea*

SUMATRA   Banjarmasin   *Timor*
Sea

Padang   *Java*   Ujungpandang   Dili

Palembang   *Sea*   **EAST**
TIMOR

Jakarta   Surabaya   Kupang   *AUSTRALIA*

Bandung   *JAVA*

PACIFIC
OCEAN

©MAPQUEST.COM

161

ATLANTIC OCEAN

AZORES (Port.)

MADEIRA (Port.)

CANARY IS. (Sp.)
Las Palmas

PORTUGAL
Lisbon
SPAIN
Madrid
Paris
FRANCE
SWITZ.
ITALY
Rome
GERMANY
CZECH REP.
AUSTRIA
SLOVE.
CRO.
BOS. & HER.
YUGO.
MAC.
ALBANIA
GREECE
Athens
SLOVAKIA
HUNGARY
SLOVENIA
ROMANIA
Bucharest
BULGARIA
MOLDOVA
UKRAINE
RUSSIA
KAZAKHSTAN
Aral Sea
UZBEKISTAN
TURKMENISTAN
Caspian Sea
GEORGIA
ARMENIA
AZERBAIJAN
Tehran
IRAN
Black Sea
TURKEY
Ankara
istanbul
CYPRUS
LEBANON
ISRAEL
SYRIA
Damascus
JORDAN
Jerusalem
IRAQ
Baghdad
KUWAIT
Persian Gulf
QATAR
BAHRAIN
Riyadh
SAUDI ARABIA
Sanaa
YEMEN
Aden
DJIBOUTI
Djibouti
Berbera
Hargeysa
SOMALIA
Kelafo
ETHIOPIA
GREAT RIFT VALLEY
Harer
Aseb
ERITREA
Asmara
Conder
Jima
ETHIOPIAN HIGHLANDS
Addis Ababa
L. Tana
Blue Nile
Wad Madani
Kassala
Atbarah
Port Sudan
NUBIAN DESERT
al-Ubayyid
Khartoum
Omdurman
Malakal
White Nile
Juba
Waw
SUDAN
CENTRAL AFRICAN REPUBLIC
Bangui
Bouar

Tropic of Cancer

OMAN

MALTA
Mediterranean Sea
MALTA
Tripoli
Misratah
Gulf of Sidra
Banghazi
al-Bayda
Tobruk
al-Jawf
LIBYA
SAHARA
LIBYAN DESERT
EGYPT
Cairo
Alexandria
Port Said
Siwah
Luxor
Aswan
L. Nasser
Nile

TUNISIA
Bizerte
Tunis
Sfax

Algiers
Annaba
Constantine
Oran
ATLAS MOUNTAINS
Oujda
Fez
Ghardaia
I-n-Salah
ALGERIA
Bechar
HAGGAR MTS.
Tamanrasset
AIR MTS.
Agadez
Zinder
NIGER
TIBESTI MTS.
Faya-Largeau
CHAD
L. Chad
N'Djamena
Maroua
Maiduguri
Sarh
Abéché
Garoua
CAMEROON
Douala
Malabo
Bouar

MOROCCO
Tangier
Rabat
Casablanca
Safi
Marrakech

WESTERN SAHARA (occ. by Morocco)
Laayoune
Nouadhibou

MAURITANIA
Nouakchott
Timbuktu
MALI
Niger
Ségou
Bamako
Kayes
SENEGAL
Dakar
Kaolack
THE GAMBIA
Banjul
GUINEA-BISSAU
Bissau
Labé
GUINEA
Kankan
Conakry
Freetown
SIERRA LEONE
Monrovia
LIBERIA
CÔTE D'IVOIRE
Yamoussoukro
Bouake
Abidjan
BURKINA FASO
Ouagadougou
Bobo-Dioulasso
GHANA
Kumasi
Accra
Sekondi-Takoradi
TOGO
Lomé
BENIN
Porto-Novo
Cotonou
NIGERIA
Niamey
Sokoto
Zaria
Kano
Abuja
Ogbomosho
Ibadan
Lagos
Enugu
Onitsha
Port Harcourt

162

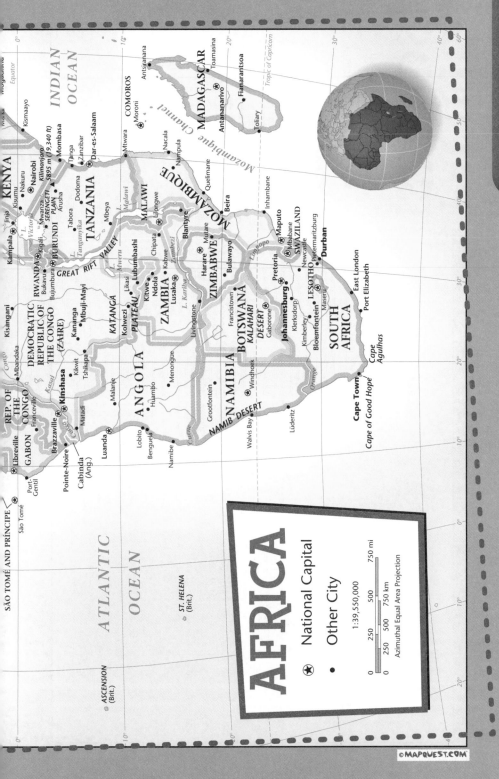

AFRICA

⊛ National Capital

• Other City

1:39,550,000

0   250   500   750 km
0   250   500   750 mi

Azimuthal Equal Area Projection

INDIAN OCEAN

ATLANTIC OCEAN

MADAGASCAR

Toamasina
Antsirañana
Antananarivo ⊛
Fianarantsoa
Toliary

COMOROS
Moroni ⊛

Mozambique Channel

MOZAMBIQUE

Mtwara
Nacala
Nampula
Quelimane
Beira
Inhambane
Maputo ⊛
Pietermaritzburg
Durban
East London
Port Elizabeth

KENYA
Mombasa
Kismaayo
Nairobi ⊛
Nakuru
Kisumu
Jinja
Kampala ⊛

TANZANIA
Dar-es-Salaam
Zanzibar
Tanga
Dodoma
Arusha
Tabora
Mbeya
Kilimanjaro
5895 m (19,340 ft)
SERENGETI PLAIN
Mwanza
L. Victoria

UGANDA

BURUNDI
Bujumbura ⊛

RWANDA
Kigali ⊛
Bukavu

L. Tanganyika

MALAWI
Lilongwe ⊛
Blantyre
L. Malawi

Chipata
GREAT RIFT VALLEY

ZAMBIA
Lusaka ⊛
Kabwe
Ndola
Kitwe
L. Kariba
Livingstone

DEMOCRATIC REPUBLIC OF THE CONGO (ZAIRE)
Kisangani
Mbuji-Mayi
Kananga
Kikwit
Tshikapa
Kinshasa ⊛
Matadi
KATANGA
PLATEAU
Lubumbashi
Likasi
Kolwezi
Mbandaka
Congo

REP. OF THE CONGO
Brazzaville ⊛
Franceville
Pointe-Noire

GABON
Libreville ⊛
Port-Gentil

SÃO TOMÉ AND PRÍNCIPE
São Tomé

ANGOLA
Luanda
Lobito
Benguela
Namibe
Huambo
Malanje
Menongue
Cabinda (Ang.)

Kasai

ZIMBABWE
Harare ⊛
Mutare
Bulawayo
Francistown
Zambezi

BOTSWANA
Gaborone ⊛
KALAHARI DESERT

NAMIBIA
Windhoek ⊛
Grootfontein
Walvis Bay
Lüderitz
NAMIB DESERT
Orange

SOUTH AFRICA
Pretoria ⊛
Johannesburg
Klerksdorp
Kimberley
Bloemfontein ⊛
Cape Town
Cape of Good Hope
Cape Agulhas
Newcastle

SWAZILAND
Mbabane ⊛

LESOTHO
Maseru ⊛

Limpopo

ASCENSION (Brit.)

ST. HELENA (Brit.)

Equator

Tropic of Capricorn

163

PACIFIC ISLANDS

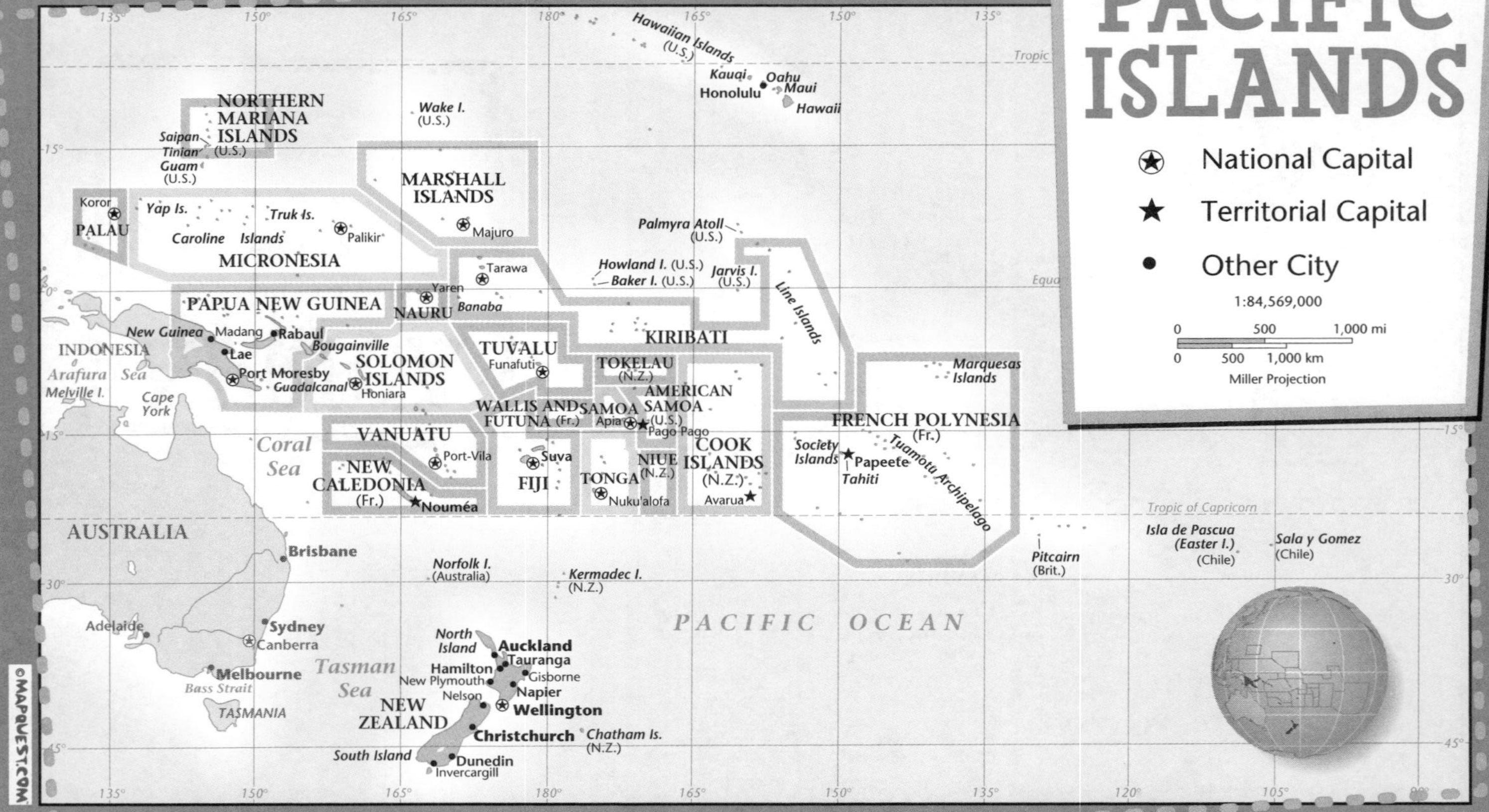

National Capital ⊛
Territorial Capital ★
Other City •

1:84,569,000

0   500   1,000 mi
0 500 1,000 km
Miller Projection

Sala y Gomez (Chile)

Isla de Pascua (Easter I.) (Chile)

Tropic of Capricorn

Pitcairn (Brit.)

FRENCH POLYNESIA (Fr.)

Marquesas Islands

Tuamotu Archipelago

Society Islands ★ Papeete Tahiti

PACIFIC OCEAN

Line Islands

Hawaiian Islands (U.S.)

Kauai • Oahu • Maui
Honolulu • Hawaii

Palmyra Atoll (U.S.)

Howland I. (U.S.)
Baker I. (U.S.)

Jarvis I. (U.S.)

KIRIBATI

TOKELAU (N.Z.)

AMERICAN SAMOA

WALLIS AND SAMOA
FUTUNA (Fr.)
Apia ★ Pago Pago (U.S.)

COOK ISLANDS (N.Z.)
Avarua ★

NIUE (N.Z.)

TONGA (N.Z.)
Nuku'alofa

Tarawa

Wake I. (U.S.)

⊛ Majuro

MARSHALL ISLANDS

Yaren NAURU Banaba

TUVALU
Funafuti

Suva
FIJI

Kermadec I. (N.Z.)

Port-Vila
VANUATU

NEW CALEDONIA (Fr.)
Nouméa

Norfolk I. (Australia)

Tasman Sea

North Island
Auckland • Tauranga
Hamilton • Gisborne
New Plymouth • Napier
Nelson Wellington ⊛
Christchurch Chatham Is. (N.Z.)
Dunedin
South Island Invercargill
NEW ZEALAND

NORTHERN MARIANA ISLANDS

Saipan Tinian (U.S.)
Guam (U.S.)

Truk Is.

Caroline Islands

MICRONESIA

Palikir ★

Yap Is.

Korror PALAU

PAPUA NEW GUINEA

Bougainville
Rabaul
Madang Lae
New Guinea
Port Moresby ⊛

SOLOMON ISLANDS
Guadalcanal Honiara

Coral Sea

Brisbane •

Sydney •
Canberra ⊛
Melbourne ⊛
TASMANIA
Bass Strait

AUSTRALIA

Adelaide •

INDONESIA

Arafura Sea

Melville I.

Cape York

Tropic

Equator

©MAPQUEST.COM

164

FLAGS of the NATIONS of the WORLD

(Afghanistan–Dominican Republic)

 AFGHANISTAN

 ALBANIA

 ALGERIA

 ANDORRA

 ANGOLA

 ANTIGUA AND BARBUDA

 ARGENTINA

 ARMENIA

 AUSTRALIA

 AUSTRIA

 AZERBAIJAN

 THE BAHAMAS

 BAHRAIN

 BANGLADESH

 BARBADOS

 BELARUS

 BELGIUM

 BELIZE

 BENIN

 BHUTAN

 BOLIVIA

 BOSNIA AND HERZEGOVINA

 BOTSWANA

 BRAZIL

 BRUNEI

 BULGARIA

 BURKINA FASO

 BURUNDI

 CAMBODIA

 CAMEROON

 CANADA

 CAPE VERDE

 CENTRAL AFRICAN REPUBLIC

 CHAD

 CHILE

 CHINA

 COLOMBIA

 COMOROS

 CONGO, DEM. REP. OF THE

 CONGO, REP. OF THE

 COSTA RICA

 CÔTE D'IVOIRE

 CROATIA

 CUBA

 CYPRUS

 CZECH REPUBLIC

 DENMARK

 DJIBOUTI

 DOMINICA

 DOMINICAN REPUBLIC

FLAGS of the NATIONS of the WORLD

(Ecuador–Lithuania)

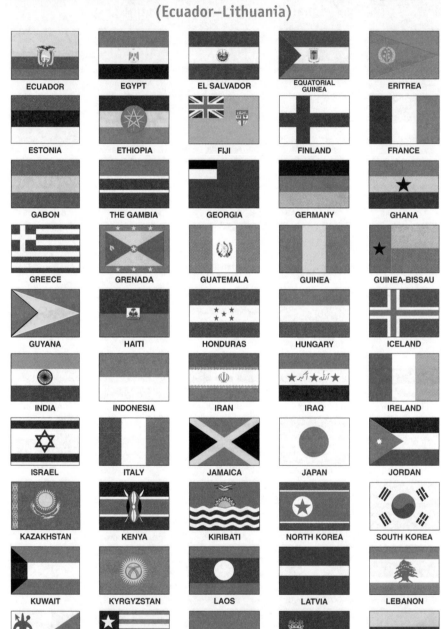

ECUADOR   EGYPT   EL SALVADOR   EQUATORIAL GUINEA   ERITREA

ESTONIA   ETHIOPIA   FIJI   FINLAND   FRANCE

GABON   THE GAMBIA   GEORGIA   GERMANY   GHANA

GREECE   GRENADA   GUATEMALA   GUINEA   GUINEA-BISSAU

GUYANA   HAITI   HONDURAS   HUNGARY   ICELAND

INDIA   INDONESIA   IRAN   IRAQ   IRELAND

ISRAEL   ITALY   JAMAICA   JAPAN   JORDAN

KAZAKHSTAN   KENYA   KIRIBATI   NORTH KOREA   SOUTH KOREA

KUWAIT   KYRGYZSTAN   LAOS   LATVIA   LEBANON

LESOTHO   LIBERIA   LIBYA   LIECHTENSTEIN   LITHUANIA

FLAGS of the NATIONS of the WORLD
(Luxembourg–Senegal)

 LUXEMBOURG

 MACEDONIA

 MADAGASCAR

 MALAWI

 MALAYSIA

 MALDIVES

 MALI

 MALTA

 MARSHALL ISLANDS

 MAURITANIA

 MAURITIUS

 MEXICO

 MICRONESIA

 MOLDOVA

 MONACO

 MONGOLIA

 MOROCCO

 MOZAMBIQUE

 MYANMAR (BURMA)

 NAMIBIA

 NAURU

 NEPAL

 NETHERLANDS

 NEW ZEALAND

 NICARAGUA

 NIGER

 NIGERIA

 NORWAY

 OMAN

 PAKISTAN

 PALAU

 PANAMA

 PAPUA NEW GUINEA

 PARAGUAY

 PERU

 PHILIPPINES

 POLAND

 PORTUGAL

 QATAR

 ROMANIA

 RUSSIA

 RWANDA

 ST. KITTS AND NEVIS

 ST. LUCIA

 ST. VINCENT AND THE GRENADINES

 SAMOA

 SAN MARINO

 SÃO TOMÉ AND PRÍNCIPE

 SAUDI ARABIA

 SENEGAL

167

FLAGS of the NATIONS of the WORLD
(Seychelles–Zimbabwe)

 SEYCHELLES

 SIERRA LEONE

 SINGAPORE

 SLOVAKIA

 SLOVENIA

 SOLOMON ISLANDS

 SOMALIA

 SOUTH AFRICA

 SPAIN

 SRI LANKA

 SUDAN

 SURINAME

 SWAZILAND

 SWEDEN

 SWITZERLAND

 SYRIA

 TAIWAN

 TAJIKISTAN

 TANZANIA

 THAILAND

 TOGO

 TONGA

 TRINIDAD AND TOBAGO

 TUNISIA

 TURKEY

 TURKMENISTAN

 TUVALU

 UGANDA

 UKRAINE

 UNITED ARAB EMIRATES

 UNITED KINGDOM (GREAT BRITAIN)

 UNITED STATES

 URUGUAY

 UZBEKISTAN

 VANUATU

 VATICAN CITY

 VENEZUELA

 VIETNAM

 YEMEN

 YUGOSLAVIA

 ZAMBIA

 ZIMBABWE

NUMBERS

How many children are born if a mother has septuplets? *You can find the answer on page 170.*

NUMERALS IN ANCIENT CIVILIZATION

People have been counting since the earliest of times. This is what some early numerals looked like.

Modern	1	2	3	4	5	6	7	8	9	10	20	50	100
Egyptian	I	II	III	IIII	|||	|||	||||	||||	||||	∩	∩∩	∩∩∩∩∩	૭
Babylonian	𐤉	𐤉𐤉	𐤉𐤉𐤉	𐤉𐤉	𐤉𐤉𐤉	𐤉𐤉𐤉	𐤉𐤉𐤉	𐤉𐤉𐤉	𐤉𐤉𐤉	<	≪	≪≪	≪<
Greek	A	B	Γ	Δ	E	F	Z	H	θ	I	K	N	P
Mayan	•	••	•••	••••	—	—·	—··	—···	—····	═	⊙	≖	👁
Chinese	一	二	三	四	五	六	七	八	九	十	二十	五十	百
Hindu	1	੨	੩	੪	੫	੬	੭	੮	੯	10	੨0	੪0	100
Arabic	1	٢	٣	٤	٥	٦	٧	٨	٩	1o	2o	6o	100

ROMAN NUMERALS

Roman numerals are still used today. The symbols used for different numbers are the letters I (1), V (5), X (10), L (50), C (100), D (500), and M (1,000). If one Roman numeral is followed by a larger one, the first is subtracted from the second. For example, IV means 5 − 1 = 4. Think of it as "one less than five." On the other hand, if one Roman numeral is followed by another that is equal or smaller, add them together. Thus, XII means 10 + 1 + 1 = 12. Can you put your age in Roman numerals?

1	I	14	XIV	90	XC
2	II	15	XV	100	C
3	III	16	XVI	200	CC
4	IV	17	XVII	300	CCC
5	V	18	XVIII	400	CD
6	VI	19	XIX	500	D
7	VII	20	XX	600	DC
8	VIII	30	XXX	700	DCC
9	IX	40	XL	800	DCCC
10	X	50	L	900	CM
11	XI	60	LX	1,000	M
12	XII	70	LXX	2,000	MM
13	XIII	80	LXXX	3,000	MMM

▼ *The Colosseum*

Gladiators fought in Rome's Colosseum until A.D. 404. Can you put that year into Roman numerals?
Answers are on pages 317–320.

169

The PREFIX Tells the Number

After each number here are one or more prefixes used to form words that include that number. Knowing what the prefix stands for will help you understand the meaning of the word. For example, a monorail has one track instead of two. A pentagon has five sides. A centipede is said to have 100 legs (though it may have more or fewer).

1	uni-, mon-, mono-	unicycle, unicorn, monarch, monotone
2	bi-	bicycle, binary, binoculars, bifocals
3	tri-	tricycle, triangle, trilogy, trio
4	quadr-, tetr-	quadrangle, quadruplet, tetrahedron
5	pent-, quint-	pentagon, pentathlon, quintuplet
6	hex-, sext-	hexagon, sextuplet, sextet
7	hept-, sept-	heptathlon, septuplet
8	oct-	octave, octet, octopus, octagon
9	non-	nonagon, nonet
10	dec-	decade, decibel, decimal
100	cent-	centipede, century
1000	kilo-	kilogram, kilometer, kilowatt
million	mega-	megabyte, megahertz
billion	giga-	gigabyte, gigawatt

◄ A centipede

READING AND WRITING BIG NUMBERS

Below are the words for some numbers, plus the number of zeros needed when each number is written out.

ten	1 zero	10
hundred	2 zeros	100
thousand	3 zeros	1,000
ten thousand	4 zeros	10,000
hundred thousand	5 zeros	100,000
million	6 zeros	1,000,000
ten million	7 zeros	10,000,000
hundred million	8 zeros	100,000,000
billion	9 zeros	1,000,000,000
trillion	12 zeros	1,000,000,000,000
quadrillion	15 zeros	1,000,000,000,000,000
quintillion	18 zeros	1,000,000,000,000,000,000
sextillion	21 zeros	1,000,000,000,000,000,000,000
septillion	24 zeros	1,000,000,000,000,000,000,000,000

Can you write the number 7 googols? (1 googol is 1 followed by 100 zeros)

How Many SiDES and FACES Do They Have?

When a figure is flat (two-dimensional), it is a **plane** figure. When a figure takes up space (three-dimensional), it is a **solid figure**. The flat surface of a solid figure is called a **face**. Plane and solid figures come in many different shapes.

TWO-DIMENSIONAL

square   circle   triangle

THREE-DIMENSIONAL

cube   sphere   tetrahedron (pyramid)

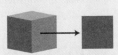

The flat surface of a cube is a square.

WHAT ARE POLYGONS?

A polygon is a two-dimensional figure with three or more straight sides (called line segments). A square is a polygon. Polygons have different numbers of sides—and each has a different name. If the sides are all the same length and all the angles between the sides are equal, the polygon is called regular. If the sides are of different lengths or the angles are not equal, the polygon is called irregular. Below are some regular and irregular polygons.

NAME & NUMBER OF SiDES	REGULAR	IRREGULAR
triangle — 3		
quadrilateral or tetragon — 4		
pentagon — 5		
hexagon — 6		
heptagon — 7		
octagon — 8		
nonagon — 9		
decagon — 10		

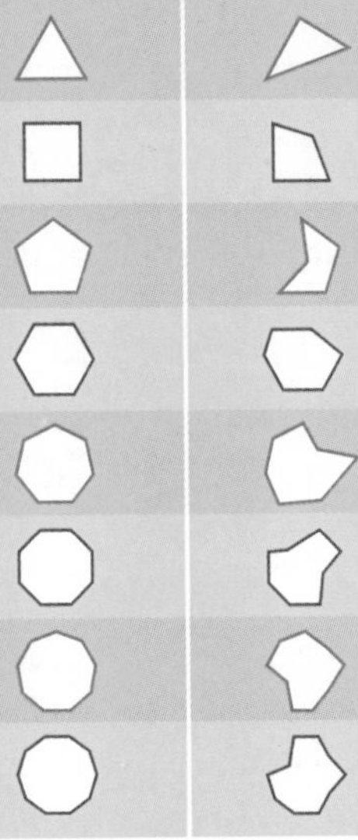

WHAT ARE POLYHEDRONS?

A polyhedron is a three-dimensional figure with four or more faces. Each face on a polyhedron is a polygon. Below are some polyhedrons with many faces.

tetrahedron 4 faces   hexahedron 6 faces   octahedron 8 faces   dodecahedron 12 faces   icosahedron 20 faces

◀ *Great Pyramid of Khefren*

EVEN vs ODD   TRY THIS GAME WITH A FRIEND.

On the count of 3 each player shows a number using the fingers of one hand. Multiply the numbers. If the answer is an odd number, your friend wins. If the answer is even, you win. How can you make sure you win every time?

From Letters to Numbers

Each of these phrases contains letters that are used as Roman numerals. Using the chart on page 169 if you need to, pick out the individual letters that are Roman numerals and add them up. For example, the total for "I LIKE TO READ" would be 552 (I=1, L=50, and D=500).

❶ **MIX MILK WITH CHOCOLATE.**
❷ **MOVE AND CLIMB.**
❸ **A LIVE DIVER.**

CENTS AND SHAPES

Arrange 10 pennies as shown.

① ② ③ ④
⑤ ⑥ ⑦ ⑧
⑨ ⑩

❶ Make them into a rectangle, moving pennies one space at a time: up, down, forwards, backwards, or diagonally. Can you do it in two moves, moving only two pennies?

❷ How many moves does it take to change them from the original pattern into a triangle with four pennies on each side?

What Am I?

► I'm the same forwards and backwards.
► My 2 parts equal 2.
► You can't divide me evenly without using fractions or decimals.

LAUGH

Q Why didn't the two 4's want any dinner?

A Because they already 8.

PLANTS

What happens to perennials in the fall? You can find the answer on page 174.

WHAT MAKES A PLANT A PLANT?

Plants were the first living things on Earth. The first plants, called algae, appeared around three billion years ago and grew in or near water. About 300 or 400 million years ago, the first land plants appeared. These were ferns, club mosses, and horsetails. After these came plants that had cones (conifers) and trees that were ancestors of the palm trees we see today.

Flowers, grass, weeds, oak trees, palm trees, and poison ivy are all plants. This means:

Bristlecone pine tree ▶

▶ *They can create their own food from air, sunlight, and water in a process called photosynthesis.*

▶ *They are rooted in one place—don't move around.*

▶ *Their cells contain cellulose, a substance that keeps them standing upright.*

All plants need some air, water, light, and warmth. But they can grow in different kinds of conditions. A cactus plant needs lots of heat and light but not much water, while a fir tree will grow in a northern forest where it is cold much of the year and light is limited.

Record Breakers

WORLD'S OLDEST LIVING PLANTS: Bristlecone pine trees in California (4,900 years old)

WORLD'S TALLEST PLANTS: The tallest tree ever measured was a eucalyptus tree in Victoria, Australia, measuring 435 feet in 1872. The tallest tree now standing is a giant sequoia tree in Redwood National Park, California, standing at 367 feet.

All About... GROWING GREAT GREENS

You can grow many kinds of plants in your house. Before you start, here are some basic rules for green thumbs.

1. Give plants room to grow.

2. Plants grow best in temperatures between 55 and 75 degrees Fahrenheit.

3. Most plants love sunlight and could use seven to twelve hours of direct light every day.

4. Roots need just the right amount of water—not too much and never too little. Some plants need to be watered from the bottom.

5. Give plants room to breathe through their roots and leaves.

6. Use soil that has nutrients plants like, such as nitrogen, phosphorus, and potassium.

7. Plants need time to grow. Be patient and caring.

PLANT TALK

agronomy The growing of plants for food.

algae single-celled plants that grow in or near water.

annual A plant that grows, flowers, and dies in one year. Most annuals produce seeds that can be planted the following spring.

biennial A plant that takes two years to mature. The first year the plant produces a stem and leaves, and the second year it produces flowers and seeds and then dies.

chlorophyll the green chemical that allows plants to make energy from the sun, and that makes plants green.

compost a mixture of decaying plants, food, and waste that is added to plants to help them grow.

conifer a tree that carries its seeds in cones, like pine, spruce, or cedar.

deciduous A tree that loses its leaves in autumn and gets new ones in the spring.

ecology the study of relationships between plants and the environment.

ecological niche the particular role that a plant plays within an environment.

evergreen A tree that keeps its leaves or needles all year long.

fertilizer A natural or chemical substance applied to the soil to help plants grow bigger and faster.

herb A plant used for flavoring or seasoning, for its scent, or as medicine. Mint, lavender, palmetto, and rosemary are all herbs.

hybrid A plant that has been scientifically combined with another plant or has been changed to make it more beautiful, larger, stronger, or better in some other way. Many roses are hybrids.

irrigation a method of supplying water to land that doesn't otherwise get enough.

legume a plant that produces a seed in a pod, like peas and beans.

mulch A covering of bark, compost (decomposed garbage), hay, or other substance used to conserve water and control weeds. Mulch can also provide nutrients for plants and keep plants warm in winter.

native A plant that has always grown in a certain place, rather than being brought there from somewhere else. Corn is native to North America.

osmosis the process by which plants absorb water through leaves and roots.

perennial A plant that stops growing and may look dead in the fall, but comes back year after year.

photosynthesis The process that allows plants to make their own food from air, sunlight, and water.

terrarium A glass box containing small plants and animals, such as moss, ferns, lizards, and turtles.

variegated having marks or patches with different colors.

wildflower A flowering plant that grows on its own in the wild, rather than being planted by a person.

LAUGH

Q What kind of vegetable is dangerous to have on a ship?

A A LEEK.

Where Do Plants Grow?

Plants grow nearly everywhere except near the South and North Poles.

FORESTS

Where Evergreens Grow. Forests cover about one-third of Earth's land surface. Evergreens, such as pines, hemlocks, firs, and spruces, grow in the cool forest regions farthest from the equator. These trees are called **conifers** because they produce cones.

Temperate Forests. Temperate forests have warm, rainy summers and cold, snowy winters. Here **deciduous trees** (which lose their leaves in the fall and grow new ones in the spring) join the evergreens. Temperate forests are home to maple, oak, beech, and poplar trees, and to wildflowers and shrubs. These forests are found in eastern United States, southeastern Canada, northern Europe and Asia, and southern Australia.

Tropical Rain Forests. Still closer to the equator are the tropical rain forests, home to the greatest variety of plants on Earth. The temperature never falls below freezing except on the mountain slopes. About 60 to 100 inches of rain fall each year. Tropical trees stay green all year. They grow close together, shading the ground. There are several layers of trees. The top, **emergent layer** has trees that can reach 200 feet in height. The **canopy,** which gets lots of sun, comes next, followed by the **understory.** The **forest floor,** covered with roots, gets little sun, and many plants cannot grow there.

Tropical rain forests are found mainly in Central America, South America, Asia, and Africa. They once covered more than 8 million square miles. Today, because of destruction by humans, fewer than 3.4 million square miles remain. More than half the plant and animal species in the world live there. Foods such as bananas and pineapples first grew there. Woods such as mahogany and teak also come from rain forests. Many kinds of plants there are used to make medicines.

When rain forests are burned, carbon dioxide is released into the air. This adds to the greenhouse effect (see page 75). As forests are destroyed, the precious soil is easily washed away by the heavy rains.

A rain forest ▼

EMERGENT LAYER

CANOPY

UNDERSTORY

FOREST FLOOR

TUNDRA REGION

In the northernmost regions of North America, Europe, and Asia surrounding the Arctic Ocean are plains called the **tundra.** The temperature rarely rises above 45 degrees Fahrenheit, and it is too cold for trees to grow there. Most tundra plants are mosses and lichens that hug the ground for warmth. A few wildflowers and small shrubs also grow where the soil thaws for about two months of the year. This kind of climate and plant life also exists on top of the highest mountains (the Himalayas, Alps, Andes, Rockies), where small Alpine flowers also grow.

What Is the Tree Line? On mountains in the north (such as the Rockies) and in the far south (such as the Andes), there is an altitude above which trees will not grow. This is the **tree line** or **timberline.** Above the tree line, you can see low shrubs and small plants, like Alpine flowers.

DESERTS

▼ Arizona desert

The driest areas of the world are the **deserts.** They can be hot or cold, but they also contain an amazing number of plants. Cactuses and sagebrush are native to dry regions of North and South America. The deserts of Africa and Asia contain plants called euphorbias. Dates have grown in the deserts of the Middle East and North Africa for thousands of years. In the southwestern United States and northern Mexico, there are many types of cactuses, including prickly pear, barrel, and saguaro.

GRASSLAND

▼ Grassland in Alberta, Canada

The areas of the world that are too dry to have green forests, but not dry enough to be deserts, are called **grasslands.** The most common plants found there are grasses. Cooler grasslands are found in the Great Plains of the United States and Canada, in the steppes of Europe and Asia, and in the pampas of Argentina. The drier grasslands are used for grazing cattle and sheep. In the **prairies,** where there is a little more rain, important grains, such as wheat, rye, oats, and barley are grown. The warmer grasslands, called **savannas,** are found in central and southern Africa, Venezuela, southern Brazil, and Australia. Most savannas have moist summers and cool, dry winters.

PLANTS THAT EAT BUGS

Bugs sometimes eat plants. But did you know that some plants trap insects and eat them? These are "carnivorous plants." The pitcher plant, Venus's-flytrap, and sundew are three examples. Most carnivorous plants live in poor soils, where they don't get enough nourishment. They digest their prey very slowly over a long period of time.

POPULATION

What country in the world has fewer than 1,000 people? *You can find the answer below.*

WHERE DO PEOPLE LIVE?

Our planet is growing—not in size, but in population. In 1999, the number of people on Earth hit six billion. Back in 1959, Earth had five billion people. By 2050, the world population is expected to grow to more than nine billion people. Much of that growth will be in the world's poorest nations. (Despite the worldwide population growth, some nations are actually losing population, such as Russia and Ukraine.)

LARGEST CITIES
(Most People)

Here are the ten cities in the world that have the most people, as of 1999. Numbers include people from the whole built-up area around each city (the metropolitan area).

CITY, COUNTRY	POPULATION
Tokyo, Japan	26,444,000
Mexico City, Mexico	18,131,000
Mumbai (Bombay), India	18,066,000
São Paulo, Brazil	17,755,000
New York City, U.S.	16,640,000
Lagos, Nigeria	13,427,000
Los Angeles, U.S.	13,140,000
Kolkata (Calcutta), India	12,918,000
Shanghai, China	12,887,000
Buenos Aires, Argentina	12,560,000

LARGEST COUNTRIES
(Most People, 2000)

POPULATION	COUNTRY
1,261,832,000	China
1,014,004,000	India
281,421,900	United States
224,784,000	Indonesia
172,860,000	Brazil
146,001,000	Russia
141,554,000	Pakistan
129,194,000	Bangladesh
126,550,000	Japan
123,338,000	Nigeria
100,350,000	Mexico
82,797,000	Germany
81,160,000	Philippines
78,774,000	Vietnam
68,360,000	Egypt
65,667,000	Turkey
65,620,000	Iran
64,117,000	Ethiopia
61,231,000	Thailand
59,508,000	Great Britain
59,330,000	France
57,634,000	Italy
51,965,000	Congo Republic
49,153,000	Ukraine
47,471,000	South Korea

SMALLEST COUNTRIES
(Fewest People, 2000)

POPULATION	COUNTRY
860	Vatican City
10,838	Tuvalu
11,845	Nauru
18,766	Palau
26,937	San Marino
31,693	Monaco
32,204	Liechtenstein

WHERE IS EVERYBODY?

► According to UN estimates, the world population reached six billion on October 12, 1999.

► India's population passed the one billion mark in 1999.

Did You KNOW?

POPULATION OF THE UNITED STATES

Total U.S. Population on April 1, 2000, based on the U.S. Census: 281,421,906.

POPULATION OF THE STATES FROM CENSUS 2000

RANK & STATE NAME	POPULATION
❶ California	33,871,648
② Texas	20,851,820
❸ New York	18,976,457
④ Florida	15,982,378
❺ Illinois	12,419,293
⑥ Pennsylvania	12,281,054
❼ Ohio	11,353,140
⑧ Michigan	9,938,444
❾ New Jersey	8,414,350
⑩ Georgia	8,186,453
⓫ North Carolina	8,049,313
⑫ Virginia	7,078,515
⓭ Massachusetts	6,349,097
⑭ Indiana	6,080,485
⓯ Washington	5,894,121
⑯ Tennessee	5,689,283
⓱ Missouri	5,595,211
⑱ Wisconsin	5,363,675
⓳ Maryland	5,296,486
⑳ Arizona	5,130,632
㉑ Minnesota	4,919,479
㉒ Louisiana	4,468,976
㉓ Alabama	4,447,100
㉔ Colorado	4,301,261
㉕ Kentucky	4,041,769
㉖ South Carolina	4,012,012
㉗ Oklahoma	3,450,654
㉘ Oregon	3,421,399
㉙ Connecticut	3,405,565
㉚ Iowa	2,926,324
㉛ Mississippi	2,844,658
㉜ Kansas	2,688,418
㉝ Arkansas	2,673,400
㉞ Utah	2,233,169
㉟ Nevada	1,998,257
㊱ New Mexico	1,819,046
㊲ West Virginia	1,808,344
㊳ Nebraska	1,711,263
㊴ Idaho	1,293,953
㊵ Maine	1,274,923
㊶ New Hampshire	1,235.786
㊷ Hawaii	1,211,537
㊸ Rhode Island	1,048,319
㊹ Montana	902,195
㊺ Delaware	783,600
㊻ South Dakota	754,844
㊼ North Dakota	642,200
㊽ Alaska	626,932
㊾ Vermont	608,827
㊿ District of Columbia	572,059
(51) Wyoming	493,782

LARGEST CITIES IN THE UNITED STATES

Cities grow and shrink in population. At right is a list of the largest cities in the United States in 2000 compared with their populations in 1950. Which seven cities increased in population? Which three decreased?

RANK & CITY	2000	1950
❶ New York, NY	8,008,278	7,891,957
❷ Los Angeles, CA	3,694,820	1,970,358
❸ Chicago, IL	2,896,016	3,620,962
❹ Houston, TX	1,953,631	596,163
❺ Philadelphia, PA	1,517,550	2,071,605
❻ Phoenix, AZ	1,321,045	106,818
❼ San Diego, CA	1,223,400	334,387
❽ Dallas, TX	1,188,580	434,462
❾ San Antonio, TX	1,144,646	408,442
❿ Detroit, MI	951,270	1,849,568

TAKING THE CENSUS: EVERYONE COUNTS

Were you counted during Census 2000? The United States takes a census every 10 years. It tries to count everyone. But in every census, some people get missed. In Census 2000, census-takers tried to track down and count people who did not send back forms, so that this census would be as accurate as possible. Census officials believe that this census was one of the most accurate ever, but that it missed about 1 out of 100 people.

WHY IS THE CENSUS NEEDED?

▶ The population of a state determines how many representatives it has in the U.S. House.

▶ Census information helps the federal government in Washington, D.C., decide which public services must be provided and where.

▶ The census provides a picture of the people. Where do they live? How old are they? What do they do? How much money do they earn? How many children do they have? What is their background?

WHEN WAS THE FIRST CENSUS TAKEN? It was in 1790 just after the American

Revolution. That year census-takers counted 3,929,200 people lived in what was then the United States. Most of them lived on farms or in small towns. (Today, three out of every four Americans live in or near cities.)

NEWS FROM CENSUS 2000

▶ Do you like being in the middle of things? Then maybe you should move to the area around Edgar Springs, Missouri. The U.S. Census Bureau says that community is the center of our nation's population. Edgar Springs is a rural community. It has 190 people, according to Census 2000. Since 1790, the population center of the U.S. moved first in a westerly direction, then southerly. The first population center was near Chestertown, Maryland. That's more than 1,000 miles from the current center!

▶ The United States population grew by 32.7 million people between 1990 and 2000. That's the largest 10-year population increase in U.S. history. All 50 states have more people today than they did 10 years ago, the first time that happened in the 20th century. Western states added 10.4 million residents in the 1990s. That made the West the fastest-growing region. Nevada has bragging rights as the fastest-growing state.

WHO ARE WE? Census 2000 was the first time a census

allowed Americans to identify themselves as being of more than one race. Almost seven million people made that choice. That is about two percent of the total population of the United States.

This list shows the percentage of Americans that felt they belonged in each of the racial groups listed here.

▶ Hispanics are the fastest-growing minority in the United States.

▶ One out of every 10 Americans was born in another country. This is the first time since the 1930s that this has been true.

▶ Thanks to the Child Citizenship Act of 2000, all children adopted overseas by Americans will automatically become U.S. citizens. Every year, Americans adopt about 20,000 children from other nations.

RACE	PERCENT OF POPULATION
One race	97.6%
White	75.1%
Black or African American	12.3%
American Indian and Alaska Native	0.9%
Asian	3.6%
Native Hawaiian and Other Pacific Islander	0.1%
Some other race	5.5%
Two or more races	2.4%
Hispanic or Latino	12.5%
Not Hispanic or Latino	87.5%

(Hispanics may be of any race.)

COUNTING THE FIRST AMERICANS

WHERE DID AMERICAN INDIANS COME FROM? American Indians, also called Native Americans, lived in North and South America long before the first European explorers arrived. Their ancestors are thought to have arrived more than 20,000 years ago, probably from Northeast Asia. American Indians are not one people, but many different peoples, each with their own traditions.

HOW MANY AMERICAN INDIANS WERE HERE IN THE 1400s? About 850,000 Native Americans lived in what is now the United States before Columbus arrived.

HOW MANY AMERICAN INDIANS ARE IN THE U.S. NOW? During the 17th, 18th, and 19th centuries, disease and wars with white settlers and soldiers caused the deaths of thousands of American Indians. By 1910 there were only about 220,000 left in the United States. Since then, the American Indian population has increased dramatically. According to Census 2000, the total number of Native Americans was about 2.5 million.

WHEN DID AMERICAN INDIANS BECOME U.S. CITIZENS? In 1924, the U.S. Congress approved a law giving citizenship to all Native Americans.

WHERE DO NATIVE AMERICANS LIVE?

Below are the states with the largest Native American populations according to Census 2000. The states are numbered in the map below.*

❶	California	333,346	❾	New York	82,461
❷	Oklahoma	273,230	❿	South Dakota	62,283
❸	Arizona	255,879	⓫	Michigan	58,479
❹	New Mexico	173,483	⓬	Montana	56,068
❺	Texas	118,362	⓭	Minnesota	54,967
❻	North Carolina	99,551	⓮	Florida	53,541
❼	Alaska	98,043	⓯	Wisconsin	47,228
❽	Washington	93,301	⓰	Oregon	45,211

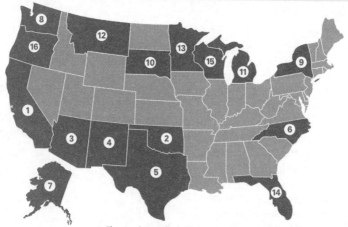

* Figures do not include people who said they were of more than one race.

THE MANY FACES OF AMERICA:
IMMIGRATION

You have probably heard it said that America is a nation of immigrants. Many Americans are descended from Europeans, Africans, or Asians.

COMING TO AMERICA

Millions of people have immigrated to the United States from all over the world—more than 40 million since 1820. Today the U.S. is experiencing a period of high immigration. Immigrants chose to come for various reasons, such as to live in freedom, to practice their religion freely, to escape poverty or oppression, and to make better lives for themselves and their children. But some people were brought here by force. In the 1600s, the British began shipping Africans to the American colonies to work as slaves. One out of every three people living in the southern colonies in the 1700s was an African slave.

WHAT COUNTRIES DO IMMIGRANTS COME FROM?

Immigrants come to the United States from many countries. Below are some of the countries immigrants came from in 1998. The name of the country is followed by the number of immigrants. In 1998, immigration from all countries to the United States totaled 660,477.

Mexico	131,575
China	36,884
India	36,482
Philippines	34,466
Dominican Republic	20,387
Vietnam	17,649
Cuba	17,375
Jamaica	15,146
El Salvador	14,590
North and South Korea	14,268
Haiti	13,449
Pakistan	13,094
Colombia	11,836
Russia	11,529
Canada	10,190
Peru	10,154

Where Do Immigrants Settle?

State	Number
California	170,126
New York	96,559
Florida	59,965
Texas	44,428
New Jersey	35,091
Illinois	33,163

The bar chart shows the states that received the highest number of immigrants in 1998.

More than two-thirds of the immigrants from Mexico went to live in California or Texas, while over half of the immigrants from China went to two states: California and New York. About 85 percent of the immigrants from Cuba went to live in Florida.

181

Becoming an AMERICAN CITIZEN

When a foreign-born person becomes a citizen of the United States, we say the person has become naturalized. To apply for American citizenship, a person:

PASSPORT

United States
of America

▶ Must be at least 18 years old.
▶ Must have lived legally in the United States for at least five years.
▶ Must be able to understand English if under the age of 55.
▶ Must be of good moral character.
▶ Must show knowledge of the history and form of government of the United States.

A CITIZENSHIP TEST

When immigrants wanting to be United States citizens are interviewed, they may be asked any of 100 questions. Here are some of them. How many can you answer correctly?

1. How many stars are there on our flag?

2. What do the stars on the flag mean?

3. Who was the first president of the United States?

4. How many Supreme Court justices are there?

5. Who selects the Supreme Court justices?

6. What are the three branches of our government?

7. How many senators are there in Congress?

8. For how long do we elect each senator?

9. What is the national anthem of the United States?

10. Who becomes president of the United States if the president and the vice president should be unable to serve?

Answers are on pages 317-320.

THE STATUE OF LIBERTY

Many of the immigrants who crossed the Atlantic Ocean and steamed into New York Harbor passed by the Statue of Liberty. Set on her own island, the "Lady With the Lamp" was given to the United States by France and has served as a welcome to Americans-to-be since she was erected in 1886. In 1903, a poem by the U.S. poet Emma Lazarus was inscribed at the base of the statue. Two of its lines read: "Give me your tired, your poor, your huddled masses yearning to breathe free...."

PRIZES & CONTESTS

What is surprising about the finalists of the 2000 Spelling and Geography bees? *You can find the answer on page 186.*

NOBEL PRIZES

Nelson Mandela

The **Nobel Prizes** are named after Alfred B. Nobel (1833–1896), a Swedish scientist who invented dynamite, and left money to be given every year to people who have helped humankind. Prizes are also given for medicine-physiology, literature, economics, and peace.

The **Nobel Peace Prize** goes to people who the judges think did the most during the past year to help achieve peace. In 2000, the prize went to Kim Dae Jung for supporting democracy and human rights in South Korea and in East Asia. His work toward peace and reconciliation with North Korea was also honored.

Past winners of the Nobel Peace Prize include:

1994 Yasir Arafat, Palestinian leader; **Shimon Peres**, foreign minister of Israel; **Yitzhak Rabin**, prime minister of Israel

1993 Nelson Mandela, leader of South African blacks; **Frederik Willem de Klerk**, president of South Africa

1989 The 14th Dalai Lama (Tenzin Gyatso), Tibet

1986 Elie Wiesel, U.S. holocaust survivor and author

1979 Mother Teresa, India, leader of the Order of the Missionaries of Charity, which helps care for the sick and dying

1978 Anwar al-Sadat, president of Egypt; **Menachem Begin**, prime minister of Israel

1973 Henry Kissinger, U.S. secretary of state; **Le Duc Tho**, of North Vietnam (declined the prize)

1964 Martin Luther King Jr., leader of the Southern Christian Leadership Conference

1952 Albert Schweitzer, missionary, surgeon

1906 Theodore Roosevelt, president of the United States

◀ *The Dalai Lama*

183

Marie Curie

Other winners of Nobel Prizes have included:

Toni Morrison, *1993 Nobel Prize in Literature* Born in Lorain, Ohio, in 1931, Toni Morrison is known for writing both fiction and nonfiction on African-American themes. Her books include *Beloved, The Song of Solomon,* and *Tar Baby.*

Francis Crick, James Watson, and Maurice Wilkins, *1962 Nobel Prize in Medicine* These scientists finally won a Nobel Prize in 1962, for discovering the double helix structure of DNA. They made the discovery in 1953.

Albert Einstein, *1921 Nobel Prize in Physics* Albert Einstein was born in Germany in 1879 and later immigrated to the United States. He won the Nobel Prize *not* for his famous theory of relativity, but for his 1905 work on the photoelectric effect.

Marie Curie, *1903 Nobel Prize in Physics, 1911 Nobel Prize in Chemistry* Madame Curie was the first woman to win a Nobel Prize. Born in Poland in 1867, she won the prize in physics with her husband, Pierre, and another scientist, Antoine Henri Becquerel. They studied the source of radiation in uranium ore. She received the Nobel Prize for Chemistry in 1911 for isolating and studying radium's chemical properties. She died in 1934 from a disorder caused by being exposed to too much radiation.

THE MEDAL OF HONOR

The Medal of Honor is given by the United States government for bravery in war against an enemy. The first medals were awarded in 1863. Since that time, nearly 3,400 people have received the award.

In 2000, Medals of Honor were awarded to 21 World War II soldiers, all Asian-Americans, for "heroic actions."

PULITZER PRIZES

The Pulitzer Prizes are named after Joseph Pulitzer (1847–1911), a journalist and publisher, who gave the money to set them up. The prizes are given yearly in the United States for journalism, drama, literature, and music.

DID YOU KNOW? *The poet Robert Frost won 4 Pulitzer Prizes, in 1924, 1931, 1937, and 1943.*

SPINGARN MEDAL

The Spingarn Medal was set up in 1914 by Joel Elias Spingarn, leader of the National Association for the Advancement of Colored People (NAACP). It is awarded every year by the NAACP for achievement by a black American. Here are some winners:

2001: Vernon E. Jordan Jr.
2000: Oprah Winfrey
1999: Publisher Earl Graves
1998: Civil rights activist
Myrlie Evers-Williams
1994: Writer and poet Maya Angelou
1991: General Colin Powell
1985: Actor Bill Cosby
1979: Civil rights activist Rosa Parks
1975: Baseball player Hank Aaron
1957: Martin Luther King Jr.

YOUR TURN

Suppose you were giving out your own prize for music. Can you think of three singers or groups who would be tops on your list?

1 _____

2 _____

3 _____

ENTERTAINMENT AWARDS

If you are interested in the movies, you probably know that an Oscar is a golden statuette that is awarded for the year's best actor, best actress, best movies, and so on. The Oscar ceremonies are watched on TV by millions of people all over the world. Among other awards given every year for the best in entertainment are the Grammys and the MTV Video Music Awards.

GRAMMY AWARDS

Grammys are given out each year by the National Academy of Recording Arts and Sciences. Some of the winners for 2000 were:

Record and Song of the Year: "Beautiful Day," U2

Album of the Year: *Two Against Nature*, Steely Dan

New Artist: Shelby Lynne

Rock Duo or Group: U2

Rock Album: *There Is Nothing Left to Lose*, Foo Fighters

Rock Song: "With Arms Wide Open," written by Scott Stapp and Mark Tremonti (of Creed)

Pop Vocal Album: *Two Against Nature*, Steely Dan

Rhythm and Blues Song: "Say My Name," written by Destiny's Child and others

Rap Soloist: Eminem

Rap Album: *Voodoo*, D'Angelo

Country Album: *Breathe*, Faith Hill

Spoken Word Album for Children: *Harry Potter and the Goblet of Fire*, Jim Dale

Film or TV Song: "When She Loved Me," from *Toy Story 2*

ACADEMY AWARDS

The Oscars are awarded every year by the Academy of Motion Picture Arts and Sciences for the best in movies. Here are some of the films and people that won Oscars for 2000.

Best Picture: *Gladiator*

Best Actor: Russell Crowe in *Gladiator*

Best Actress: Julia Roberts in *Erin Brockovich*

Best Supporting Actor: Benicio Del Toro in *Traffic*

Best Supporting Actress: Marcia Gay Harden in *Pollock*

Best Director: Steven Soderbergh for *Traffic*

Best Original Screenplay: Cameron Crowe for *Almost Famous*

MTV VIDEO MUSIC AWARDS

The MTV Video Music Awards are presented each year in a variety of music video categories. Here are some winners for 2000:

Best New Artist: Macy Gray, "I Try" ▶

Best Male Video: Eminem, "The Real Slim Shady"

Best Female Video: Aaliyah, "Try Again"

Best Group Video: Blink 182, "All the Small Things"

Best Pop Video: 'N Sync, "Bye, Bye, Bye"

CONTESTS

If you have a special talent or interest and you like to compete, why not enter a contest? Here are a few examples:

How do you spell WINNER?

Twelve-year-old George Thampy from Maryland Heights, Missouri, won the 2000 National Spelling Bee. If you're a good speller, maybe you could follow in his footsteps. Newspapers across the country run local spelling bees for kids ages 15 and under. Winners may qualify for the Scripps Howard National Spelling Bee held in Washington, D.C., in late May or early June every year. If you're interested, ask your school principal to contact your local newspaper.

George won $10,000, which he said he would give to his parents.

Here are the words he had to spell correctly. Can you find them in a dictionary?

How many would you have gotten right? One of our editors only got 3 out of 15 right.

WEB SITE http://www.spellingbee.com

ROUND	SPELLING WORD	ROUND	SPELLING WORD
1	fondu	9	trophobiosis
2	waiver	10	psilosis
3	serendipity	11	quodlibet
4	ersatz	12	eudaemonic
5	surfactant	13	ditokous
6	vesicant	14	propaedeutic
7	emmetropia	15	demarche
8	annelid		

LOVE GEOGRAPHY? HERE'S WHERE TO GO!

Felix Peng, a 13-year-old from Guilford, Connecticut, won the National Geographic Bee in 2000. He won a $25,000 college scholarship by coming in first place in the annual competition.

Felix first got interested in geography when his parents showed him their birthplace, Taiwan, on a globe.

The winning question was: *Name two of the three largest sections of Denmark, which includes its mainland peninsula and two largest islands.*

The answer? **Jutland, Sjaelland, and Fyn.**

Second place went to 12-year-old George Thampy. Does his name sound familiar? That's because he also came in first place in the National Spelling Bee! George had quite a year!

If you want to enter this contest, you must be a fourth-through eighth-grader. School-level bees are followed by state-level bees, then the national competition. For more information, ask your school principal to write to: National Geographic Bee; National Geographic Society; 1145 17th St., NW; Washington, D.C. 20036-4688. The registration deadline each year is October 15. You can also visit the web site:

WEB SITE http://www.nationalgeographic.com

CASTLES IN SAND

Everyone who's been to the beach has felt the urge to play in the sand—to dig holes in it, pile it into towers, even build sand castles. Some people like it so much that they travel all over the world to compete in contests. Professional teams have built towers more than 33 feet high!

But you don't have to live near the ocean (or be a professional). Most contests have separate divisions for kids and/or families, and many are held on lakeshores, or anywhere that water and sand can be found—or brought in.

The secret is to pile up and pack a big mound of wet sand, then carve it using tools. Sticks or shells from the beach make good tools and so do plastic forks, spoons, and knives. You can make animals, cartoon characters, or almost anything. All it takes (besides water and sand) is imagination and practice. For more information, visit

WEB SITE *http://sandcastlecentral.com*

A BRIGHT WAY TO BAKE

Nine-year-old Alexandra Stewart from Austin, Texas, was named Easy-Bake "Baker of the Year 2000" thanks to her recipe for chocolate mousse cake. Easy-Bake Ovens, first made in 1963, let kids bake safely by using a light bulb to cook the food.

Alexandra was one of the five finalists who was flown to New York City to compete at the Four Seasons Hotel. She won a $5,000 savings bond, a dinner party for 10 people in her home, and a two-year supply of Easy-Bake bake sets. The runners-up each received a $1,000 savings bond and a one-year supply of Easy-Bake bake sets.

A panel of experts judged the five finalists on creative use of ingredients, ease of preparation, presentation, and taste.

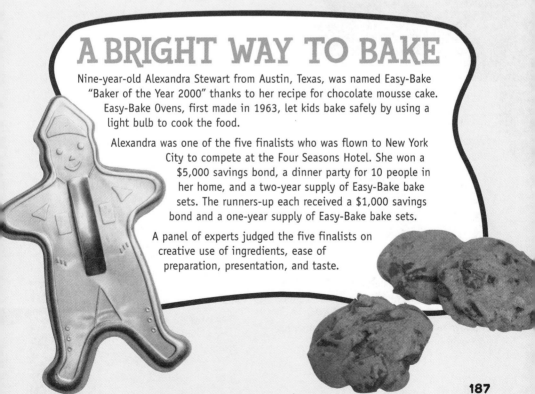

RELIGION

What book is considered sacred by both Jews and Christians? *You can find the answer on page 190.*

WORLD RELIGIONS

How did the universe begin? Why are we here on Earth? What happens to us after we die? For many people, religion is a way of answering questions like these. Believing in a God or gods, or in a Divine Being, is one way of making sense of the world around us. Religions can also help guide people's lives.

About six billion people all over the world belong to some group. Different religions have different beliefs. For example, Christians, Jews, and Muslims all believe in one God, while Hindus believe in many gods. On this page and the next are some facts about the world's major religions.

CHRISTIANITY

Who Started Christianity? Jesus Christ, in the first century. He was born in Bethlehem between 8 B.C. and 4 B.C. and died about A.D. 29.

What Do Christians Believe? That there is one God. That Jesus Christ is the Son of God, who came on Earth, died to save humankind, and rose from the dead.

How Many Are There? Christianity is the world's biggest religion. In 2001 there were almost two billion Christians, in nearly all parts of the world. More than one billion of the Christians were **Roman Catholics**, who follow the leadership of the pope in Rome. Other groups of Christians include **Orthodox Christians**, who accept most of the same teachings as Roman Catholics but follow different leadership, and **Protestants**, who often disagree with Catholic teachings. Protestants rely especially on the Bible itself. They belong to many different groups.

BUDDHISM

Who Started Buddhism? Gautama Siddhartha (the Buddha), around 525 B.C.

What Do Buddhists Believe? Buddha taught that life is filled with suffering. In order to be free of that suffering, believers have to give up worldly possessions and worldly goals and try to achieve a state of perfect peace known as *nirvana*.

How Many Are There? In 2001, there were more than 350 million Buddhists, mostly in Asia.

What Kinds Are There? There are two main kinds of Buddhists. **Theravada** ("Path of the Elders") **Buddhism,** the older kind, is more common in the southern part of Asia. **Mahayana** ("Great Vessel") **Buddhism** is more common in northern Asia.

HINDUISM

Who Started Hinduism?

Aryan beliefs spread into India, around 1500 B.C. These beliefs were mixed with the beliefs of the people who already lived there.

What Do Hindus Believe?

That there are many gods and many ways of worshipping. That people die and are reborn many times as other living things. That there is a universal soul or principle known as **Brahman**. That the goal of life is to escape the cycle of birth and death and become part of the **Brahman**. This is achieved by leading a pure and good life.

How Many Are There?

In 2001, there were nearly 800 million Hindus, mainly in India and places where people from India have gone to live.

What Kinds Are There?

There are many kinds of Hindus, who worship different gods or goddesses.

ISLAM

Who Started Islam?

Muhammad, the Prophet, in A.D. 610.

What Do Muslims Believe?

People who believe in Islam are known as Muslims. The word "Islam" means submission to God. Muslims believe that there is no other god than the one God; that Muhammad is the prophet and lawgiver of his community; that they should pray five times a day, fast during the month of Ramadan, give to the poor, and once during their life make a pilgrimage to Mecca in Saudi Arabia if they can afford it.

How Many Are There?

In 2001, there were about one billion Muslims, mostly in parts of Africa and Asia. The two main branches are: **Sunni Muslims**, who make up over 80 percent of all Muslims today, and **Shiite Muslims**, who broke away in a dispute over leadership after Muhammad died in 632.

JUDAISM

Who Started Judaism?

Abraham is considered to be the founder of Judaism. He lived around 1300 B.C.

What Do Jews Believe?

That there is one God who created the universe and rules over it. That they should be faithful to God and carry out God's commandments.

How Many Are There?

In 2001, there were about 14 million Jews living around the world. Many live in Israel or the United States.

What Kinds Are There?

In the United States there are three main kinds: **Orthodox**, **Conservative**, and **Reform**. Orthodox Jews are the most traditional. Traditional means that they follow strict laws about how they dress, what they can eat, and how they conduct their lives. Conservative Jews follow many of the traditions. Reform Jews are the least traditional.

RELIGIOUS MEMBERSHIP in the United States

Did you know that Protestants are the largest religious group in the United States, and that Catholics are the second largest? The pie chart below shows how many people belong to the major religious groups. These numbers are recent estimates; no one knows exactly how many people belong to each group.

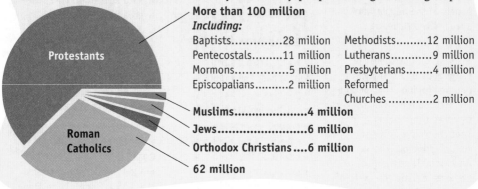

More than 100 million
Including:

Baptists	28 million	Methodists	12 million
Pentecostals	11 million	Lutherans	9 million
Mormons	5 million	Presbyterians	4 million
Episcopalians	2 million	Reformed Churches	2 million

Muslims....................4 million

Jews........................6 million

Orthodox Christians ....6 million

62 million

RELIGIOUS WRITINGS

Every religion has its writings or sacred texts that set out its laws and beliefs. Among them are:

THE BIBLE

The Old Testament

Also known as the Hebrew Bible, this is a collection of laws, history, and other writings that are holy books for Jews and also for Christians. The first five books of the Old Testament are known by Jews as the Torah. These contain the stories of creation and the beginnings of human life, as well as the laws handed down by the prophet Moses.

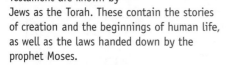

The New Testament

A collection of Gospels (stories about Jesus), epistles (letters written to guide the early Christians), and other writings. The Old Testament and New Testament together make up the Bible that is read by Christians.

THE KORAN

The Koran (al-Qur'an in Arabic) sets out the main beliefs and practices of Islam, the religion of Muslims. Muslims believe that the Koran was revealed by God to the prophet Muhammad through the angel Gabriel.

THE BHAGAVAD GHITA

The Bhagavad Ghita is one of several Hindu religious writings. Part of a long poem about war, it is familiar to almost every Hindu. In it the god Krishna, in the form of a man, drives the chariot of Prince Arjuna into battle and teaches him how to live.

THE *TRIPITAKA*

The three main collections of Buddhist writings are called the *Tripitaka*, or "Three Baskets." They describe the Buddha's teachings, philosophers' thoughts on these teachings, and rules for living as a Buddhist monk or nun. Parts of the *Tripitaka* and other important Buddhist writings are called *sutras*.

MAJOR HOLY DAYS
for Christians, Jews, and Muslims

CHRISTIAN HOLY DAYS

	2001	2002	2003
Ash Wednesday	February 28	February 13	March 5
Good Friday	April 13	March 29	April 18
Easter Sunday	April 15	March 31	April 20
Easter for Orthodox Churches	April 15	May 5	April 27
Christmas	December 25	December 25	December 25

JEWISH HOLY DAYS
The Jewish holy days begin at sundown the night before the first full day of the observance. The dates of these evenings are listed below.

	2001 (5761-5762)	2002 (5762-5763)	2003 (5763-5764)
Passover	April 7	March 27	April 16
Rosh Hashanah (New Year)	September 17	September 6	September 26
Yom Kippur	September 26	September 15	October 5
Hanukkah	December 9	November 29	December 19

ISLAMIC (MUSLIM) HOLY DAYS

	2001-2002 (1422)	2002-2003 (1423)	2003-2004 (1424)
Muharram, 1st day (New Year)	March 26	March 15	March 4
Mawlid (Birthday of Muhammad)	June 4	May 24	May 13
Ramadan, 1st day	November 16	November 6	October 26
Id al-Adha Dhu al-Hijjah, 10th day	February 22	February 11	February 1

SCIENCE

Which mineral is the hardest? You can find the answer on page 194.

WHAT EVERYTHING IS MADE OF

Everything we see and use is made up of basic ingredients called elements. There are at least 112 elements. Most have been found in nature. Some are created by scientists in labs.

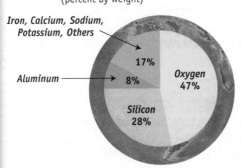

Elements Found in Earth's Crust
(percent by weight)

Iron, Calcium, Sodium, Potassium, Others — 17%

Aluminum — 8%

Oxygen 47%

Silicon 28%

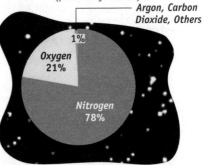

Elements Found in the Atmosphere
(percent by volume)

Argon, Carbon Dioxide, Others — 1%

Oxygen 21%

Nitrogen 78%

IT ALL STARTS WITH AN ATOM

The smallest possible piece of an element that has all the properties of the original element is called an **atom**. Each tiny atom is made up of even smaller particles called **protons**, **neutrons**, and **electrons**.

To tell one element from another, scientists count the number of protons in an atom. The total number of protons is called the element's **atomic number**. All of the atoms of an element have the same number of protons and electrons, but some atoms have a different number of neutrons. For example, carbon-12 has six protons and six neutrons, and carbon-13 has six protons and seven neutrons.

We call the amount of matter in an atom its **atomic mass**. Carbon-13 has a greater atomic mass than carbon-12. The average atomic mass of all of the different atoms of the same element is called the element's **atomic weight**. Every element has a different atomic number and a different atomic weight.

CHEMICAL SYMBOLS ARE SCIENTIFIC SHORTHAND

When scientists write the names of elements, they often use a symbol instead of spelling out the full name. The symbol for each element is one or two letters. Scientists write O for oxygen and He for helium. The symbols usually come from the English name for the element (C for carbon). The symbols for some of the elements come from the element's Latin name. For example, the symbol for gold is Au, which is short for *Aurum*, the Latin word for gold.

How Elements are Named

How many of these elements have you heard of?

NAME	SYMBOL	WHAT IT IS	WHEN FOUND	NAMED FOR
Californium	Cf	radioactive metal	1950	the state and Universities of California
Helium	He	gas	1868	the Greek word *helios*, meaning sun
Mercury	Hg	liquid metal	B.C.	the Roman god Mercury
Neon	Ne	gas	1898	the Greek word *neon*, meaning new
Oxygen	O	gas	1774	Greek words *oxy* and *genes*, meaning acid former
Seaborgium	Sg	synthetic—not found in nature	1974	Chemist Glenn T. Seaborg, creator of plutonium and eight other elements, and Nobel prize winner
Silicon	Si	transitional metal	1824	The latin word *silicus*, meaning flint
Uranium	U	radioactive metal	1789	the planet Uranus

The elements 110-112 were discovered in recent years and have not yet been named. Reports of the discoveries of elements 114, 116, and 118 were made in 1999, but have not yet been confirmed. Discoveries of elements 113 and 115 have not yet been reported. Elements are named after places, scientists, myths, or properties of the element. But no element gets a new name until the International Union of Pure and Applied Chemistry (IUPAC) accepts it. Do you have any suggestions for the nameless elements?

All About... COMPOUNDS

Carbon, hydrogen, nitrogen, and oxygen are the most common chemical elements in the human body. Many other elements may be found in small amounts. These include calcium, iron, phosphorus, potassium, and sodium.

When elements join together, they form *compounds*. Water is a compound made up of hydrogen and oxygen. Salt is a compound made up of sodium and chlorine.

Common Name	Contains the Compound	Contains the Elements
Baking soda	sodium bicarbonate	sodium, hydrogen, carbon, oxygen
Alcohol	hydroxyl	carbon, oxygen, hydrogen
Rust	iron oxide	iron, oxygen
Peroxide	hydrogen peroxide	hydrogen, oxygen
Chalk	calcium carbonate	calcium, carbon, oxygen
Laughing gas	nitrous oxide	nitrogen, oxygen
Soda bubbles	carbon dioxide	carbon, oxygen

MINERALS, ROCKS, AND GEMS

WHAT ARE MINERALS?

Minerals are solid materials in the soil that were never alive. All the land on our planet—even the ocean floor—rests on a layer of rock made up of minerals. Minerals have also been found on other planets, on our moon, and in meteorites that landed on Earth. Some minerals, such as **gold** and **silver,** are made up entirely of one element. But most are formed from two or more elements joined together.

The most common mineral is **quartz,** which is made of silicon and oxygen and is found all over the world. **Sand** is made up mostly of quartz. **Graphite,** which is used in pencils, is another common mineral. Other minerals, like **diamonds,** are very rare and valuable. Amazingly, diamonds and graphite are different forms of the same element— carbon.

Diamond

WHAT ARE ROCKS?

Rocks are combinations of minerals. The three kinds of rocks are:

❶ **Igneous rocks**—rocks that form from melted minerals deep in the Earth that cool and become solid. Granite is an igneous rock made from quartz, feldspar, and mica.

❷ **Sedimentary rocks**—rocks that usually form in the beds of seas, lakes, and rivers from tiny pieces of other rocks, sand, and shells packed together. It takes millions of years for these pieces to form sedimentary rocks. Limestone is a kind of sedimentary rock.

❸ **Metamorphic rock**—Over millions of years, the heat and pressure inside Earth can change the minerals in igneous and sedimentary rocks. When the minerals in a rock change, the new rock is called a **metamorphic rock**. Marble is a metamorphic rock formed from limestone.

WHAT ARE GEMS?

Most **gems** are minerals that have been cut and polished to be used as jewelry or other kinds of decoration. Some gems are not minerals. A pearl is a gem that is not a mineral, because it comes from an oyster, which is a living thing. The most valued gems—diamonds, emeralds, rubies, and sapphires—are minerals called **precious stones**. Below are some popular gems, the kind of mineral each one is, the elements each is made up of, and the usual colors for the gem.

GEM NAME	MINERAL	ELEMENT IT IS MADE OF	USUAL COLORS
Topaz	aluminum, fluosilicate	aluminum, silicon, oxygen, fluorine, hydrogen	red, pink
Diamond	carbon	carbon	bluish white
Emerald	beryl	beryllium, silicon, aluminum, oxygen	green
Aquamarine	beryl	beryllium, silicon, aluminum, oxygen iron	blue-green
Ruby	corundum	aluminum, oxygen	red
Sapphire	corundum	aluminum, oxygen	blue

Did You Know?

OF ALL THE KNOWN MINERALS, DIAMONDS ARE THE HARDEST. *They are also hard to get because they are buried deep in the Earth's crust. Miners must dig out about 500 tons of ore just to get one ounce of diamond! This helps explain why diamonds cost so much money.*

WHAT IS DNA?

Every cell in every living thing (or organism) has DNA, a molecule that contains all the information about that organism. Lengths of connected DNA molecules, called genes, are like tiny pieces of a secret code. They determine what each organism is like in great detail.

Genes are passed on from parents to children, and no two organisms (except identical twins) have the same DNA. Many things about us—the color of our eyes or hair, whether we're tall or short, the size of our feet—depend on the genes we inherited from our parents.

DNA "FINGERPRINTS"

DNA is located in each of your cells, including your blood, saliva, hair follicles, and skin. No one else has a DNA pattern exactly like yours. For these reasons DNA evidence can be collected from a crime scene and then linked to a suspect. Scientists can match the DNA from skin or hair collected at a crime scene, for instance, to DNA from a suspect. They analyze the exact makeup of the two sets of DNA, and if they are identical, chances are that they are from the same person. Cells from a person at a crime scene can be evidence enough to convince a jury that that person was present at the crime.

DNA evidence is also helping show that some wrongly accused and convicted people are innocent. Since 1992, DNA evidence has helped reverse at least 78 convictions (including 10 cases where the death penalty was involved). In January 2001, a man imprisoned for murder in Texas was released because of DNA tests. Another man, sentenced to death for a murder in Virginia in 1982, was set free in February. New evidence based on DNA tests cleared him of the crime.

THE HUMAN GENOME

The DNA code for the human species, called the human genome, is what makes us all human beings.

In 2000, the Human Genome Project reached a milestone in a 15-year study of the human genome. It identified the 3.1 billion separate codes in human DNA. In early 2001, researchers reported that the human genome contains about 30,000 to 40,000 genes. For the first time we have an outline of the genetic code for the human race. (Surprisingly, humans don't have that many more genes than the roundworm, which has about 20,000!) Scientists will use this knowledge to learn more about hereditary diseases and gain a better understanding of how human beings evolved.

All About... CLONING

A clone is an organism that has developed from a cell of just one other organism. This means it has the exact same DNA as its parent. Scientists have been able to clone mammals artificially. The most famous clone was a sheep named Dolly, born in Scotland in 1996. More recently, researchers have tried to use cloning to preserve endangered species. In 2000, Noah, a clone of a rare wild ox, was born in a lab. But he only lived for two days before dying of an infection. Human cloning may also be possible one day. But many people believe human cloning would be wrong.

SOME FAMOUS SCIENTISTS

CHARLES DARWIN (1809-1882), a British scientist best known for his theory of evolution. According to this theory, living creatures slowly develop over millions of years.

THOMAS EDISON (1847-1931), Ohio-born inventor who only attended school for three months. He created devices that transformed society, such as a reliable electric lightbulb, the electric generator, phonograph, wireless telegraph, motion-picture projector, and alkaline, iron-nickel batteries.

ALBERT EINSTEIN (1879-1955), a German-American physicist who developed a revolutionary theory about the relationships between time, space, matter, and energy.

Thomas Edison

JAMES HARRIS (1932-), Nobel-Prize-winning physicist who co-discovered elements 104 and 105 at the University of California, Berkeley, and pushed to finish the periodic table.

FREDERICK JONES (1892-1961), changed our eating habits by inventing refrigerated trucks, eliminating the problem of food spoilage. These also allow for transporting blood long distances, which makes medical operations much safer.

JOHANNES KEPLER (1571-1630), German astronomer who developed three laws of planetary motion. He was the first to propose a force (later named gravity) that governs planets' orbits around the sun, and he invented a form of mathematics that led to calculus.

ADA LOVELACE (1815-1852), British mathematical genius who is considered the first computer programmer. She designed a "language" for the first computing machine (invented by Charles Babbage), and published important papers on the theory behind analytical engines.

LISE MEITNER (1878-1968), physicist who first discovered nuclear fission. She helped find the element protactinium, and later predicted the chain reaction, which eventually led to the development of the atomic bomb, along with other nuclear power.

LOUIS EUGENE NEEL (1904-2000), a French physicist who discovered that certain materials that do not conduct electricity can still be magnetized. This allowed the development of the silicon computer chip and other communications devices. His work on magnetism also led to the theory of plate tectonics.

WOLFGANG PAULI (1900-1958), Austrian-American physicist who invented a rule of physics called the exclusion principle. It says that two electrons cannot occupy the same energy state in an atom at the same time. This principle helps explain why objects do not blend into each other. He also first proposed in 1931 the existence of a tiny particle, called a neutrino, that scientists confirmed 25 years later exists.

All About... JUMPING GENES

Barbara McClintock was an American biologist who discovered that genes don't always stay in one place. She lived from 1902 to 1992. In 1944, through experiments with corn of different colors, she showed that genes sometimes switch places. Other scientists ignored her "jumping genes" theory at the time. But McClintock won a Nobel Prize in 1983, almost 40 years later. Jumping genes may offer clues to how cancer develops and how one species evolves into another.

Ocean exhibit at COSI Columbus

SCIENCE MUSEUMS

If you like hands-on exhibits and want to learn about science, here are three terrific museums you might visit. More activities and information can be found on their Web sites.

The Center of Science and Industry. Toledo and Columbus, Ohio.

COSI Toledo: The Water Works exhibit explores everything to do with water: plumbing, rainstorms, maritime shipping—even building a sailboat. Mind Zone highlights optical illusions, distorted perspective and gravity, and three-dimensional sound.

COSI Columbus: Exhibits are arranged in eight learning worlds, including: ocean (with deep-sea exploration); life (human biology); space (3-D laser show, virtual voyage to Mars); and i/o (input/output—the wired world of high-tech).

WEB SITE *http://www.cosi.org* (for both)

Franklin Institute Science Museum. Philadelphia,

Pennsylvania. Benjamin Franklin has his own exhibit hall in which visitors can experiment with some of his inventions. The bioscience exhibit invites visitors to listen to their own heartbeats and experience what it's like inside a human heart (enlarged 220 times). "It's All in the Brain" uses demonstrations and interactive exhibits to test reflexes and help visitors experience how the brain reacts to the outside world.

WEB SITE *http://www.fi.edu*

DID YOU KNOW? *Benjamin Franklin invented swim fins.*

Oregon Museum of Science and Industry. Portland, Oregon. Find out what an

earthquake of magnitude 5.5 feels like, in the Earthquake Room. Computers, electronics, and other gadgets are on display in the ever-changing High Tech Hall. Climb aboard the Navy's last non-nuclear submarine, the *U.S.S. Blueback* (featured in the movie *The Hunt for Red October*).

WEB SITE *http://www.omsi.edu*

MYSTERY BUBBLES EXPERIMENT

Air expands when it is heated. You don't usually see this unless the air is trapped in a tight space and tries to burst out. When air escapes into water, you see bubbles.

YOU NEED:

▶ one small cardboard juice container, with straw
▶ a glass of water
▶ food coloring
▶ a small bit of modeling clay or Silly Putty

WHAT TO DO:

1. Punch a hole in the top of the juice carton with the straw. Drink the juice or put it in another container.
2. Place the clay around the base of the straw to make the opening airtight.
3. Add a few drops of food coloring to the glass of water.
4. Hold the carton in both hands, upside down. Place the end of the straw into the glass of water, about 3 inches below the water surface.
5. Wait for two or three minutes and watch what happens.

WHAT HAPPENED:

When you held the carton in your hands, you were heating the air inside. The air expanded and filled whatever space there was. The expanded air came out of the carton through the straw. You would see it as a series of bubbles in the colored water.

TRY IT!

Try an experiment that's a little different. What do you think would happen if you didn't use the clay? What if you placed the carton on top of the glass without holding it in your hands? Can you think up another experiment that might show the same effect using a balloon?

SCIENCE Q&A

WHAT DO ALL LIVING THINGS HAVE IN COMMON? All living things are made of **cells**. These are the basic building blocks of life. Cells carry out all the basic functions of life: eating, processing energy, reproducing, and disposing waste.

WHY ISN'T ALL MATTER HARD AND SOLID? On Earth matter exists mainly in three states: **solid**, **liquid**, and **gas**. Matter will change from solid to liquid and then from liquid to gas as temperatures get hotter. The fourth state of matter, more common in space than on Earth, is **plasma**. Gas becomes plasma when it is heated to a high enough temperature.

CAN YOU HEAR THE OCEAN THROUGH A CONCH SHELL? No. What you really hear are sounds from the air around you. The shell acts as a mini-echo chamber, increasing and distorting the sounds so that they resemble the roar of ocean waves.

HOW STRONG IS GRAVITY? Compared to other forces, **gravity** is weak. It may feel powerful on Earth, where it takes lots of energy for airplanes and rockets to leave the ground. But this is only because the planet is so massive that it pulls everything toward its center. **Magnets** use a force stronger than gravity when they stick on metal. And **static electricity** defies gravity when it makes your hair stand on end.

WHAT IS AN ECHO? An **echo** is a reflection of a sound, just as a mirror shows a visual reflection. Sound travels in waves, which can bounce off another surface. The speed of sound is slow enough so that you can hear a repeat of the sound after a slight delay when the sound waves bounce back to you. When sound waves bounce off many surfaces, such as in a cave or a canyon, you'll hear echoes.

WHY IS THE SKY BLUE? **Sunlight** makes the sky blue. The light from the Sun is really white until it reaches Earth's atmosphere. Then it hits water vapor, dust, and other particles in the air and scatters in different directions. The white light is actually made of different colors of the spectrum. **Blue** is scattered much more than any other color, so blue is what we see when we look up at a clear sky. During sunrises and sunsets, we see **red** and **orange** because the Sun is closer to the horizon, scattering the blue light out of our line of vision.

WHY CAN'T YOU SEE MORE STARS AT NIGHT IN THE CITY? Heavily populated areas cause light pollution, or "sky glow," at night. Outdoor lights bounce off dust, water vapor, and pollution in the atmosphere, scattering light so that the night sky no longer looks very dark. This glow prevents people from seeing many of the stars and planets.

CAN ROCKS MELT? At very hot temperatures, they can. Molten rock is called **magma**. It is usually found way below the Earth's surface. Magma comes out from under the Earth's crust in the form of lava when volcanoes erupt.

SIGNS & SYMBOLS

S W T H H A I T S D S O A E Y?
To figure this out, look on page 203.

signs & symbols give us information at a glance. In the days when most people could not read, pictures helped them find their way around. Today, many of the same symbols are used the world over.

Handicapped Access

Men's Rest Room

Women's Rest Room

Food

Lodging

Picnic Area

Camping

Swimming

Fishing

Hiking Trail

No Smoking

Flammable

Poison

Radioactive

Make your own sign

THE ENIGMA CODE

The small group of men and women looked as if they were out for a day's sport that summer of 1939. But their purpose was far different. They were a team of codebreakers—mostly professors—and they went to Bletchley Park, a house near London, England, to help Britain win World War II. Their mission: to crack the Enigma code, invented by Nazi Germany and said to be the most complex code yet created. The odds against the codebreakers were 150 quintillion (150,000,000,000,000,000,000) to one. Why?

The Enigma code was set up by machine and changed daily. The rotors and wires of the machine that produced each coded letter could be arranged in a multitude of ways. But the British had Alan Turing on their side. A brilliant mathematician, he invented a complex electro-mechanical machine of his own that allowed codebreakers to decipher German messages with speed and accuracy. Turing's success in breaking this "unbreakable" code has been called one of the greatest mental achievements of the 20th century.

SOME USEFUL SYMBOLS

$ Dollar

¢ Cent

% Percent

℞ Prescription

♂ Male

♀ Female

& Ampersand (and)

± Plus or minus

= Is Equal To

≠ Is Not Equal To

< Is Less Than

> Is Greater Than

( ) Parentheses

© Copyright

® Registered Trademark

All About... COMANCHE CODE TALKERS

From 1941 to 1945, during World War II, seventeen Comanche Indians—known as Comanche code talkers—helped to keep enemy Germans from learning U.S. military secrets. The code talkers used their own language to send U.S. Army messages over the radio. Since there are no Comanche words for many military terms, they used other words instead. To talk about tanks, for example, the Comanches used their word for turtle. The Germans had no knowledge of the Comanche language to start with, and this sort of double code baffled them even more.

ROAD SIGNS

 Stop

 One Way

 No Entry

 No U-Turn

 No Parking

 Right Turn

 No Left Turn

 Hill

 Signal Ahead

 School Zone

 Pedestrian Crossing

 Deer Crossing

 Railroad Crossing

 Road Work Ahead

 Cross Road

 Winding Road

 Slippery Road

 Divided Highway

 Yield

 Merging Traffic

GATOR XING
NEXT 1/2 MILE

SASQUATCH XING

BRAILLE

Many blind people read with their fingers using a system of raised dots called Braille. Braille was developed by Louis Braille (1809-1852) in France in 1826, when he was a teenager.

The Braille alphabet, numbers, punctuation, and speech sounds are represented by 63 different combinations of 6 raised dots arranged in a grid like this:

```
① ④
② ⑤
③ ⑥
```

All the letters in the basic Braille alphabet are lowercase. Special symbols are added to show that what follows is a capital letter or a number. The white circles on the grid below show the raised dots.

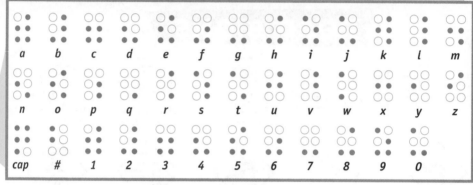

▲ Braille alphabet and numbers

SIGN LANGUAGE

Many people who are deaf or hearing-impaired, and cannot hear spoken words, talk with their fingers instead of their voices. To do this, they use a system of manual signs (the manual alphabet), or finger spelling, in which the fingers are used to form letters and words. Originally developed in France by Abbe Charles Michel De l'Epee in the late 1700s, the manual alphabet was later brought to the United States by Laurent Clerc (1785-1869), a Frenchman who taught people who were deaf.

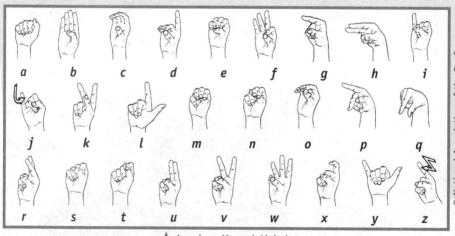

▲ American Manual Alphabet

◄ TSCEOCDREES ►

Can you guess what the title of this page says? You can find out by solving the "Take a Second Look" code below. This is one simple way to create a secret code. Different kinds of codes have been used since ancient times to keep military plans secret. Secret codes are still used today by the military, by banks for ATM machines, and on the Internet.

❶ TAKE A SECOND LOOK

To solve this secret code, look at the letters in it not once, but twice! That's right—in each coded message, read every second letter. You'll begin to see the sense in the message. Then start again on the letters you missed the first time. The secret of the message will be revealed to you!

The title on this page uses the take-a-second-look code. Can you figure out what it says?

Here's another hidden message. Look twice, it's all right!

I' A L F L T S E E R E S Y C O H U O A O T L 3

❷ THE HORSE CORRAL CODE

When pairs of letters are squeezed into a grid, they look like horses in a corral—at least they did to creators of this secret code. The horse corral code depends on how you look at it! First you write out the whole alphabet in two grids, as shown:

Each letter is represented by the part of the corral that surrounds it. If it's the second letter in the box, then it has a dot in the middle.

An **A** looks like this: ⌐ A **B** looks like this: •⌐

Can you decipher the two messages below?

A.

B.

Now write a secret message of your own. Use a different code. Here's one for example: one two *use* two dog *every* cat fourth *third* or cat *word*

SPACE

Who was the first person to walk on the moon? *You can find the answer on page 211.*

THE SOLAR SYSTEM

Nine planets, including Earth, travel around the Sun. These planets, together with the Sun, form the solar system.

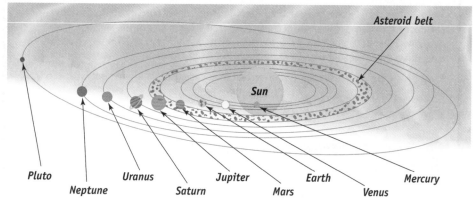

Asteroid belt

Sun

Pluto
Neptune
Uranus
Saturn
Jupiter
Mars
Earth
Venus
Mercury

THE SUN IS A STAR

Did you know that the Sun is a star, like the other stars you see at night? It is a typical, medium-size star. But because the Sun is much closer to our planet than any other star, we can study it in great detail. The diameter of the Sun is 864,000 miles—more than 100 times Earth's diameter. The gravity of the Sun is nearly 28 times the gravity of Earth.

How Hot Is the Sun? The surface temperature of the Sun is close to 10,000°F, and it is believed that the sun's inner core may reach temperatures near 35 million degrees! The Sun provides enough light and heat energy to support all forms of life on our planet.

THE PLANETS ARE IN MOTION

The planets move around the Sun along oval-shaped paths called **orbits**. One complete path around the Sun is called a **revolution**. Earth takes one year, or 365¼ days, to make one revolution around the Sun. Planets that are farther away from the Sun take longer. Some planets have one or more **moons**. A moon orbits a planet in much the same way that the planets orbit the Sun.

Each planet also spins (or rotates) on its axis. An **axis** is an imaginary line running through the center of a planet. The time it takes Earth to rotate on its axis equals one day. Here are some other facts about the planets and the symbol for each planet.

THE PLANETS

❶ MERCURY

Average distance from the Sun: 36 million miles
Diameter: 3,032 miles
Time to revolve around the Sun: 88 days
Time to rotate on its axis: 58 days, 15 hours, 30 minutes
Number of moons: 0

DID YOU KNOW? *So far, Mariner 10 has been the only spacecraft to visit Mercury. The Messenger spacecraft will be launched in 2004 and orbit Mercury starting in 2009.*

❷ VENUS

Average distance from the Sun: 67 million miles
Diameter: 7,521 miles
Time to revolve around the Sun: 224.7 days
Time to rotate on its axis: 243 days
Number of moons: 0

DID YOU KNOW? *Stormy Venus rotates clockwise, unlike other planets. A person on Venus would see the sun rise in the west and set in the east.*

❸ EARTH

Average distance from the Sun: 93 million miles
Diameter: 7,926 miles
Time to revolve around the Sun: 365 ¼ days
Time to rotate on its axis: 23 hours, 56 minutes, 4.2 seconds
Number of moons: 1

DID YOU KNOW? *We live at the bottom of an ocean of air. Seventy-eight percent of it is nitrogen.*

❹ MARS

Average distance from the Sun: 142 million miles
Diameter: 4,213 miles
Time to revolve around the Sun: 687 days
Time to rotate on its axis: 24 hours, 37 minutes, 22 seconds
Number of moons: 2

DID YOU KNOW? *Mars has a reddish color because its soil has so much iron oxide, or rust.*

❺ JUPITER

Average distance from the Sun: 484 million miles
Diameter: 88,732 miles
Time to revolve around the Sun: 11.9 years
Time to rotate on its axis: 9 hours, 55 minutes, 30 seconds
Number of moons: 16

DID YOU KNOW? *Jupiter's four largest moons—Io, Europa, Ganymede, and Callisto— were first seen by Galileo in the 17th century.*

❻ SATURN

Average distance from the Sun: 888 million miles
Diameter: 74,975 miles
Time to revolve around the Sun: 29.5 years
Time to rotate on its axis: 10 hours, 30 minutes
Number of moons: at least 18

DID YOU KNOW? *More than 1,000 rings circle Saturn. They look like CDs twirling in space.*

◀ Jupiter

Saturn ▶

⑦ URANUS

Average distance from the Sun: 1.8 billion miles

Diameter: 31,763 miles

Time to revolve around the Sun: 84 years

Time to rotate on its axis: 17 hours, 14 minutes

Number of moons: 18

DID YOU KNOW? *Because Uranus is tipped way over on its axis, its north pole is in darkness for 42 Earth years.*

⑧ NEPTUNE

Average distance from the Sun: 2.8 billion miles

Diameter: 30,603 miles

Time to revolve around the Sun: 164.8 years

Time to rotate on its axis: 16 hours, 6 minutes

Number of moons: 8

DID YOU KNOW? *In 2010, Neptune will complete its first full trip around the Sun since its discovery in 1846.*

⑨ PLUTO

Average distance from the Sun: 3.6 billion miles

Diameter: 1,413 miles

Time to revolve around the Sun: 247.7 years

Time to rotate on its axis: 6 days, 9 hours, 18 minutes

Number of moons: 1

DID YOU KNOW? *Some scientists do not consider Pluto a planet, but rather one of many large objects orbiting the Sun outside Neptune's orbit.*

FACTS About the PLANETS

Largest planet: Jupiter

Smallest planet: Pluto

Planet closest to the Sun: Mercury

Planet that comes closest to Earth: Venus (Every 19 months, it gets closer to Earth than any other planet does.)

Fastest-moving planet: Mercury (107,000 miles per hour)

Slowest planet: Pluto (10,600 mph)

Warmest planet: Venus

Coldest planet: Pluto

Longest days: Mercury

Shortest days: Jupiter

THE MOON

The moon is about 238,900 miles from Earth. It is 2,160 miles in diameter and has no atmosphere. The dusty surface is covered with deep craters. It takes the same time for the moon to rotate on its axis as it does to orbit Earth (27 days, 7 hours, 43 minutes). This is why one side of the moon is always facing Earth. The moon has no light of its own, but reflects light from the Sun. The fraction of the lighted part of the moon that we see is called a *phase*. It takes the moon about 29½ days to go through all its phases.

PHASES OF THE MOON

| New Moon | Crescent Moon | First Quarter | Full Moon |

| Last Quarter | Crescent Moon | New Moon |

Did You KNOW?

THE MOON HAS NO ATMOSPHERE. *This means it has no wind or weather, so everything on its surface stays the same. The footprints and American flag left by astronauts in 1969 are still there!*

EXPLORING THE SOLAR SYSTEM

American space exploration began in January 1958, when the *Explorer I* satellite was launched into orbit. In 1958, NASA (the National Aeronautics and Space Administration) was formed.

SEARCHING for LIFE

For years scientists have tried to discover if there is life on other planets in our solar system or elsewhere. They look for signs of what is needed for life on Earth—basics like water and proper temperature.

NASA is searching for signs of life on Mars. The search will continue until at least 2013. Some spacecraft will fly around Mars taking pictures. Others will land there to study soil and rocks and look for living things. *Mars Pathfinder* and *Mars Global Surveyor*, launched in 1996, reached Mars in 1997. Unfortunately, two later missions to Mars failed. Scientists aren't sure what happened.

In 1996, scientists examined two meteorites that may have come from Mars and found evidence that some form of life may have existed there billions of years ago. In 2000, the spacecraft *Galileo* provided strong evidence that there might be life in the icy waters of Europa, one of the 16 moons orbiting Jupiter.

Outside of NASA, another program is looking for life on other worlds. It is called SETI (Search for Extraterrestrial Intelligence). Most often it uses powerful radio telescopes to detect signs of life. Recently, however, astronomers began searching for light signals as signs of extraterrestrial life.

Astronomers have found evidence of several planets outside our solar system. In 1999, astronomers reported the first evidence of a group of planets orbiting one star, a star not very different from our Sun. Since then they have found over 45 planets outside our solar system. There could be life on one of those planets, or on a planet we have not found yet.

UNMANNED SPACE MISSIONS

1962 Mariner 2 *First successful flyby of Venus.*

1964 Mariner 4 *First probe to reach Mars, 1965.*

1972 Pioneer 10 *First probe to reach Jupiter, 1973.*

1973 Mariner 10 *Only U.S. probe to Mercury, 1974.*

1975 Viking 1 and 2 *Landed on Mars in 1976.*

1977 Voyager 1 *Reached Jupiter in 1979 and Saturn in 1980.*

1977 Voyager 2 *Reached Jupiter in 1979, Saturn in 1981, Uranus in 1986, Neptune in 1989.*

1978 Pioneer Venus 1 *Operated in Venus orbit 14 years.*

1989 Magellan *Orbited and mapped Venus.*

1989 Galileo *Reached Jupiter, 1995.*

1996 Mars Pathfinder *Landed on Mars, sent a roving vehicle (Sojourner) to explore the surface.*

1997 Cassini *Expected to reach Saturn in 2004.*

1998 Lunar Prospector *Began yearlong orbit.*

1999 Stardust *Expected to reach Comet Wild-2 in 2004 to collect dust samples and return them to Earth in 2006.*

2001 Mars Odyssey *Launched in April 2001 to study mineralogy and radiation of the planet's surface. Odyssey will orbit Mars for five years and act as a communications relay for future Mars missions.*

A composite of photos taken by Pathfinder on the surface of Mars. Sojourner is to the right.

Comets, Asteroids, and Satellites

What else is in the solar system?

COMETS are fast-moving chunks of ice, dust, and rock that form huge gaseous heads as they move nearer to the Sun. One of the most well-known is **Halley's Comet**. It can be seen about every 76 years and will appear in the sky again in the year 2061.

Comet Hale-Bopp ▲

ASTEROIDS (or minor planets) are solid chunks of rock or metal that range in size from very small, like grains of sand, to very large. **Ceres**, the largest, is about 600 miles across. Thousands of asteroids orbit the Sun between Mars and Jupiter.

SATELLITES are objects that move in an orbit around a planet. Moons are natural satellites. Satellites made by humans are used as space stations and astronomical observatories. They are also used to photograph Earth's surface and to transmit communications signals.

WHAT IS AN ECLIPSE?

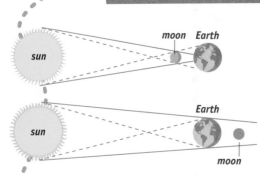

A **solar eclipse** occurs when the moon moves between the Sun and Earth, casting a shadow over part of Earth. When the moon completely blocks out the Sun, it is called a **total** solar eclipse. When this happens, a halo of gas can be seen around the Sun. This is called the **corona**.

Sometimes Earth casts a shadow on the moon. This is called a **lunar eclipse**. Usually, it lasts longer than a solar eclipse. The moon remains visible, but becomes dark, often with a reddish tinge (from sunlight bent through Earth's atmosphere).

UPCOMING TOTAL SOLAR ECLIPSES

DECEMBER 4, 2002
Will be seen in southern Africa, over the Indian Ocean, and in Australia.

AUGUST 21, 2017
Will be seen from Oregon to South Carolina.

APRIL 8, 2024
Will be seen from Mexico to the Northeastern United States and Canada.

Did You KNOW?

IN 1996, NASA LAUNCHED *NEAR SHOEMAKER* TO STUDY ASTEROIDS. *In February 2001, NEAR became the first spacecraft to land on an asteroid. It came to rest on Eros, a 21-mile-long asteroid and the second-largest near Earth.*

CONSTELLATIONS

Ancient cultures used myths to explain how constellations came to be. The constellation of **Cassiopeia** looks like the letter "W" in the sky. In Greek mythology, Cassiopeia was an Ethiopian queen. She was the wife of **Cepheus** and the mother of **Andromeda**. According to tradition, when she died, she was changed into the constellation that is named after her.

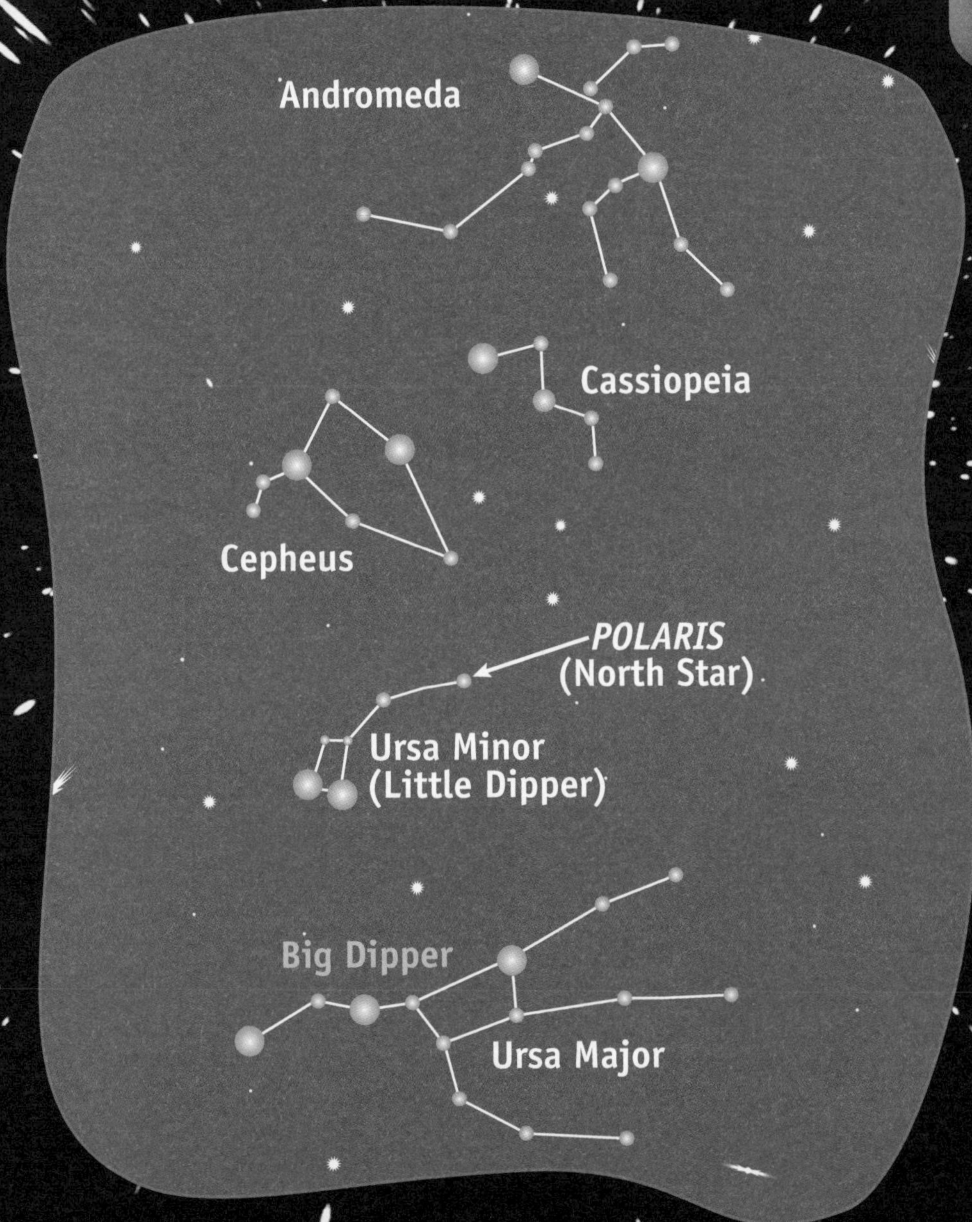

Andromeda

Cassiopeia

Cepheus

POLARIS (North Star)

Ursa Minor (Little Dipper)

Big Dipper

Ursa Major

BIG QUESTIONS

HOW OLD IS THE UNIVERSE? Scientists estimate the universe began about 13 to 15 billion years ago. Many experts believe it formed from the Big Bang. According to this theory, everything—all matter and energy—was packed together into a tiny space. This blew apart in a huge explosion, and the universe was born. Ever since, the universe has been expanding. Some astronomers believe the universe will eventually get so big it will start to collapse on itself. (They call that collapse "The Gnab Gib," "Big Bang" spelled backwards.) Others expect it to expand forever. Maybe *The World Almanac for Kids 2999* will have the answer!

WHAT IS A LIGHT-YEAR? Nothing moves faster than light, which travels 186,000 miles a second. A light-year is the distance light travels in a year—about 5.9 trillion miles. The nearest star to Earth, Alpha Centauri, is four light-years away. When we see Alpha Centauri in the night sky, the light we see is from four years ago.

IS EARTH THE ONLY PLACE WITH WATER? No. For example, Mars has ice at its north pole. Dry canyons on its surface suggest Mars also may have had liquid water. One of Jupiter's moons, Europa, is covered with ice. Below this layer may be a large salty ocean. Another of its moons, Ganymede, may have thick layers of ice floating in deep seas. Astronomers are especially interested in signs of water as they search for evidence of life outside of Earth.

WHAT IS A GALAXY? A **galaxy** is a group of billions of stars held together by gravity. Galaxies also contain interstellar gas and dust. The universe may have about 50 billion galaxies. The one we live in is called the **Milky Way**. The Sun and the stars we see are just a few of the 200 billion stars in the Milky Way. Light from a star along one edge of the galaxy would take about 100,000 years to reach the other edge.

WHAT ARE METEORS, METEORITES, AND METEOR SHOWERS? On a clear night, you may see a sudden streak of light in the sky. It may be caused by chunks of rock or metal called **meteoroids** speeding through space. When a meteoroid enters Earth's atmosphere, friction with air molecules causes it to burn brightly. The streak we see is called a **meteor**, or **shooting star**.

Many meteoroids follow in the path of a comet as it orbits the sun. As these meteoroids enter Earth's atmosphere, many can be seen coming from about the same area. These streaks are called **meteor showers**. If a meteoroid is big enough to land without burning up completely, it is called a **meteorite**.

Did You KNOW?

▶ Other planets exist outside our solar system. These are too far away to see. But astronomers know where the planets are by studying movements of the stars they orbit. A revolving planet's gravity can pull on a star, causing it to wobble.

▶ Earth's largest telescopes are hundreds of miles off the ground, in Earth's orbit. The Hubble Space Telescope, launched in 1990, has located whirlpools of gas in space, offering proof of the existence of black holes—remains of exploded stars, so heavy that they pull in light around them and can't be seen. This telescope has also found signs of oxygen in the atmosphere of one of Jupiter's moons.

ASTRONAUTS IN OUTER SPACE

The rapid entry of the United States into space in 1958 was in response to the Soviet Union's launching of its satellite *Sputnik I* into orbit on October 4, 1957. In 1961, three years after NASA was formed, President John F. Kennedy promised Americans that the United States would land a person on the moon by the end of the 1960s. NASA landed a human on the moon in July 1969. Since then, many astronauts have made trips into outer space. This time line gives some of the major flights of astronauts into space.

1961 — On April 12, Soviet cosmonaut Yuri Gagarin, in *Vostok 1*, became the **first human to orbit Earth.** On May 5, U.S. astronaut Alan B. Shepard Jr. of the *Mercury 3* mission became the **first American in space.**

1962 — On February 20, U.S. astronaut John H. Glenn Jr. of *Mercury 6* became the **first American to orbit Earth.**

1963 — From June 16 to 19, the Soviet spacecraft *Vostok 6* carried the **first woman in space**, Valentina V. Tereshkova.

1965 — On March 18, Soviet cosmonaut Aleksei A. Leonov became the **first person to walk in space.** He spent 10 minutes outside the spaceship. On December 15, U.S. *Gemini 6A* and *7* (with astronauts) became the **first vehicles to rendezvous** (approach and see each other) **in space.**

1966 — On March 16, U.S. *Gemini 8* became the **first craft to dock with** (become attached to) **another vehicle** (an unmanned *Agena* rocket).

1967 — On January 27, a fire in a U.S. *Apollo* spacecraft on the ground killed astronauts Virgil I. Grissom, Edward H. White, and Roger B. Chaffee. On April 24, *Soyuz 1* crashed to the Earth, killing Soviet cosmonaut Vladimir Komarov.

1969 — On July 20, after successful flights of *Apollo 8, 9,* and *10*, U.S. *Apollo 11's* **lunar module** *Eagle* **landed on the moon's surface** in the area known as the Sea of Tranquility. Neil Armstrong became the **first person ever to walk on the moon.**

1970 — In April, *Apollo 13* astronauts returned safely to Earth after an explosion damaged their spacecraft and prevented them from landing on the moon.

1971 — In July and August, U.S. *Apollo 15* astronauts tested the **Lunar Rover** on the moon.

1972 — In December, *Apollo 17* was the sixth and **final U.S. space mission to land successfully on the moon.**

1973 — On May 14, the U.S. put its **first space station**, **Skylab**, **into orbit.** The last Skylab crew left in January 1974.

1975 — On July 15, the U.S. launched *Apollo 18* and the U.S.S.R. launched *Soyuz 19*. Two days later, the **American and Soviet spacecraft docked**, and for several days their crews worked and spent time together in space. This was NASA's last space mission with astronauts until the space shuttle.

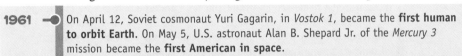

SHUTTLES and SPACE STATIONS

In the 1970s, NASA developed the space shuttle program. Earlier space capsules could not be used again after returning to Earth.

In 1986, the Soviet Union launched its *Mir* space station. By the mid-1990s, the United States and Russia were sharing projects in space. By the late 1990s, they had joined other nations in planning an International Space Station.

1977 — The first shuttle, **Enterprise**, took off from the back of a 747 jet airliner.

1981 — **Columbia** was launched and became the first shuttle to reach Earth's orbit.

1983 — In April, NASA began using a third shuttle, **Challenger**. Two more **Challenger** flights in 1983 included astronauts Sally K. Ride and Guion S. Bluford Jr., the first American woman and first African-American man in space. In November, **Columbia** was launched carrying Spacelab, a European scientific laboratory.

1984 — In August, the shuttle **Discovery** was launched for the first time.

1985 — In October, the shuttle **Atlantis** was launched for the first time.

1986 — On January 28, after 24 successful missions, **Challenger** exploded 73 seconds after takeoff. Astronauts Dick Scobee, Michael Smith, Ellison Onizuka, Judith Resnik, Greg Jarvis, and Ron McNair, and teacher Christa McAuliffe died. In February, the Soviet space station **Mir** was launched into orbit.

1988 — In September new safety procedures led to a successful launch of **Discovery**.

1990 — On April 24, the **Hubble Space Telescope** was launched from **Discovery**, but the images sent back to Earth were fuzzy.

1992 — In May, NASA launched a new shuttle, **Endeavour**.

1993 — In December, a crew aboard **Endeavour** repaired the Hubble telescope.

1995 — In March, astronaut Norman Thagard became the first American to travel in a Russian spacecraft; he joined cosmonauts on **Mir**. In June, **Atlantis** docked with **Mir** for the first time.

1996 — In March, Shannon Lucid joined the **Mir** crew. She spent 188 days in space, setting the record for all American and all female astronauts.

1998 — In October astronaut John Glenn was launched into space a second time, aboard the shuttle **Discovery**. In December, **Endeavour** was launched with **Unity**, a U.S.-built part of the International Space Station. The crew attached it to the Russian-built **Zarya** control module.

1999 — In June, **Discovery** astronauts docked with the International Space Station and unloaded 2 tons of supplies. In July, Eileen Collins became the first woman to command a shuttle, the **Columbia.** In December, space shuttle astronauts repaired the **Hubble Space Telescope.**

2000 — In February, **Endeavour** used radar to produce a very accurate map of Earth's features.

2001 — In February, **Atlantis** carried the lab module **Destiny** to the International Space Station (see page 213). **Mir** parts splashed down in the Pacific Ocean east of New Zealand in March, ending the 15-year Russian program.

Astronauts repair the Hubble Space Telescope ▶

INTERNATIONAL SPACE STATION

After years of research and planning, a permanent space research laboratory in orbit around Earth is being built. The International Space Station is a project that 16 countries, including the United States and Russia, are working on together. Three astronauts arrived by space shuttle to live on the station in November 2000. In February 2001, the U.S. laboratory *Destiny* was delivered and installed. It will let astronauts conduct year-round experiments. New parts of the station were delivered in March 2001, along with a new crew.

Four more shuttle missions to the station were scheduled through the rest of 2001. The completed station will weigh almost 500 tons. It will be as long as a football field, including end zones. Fifty-two computers will control its systems and six scientific laboratories.

To find out when you might see the Space Station in orbit over your town, go to *http://spaceflight.nasa.gov*

THE ZODIAC

The zodiac is an imaginary belt that goes around the sky. The orbits of the sun, moon, and most planets are within it. It crosses parts of 21 constellations. Below are the symbols for the 12 constellations most commonly associated with the zodiac.

ARIES (Ram)
March 21–April 19

TAURUS (Bull)
April 20–May 20

GEMINI (Twins)
May 21–June 21

CANCER (Crab)
June 22–July 22

LEO (Lion)
July 23–August 22

VIRGO (Maiden)
August 23–Sept. 22

LIBRA (Balance)
Sept. 23–Oct. 23

SCORPIO (Scorpion)
Oct. 24–Nov. 21

SAGITTARIUS
(Archer)
Nov. 22–Dec. 21

CAPRICORN (Goat)
Dec. 22–Jan. 19

AQUARIUS
(Water Bearer)
Jan. 20–Feb. 18

PISCES (Fishes)
Feb. 19–March 20

All About... PLANETARIUMS

Planetariums are theaters with big domes, where you can see images of space and the night sky. Today, these shows are more spectacular than ever—using advanced technology to show billions of stars and the entire universe in three dimensions. Many new or redesigned planetariums opened in the United States in 2000 and 2001.

Here are two of the newest planetariums:

The Rose Center for Earth and Space, American Museum of Natural History, New York, New York.
WEB SITE *http://www.amnh.org*

Exploration Place, Wichita, Kansas.
WEB SITE *http://www.exploration.org*

What was unusual about Mario Lemieux's comeback? *You can find the answer on page 223.*

SPORTS

BASEBALL

In 2000 the New York Yankees beat the New York Mets in five close games to win their third championship in a row. It was their fourth World Series win in five years and their 26th overall. The Yankees have won more championships than any other major pro sports franchise in North America. The 2000 World Series was called a "subway series" because all the games could be reached by riding the New York City subways—for the first time in 44 years.

▼ Kazuhiro Sasaki, voted 2000 AL Rookie of the Year at age 32, after pitching 10 seasons in Japan

2000 MAJOR LEAGUE LEADERS

MVP AWARD
AL: Jason Giambi, Oakland
NL: Jeff Kent, San Francisco

CY YOUNG AWARD (top pitcher)
AL: Pedro Martinez, Boston
NL: Randy Johnson, Arizona

ROOKIE OF THE YEAR
AL: Kazuhiro Sasaki, Seattle
NL: Rafael Furcal, Atlanta

BATTING CHAMPS
AL: Nomar Garciaparra, Boston, .372
NL: Todd Helton, Colorado, .372

HOME RUN LEADERS
AL: Troy Glaus, Anaheim, 47
NL: Sammy Sosa, Chicago, 50

EARNED RUN AVERAGE LEADERS
AL: Pedro Martinez, Boston, 1.74
NL: Kevin Brown, Los Angeles, 2.58

COOL FEATS, FACTS, AND FIRSTS

▶ Don Baylor was hit by a pitch 267 times in his career—a major-league record.

▶ On August 10, 1944, Charley "Red" Barrett of the (Boston) Braves pitched a complete 9-inning shutout against the Reds—and only threw 58 pitches!

▶ A Reds-Dodgers doubleheader on August 26, 1930, was the first pro baseball game on TV.

▶ Harvey Haddix pitched 12 perfect innings for the Pirates in a 1959 game against the (Milwaukee) Braves—and lost, 1-0, in the 13th!

▶ To celebrate his 100th homer in 1963, N.Y. Met Jimmy Piersall ran the bases backward.

▶ Only 4 players have ever played all 9 positions in one game. In 2000, it happened twice! The Rangers' Scott Sheldon did it (September 6) and then Shane Halter did it for the Tigers (October 1).

▶ Hall of Famer Robin Roberts gave up more homers in his career than any other pitcher—505.

▶ Super slugger Mark McGwire was originally drafted by the Expos as a pitcher!

MEMORABLE MOMENT

October 3, 1951—"The Shot Heard 'Round the World" The N.Y. Giants had trailed the Brooklyn Dodgers all summer and were 13½ games behind on August 11, but they began a 16-game winning streak the next day. The Giants won 37 of their last 44 regular-season games to force a 3-game playoff with the Dodgers. After each team won a game, the Giants were trailing 4-2 in the bottom of the 9th in the third game, at the Polo Grounds. With 1 out and 2 men on base, Bobby Thomson hit a home run off pitcher Ralph Branca to win the game and the National League pennant.

As famous as Thomson's dramatic homer is announcer Russ Hodges's excited reaction: "The Giants win the pennant! The Giants win the pennant! The Giants win the pennant! The Giants win the pennant!"

All About... THE NEGRO LEAGUES

In the early 20th century Major League Baseball, like America, was segregated. Black and Latino players weren't allowed in the majors. They formed their own teams and traveled around, playing exhibition games against each other and any other teams they could find. This was called "barnstorming." In the 1920s and '30s, pro leagues such as the Negro National League, the Eastern Colored League, and the Negro American League were formed. The Homestead Grays (Pennsylvania), Pittsburgh Crawfords, and Kansas City

Willie Mays (left)
Roy Campanella

Monarchs were some of the more successful teams. Famous players included Josh Gibson, a powerful home run hitter called the "black Babe Ruth"; James "Cool Papa" Bell, a base-stealer said to be so fast he could "turn out the light and get in bed before the room got dark"; and the legendary Leroy "Satchel" Paige who pitched into his 50s.

In 1947, a young infielder named Jackie Robinson took the field for the Brooklyn Dodgers, and the "color line" was finally broken. Facing slurs from fans, opponents, and even teammates, Robinson led the National League in stolen bases and was named Rookie of the Year. His courage and talent helped change attitudes in baseball and in America. Some of the greatest names in baseball—such as Hank Aaron (Indianapolis Clowns), Ernie Banks (Kansas City Monarchs), Roy Campanella (Baltimore Elite Giants), Willie Mays (Birmingham Black Barons), and Don Newcombe (Newark Eagles)—started out in the Negro Leagues and followed Robinson into the majors.

Baseball Hall of Fame

The National Baseball Hall of Fame and Museum opened in 1939, in Cooperstown, New York. To be eligible for membership, players must be retired from baseball for five years.

Address: 25 Main Street, PO Box 590, Cooperstown, NY 13326
Phone: (607) 547-7200; toll-free: (888) 425-5633
WEBSITE http://www.baseballhalloffame.org

LITTLE LEAGUE

Little League Baseball is the largest youth sports program in the world. It began in 1939 in Williamsport, Pennsylvania, with 45 boys playing on three teams. Now nearly three million boys and girls ages 5 to 18 play on 200,000 Little League teams in more than 80 countries.

WEBSITE http://www.littleleague.org

BASKETBALL

Basketball began in 1891 in Springfield, Massachusetts, when Dr. James Naismith invented it, using peach baskets as hoops. At first, each team had nine players instead of five. Big-time pro basketball started in 1949, when the National Basketball Association (NBA) was formed. The Women's National Basketball Association (WNBA) began play in 1997.

HIGHLIGHTS OF THE 2000-2001 NBA SEASON

MVP & SCORING LEADER: Allen Iverson, Philadelphia 76ers
Games: 71   Points: 2,207   Average: 31.1

REBOUNDING LEADER: Dikembe Mutombo, Philadelphia 76ers
Games: 75   Rebounds: 1,015   Average: 13.5

ASSISTS LEADER: Jason Kidd, Phoenix Suns
Games: 77   Assists: 753   Average: 9.8

STEALS LEADER: Allen Iverson, Philadelphia 76ers
Games: 71   Steals: 178   Average: 2.51

BLOCKED SHOTS LEADER: Theo Ratliff, Atlanta Hawks
Games: 50   Blocks: 187   Average: 3.74

NBA HALL OF FAME

The Naismith Memorial Basketball Hall of Fame was founded in 1959 to honor great basketball players, coaches, referees, and others important to the history of the game.

Address: 1150 W. Columbus Ave., Springfield, MA 01105.
Phone: (413) 781-6500.
WEB SITE *http://www.hoophall.com*

Two Players: 17 Rings

Michael Jordan's storybook career ended with a last-second shot that gave the Chicago Bulls their 6th NBA championship of the '90s. Many fans consider Air Jordan the greatest player ever. His accomplishments are impressive: 5-time NBA MVP, 6-time Championship MVP, 10 scoring titles—to name a few. His soaring dunks and amazing moves have made him one of the world's most recognizable stars.

▲ *Bill Russell (left) presenting Michael Jordan his 5th MVP award*

But another NBA superstar led his team to almost *twice* as many titles as his "Airness." During his 13-year career, Bill Russell and the Boston Celtics won 11 NBA championships between 1957 and 1969, including an amazing 8 in a row! In 1966, Russell became the first African-American head coach in the NBA, and as a player-coach led the Celtics to championships in 1968 and 1969. Russell was also a 5-time NBA MVP and is considered the greatest defensive center ever.

The Harlem Globetrotters

When Abe Saperstein founded the Globetrotters in Chicago in 1927, they were a serious team. The fun-loving style of today's Globetrotters didn't develop until 1939. One night, with a 107-point lead, players clowned around and the crowd loved it! They began to work comic sketches and displays of basketball wizardry into their games every night. In the 1940s Reece "Goose" Tatum developed many routines and the role of the "Clown Prince"—later played by "Meadowlark" Lemon, then "Geese" Ausbie. Another famous trotter was "Curly" Neal, one of the world's greatest dribblers. Now in their 75th year, the Trotters have entertained more than 100 million fans in 115 countries. On November 13, 2000, Michigan State beat the Trotters, 72-68, snapping a 1,270-game winning streak. For the record, the Globetrotters once won 8,829 games in a row!

Did You KNOW? Among sports stars who once played for the Globetrotters were NBA Hall of Famers Wilt Chamberlain and Connie Hawkins, baseball Hall of Fame pitcher Bob Gibson, and boxing great Sugar Ray Robinson.

HIGHLIGHTS OF THE 2000 WNBA SEASON

MOST VALUABLE PLAYER: Sheryl Swoopes, Houston Comets
DEFENSIVE PLAYER OF THE YEAR: Sheryl Swoopes, Houston Comets
ROOKIE OF THE YEAR: Bettie Lennox, Minnesota Lynx
COACH OF THE YEAR: Michael Cooper, Los Angeles Sparks
SCORING LEADER: Sheryl Swoopes, Houston Comets
Games: 31   Points: 643   Average: 20.7
REBOUNDING LEADER: Natalie Williams, Utah Starzz
Games: 29   Rebounds: 336   Average: 11.6
ASSISTS LEADER: Ticha Penicheiro, Sacramento Monarchs
Games: 30   Assists: 236   Average: 7.9

SUPER-DUPER COOPER

Long before her success in the WNBA, Cynthia Cooper was a winner. Her high school team won the California state championship (Locke High, 1981). In college, she led the USC Lady Trojans to the Final Four three times, winning the national title twice (1983, '84). Playing for Team USA, she won an Olympic gold medal in 1988 and a bronze in 1992. After playing in Europe, Cooper came to the WNBA, where she led the Houston Comets to four consecutive championships and was named MVP of the finals each time. Cooper was also named WNBA MVP twice (1997, '98) and led the league in scoring for three years. What's next for this superstar? You can bet it involves basketball! Now retired as a player, she became the coach of the Phoenix Mercury in January 2001.

COLLEGE BASKETBALL

The National Collegiate Athletic Association (NCAA) Tournament began in 1939. Today, it is a spectacular 65-team extravaganza. The Final Four weekend, when the semi-finals and finals are played, is one of the most-watched sports events in the U.S. The Women's NCAA Tournament began in 1982. Since then, the popularity of the women's game has grown by leaps and (re)bounds.

THE 2001 NCAA TOURNAMENT RESULTS

MEN'S FINAL FOUR

SEMI-FINALS:
Arizona 80, Michigan State 61
Duke 95, Maryland 84

CHAMPIONSHIP GAME:
Duke 82, Arizona 72

MOST OUTSTANDING PLAYER:
Shane Battier, Duke

WOMEN'S FINAL FOUR

SEMI-FINALS:
Purdue 81, Southwest Missouri State 64
Notre Dame 90, Connecticut 75

CHAMPIONSHIP GAME:
Notre Dame 68, Purdue 66

MOST OUTSTANDING PLAYER:
Ruth Riley, Notre Dame

THE JOHN R. WOODEN AWARD

Awarded to the nation's outstanding male college basketball player by the Los Angeles Athletic Club.
2001 winner: Shane Battier, Duke

THE WADE TROPHY

Awarded to the nation's outstanding female college basketball player by the National Association for Girls and Women in Sport.
2001 winner: Jackie Stiles, Southwest Missouri State

NAISMITH AWARD WINNERS 2000-2001

Presented by the Atlanta Tipoff Club to honor the nation's best in college basketball.

MEN
Player of the Year: Shane Battier, Duke
Coach of the Year: Rod Barnes, Ole Miss

WOMEN
Player of the Year: Ruth Riley, Notre Dame
Coach of the Year: Muffet McGraw, Notre Dame

All About... JACKIE STILES

In March 2001, All-American Jackie Stiles led Southwest Missouri State to the Final Four (where they lost to Purdue) and finished her career with 3,393 points—the most ever in women's NCAA Division I. Her 1,062 points for the season was also a record. From tiny Clafin, Kansas (pop. 600), Jackie has been a regional superstar since she was 15. Fans lined up hours before her games and waited for autographs afterward. She's the all-time leading scorer—boy or girl—in Kansas high school history. She once scored 61 points in one half! Jackie, whose dedication is legendary, is said to have made 1,000 shots a day in practice. In April, she became only the 6th woman ever drafted by a men's professional team (U.S. Basketball League) and she was selected 4th in the WNBA draft by the Portland Fire. Jackie is finally getting the national attention she deserves!

FOOTBALL

American football began as a college sport. The first game that was like today's football took place between Yale and Harvard in New Haven, Connecticut, on November 13, 1875. The National Football League started in 1922. The rival American Football League began in 1960. The two leagues played the first Super Bowl in 1967. In 1970, the AFL merged with the NFL.

DEE-FENSE WINS SUPER BOWL

At Super Bowl XXXV in Tampa, Florida, the AFC's Baltimore Ravens dominated the NFC's New York Giants, 34-7. Baltimore's All-Pro linebacker Ray Lewis, who had five tackles and 4 pass deflections, was named Super Bowl MVP. The Ravens' smothering defense—which set an NFL record by allowing only 165 points in a 16-game season—intercepted the Giants 4 times, tying a Super Bowl record. The Ravens join the Oakland Raiders (1981) and Denver Broncos (1998) as the only wild-card teams to win a Super Bowl.

2000 NFL LEADERS & AWARDS

▲ *Peyton Manning*

RUSHING LEADER: Edgerrin James, Indianapolis Colts • 1,709

RUSHING TDs: Marshall Faulk, St. Louis Rams • 18

RECEPTIONS: Marvin Harrison, Indianapolis Colts; Muhsin Muhammad, Carolina Panthers (tie) • 102

RECEIVING YARDS: Torry Holt, St. Louis Rams • 1,635

RECEIVING TDs: Randy Moss, Minnesota Vikings • 15

PASSING YARDS: Peyton Manning, Indianapolis Colts • 4,413

PASSER RATING: Brian Griese, Denver Broncos • 102.9

PASSING TDs: Daunte Culpepper, Minnesota Vikings; Peyton Manning, Indianapolis Colts (tie) • 33

PASS INTERCEPTIONS: Darren Sharper, Green Bay Packers • 9

SACKS: La'Roi Glover, New Orleans • 17

2000 ASSOCIATED PRESS AWARDS
Most Valuable Player: Marshall Faulk, St. Louis Rams
Offensive Player of the Year: Marshall Faulk, St. Louis Rams
Defensive Player of the Year: Ray Lewis, Baltimore Ravens
Coach of the Year: Jim Haslett, New Orleans, Saints
Offensive Rookie of the Year: Mike Anderson, Denver Broncos
Defensive Rookie of the Year: Brian Urlacher, Chicago Bears
Comeback Player of the Year: Joe Johnson, New Orleans Saints
Super Bowl Most Valuable Player: Ray Lewis, Baltimore Ravens

WEB SITE *http://www.nfl.com*

FANTASTIC FINISHES

"The Greatest Game Ever Played" **December 28, 1958, NFL Championship, New York, New York (Yankee Stadium): Baltimore Colts 23, New York Giants 17** With a 14-3 lead in the 3rd quarter, the Colts had the ball on the Giants' 1-yard line and seemed to be on their way to an easy win. But the Giants made a determined goal-line stand, got the ball on their own 5-yard line, and drove downfield for a TD. In the 4th quarter, Frank Gifford caught a TD pass to give the Giants a 17-14 lead. But Colts star quarterback Johnny Unitas passed his team down the field, completing 3 to Ray Berry for 62 yards. With 7 seconds left, the Colts kicked a field goal to force the first post-season overtime. In the extra period, the Giants punted and Unitas went to work. He took the Colts 80 yards before fullback Alan "The Horse" Ameche bulled into the end zone from the 1-yard line to end what many still call "the greatest game ever played."

"The Immaculate Reception" **December 23, 1972, AFC Divisional Playoffs, Pittsburgh, Pennsylvania: Pittsburgh Steelers 13, Oakland Raiders 7** Down 7-6, with just over a minute left, the Steelers' Terry Bradshaw fired a pass downfield to halfback John Fuqua, who was hit hard by Raiders defender Jack Tatum just as the ball arrived. It hit one of the players and bounced in the air and, luckily for the Steelers, into the hands of rookie running back Franco Harris. After his "immaculate reception," Harris ran 42 yards to score with 5 seconds left.

"The Drive" **January 11, 1987, AFC Championship, Cleveland, Ohio: Denver Broncos 23, Cleveland Browns 20 (OT)** Bronco quarterback John Elway led his team to so many 4th-quarter victories that he became known as the "Comeback Kid." This comeback was one of his most famous. Down 20-13 with 5:30 left in the game, Elway drove the Broncos from their own 2-yard line to the Browns' 6. With 39 seconds left, he hit Mark Jackson for a game-tying touchdown. An overtime field goal sent the Broncos to the Super Bowl.

"The Music City Miracle" **January 8, 2000, AFC Wildcard Playoff, Nashville, Tennessee: Tennessee 22, Buffalo Bills 16** After a field goal gave them a 16-15 lead, the Bills kicked off to the Titans with just 16 seconds left in the game. Lorenzo Neal fielded the kick at the Titan 24-yard line, took a step, then handed off to Frank Wycheck. Wycheck ran to his right, stopped, and threw the ball back across the field to a wide open Kevin Dyson. Dyson had a wall of blockers in front of him and raced 75 yards for a TD and a "miracle" win in the "Music City."

PRO FOOTBALL HALL OF FAME

Football's Hall of Fame was founded in 1963 by the National Football League to honor outstanding players, coaches, and contributors. **Address:** Pro Football Hall of Fame, 2121 George Halas Drive NW, Canton, OH 44708. **Phone:** (330) 456-8207.

WEB SITE *http://www.profootballhof.com*

Marshall Faulk, the St. Louis Rams running back, had another big year in 2000. His team failed to repeat as Super Bowl champions (losing to the New Orleans Saints in the first round of the NFC playoffs). Yet Faulk broke Emmitt Smith's record for the most touchdowns scored in a season. He ran for 18 touchdowns and scored another 8 as a receiver, for a total of 26.

COLLEGE FOOTBALL

College football is one of America's most colorful and exciting sports. The National Collegiate Athletic Association (NCAA), founded in 1906, oversees college football today.

The Oklahoma Sooners won the Orange Bowl and the national championship when they defeated the Florida State Seminoles, 13-2, January 3, 2001.

2000 TOP 5 COLLEGE TEAMS
Chosen by the Associated Press Poll and the USA Today/ESPN Poll

RANK	AP	USA TODAY/ESPN
1	Oklahoma	Oklahoma
2	Miami	Miami
3	Washington	Washington
4	Oregon State	Florida State
5	Florida State	Oregon State

HEISMAN TROPHY

The Heisman Trophy goes to the most outstanding U.S. college football player. The 2000 winner was 28-year-old Chris Weinke of Florida State University. Weinke, first recruited as a college player in 1990, is the oldest winner ever. He spent six years in minor league baseball before returning to college in 1997. In 2000, the 6'5", 229-pounder threw 33 touchdowns, with only 11 interceptions, and led the nation in passing with 4,167 yards.

DID YOU KNOW? *Facing unbeaten Army at Yankee Stadium in 1928, Notre Dame coach Knute Rockne knew he had to inspire his team. At halftime, he told them about a visit he had made to the hospital in 1920 to see George Gipp, the All-American halfback for Notre Dame, who died of pneumonia his senior year. In the 1940 film* Knute Rockne, All American, *it is Ronald Reagan, as George Gipp, who says the famous words: "Some day when the going is tough, ask the boys to win one for the Gipper." They did, 12-6.*

Great College Football Moments

November 23, 1984: Boston College 47, Miami 45 This game featured one of college football's greatest head-to-head passing performances. Boston College quarterback Doug Flutie, on the way to a Heisman Trophy, completed 34 of 46 passes for 472 yards. Miami's Bernie Kosar threw for 447 yards. Flutie won the game for BC by throwing a 64-yard "Hail Mary" touchdown pass to receiver Gerard Phelan in the last seconds!

November 20, 1982: California 25, Stanford 20 The Stanford Cardinals kicked off to the California Golden Bears with only four seconds left in the game and a 20-19 lead. After Cal got the kickoff, the ball was lateraled among four players. Thinking the game was over, Stanford's marching band started onto the field. The ball ended up with Cal's Kevin Moen, who had received the kickoff. Moen ran into the end zone, where he knocked over a Stanford trombone player. Cal won!

December 31, 1973, Sugar Bowl: Notre Dame 24, Alabama 23 This New Year's Eve game pitted the No. 1 Alabama Crimson Tide against the No. 3 Notre Dame Fighting Irish. The game was close from start to finish, and the lead changed hands 6 times. With 9:30 left, the Tide scored a touchdown to take the lead 23-21. But their kicker missed the extra point. With 4:26 to go, the Irish kicked a field goal and held on to win by one point.

GOLF

Golf began in Scotland as early as the 1400s. The first golf course in the U.S. opened in 1888 in Yonkers, NY. The sport has grown to include both men's and women's professional tours. And millions play golf just for fun.

The men's tour in the U.S. is run by the Professional Golf Association (PGA). The four major championships (with the year first played) are:

British Open (1860)
United States Open (1895)
PGA Championship (1916)
Masters Tournament (1934)

The women's tour in the U.S. is guided by the Ladies Professional Golf Association (LPGA). The four major championships are:

United States Women's Open (1946)
McDonald's LPGA Championship (1955)
Nabisco Championship (1972)
*Women's British Open (1976)

*Replaced the du Maurier Classic as a major in 2001.

All About... THE TIGER AND THE BEAR

His real name is Eldrick, but the world knows him as "Tiger" and he's chasing a legend called the "Golden Bear." That's Jack Nicklaus—golf's greatest champion and Tiger's idol. Jack won *18* majors in his career, a feat that seemed untouchable. Great golfers like Walter Hagen (11), Ben Hogan (9), Gary Player (9), Tom Watson (8), and Arnold Palmer (7) never came close. But Tiger is hot on the Bear's trail. In 2000, at 24, he replaced Jack as the youngest golfer ever to complete a career Grand Slam (win all 4 majors). By the time Jack was 28, he'd won 7 majors. Tiger is 25, and has already won 6! And at The Masters in 2001, Tiger did something no other golfer has *ever* done: he won his 4th major in a row.

WEB SITE http://tigerwoods.com • http://www.pga.com

Swedish Sensation

By April, the year 2001 was already an incredible one for Sweden's Annika Sorenstam. On March 16, she became only the fourth pro golfer ever—and the first woman—to shoot an 18-hole score of 59. Her winning total of 27-under-par was also an LPGA record for a 72-hole tournament. She won her third career major, the Nabisco Championship, on March 25. On April 14, she came from 10 strokes behind in the last round—another LPGA record—to win her fourth consecutive Tour event.

GYMNASTICS

It takes strength, coordination, and grace to become a top gymnast. Although the sport goes back to ancient Greece, modern-day gymnastics began in Sweden in the early 1800s. The sport has been part of the Olympics since 1896. The 2001 World Gymnastics Championships are scheduled for October 27 to November 4 in Ghent, Belgium.

ICE HOCKEY

Ice hockey began in Canada in the mid-1800s. The National Hockey League (NHL) was formed in 1916. With the addition of the Minnesota Wild and the Columbus (Ohio) Bluejackets, the NHL had 30 teams—24 in the U.S. and 6 in Canada—in the 2000-2001 season.

In 2000 the New Jersey Devils won their second Stanley Cup, defeating the defending champion Dallas Stars four games to two. Devils defenseman and team captain Scott Stevens won the Conn Smythe Trophy (Playoff MVP) for 2000. At right is a list of Stanley Cup winners since 1990.

SEASON	WINNER	RUNNER-UP
1990-91	Pittsburgh Penguins	Minnesota North Stars
1991-92	Pittsburgh Penguins	Chicago Black Hawks
1992-93	Montreal Canadiens	Los Angeles Kings
1993-94	New York Rangers	Vancouver Canucks
1994-95	New Jersey Devils	Detroit Red Wings
1995-96	Colorado Avalanche	Florida Panthers
1996-97	Detroit Red Wings	Philadelphia Flyers
1997-98	Detroit Red WIngs	Washington Capitals
1998-99	Dallas Stars	Buffalo Sabres
1999-2000	New Jersey Devils	Dallas Stars

All About...
LORD STANLEY'S CUP

In 1892, Lord Stanley, the British governor general of Canada, bought a silver cup (actually a bowl) as an annual prize for the best amateur hockey team in Canada.

Today, NHL champions have their names engraved on one of the silver rings around the cup's base. When all the bands are filled, the oldest one is retired to the Hockey Hall of Fame and a new ring is added.

The Stanley Cup is the only professional sports trophy that each player on the winning team gets to take home. The Cup has had many interesting adventures:

► In 1980, New York Islander Clark Gillies fed his dog from it. Gillies's teammate Bryan Trottier slept with it.

► In 1991, the cup turned up at the bottom of Mario Lemieux's swimming pool.

► In 1994, members of the New York Rangers took the cup on *The Late Show with David Letterman*. There it was used in a sketch called "Stupid Cup Tricks." The cup took such a beating from the Rangers that the NHL hired 2 "cup cops" to accompany the trophy at all times.

SUPER MARIO RETURNS

On December 27, 2000, the great Mario Lemieux returned to the ice with the Pittsburgh Penguins. Almost four years ago injuries and illness had forced him to retire from the NHL and he was inducted into the Hall of Fame in 1997. In 1999 he bought the Penguins. He is the only owner-player in the history of modern U.S. professional sports. There were thousands of fans in the sold-out Mellon Arena, but none was more important to Mario than his four-year-old son Austin. For the first time, he got to see his father play professionally.

HOCKEY HALL OF FAME

The Hockey Hall of Fame was opened in 1961 to honor hockey greats.
Address: BCE Place, 30 Yonge Street, Toronto, Ontario, Canada M5E 1X8.
Phone: (416) 360-7735
WEB SITE http://www.hhof.com

THE OLYMPIC GAMES

The first Olympics were held in Greece more than 2,500 years ago. In 776 B.C. they featured just one event—a footrace. Boxing, wrestling, chariot racing, and the pentathlon (which consists of five different events) came later. The Olympic Games were held every four years for more than 1,000 years, until A.D. 393, when a Roman emperor stopped them.

SOME MODERN OLYMPIC FIRSTS

1896 — **The first modern Olympic Games were held in Athens, Greece.** A total of 312 athletes from 13 nations participated in nine sports.

1900 — **Women competed in the Olympic Games for the first time.**

1908 — **For the first time, medals were awarded to the first three people to finish each event**—a gold for first, a silver for second, and a bronze for third.

1920 — **The Olympic flag was raised for the first time, and the Olympic oath was introduced.** The five interlaced rings of the flag represent: Africa, America, Europe, Asia, and Australia.

1924 — **The first Winter Olympics, featuring skiing and skating events, were held.**

The Olympic flame was introduced at the Olympic Games. A relay of runners carries a torch with the flame from Olympia, Greece, to the site of each Olympics.

1994 — **Starting with the 1994 Winter Olympics, the winter and summer Games have been held two years apart,** instead of in the same year.

2002 WINTER OLYMPICS: Salt Lake City

From February 8 to February 24, the world's attention will be focused on Utah's capital, which is nestled in a valley 4,300 feet above sea level, along the southern shore of the Great Salt Lake. About 3,500 athletes and officials from 80 countries are expected to take part. There will be 78 medal events in 7 sports. The mascots for the 2002 Games, symbolizing the Olympic motto of "Citius, Altius, Fortius"—Swifter, Higher, Stronger—are Powder, the snowshoe hare; Copper, the coyote; and Coal, the black bear. The next Olympics will be held in Athens, Greece (Summer 2004), and Turin, Italy (Winter 2006).

2000 SUMMER OLYMPIC HIGHLIGHTS FROM SYDNEY

▶ Greco-Roman wrestler Rulon Gardner upset Russian Aleksandr Karelin (9-time world champ and 3-time Olympic champ) for the super-heavyweight gold.

▶ Sprinter Marion Jones's 5 track and field medals for the U.S. (3 gold, 2 bronze) set a record for women at a single Olympics.

▶ Australia's Cathy Freeman, who lit the torch in the opening ceremonies, won the 400-meter dash, becoming the first Aborigine to win an individual gold medal.

▶ Made up largely of unknown minor leaguers, the U.S. baseball team won its first-ever gold and stopped Cuba's 20-year domination of international baseball.

▶ Competing with a broken foot, diver Laura Wilkinson won the first U.S. gold in 36 years in the 10-meter platform.

OLYMPIC SPORTS

SUMMER OLYMPIC SPORTS

Archery
Badminton
Baseball
Basketball
Boxing
Canoe/Kayak
  (slalom, sprint)
Cycling
  (road, mountain
  bike, track)
Diving
Equestrian
  (dressage, jumping,
  3-day event)

Fencing
Field Hockey
Football (Soccer)
Gymnastics
  (artistic, rhythmic, trampoline)
Handball
Judo
Modern Pentathlon
  (show jumping, running, fencing,
  pistol shooting, swimming—one
  event per day for 5 days)
Rowing
Sailing
Shooting

Softball
Swimming
Synchronized
  Swimming
Table Tennis
  (Ping-Pong)
Taekwondo
Tennis
Track and Field
Triathlon
Volleyball
  (beach, indoor)
Water Polo
Weightlifting
Wrestling

2002 WINTER OLYMPIC SPORTS

Alpine Skiing
  (downhill, slalom,
  giant slalom, super-G,
  Alpine combined)
Biathlon
  (cross-country
  skiing, rifle
  marksmanship)
Bobsled

Curling
Figure Skating
Freestyle Skiing
  (moguls, aerials)
Ice Hockey
Luge

Nordic Skiing
  (cross-country skiing, ski
  jumping, Nordic combined)
Skeleton
Snowboarding
  (parallel giant slalom,
  halfpipe)
Speed Skating
  (long track, short track)

All About... SNOWBOARDING

Sherman Poppen of Michigan produced a "Snurfer" back in 1965. It was just 2 skis bolted together, with a rope on the front to hold on to. Jake Burton had a Snurfer when he was a teenager, and in 1977 he started a company—Burton Snowboards—to improve on the concept. It took more than 100 different designs before Burton got the "snowboard" he wanted. Out west, another pioneering "snow-surfer," Tom Sims—of Sims Snowboards—was building boards as well. But it wasn't until 1983, when Stratton Mountain Resort in Vermont finally allowed snowboards on the slopes, that the sport really began to grow. Other resorts soon followed, and today, resorts that don't allow snowboards are rare.

Snowboarding became an Olympic sport in 1998. In 2002, there will be two events. In the *halfpipe*, a freestyle competition similar to skateboarding, individuals perform tricks off the walls of a U-shaped course and receive scores from a panel of judges. In the *parallel giant slalom*, an alpine (downhill) race, boarders compete side-by-side on separate courses, with the winner going on to the next round until there is a champion.

SKATING

Recreational skating began with highly waxed wooden blades. The first all-steel skate was invented by E.W. Bushnell of Philadelphia around 1850. There are two types of competitive ice skating today: figure skating and speed skating.

FIGURE SKATING

Figure skating, which is almost like ballet, is judged by the way the skaters perform certain turns and jumps and by the creative difficulty of their programs. There are singles competitions for both men and women, pairs skating, and ice dancing.

2001 WORLD CHAMPIONSHIPS

	WOMEN'S SINGLES	MEN'S SINGLES
Gold Medal:	Michelle Kwan, United States	Alexei Yagudin, Russia
Silver Medal:	Irina Slutskaya, Russia	Yevgeny Plushchenko, Russia
Bronze Medal:	Sarah Hughes, United States	Todd Eldredge, United States

All About... MICHELLE KWAN

Michelle has dreamed of winning Olympic gold since she started skating at age 5. At age 12, she was so determined that she passed the test for senior levels while her coach was out of town. At 13, she was an alternate on the 1994 U.S. Olympic team. In 2001, she won her *fifth* U.S. title and her *fourth* world championship. Now 21, Michelle has won about every title there is in figure skating—except that Olympic gold (she took silver at Nagano, Japan, in 1998). She hopes to finish her career as an Olympic champion. Next stop: Salt Lake City!

A native of Torrance, California, Michelle trains in nearby Lake Arrowhead with legendary coach Frank Carroll. She attends UCLA when she's not skating.

WEBSITE http://www.usfsa.org

AMERICA'S OLYMPIC CHAMPIONS
(for figure skating in singles competition)

MEN: Dick Button (1948, 1952), Hayes Alan Jenkins (1956), David Jenkins (1960), Scott Hamilton (1984), Brian Boitano (1988)

WOMEN: Tenley Albright (1956), Carol Heiss (1960), Peggy Fleming (1968), Dorothy Hamill (1976), Kristi Yamaguchi (1992), Tara Lipinski (1998)

SPEED SKATING

Speed skating is divided into two types: long track and short track. In long track, competitors race the clock skating around a 400-meter oval. This became an Olympic sport for men in 1942, for women in 1960. Short track skating only became an official Olympic sport in 1992. The track is much smaller (111 meters), with a pack of four to six skaters racing against each other instead of the clock.

WEBSITE http://www.usspeedskating.org

SOCCER

Soccer, which is called football in many countries, is the number one sport worldwide. It's played by more than 100 million people in some 150 countries. The first rules for the game were published in 1863 by the London Football Association. Since then, the sport has spread rapidly from Europe to almost every part of the world.

Nearly 18 million children (6 years old and up) and adults play soccer in the U.S., according to the 2000 Soccer Industry Council of America survey. Nearly 14 million are under the age of 18—the sport is growing fastest among young people between the ages of 12 and 17.

MAJOR LEAGUE SOCCER Kansas City Wizards goalkeeper Tony Meola was truly a wizard in 2000. He made 10 saves and won the MVP Award as the Wizards won the Major League Soccer (MLS) Cup 1-0 over the Chicago Fire. The 31-year-old Meola also set an MLS record with 16 regular-season shutouts and was named league MVP, Goalkeeper of the Year, and Comeback Player of the Year.

WEB SITE http://www.mlsnet.com

WOMEN'S PRO SOCCER Professional women's soccer came to the U.S. in April 2001, as teams from the Women's United Soccer Association (WUSA) took the field. The WUSA's eight teams are the Atlanta Beat, Bay Area CyberRays (who play in San Jose, California), Boston Breakers, Carolina Tempest, New York Power, Philadelphia Charge, San Diego Spirit, and Washington Freedom. Former Women's U.S. World Cup teammates Brandi Chastain, Julie Foudy, Mia Hamm, Kristine Lilly, and Briana Scurry all play in the WUSA now.

More than 34,000 fans attended the season opener on April 14, at RFK Stadium in Washington, D.C. The contest featured former U.S. national teammates Mia Hamm, now with the Freedom, and Brandi Chastain, of the CyberRays. The game was decided by a penalty in the 70th minute. Brandi, defending against Mia, was called for tripping. Freedom forward Pretinha, of Brazil, scored on the penalty kick to give the Freedom a 1-0 victory.

WEB SITE http://www.wusa.com

THE WORLD CUP The men's World Cup, the biggest soccer tournament in the world, was last held in France in 1998. On July 11, in St. Denis, a crowd of 80,000 watched the home country, France, upset 1994 champions Brazil, 3-0, to win their first World Cup. The French gave up just two goals in seven matches, the lowest number ever for a winner. The next Cup will be held in 2002, hosted by Japan and South Korea.

Did You Know?

THE WOMEN'S WORLD CUP *has been held three times (1991, 1995, 1999), with Team USA winning in 1991 and 1999. The next Women's World Cup is scheduled for 2003.*

SPECIAL OLYMPICS

The Special Olympics is the world's largest program of sports training and athletic competition for children and adults with special needs. Founded in 1968, Special Olympics International has offices in all 50 U.S. states and Washington, D.C., and throughout the world. The organization offers training and competition to 1.5 million athletes in 150 countries.

The first Special Olympics competition took place in Chicago in 1968. After national events in individual countries, Special Olympics International holds World Games. These alternate between summer and winter sports every two years. In March 2001, more than 2,500 athletes and coaches from 80 countries gathered in Anchorage, Alaska, for the World Winter Games. More than 7,000 athletes from 160 countries are expected at the 2003 World Summer Games in Dublin, Ireland, the first to be held outside of the U.S.

SPECIAL OLYMPICS OFFICIAL SPORTS

▶ **Winter:** alpine and cross-country skiing, figure and speed skating, floor hockey, snowshoeing, snowboarding

▶ **Summer:** aquatics (swimming and diving), athletics (track and field), basketball, bowling, cycling, equestrian, golf, gymnastics, powerlifting, roller skating, soccer, softball, tennis, volleyball

▶ **Demonstration sports:** badminton, bocce, sailing

For more information, contact Special Olympics International Headquarters, 1325 G Street NW, Suite 500, Washington, D.C. 20005. Phone: (202) 628-3630.

WEB SITE *http://www.specialolympics.org*

Swimming

When the modern Olympic Games began in Athens, Greece, in 1896, the only racing stroke was the breaststroke. Today, men and women at the Olympics swim the backstroke, breaststroke, butterfly, and freestyle, in events ranging from 50 meters to 1,500 meters.

SOME GREAT U.S. OLYMPIC SWIMMERS

MARK SPITZ made history by winning seven gold medals at the 1972 Games in Munich. He won 11 medals—nine gold—in his Olympic career.

MATT BIONDI won seven medals—five gold—at the 1988 Olympics in Seoul. He won eight gold medals, 11 overall, in his Olympic career from 1984 to 1992.

JANET EVANS, at age 17, won three golds at the 1988 Olympics in Seoul. In 1992 she won another gold and a silver at Barcelona.

DARA TORRES won five golds at the 2000 Games in Sydney, the most by a U.S. woman at one Olympiad. Seven years after retiring, she returned to become the first American to swim in four Olympics (1984, 1988, 1992, 2000).

AMERICAN SWIMMERS A SPLASHING SUCCESS

Team USA dominated the 2000 Olympics in Sydney, winning 14 golds (33 total medals), more than twice as many as host-country Australia (5 golds, 18 total medals) or the Netherlands (5 golds, 8 total medals). Brooke Bennett (400m, 800m freestyle) and Lenny Krayzelburg (100m, 200m backstroke) were two-time individual winners for the U.S.

TENNIS

Modern tennis began in 1873. It was based on court tennis. In 1877 the first championships were held in Wimbledon, near London. In 1881 the first official U.S. men's championships were held at Newport, Rhode Island. Six years later, the first women's championships took place, in Philadelphia. The four most important ("grand slam") tournaments today are the Australian Open, the French Open, the All-England (Wimbledon) Championships, and the U.S. Open.

GRAND SLAM TOURNAMENTS

ALL-TIME GRAND SLAM SINGLES WINNERS					
MEN	Australian	French	Wimbledon	U.S.	Total
Pete Sampras (b. 1971)	2	0	7	4	13
Roy Emerson (b. 1936)	6	2	2	2	12
Bjorn Borg (b. 1956)	0	6	5	0	11
Rod Laver (b. 1938)	3	2	4	2	11
Bill Tilden (1893–1953)	*	0	3	7	10
WOMEN					
Margaret Smith Court (b. 1942)	11	5	3	5	24
Steffi Graf (b. 1969)	4	6	7	5	22
Helen Wills Moody (1905–1998)	*	4	8	7	19
Chris Evert (b. 1954)	2	7	3	6	18
Martina Navratilova (b. 1956)	3	2	9	4	18

*Never played in tournament.

All About...
VENUS AND SERENA WILLIAMS

Sometimes their hair and clothes get as much attention as their tennis game—and that gets a lot of attention. Venus can serve the ball 127 miles per hour! And they're almost unstoppable as doubles partners—the hard-hitting sisters have already racked up championships at the Australian Open (2001), French Open (1999, 2000), Wimbledon (2000), U.S. Open (1999), and the Sydney Olympics (2000). Younger sister Serena was the first of the pair to win a Grand Slam singles title, taking the U.S. Open in 1999. But Venus was the star of 2000, winning singles titles at Wimbledon, the U.S. Open, and the Sydney Olympics. Venus and Serena finished the 2000 season with world rankings of third and sixth, respectively. They live in Palm Beach, Florida, where they are managed and coached by their father, Richard Williams.

"KING OF CLAY"

Brazilian Gustavo Kuerten finished the 2000 season as the first South American player ever to be ranked number-one in the world. Gustavo, nicknamed "Guga," has been called the "King of Clay" because all ten of his professional wins (by early 2001) were on clay courts. In 2000, he won his second French Open—the only Grand Slam event held on clay—in four years and had a 28-6 record in matches played on the tricky surface.

TRANSPORTATION

How can a pig fly? You can find the answer on page 232.

Can you imagine life without bikes, buses, cars, planes, trains, or boats? Can you imagine a time when people could go only as fast and far as their legs or their animals' legs could carry them?

A SHORT HISTORY OF TRANSPORTATION
WIND, WHEELS, AND WATER

5000 B.C.
People discover animal-muscle power. Oxen and donkeys carry heavy loads.

3500 B.C.
Egyptians create the first sailboat. Before this, people made rafts or canoes and paddled them with poles or their hands.

1450s
Portuguese build fast ships with three masts. These plus the compass usher in an age of exploration.

1730s
Stagecoach service begins in the U.S.

 5000 B.C.

3500 B.C.
In Mesopotamia (modern-day Iraq), people invent vehicles with wheels. But the first wheels are made of heavy wood, and the roads are terrible.

1100 B.C.
Chinese invent the magnetic compass. It allows them to sail long distances.

1660s
Horse-drawn stagecoaches begin running in France. They stop at stages to switch horses and passengers—the first mass transit system.

1769
James Watt patents the first successful steam engine.

HOW LONG DID IT TAKE?

1492	Christopher Columbus's first trip across the Atlantic Ocean took 70 days. (Part of it was spent on the Canary Islands waiting for good winds.)
1650s	It took 50 days to sail across the Atlantic Ocean from London, England, to Boston, Massachusetts.
1819	The first Atlantic Ocean crossing by a ship powered in part by steam (*Savannah*, from Savannah, Georgia, to Liverpool, England) took 27 days.
1927	Charles Lindbergh flew from New York to Paris in 33½ hours. It was the first nonstop flight made across the Atlantic Ocean by one person.
1986	Richard Rutan and Jeana Yeager made the first nonstop flight around the world without refueling, in 9 days, 3 minutes.
1999	Bertrand Piccard and Brian Jones, in the *Breitling Orbiter 3*, completed the first around-the-world balloon flight, in 19 days, 21 hours, 55 minutes.

AGE OF MACHINES

1807
Robert Fulton patents a highly efficient steamboat.

1903
At Kitty Hawk, North Carolina, Orville Wright pilots the first powered heavier-than-air machine on a 12-second flight.

1939
The first practical helicopter and first jet plane are invented. The jet flies up to 434 mph. Jet passenger service began in 1958.

1981
The Space Shuttle *Columbia* is the first reusable spacecraft with a human crew.

1997
British driver Andy Green breaks the sound barrier on land for the first time, going 763 mph.

1839
Kirkpatrick Macmillan of Scotland invents the first pedaled bicycle.

1908
Henry Ford builds the first Model T, a practical car for the general public.

1961
Russian cosmonaut Yuri Gagarin orbits the Earth in a spaceship.

1830
Passenger rail service begins in England with the *Rocket,* a steam train built by George Stephenson. It goes about 24 miles an hour.

1862
Étienne Lenoir of Belgium builds the first car with an internal-combustion engine.

1947
Flying 700 mph, U.S. Air Force Capt. Charles "Chuck" Yeager breaks the sound barrier in the jet-powered Bell X-1.

1969
U.S. astronauts aboard *Apollo 11* land on the Moon.

2000
Amtrak runs its northeast high-speed *Acela* train. It can go 150 miles an hour.

All About... NAVIGATION SYSTEMS

Suppose you and your family are on the road, driving to somewhere you've never been. And you left your map at home! It's no problem if you have an on-board navigation system. This system can tell you how to get to where you want to go. A built-in computer receives information from the Global Positioning System (GPS), a network of 24 satellites orbiting the earth that uses radio waves to pinpoint your location. When the driver enters an address on a keypad, a map shows up on a dashboard computer screen. It lights up, showing which streets to take. More advanced systems can even "speak" the directions!

FLYING PIGS AND OTHER WEIRD BUT TRUE TALES

Pigs Can Fly! On October 17, 2000, one of the passengers aboard USAirways Flight 107 was a 300-pound pig. He was allowed on board when his owners showed a doctor's note. It said the pig helped relieve their stress and was, therefore, a medical aid.

Stuffed Goose *Spruce Goose*, the largest seaplane ever built, was 79 feet high with a 320-foot wing span. It was flown for about a mile and then placed in storage—never to fly again. Built in 1947 by Howard Hughes, an eccentric billionaire, the *Spruce Goose* got its name from its wooden skin. Many considered it a big waste. But it did show that very big airplanes could fly.

Last Tune-up The Cadillac Ranch, just outside Amarillo, Texas, consists of 10 old Cadillac cars buried nose down in a wheat field. The ranch began in 1974 as a tribute to the one of America's most admired cars. It remains a big tourist attraction.

Retro Ship Trip Around A.D. 1000, Viking explorers sailing from Iceland came to North America, first landing in Greenland. In 2000, a group of modern-day explorers re-created that feat in a replica of a Viking ship called the *Icelander*. The Viking re-enactors had to brave the cold, stormy North Atlantic in an open ship to make the 2,600-mile voyage.

Fuel of the Future? What kind of fuel could substitute for gasoline? **A.** solar power; **B.** pond scum; **C.** both? The answer is **C.** A few solar-powered cars are already on the road. As for the pond scum, scientists at the University of California at Berkeley found a way to make green algae produce large amounts of hydrogen. That hydrogen could be used in new fuel cells—or batteries—that already power some cars. In theory, a one-acre pond of algae could produce enough hydrogen to drive a car 900 miles.

All Gone The Reliant Robin, a three-wheeled car, is now history. The last ones came off the assembly line at a British factory in 2000, five years after the first was built. The earliest versions had handlebars instead of steering wheels. That meant drivers needed only easy-to-get motorcycle licenses to drive Robins. But stricter laws put an end to that. The cars get 65 miles to the gallon—nothing to laugh at. But there are lots of jokes about Robins. Here's a sample: **Q:** What do you call a Robin at the top of a hill? **A:** A miracle.

UNDER THE SEA

The Navy's largest **submarines** are powered by nuclear energy. They carry missiles that can hit targets 4,000 miles away. They make their own drinking water out of seawater and can stay under for months at a time.

MOST POPULAR CAR COLORS
(FOR 2000)

COMPACT/ SPORTS CARS	FULL-SIZE CARS	LUXURY CARS
❶ Silver	Silver	White Metallic
❷ Black	White	Silver
❸ White	Black	Black
❹ Light Brown	Med./ Dark Green	Light Brown
❺ Med./ Dark Green	Light Brown	White

DID YOU KNOW? The three top-selling cars in the U.S. are the Toyota Camry, the Honda Accord, and the Ford Taurus.

TRANSPORTATION IN THE FUTURE

Land

Paul Moller, inventor of Skycar, hopes his **flying car** will be on sale by 2002. It is designed to take off like a helicopter and fly up to 350 miles an hour. Computers do the piloting while passengers enjoy the ride.

Also possibly down the road:

- ► The Futura, a car that parks itself.
- ► Cars driven entirely by computers.
- ► Sensors on roads and autos that prevent cars from driving too close to each other.

The **Maglev** (MAGnetic LEVitation Vehicle) can provide high-speed, clean, energy-efficient **train** service. Japan has this system already. Huge magnetic forces lift the train above the track and send it forward on electrical currents. There is no friction between train and track, so it can go 300 miles per hour.

CHALLENGE: What kinds of cars would you like to see in your lifetime? What will they look like? What will they do? How fast will they go?

Air

Scientists are working on a **hypersonic** (at least five times the speed of sound) **aircraft** that would run on hydrogen and oxygen, giving off water vapor rather than harmful pollutants. The Orient Express—a **Trans-Atmospheric Vehicle** (TAV)—would fly 10,000 miles per hour, taking only two hours to travel from New York to Japan.

A new **Boeing 777** is due to fly in 2003. It will go nonstop for 10,500 miles, about the distance from Atlanta, Georgia, to Hong Kong, China. (The 747-400, the largest commercial passenger plane now flying, goes 8,430 miles.) The new 777 will be able to stay in the air for 18 hours—two hours longer than today's longest flight.

In 2004 look for the huge **Airbus A-380.** Early plans show it with gyms, shops, and fast-food restaurants. But some people doubt that will happen. They think the space will be filled with more seats.

Sea

Sea vessels will be even larger and made of **aluminum** or another material that can hold up better in ocean water. More ships may be powered by **nuclear energy**, and even very large ships will have crews of fewer than 20 people. Computers do everything from setting the course to running the engines.

◄TRANSPORTATION PUZZLE►

The letters in the boxes are in the right order, but they are not grouped correctly into words. Can you write out the words correctly so each sentence tells a fact?

1. T HEF IRS TWHE ELS WE REM ADEO FW OOD.

2. TH EFI RSTMA SS PR ODU CED C ARW AST HEM ODELT.

3. TH EFIR STM AS STRA NSIT SY ST EM US EDH OR SED RAW NST AGEC OAC HES.

TRAVEL

How fast is the world's fastest roller coaster? *You can find the answer on page 237.*

COOL PLACES TO VISIT

Pack your suitcase. Put some film in the camera. It's vacation time. Here are some interesting and unusual places you can visit.

AUSTRALIA The **Great Barrier Reef** off the coast of Australia is made of billions of coral polyps. The coral form a large underwater ridge 1,200 miles long and 50 miles wide. Snorkeling or scuba diving are great ways to see the millions of plants and animals that live there.

AUSTRIA Watch the **Lippizaner Stallions** perform at the Spanish Riding School in the city of Vienna. These beautiful white horses are trained to perform leaps and other exciting movements as their riders give them directions.

On Sunday, you can attend a performance of the **Vienna Boys' Choir**. The Choir was created back in 1498 by the Emperor Maximilian I. Visit the **Circus and Clown Museum** and the **Streetcar Museum** in Vienna, too.

BRAZIL Alligators, jaguars, anaconda snakes, and giant red-necked storks will welcome you to **The Pantanal**, an open swampland in the states of Mato Grosso and Mato Grosso do Sul. Visit **Iguaçu Falls**, a group of 275 tall and powerful waterfalls. This great natural attraction is in the Parque Nacional do Iguaçu.

▲ *Scuba diving in the Great Barrier Reef in Queensland, Australia*

CANADA One of the best places to see the **Northern Lights** (aurora borealis) is in northern Alberta, a province in western Canada. The Northern Lights is a spectacular natural display of color and light which appears in the sky at night. At the end of the display, rays of light and color flare out in every direction. The Northern Lights are most visible from December to March, but you can often see them at other times.

HUNGARY Take a ride on the cable railway to the top of **Castle Hill** for the best view of the capital city of Budapest. Visit the Royal Palace and the old forts at the top of the hill.

INDONESIA Komodo National Park is a group of islands famous for being home to the **komodo dragon**. Komodo dragons are the largest lizards in the world and they are an endangered species. Males often weigh 200 pounds and are 8 feet, 6 inches long. Some dragons weigh as much as 300 pounds and are 10 feet long.

JAPAN Take a ride on a riverboat to the Asakusa section of the city of Tokyo. Visit Tokyo's most famous Buddhist temple, **Senso-ji**. Outside the temple are old-fashioned crafts shops and stalls where people sell souvenirs. Visit the Kabuki-za Theatre to see one of the famous **Kabuki** plays with singing, dancing, and beautiful costumes.

Japanese Kabuki performer ▶

KENYA Only two miles from the center of the capital city of Nairobi is the huge **Nairobi National Park**, where it is easy to spot lions, zebra, and buffalo. Visit **Mount Kenya**, an extinct volcano that is 3 1/2 million years old. The mountain is now covered with snow and glaciers. On the upper slopes you can see plants with unusual names like "water-holding cabbage" and "ostrich plume."

MOROCCO **Fes al Bali** (the old section of the city of Fes) is home to busy and colorful **marketplaces** called *souks*, where people buy and sell everything from food to handmade rugs. On another street, people stir multi-colored dyes in large pots and hang up brightly colored yarn and cloth to dry.

▲ *Moroccan market booth*

NEW ZEALAND Walk through the craters of the **Waimangu Volcanic Valley**, which was formed just over 100 years ago. Take a boat trip on a lake formed inside a crater and visit the two huge hot water springs in Inferno Crater and Echo Crater.

▼ *Macchu Picchu*

PERU High in the Andes Mountains are the ancient cities of **Cuzco** and **Macchu Picchu**. Cuzco is more than nine centuries old. Once it was an Inca capital. Macchu Picchu, the "lost city of the Incas," is nearby.

SWEDEN The Treasury in the city of Stockholm has lots of jewel-covered crowns. The oldest belonged to King Karl X, who lived in the 1600s. At Stockholm's Armory, you can see old suits of armor, costumes, and horse-drawn coaches from long ago.

TURKEY Take a walk through the **Sunken Palace**, an underground well that supplied water long ago to the Great Palace of the ancient emperors. In the ancient district of **Cappadocia**, worn-away volcanic rock has created strange and interesting land formations. Here you can see the fairy chimneys where rocks and valleys hide very old churches and homes. Some of them are still in use today.

UNITED STATES Here's a great way to see the U.S.A. Take a **train ride** all the way across the country. Get on board the **Cardinal** in Washington, D.C., and travel through the eastern states to downtown Chicago. Then all aboard the **California Zephyr** for the ride west. You'll see the Rocky Mountains, the city of Denver, and Lake Tahoe. Oakland, California, is the last stop on your ride.

⋯ And Here's a Trip That's Out of This World!

Dennis Tito, an American millionaire, became the world's first space tourist after he agreed to pay Russia a reported $20 million to visit the International Space Station. Some day you too may be able to travel outside the Earth's atmosphere. There you'll see the bright blue curve of the Earth's surface. You'll even be weightless for part of the trip. Start saving up your money!

235

AMUSEMENT PARKS: Then and Now

Amusement parks today are filled with bright lights, food, fun, and thrilling rides. But the earliest amusement parks, which appeared in Europe more than 400 years ago, were very different. Some of the attractions were flower gardens, bowling, music, and a few simple rides.

By 1884, amusement parks began to get more exciting. That's when the Switchback Gravity Pleasure Railway came to Coney Island in Brooklyn, New York. In 1893, the George Ferris Great Wheel was introduced in Chicago. The "Ferris" Wheel weighed more than four million pounds and stood 264 feet high. A year later, Chutes Park opened in Chicago. It was the first park to charge admission.

In the 1920s, some of the best roller coasters of all time were built. Many large cities had as many as six amusement parks. But the stock market crash and the Great Depression in the 1930s caused many parks to close.

In 1955, Disneyland opened in Anaheim, California. Different sections of the park, such as Tomorrowland and the Magic Kingdom, had their own themes. Disneyland became known as the country's first theme park.

These days amusement parks are more popular than ever, with thrill-seekers flocking to places like Six-Flags Great Adventure in New Jersey. Those with strong stomachs can brave the sleek, ultramodern, gravity-defying rides like Medusa, while others can stick to less scary kinds of fun.

POPULAR PARKS

PARK	LOCATION
Blackpool Pleasure Beach	England
Cedar Point	Ohio, USA
Disneyland	California, USA
Everland, Kyunggi-Do	South Korea
Lotte World	South Korea
Ocean Park, Hong Kong	China
Six Flags Great Adventure	New Jersey, USA
Tokyo Disneyland	Japan
Walt Disney World	Florida, USA
Yokohama Hakkejima Sea Paradise	Japan

FABULOUS FACTS

Largest amusement park: Walt Disney World, Lake Buena Vista, Florida, 28,000 acres

Park with the most rides: Cedar Point, Sandusky, Ohio, 68

Park with the most roller coasters: Cedar Point, Sandusky, Ohio, 14 roller coasters

Oldest operating ferris wheel: Wonderland, Gaultier, Mississippi (The wheel opened in New Jersey in 1895 and moved to Wonderland in 1990.)

Oldest operating water ride: The Old Mill, Kennywood, West Mifflin, Pennsylvania. Built in 1901, it was rebuilt in 1926.

Oldest operating merry-go-round: Flying Horses, Martha's Vineyard, Oak Bluff, Massachusetts, built in 1876

Talk Like an Expert

Amusement parks have their own lingo.

Airtime: the feeling of rising out of your seat while riding on a roller coaster

Hyper coaster: a roller coaster with at least one drop of over 200 feet

Inversion: part of a roller coaster ride that turns riders upside down

Inverted coaster: a roller coaster that travels underneath the track

Multi-looper: a roller coaster with several inversions

Theme park: a place in which the rides, attractions, shows, and buildings all have the same theme or subject, such as Sea World

All About...
ROLLER COASTERS

Close your eyes. You are in a chair on top of a mountain. You come rushing down at top speed. Your heart beats wildly. The wind whips back your hair and pins you to your seat. Your stomach drops and you let out a shriek! Does this sound like fun to you? If so, you are not alone. People have found ways to whoosh down hills since the 1400s, when ice slides were built in Russia. In the late 1700s, Catherine the Great, Russia's ruler, placed wheels on sleds so that she could coast during the summer.

The first roller coaster came to the United States in 1827. "Gravity Road," in the mountains of Pennsylvania, was 18 miles long and dropped more than 1,200 feet. The highest, longest roller coaster ever built, it was made to carry coal from a mountaintop mine to boats along the canal below. But fascinated crowds clamored for rides.

In 1884, La Marcus A. Thompson built the "Switchback Railway" at Coney Island in Brooklyn, New York. This was the first roller coaster built purely for fun. Since then, hundreds more have been built. They are made of steel as well as wood, and some have loops that turn riders upside-down. Today, roller coaster popularity seems to be at an all-time high! Here are some of the world's biggest and best.

WORLD'S FASTEST ROLLER COASTERS
1. **Superman: The Escape:** 100 mph, Valencia, California
   Tower of Terror: 100 mph, Gold Coast, Australia
2. **Steel Dragon 2000:** 95 mph, Mie, Japan
3. **Millennium Force:** 92 mph, Sandusky, Ohio
4. **Goliath:** 85 mph, Valencia, California
   Titan: 85 mph, Arlington, Texas
5. **Fujiyama:** 83 mph, Tokyo, Japan

WORLD'S LONGEST ROLLER COASTERS
1. **Steel Dragon 2000:** 8,133 ft, Mie, Japan
2. **The Ultimate:** 7,498 ft, North Yorkshire, England
3. **The Beast:** 7,400 ft, Cincinnati, Ohio
4. **Son of Beast:** 7,032 ft, Cincinnati, Ohio
5. **Millennium Force:** 6,595 ft, Sandusky, Ohio

WORLD'S TALLEST ROLLER COASTERS
1. **Superman: The Escape:** 415 ft, Valencia, California
2. **Tower of Terror:** 380 ft, Gold Coast, Australia
3. **Steel Dragon 2000:** 318 ft, Mie, Japan
4. **Fujiyama:** 259 ft, Tokyo, Japan
5. **Titan:** 245 ft, Arlington, Texas

UNITED NATIONS

What tiny country joined the UN in 2000?
You can find the answer below.

A COMMUNITY of NATIONS

The United Nations (UN) was started in 1945 after World War II. The first members of the UN were 50 nations that met in San Francisco, California. They signed an agreement known as the UN Charter. In 2001, the UN had 189 countries as members. Only three independent nations—Switzerland, Taiwan, and Vatican City—were not members.

The UN Charter lists these purposes:

► to keep worldwide peace and security

► to develop friendly relations among countries

► to help countries cooperate in solving economic and social problems

► to promote respect for human rights and basic freedoms

► to be a center that helps countries achieve their goals

▼ *Flags fly at the UN*

FAST FACTS ABOUT THE UN

► The secretary-general is the chief officer of the UN. He or she is appointed by the General Assembly to serve a five-year term. The current secretary general is Kofi Annan of Ghana. His term began in 1997.

► Six official languages are used at the UN: Arabic, Chinese, English, French, Russian, and Spanish.

► The UN has its own fire department, security force, and postal service. The UN post office sells stamps that can be used only to send mail from the UN.

DID YOU KNOW? *In 2000, the tiny island of Tuvalu became the newest member of the UN. Once part of a larger British colony, it gained independence in 1978.*

► Although UN Headquarters is located on 18 acres of land in New York City, the land and buildings are not part of the United States. They belong to the UN member nations.

► The flags of all 189 member nations fly in front of UN headquarters. They are arranged in alphabetical order beginning with Afghanistan and ending with Zimbabwe.

► The budget for the UN's main operations is $2.5 billion a year. The money is paid by member countries. The United States, which has higher dues than any other country, is required to pay about one-fourth of the UN budget.

UN PEACEKEEPERS

Keeping peace is one of the UN's main purposes. The Security Council sets up and directs UN peacekeeping missions, to try to stop people from fighting while the countries or groups try to work out their differences. UN nations provide troops and equipment. UN peacekeepers wear blue helmets or berets with white UN letters.

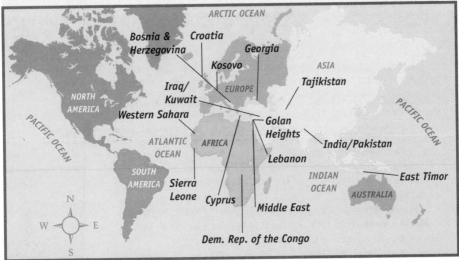

HOW THE UN IS ORGANIZED

The work of the UN is done through five main organizations:

GENERAL ASSEMBLY What It Does: discusses world problems, admits new members, appoints the secretary-general, decides the UN budget **Members:** All members of the UN belong to the General Assembly; each country has one vote.

SECURITY COUNCIL What It Does: discusses questions of peace and security **Members:** Five permanent members (China, France, Great Britain, Russia, and the United States), and ten members elected by the General Assembly for two-year terms. In early 2001 the ten were Bangladesh, Jamaica, Mali, Tunisia, and Ukraine (ending that year) and Colombia, Mauritius, Singapore, Ireland, and Norway (ending in 2002).

ECONOMIC AND SOCIAL COUNCIL What It Does: deals with issues related to trade, economic development, industry, population, children, food, education, health, and human rights **Members:** Fifty-four member countries elected for three-year terms.

INTERNATIONAL COURT OF JUSTICE (WORLD COURT) located at The Hague, Netherlands **What It Does:** highest court of law for legal disputes between countries; countries that come before the court promise to obey the court's decisions **Members:** Fifteen judges, each from a different country, elected to nine-year terms.

SECRETARIAT What It Does: carries out day-to-day operations of the UN, such as doing research and helping implement UN decisions **Members:** UN staff, headed by the secretary-general.

For more information about the UN, you can write to:
Public Inquiries Unit, Room GA-57, United Nations, NY 10017.
WEBSITE http://www.un.org

UNITED STATES

Why does the U.S. flag have 50 stars and 13 stripes? You can find the answer on page 241.

UNITED STATES: FACTS & FIGURES

AREA: 50 states and Washington, D.C.	LAND 3,536,278 square miles	WATER 181,518 square miles	TOTAL 3,717,796 square miles

POPULATION (2000): 281,421,906   **CAPITAL:** Washington, D.C.

LARGEST, HIGHEST, AND OTHER STATISTICS

▲ Sears Tower

Largest state: Alaska (615,230 square miles)
Smallest state: Rhode Island (1,231 square miles)
Northernmost city: Barrow, Alaska (71°17′ north latitude)
Southernmost city: Hilo, Hawaii (19°44′ north latitude)
Easternmost city: Eastport, Maine (66°59′05″ west longitude)
Westernmost city: Atka, Alaska (174°12′ west longitude)
Highest settlement: Climax, Colorado (11,360 feet)
Lowest settlement: Calipatria, California (184 feet below sea level)
Oldest national park: Yellowstone National Park (Idaho, Montana, Wyoming), 2,219,791 acres, established 1872
Largest national park: Wrangell-St. Elias, Alaska (8,323,618 acres)
Longest river system: Mississippi-Missouri-Red Rock (3,710 miles)
Deepest lake: Crater Lake, Oregon (1,932 feet)
Highest mountain: Mount McKinley, Alaska (20,320 feet)
Lowest point: Death Valley, California (282 feet below sea level)
Rainiest spot: Mount Waialeale, Hawaii (average annual rainfall, 460 inches)
Tallest building: Sears Tower, Chicago, Illinois (1,450 feet)
Tallest structure: TV tower, Blanchard, North Dakota (2,063 feet)
Longest bridge span: Verrazano-Narrows Bridge, New York (4,260 feet)
Highest bridge: Royal Gorge, Colorado (1,053 feet above water)

INTERNATIONAL BOUNDARY LINES OF THE U.S.

U.S.-Canadian border ...... 3,987 miles
(excluding Alaska)
Alaska-Canadian border ..... 1,538 miles
U.S.-Mexican border .... 1,933 miles
(Gulf of Mexico to Pacific Ocean)

Atlantic coast .... 2,069 miles
Gulf of Mexico coast .... 1,631 miles
Pacific coast .... 7,623 miles
Arctic coast, Alaska .... 1,060 miles

TERRITORIAL SEA OF THE U.S.
The territorial sea of the United States is the surrounding waters that the country claims as its own. A proclamation made by President Ronald Reagan on December 27, 1988, said that the territorial sea of the United States extends 12 nautical miles from the shores of the country.

SYMBOLS of the United States

THE U.S. NATIONAL MOTTO

The U.S. motto, "In God We Trust," was originally put on coins during the Civil War (1861-1865). It disappeared and reappeared on various coins until 1955, when Congress ordered it placed on all paper money and coins.

THE GREAT SEAL OF THE UNITED STATES

The Great Seal of the United States shows an American bald eagle with a ribbon in its mouth bearing the Latin words "e pluribus unum" (out of many, one). In its talons are the arrows of war and an olive branch of peace. On the back of the Great Seal is an unfinished pyramid with an eye (the eye of Providence) above it. The seal was approved by Congress on June 20, 1782.

THE FLAG

The flag of the United States has 50 stars (one for each state) and 13 stripes (one for each of the original 13 states). It is called unofficially the "Stars and Stripes."

The first U.S. flag was commissioned by the Second Continental Congress in 1777 but did not exist until 1783, after the American Revolution. Historians are not certain who designed the Stars and Stripes. Many different flags are believed to have been used during the American Revolution.

The flag of 1777 was used until 1795. In that year Congress passed an act ordering that a new flag have 15 stripes, alternate red and white, and 15 stars on a blue field. In 1818, Congress directed that the flag have 13 stripes and that a new star be added for each new state of the Union. The last star was added in 1960 for the state of Hawaii.

1777

1795

1818

PLEDGE OF ALLEGIANCE TO THE FLAG

"I pledge allegiance to the flag of the United States of America and to the republic for which it stands, one nation under God, indivisible, with liberty and justice for all."

NATIONAL ANTHEM: "THE STAR-SPANGLED BANNER"

"The Star-Spangled Banner" was a poem written in 1814 by Francis Scott Key as he watched British ships bombard Fort McHenry, Maryland, during the War of 1812. It became the National Anthem by an act of Congress in 1931. Although it has four stanzas, the one most commonly sung is the first one. The music to "The Star-Spangled Banner" was originally a tune called "Anacreon in Heaven."

THE U.S. CONSTITUTION
THE FOUNDATION OF AMERICAN GOVERNMENT

The Constitution is the document that created the present government of the United States. It was written in 1787 and went into effect in 1789. It establishes the three branches of the U.S. government, which are the executive (headed by the president), the legislative (the Congress), and the judicial (the Supreme Court and other federal courts). The first 10 amendments to the Constitution (the **Bill of Rights**) explain the basic rights of all American citizens.

You can find the constitution on-line at:

WEBSITE *http://www.nara.gov/exhall/charters/constitution*

THE PREAMBLE TO THE CONSTITUTION

The Constitution begins with a short statement called the Preamble. The Preamble states that the government of the United States was established by the people.

"We, the people of the United States, in order to form a more perfect Union, establish justice, insure domestic tranquility, provide for the common defense, promote the general welfare, and secure the blessings of liberty to ourselves and our posterity do ordain and establish this Constitution for the United States of America."

THE ARTICLES

The original Constitution contained seven articles. The first three articles of the Constitution establish the three branches of the U.S. government.

Article 1, Legislative Branch
Creates the Senate and House of Representatives and describes their functions and powers.

Article 2, Executive Branch
Creates the office of the President and the Electoral College and lists their powers and responsibilities.

Article 3, Judicial Branch
Creates the Supreme Court and gives Congress the power to create lower courts. The powers of the courts and certain crimes are defined.

Article 4, The States
Discusses the relationship of the states to one another and to the citizens. Defines the states' powers.

Article 5, Amending the Constitution
Describes how the Constitution can be amended (changed).

Article 6, Federal Law
Makes the Constitution the supreme law of the land over state laws and constitutions.

Article 7, Ratifying the Constitution
Establishes how to ratify (approve) the Constitution.

AMENDMENTS TO THE CONSTITUTION

The writers of the Constitution understood that it might need to be amended, or changed, in the future. Article 5 describes how the Constitution can be amended. In order to pass, an amendment must be approved by a two-thirds majority in the House of Representatives and a two-thirds majority in the Senate. The amendment must then be approved by three-fourths of the states (38 states). So far, the Constitution has been amended 27 times.

The Bill of Rights: The First Ten Amendments

The first ten amendments were adopted in 1791 and contain the basic freedoms Americans enjoy as a people. These amendments are known as the Bill of Rights. They are summarized below.

1 Guarantees freedom of religion, speech, and the press.

2 Guarantees the right of the people to have firearms.

3 Guarantees that soldiers cannot be lodged in private homes unless the owner agrees.

4 Protects citizens against being searched or having their property searched or taken away by the government without a good reason.

5 Protects rights of people on trial for crimes.

6 Guarantees people accused of crimes the right to a speedy public trial by jury.

7 Guarantees people the right to a trial by jury for other kinds of cases.

8 Prohibits "cruel and unusual punishments."

9 Says that specific rights listed in the Constitution do not take away rights that may not be listed.

10 Establishes that any powers not given specifically to the federal government belong to states or the people.

Other Important Amendments

13 (1865): Ends slavery in the United States.

14 (1868): Establishes the Bill of Rights as protection against actions by a state government; guarantees equal protection under the law for all citizens.

15 (1870): Guarantees that a person cannot be denied the right to vote because of race or color.

19 (1920): Gives women the right to vote.

22 (1951): Limits the president to two four-year terms of office.

24 (1964): Outlaws the poll tax (a tax people had to pay before they could vote) in federal elections. (The poll tax had been used to keep African Americans in the South from voting.)

25 (1967): Gives the president the power to appoint a new vice president, with the approval of Congress, if a vice president dies or leaves office in the middle of a term.

26 (1971): Lowers the voting age to eighteen.

THE EXECUTIVE BRANCH:
The PRESIDENT and the CABINET

The executive branch of the federal government is headed by the president. It also includes the vice president, people who work for the president or vice president, the major departments of the federal government, and special agencies. The cabinet is made up of the vice president, heads of the major departments, and other top officials. It meets when the president asks for its advice. As head of the executive branch, the president is responsible for enforcing the laws passed by Congress and is commander in chief of U.S. armed forces. The chart at right shows cabinet departments in the order in which they were created.

PRESIDENT

VICE PRESIDENT

CABINET DEPARTMENTS

1. State
2. Treasury
3. Defense
4. Justice
5. Interior
6. Agriculture
7. Commerce
8. Labor
9. Housing and Urban Development
10. Transportation
11. Energy
12. Education
13. Health and Human Services
14. Veterans Affairs

HOW LONG DOES THE PRESIDENT SERVE?

The president serves a four-year term, starting on January 20. No president can be elected more than twice.

WHAT HAPPENS IF THE PRESIDENT DIES?

▲ The White House, home of the U.S. president

If the president dies in office or cannot complete the term, the vice president becomes president. If the president is disabled, the vice president can become acting president until the president is able to work again. The next person to become president after the vice president would be the Speaker of the House of Representatives. A person who finishes more than two years of a president's term can be elected to only one more term.

The White House has an address on the World Wide Web especially for kids. It is:

WEBSITE http://www.whitehousekids.gov

You can send e-mail to the president at:

EMAIL president@whitehouse.gov

DID YOU KNOW? The White House has 132 rooms and 32 bathrooms for all the people who live, work, and visit there.

ELECTIONS
Electing the President and Vice President

Every four years on the first Tuesday after the first Monday in November, American voters go to the polls and elect a president and vice president. Right? Well, sort of. The president and vice president are the only elected U.S. officials who are not actually chosen by a direct vote of the people. They are really elected by the 538 members of the Electoral College.

The Electoral College is not really a college, but a group of people chosen in each state. In 1787 the men writing the Constitution did not agree on how a president should be selected. Some did not trust ordinary people to make a good choice. So they compromised and agreed to have the Electoral College do it.

In the early days before political parties became important, electors voted for whomever they wanted. In modern times the political parties hold primary elections and conventions to choose candidates for president and vice president. When voters choose the candidates of a particular party, they are actually choosing electors from that party. The electors have agreed to vote for their party's candidate, and except in very rare cases this is what they do.

2000 Election
- Won by Bush
- Won by Gore

THE ELECTORAL COLLEGE STATE BY STATE

The number of electors for each state is equal to the total number of senators and representatives each has in Congress. For example, Minnesota has eight representatives and two senators, for a total of ten. (In the 2004 election, numbers of representatives will change because of 2000 Census results.) The electors chosen in November meet in state capitals in December. In almost all states, the party that got the most votes in November wins all the electors and electoral votes for the state. This happens even if the results of the election in the state are very close.

In early January the electors' votes are officially opened during a special session of Congress. If no presidential candidate wins a majority (at least 270) of the electoral votes, the House of Representatives chooses the president. This happened in 1800, 1824, and 1877.

Can a candidate who didn't win the most popular votes still win a majority of electoral votes? Yes. That's what happened in 1876, 1888, and again in 2000.

THE PRESIDENTIAL ELECTION OF 2000

A U.S. presidential race is rough and tough. So much is at stake. In 2000, Al Gore, the Democratic U.S. vice president, and George W. Bush, the Republican governor of Texas, were the candidates for the presidency. In the fall of 2000 they traveled the country nonstop as they took their campaign to the people. Gore and Bush made speeches to crowds of excited voters, explaining how they would work for their country and improve the lives of their fellow Americans.

In a presidential election, each state has a certain number of electoral votes. Whoever gets the most of these wins. When November 7, Election Day, came, most Americans expected to end the day knowing who their new president would be. By early in the evening, most states were decided. Because of how the numbers were adding up, the winner of Florida's 25 electoral votes would win the election. By about 8 P.M. in the East, most television networks announced that Al Gore had won Florida. But later that night Gore's lead shrank. Bush was announced as Florida's winner. Still later, Bush's lead shrank. People went to bed not knowing who the next president would be!

Another fight was on. This battle was for those 25 electoral votes. It didn't matter that, nationwide, Al Gore had definitely won more popular votes than George W. Bush. (In the end, Gore officially won 544,683 more popular votes out of more than 100 million counted.)

▲ *George W. and Laura Bush at an inaugural event*

Each man sent teams of lawyers to Florida, where they fought over a recount of votes. Florida courts held many hearings. Five weeks later the U.S. Supreme Court, in a case called *Bush versus Gore*, ended the arguments. It ruled, in effect, that George W. Bush won Florida's 25 electoral votes and therefore would be president-elect. On January 20, 2001, George W. Bush took office as the 43rd president of the United States.

George H.W. Bush was the 41st president. George W. Bush is only the second son of a president to win the White House. John Quincy Adams, the son of John Adams, the second president, was elected in 1824.

All About... GEORGE W. BUSH

George W. Bush graduated from Yale University in Connecticut and received a master's degree from Harvard University School of Business in Massachusetts. But he had grown up in Texas and later worked there in the oil business. He even bought part of a major league baseball team, the Texas Rangers. In 1994 he won the governorship of Texas. Although he is a Republican, he got along well with members of the Democratic Party in Texas. In 1998 he easily won a second term as governor. In 1999 he announced his run for the White House.

PRESIDENTS AND VICE PRESIDENTS OF THE UNITED STATES

PRESIDENT / VICE PRESIDENT	YEARS IN OFFICE
① George Washington	1789–1797
John Adams	1789–1797
② John Adams	1797–1801
Thomas Jefferson	1797–1801
③ Thomas Jefferson	1801–1809
Aaron Burr	1801–1805
George Clinton	1805–1809
④ James Madison	1809–1817
George Clinton	1809–1812
Elbridge Gerry	1813–1814
⑤ James Monroe	1817–1825
Daniel D. Tompkins	1817–1825
⑥ John Quincy Adams	1825–1829
John C. Calhoun	1825–1829
⑦ Andrew Jackson	1829–1837
John C. Calhoun	1829–1832
Martin Van Buren	1833–1837
⑧ Martin Van Buren	1837–1841
Richard M. Johnson	1837–1841
⑨ William H. Harrison	1841
John Tyler	1841
⑩ John Tyler	1841–1845
No Vice President	
⑪ James Knox Polk	1845–1849
George M. Dallas	1845–1849
⑫ Zachary Taylor	1849–1850
Millard Fillmore	1849–1850
⑬ Millard Fillmore	1850–1853
No Vice President	
⑭ Franklin Pierce	1853–1857
William R. King	1853
⑮ James Buchanan	1857–1861
John C. Breckinridge	1857–1861
⑯ Abraham Lincoln	1861–1865
Hannibal Hamlin	1861–1865
Andrew Johnson	1865
⑰ Andrew Johnson	1865–1869
No Vice President	
⑱ Ulysses S. Grant	1869–1877
Schuyler Colfax	1869–1873
Henry Wilson	1873–1875
⑲ Rutherford B. Hayes	1877–1881
William A. Wheeler	1877–1881
⑳ James A. Garfield	1881
Chester A. Arthur	1881
㉑ Chester A. Arthur	1881–1885
No Vice President	
㉒ Grover Cleveland	1885–1889
Thomas A. Hendricks	1885
㉓ Benjamin Harrison	1889–1893
Levi P. Morton	1889–1893
㉔ Grover Cleveland	1893–1897
Adlai E. Stevenson	1893–1897
㉕ William McKinley	1897–1901
Garret A. Hobart	1897–1899
Theodore Roosevelt	1901
㉖ Theodore Roosevelt	1901–1909
Charles W. Fairbanks	1905–1909
㉗ William Howard Taft	1909–1913
James S. Sherman	1909–1912
㉘ Woodrow Wilson	1913–1921
Thomas R. Marshall	1913–1921
㉙ Warren G. Harding	1921–1923
Calvin Coolidge	1921–1923
㉚ Calvin Coolidge	1923–1929
Charles G. Dawes	1925–1929
㉛ Herbert Hoover	1929–1933
Charles Curtis	1929–1933
㉜ Franklin D. Roosevelt	1933–1945
John Nance Garner	1933–1941
Henry A. Wallace	1941–1945
Harry S. Truman	1945
㉝ Harry S. Truman	1945–1953
Alben W. Barkley	1949–1953
㉞ Dwight D. Eisenhower	1953–1961
Richard M. Nixon	1953–1961
㉟ John F. Kennedy	1961–1963
Lyndon B. Johnson	1961–1963
㊱ Lyndon B. Johnson	1963–1969
Hubert H. Humphrey	1965–1969
㊲ Richard M. Nixon	1969–1974
Spiro T. Agnew	1969–1973
Gerald R. Ford	1973–1974
㊳ Gerald R. Ford	1974–1977
Nelson A. Rockefeller	1974–1977
㊴ Jimmy Carter	1977–1981
Walter F. Mondale	1977–1981
㊵ Ronald Reagan	1981–1989
George Bush	1981–1989
㊶ George Bush	1989–1993
Dan Quayle	1989–1993
㊷ Bill Clinton	1993–2001
Al Gore	1993–2001
㊸ George W. Bush	2001–
Richard B. Cheney	2001–

PRESIDENTS
of the United States

GEORGE WASHINGTON Federalist Party   **1789-1797**
Born: Feb. 22, 1732, at Wakefield, Westmoreland County, Virginia
Married: Martha Dandridge Custis (1731-1802); no children
Died: Dec. 14, 1799; buried at Mount Vernon, Fairfax County, Virginia
Early Career: Soldier; head of the Virginia militia; commander of the
    Continental Army; chairman of Constitutional Convention (1787)

JOHN ADAMS Federalist Party   **1797-1801**
Born: Oct. 30, 1735, in Braintree (now Quincy), Massachusetts
Married: Abigail Smith (1744-1818); 3 sons, 2 daughters
Died: July 4, 1826; buried in Quincy, Massachusetts
Early Career: Lawyer; delegate to Continental Congress; signer of the
    Declaration of Independence; first vice president

THOMAS JEFFERSON Democratic-Republican Party   **1801-1809**
Born: Apr. 13, 1743, at Shadwell, Albemarle County, Virginia
Married: Martha Wayles Skelton (1748-1782); 1 son, 5 daughters
Died: July 4, 1826; buried at Monticello, Albemarle County, Virginia
Early Career: Lawyer; member of the Continental Congress; author of the
    Declaration of Independence; governor of Virginia; first secretary of
    state; author of the Virginia Statute on Religious Freedom

JAMES MADISON Democratic-Republican Party   **1809-1817**
Born: Mar. 16, 1751, at Port Conway, King George County, Virginia
Married: Dolley Payne Todd (1768-1849); no children
Died: June 28, 1836; buried at Montpelier Station, Virginia
Early Career: Member of the Virginia Constitutional Convention (1776);
    member of the Continental Congress; major contributor to the U.S.
    Constitution; writer of the *Federalist Papers*; secretary of state

JAMES MONROE Democratic-Republican Party   **1817-1825**
Born: Apr. 28, 1758, in Westmoreland County, Virginia
Married: Elizabeth Kortright (1768-1830); 2 daughters
Died: July 4, 1831; buried in Richmond, Virginia
Early Career: Soldier; lawyer; U.S. senator; governor of Virginia;
    secretary of state

JOHN QUINCY ADAMS Democratic-Republican Party   **1825-1829**
Born: July 11, 1767, in Braintree (now Quincy), Massachusetts
Married: Louisa Catherine Johnson (1775-1852); 3 sons, 1 daughter
Died: Feb. 23, 1848; buried in Quincy, Massachusetts
Early Career: Diplomat; U.S. senator; secretary of state

ANDREW JACKSON Democratic Party   **1829-1837**
Born: Mar. 15, 1767, in Waxhaw, South Carolina
Married: Rachel Donelson Robards (1767-1828); 1 son
Died: June 8, 1845; buried in Nashville, Tennessee
Early Career: Lawyer; U.S. representative and senator; soldier in the
      U.S. Army

MARTIN VAN BUREN Democratic Party   **1837-1841**
Born: Dec. 5, 1782, at Kinderhook, New York
Married: Hannah Hoes (1783-1819); 4 sons
Died: July 24, 1862; buried at Kinderhook, New York
Early Career: Governor of New York; secretary of state; vice president

WILLIAM HENRY HARRISON Whig Party   **1841**
Born: Feb. 9, 1773, at Berkeley, Charles City County, Virginia
Married: Anna Symmes (1775-1864); 6 sons, 4 daughters
Died: Apr. 4, 1841; buried in North Bend, Ohio
Early Career: First governor of Indiana Territory; superintendent of
      Indian affairs; U.S. representative and senator

JOHN TYLER Whig Party   **1841-1845**
Born: Mar. 29, 1790, in Greenway, Charles City County, Virginia
Married: Letitia Christian (1790-1842); 3 sons, 5 daughters
      Julia Gardiner (1820-1889); 5 sons, 2 daughters
Died: Jan. 18, 1862; buried in Richmond, Virginia
Early Career: U.S. representative and senator; vice president

JAMES KNOX POLK Democratic Party   **1845-1849**
Born: Nov. 2, 1795, in Mecklenburg County, North Carolina
Married: Sarah Childress (1803-1891); no children
Died: June 15, 1849; buried in Nashville, Tennessee
Early Career: U.S. representative; Speaker of the House; governor
      of Tennessee

ZACHARY TAYLOR Whig Party   **1849-1850**
Born: Nov. 24, 1784, in Orange County, Virginia
Married: Margaret Smith (1788-1852); 1 son, 5 daughters
Died: July 9, 1850; buried in Louisville, Kentucky
Early Career: Indian fighter; general in the U.S. Army

MILLARD FILLMORE Whig Party   **1850-1853**
Born: Jan. 7, 1800, in Cayuga County, New York
Married: Abigail Powers (1798-1853); 1 son, 1 daughter
      Caroline Carmichael McIntosh (1813-1881); no children
Died: Mar. 8, 1874; buried in Buffalo, New York
Early Career: Farmer; lawyer; U.S. representative; vice president

FRANKLIN PIERCE Democratic Party   **1853-1857**
Born: Nov. 23, 1804, in Hillsboro, New Hampshire
Married: Jane Means Appleton (1806-1863); 3 sons
Died: Oct. 8, 1869; buried in Concord, New Hampshire
Early Career: U.S. representative, senator

JAMES BUCHANAN Democratic Party   **1857-1861**
Born: Apr. 23, 1791, Cove Gap, near Mercersburg, Pennsylvania
Married: Never
Died: June 1, 1868, buried in Lancaster, Pennsylvania
Early Career: U.S. representative; secretary of state

ABRAHAM LINCOLN Republican Party   **1861-1865**
Born: Feb. 12, 1809, in Hardin County, Kentucky
Married: Mary Todd (1818-1882); 4 sons
Died: Apr. 15, 1865; buried in Springfield, Illinois
Early Career: Lawyer; U.S. representative

ANDREW JOHNSON Democratic Party   **1865-1869**
Born: Dec. 29, 1808, in Raleigh, North Carolina
Married: Eliza McCardle (1810-1876); 3 sons, 2 daughters
Died: July 31, 1875; buried in Greeneville, Tennessee
Early Career: Tailor; member of state legislature; U.S. representative;
    governor of Tennessee; U.S. senator; vice president

ULYSSES S. GRANT Republican Party   **1869-1877**
Born: Apr. 27, 1822, in Point Pleasant, Ohio
Married: Julia Dent (1826-1902); 3 sons, 1 daughter
Died: July 23, 1885; buried in New York City
Early Career: Army officer; commander of Union forces during Civil War

RUTHERFORD B. HAYES Republican Party   **1877-1881**
Born: Oct. 4, 1822, in Delaware, Ohio
Married: Lucy Ware Webb (1831-1889); 5 sons, 2 daughters
Died: Jan. 17, 1893; buried in Fremont, Ohio
Early Career: Lawyer; general in Union Army; U.S. representative;
    governor of Ohio

JAMES A. GARFIELD Republican Party   **1881**
Born: Nov. 19, 1831, in Orange, Cuyahoga County, Ohio
Married: Lucretia Rudolph (1832-1918); 5 sons, 2 daughters
Died: Sept. 19, 1881; buried in Cleveland, Ohio
Early Career: Teacher; Ohio state senator; general in Union Army;
    U.S. representative

21

CHESTER A. ARTHUR Republican Party 1881-1885
Born: Oct. 5, 1829, in Fairfield, Vermont
Married: Ellen Lewis Herndon (1837-1880); 2 sons, 1 daughter
Died: Nov. 18, 1886; buried in Albany, New York
Early Career: Teacher; lawyer; vice president

22

GROVER CLEVELAND Democratic Party 1885-1889
Born: Mar. 18, 1837, in Caldwell, New Jersey
Married: Frances Folsom (1864-1947); 2 sons, 3 daughters
Died: June 24, 1908; buried in Princeton, New Jersey
Early Career: Lawyer; mayor of Buffalo; governor of New York

23

BENJAMIN HARRISON Republican Party 1889-1893
Born: Aug. 20, 1833, in North Bend, Ohio
Married: Caroline Lavinia Scott (1832-1892); 1 son, 1 daughter
Mary Scott Lord Dimmick (1858-1948); 1 daughter
Died: Mar. 13, 1901; buried in Indianapolis, Indiana
Early Career: Lawyer; general in Union Army; U.S. senator

24

GROVER CLEVELAND 1893-1897
See 22, above

25

WILLIAM MCKINLEY Republican Party 1897-1901
Born: Jan. 29, 1843, in Niles, Ohio
Married: Ida Saxton (1847-1907); 2 daughters
Died: Sept. 14, 1901; buried in Canton, Ohio
Early Career: Lawyer; U.S. representative; governor of Ohio

26

THEODORE ROOSEVELT Republican Party 1901-1909
Born: Oct. 27, 1858, in New York City
Married: Alice Hathaway Lee (1861-1884); 1 daughter
Edith Kermit Carow (1861-1948); 4 sons, 1 daughter
Died: Jan. 6, 1919; buried in Oyster Bay, New York
Early Career: Assistant secretary of the Navy; cavalry leader in
Spanish-American War; governor of New York; vice president

27

WILLIAM HOWARD TAFT Republican Party 1909-1913
Born: Sept. 15, 1857, in Cincinnati, Ohio
Married: Helen Herron (1861-1943); 2 sons, 1 daughter
Died: Mar. 8, 1930; buried in Arlington National Cemetery, Virginia
Early Career: Reporter; lawyer; judge; secretary of war

28

WOODROW WILSON Democratic Party 1913-1921
Born: Dec. 28, 1856, in Staunton, Virginia
Married: Ellen Louise Axson (1860-1914); 3 daughters
Edith Bolling Galt (1872-1961); no children
Died: Feb. 3, 1924; buried in Washington, D.C.
Early Career: College professor and president; governor of New Jersey

WARREN G. HARDING Republican Party   **1921-1923**
Born: Nov. 2, 1865, near Corsica (now Blooming Grove), Ohio
Married: Florence Kling De Wolfe (1860-1924); 1 daughter
Died: Aug. 2, 1923; buried in Marion, Ohio
Early Career: Ohio state senator; U.S. senator

CALVIN COOLIDGE Republican Party   **1923-1929**
Born: July 4, 1872, in Plymouth, Vermont
Married: Grace Anna Goodhue (1879-1957); 2 sons
Died: Jan. 5, 1933; buried in Plymouth, Vermont
Early Career: Massachusetts state legislator; lieutenant governor and
    governor; vice president

HERBERT HOOVER Republican Party   **1929-1933**
Born: Aug. 10, 1874, in West Branch, Iowa
Married: Lou Henry (1875-1944); 2 sons
Died: Oct. 20, 1964; buried in West Branch, Iowa
Early Career: Mining engineer; secretary of commerce

FRANKLIN DELANO ROOSEVELT Democratic Party   **1933-1945**
Born: Jan. 30, 1882, in Hyde Park, New York
Married: Anna Eleanor Roosevelt (1884-1962); 4 sons, 1 daughter
Died: Apr. 12, 1945; buried in Hyde Park, New York
Early Career: Lawyer; New York state senator; assistant secretary of the
    Navy; governor of New York

HARRY S. TRUMAN Democratic Party   **1945-1953**
Born: May 8, 1884, in Lamar, Missouri
Married: Elizabeth Virginia "Bess" Wallace (1885-1982); 1 daughter
Died: Dec. 26, 1972; buried in Independence, Missouri
Early Career: Farmer; haberdasher (ran men's clothing store); judge; U.S.
    senator; vice president

DWIGHT D. EISENHOWER Republican Party   **1953-1961**
Born: Oct. 14, 1890, in Denison, Texas
Married: Mary "Mamie" Geneva Doud (1896-1979); 2 sons
Died: Mar. 28, 1969; buried in Abilene, Kansas
Early Career: Commander, Allied landing in North Africa and later
    Supreme Allied Commander in Europe during World War II; president of
    Columbia University

JOHN FITZGERALD KENNEDY Democratic Party   **1961-1963**
Born: May 29, 1917, in Brookline, Massachusetts
Married: Jacqueline Lee Bouvier (1929-1994); 2 sons, 1 daughter
Died: Nov. 22, 1963; buried in Arlington National Cemetery, Virginia
Early Career: U.S. naval commander; U.S. representative and senator

LYNDON BAINES JOHNSON Democratic Party   **1963-1969**
Born: Aug. 27, 1908, near Stonewall, Texas
Married: Claudia "Lady Bird" Alta Taylor (b. 1912); 2 daughters
Died: Jan. 22, 1973; buried in Johnson City, Texas
Early Career: U.S. representative and senator; vice president

RICHARD MILHOUS NIXON Republican Party   **1969-1974**
Born: Jan. 9, 1913, in Yorba Linda, California
Married: Thelma "Pat" Ryan (1912-1993); 2 daughters
Died: Apr. 22, 1994; buried in Yorba Linda, California
Early Career: Lawyer; U.S. representative and senator; vice president

GERALD R. FORD Republican Party   **1974-1977**
Born: July 14, 1913, in Omaha, Nebraska
Married: Elizabeth "Betty" Bloomer (b. 1918); 3 sons, 1 daughter
Early Career: Lawyer; U.S. representative; vice president

JIMMY (JAMES EARL) CARTER Democratic Party   **1977-1981**
Born: Oct. 1, 1924, in Plains, Georgia
Married: Rosalynn Smith (b. 1927); 3 sons, 1 daughter
Early Career: Peanut farmer; Georgia state senator; governor
of Georgia

RONALD REAGAN Republican Party   **1981-1989**
Born: Feb. 6, 1911, in Tampico, Illinois
Married: Jane Wyman (b. 1914); 1 son, 1 daughter
Nancy Davis (b. 1923); 1 son, 1 daughter
Early Career: Film and television actor; governor of California

GEORGE BUSH Republican Party   **1989-1993**
Born: June 12, 1924, in Milton, Massachusetts
Married: Barbara Pierce (b. 1925); 4 sons, 2 daughters
Early Career: U.S. Navy pilot; businessman; U.S. representative; U.S.
ambassador to the United Nations; vice president

BILL (WILLIAM JEFFERSON) CLINTON Democratic Party   **1993-2001**
Born: Aug. 19, 1946, in Hope, Arkansas
Married: Hillary Rodham (b. 1947); 1 daughter
Early Career: College professor; Arkansas state attorney general;
governor of Arkansas

GEORGE W. BUSH Republican Party   **2001-**
Born: July 6, 1946, in New Haven, Connecticut
Married: Laura Welch (b. 1946); 2 daughters
Early Career: Political adviser; businessman; governor of Texas

PRESIDENTS AND FIRST LADIES

PRESIDENTIAL FACTS

The White House George Washington chose the site for the president's house, at 1600 Pennsylvania Avenue. But John Adams was the first president to live there. Calvin Coolidge liked to sit on the front porch of the White House after dinner and watch the people go by. Abraham Lincoln's son Tad sold refreshments to White House visitors to raise money for Civil War charities.

Longest-lasting President Franklin D. Roosevelt was elected president four times. He and First Lady Eleanor Roosevelt lived in the White House for more than 12 years, from 1933 until his death in 1945.

Presidential Inaugurals Thomas Jefferson held the first inaugural open house at the White House, in 1805. In 1829, a crowd of 20,000 sometimes rowdy visitors forced the new president, Andrew Jackson, to flee to a hotel. In 1993, Bill Clinton welcomed 2,000 visitors chosen by lottery to a White House inaugural party.

Presidential Purchase Thomas Jefferson doubled the size of the country with the Louisiana Purchase (from France) in 1803. Then he sent Lewis and Clark to explore the new lands.

Thomas Jefferson

MEET THE FIRST LADIES

ABIGAIL ADAMS, wife of John Adams, did not have much formal education. But her reading formed a bond between her and her husband. Her letters to him, written while he was away serving their country, are also a history of life during times of revolution.

EDITH ROOSEVELT, wife of Theodore Roosevelt, raised six active children. Family life, in and out of the White House, was delightful and full of surprises. One of the young Roosevelt sons said one day, "When Mother was a little girl, she must have been a boy!"

LAURA BUSH became the newest first lady in January 2001. A former librarian and teacher, she is interested in books, history, art, and the well-being of children. She and her husband have twin daughters, who are both college students.

DID YOU KNOW? *Hillary Rodham Clinton, wife of Bill Clinton, was elected in 2000 to be a U.S. senator from New York. She is the first first lady ever elected to public office.*

THE LEGISLATIVE BRANCH

CONGRESS

The Congress of the United States is the legislative branch of the federal government. Congress's major responsibility is to pass the laws that govern the country and determine how money collected in taxes is spent. It is the president's responsibility to enforce the laws. Congress consists of two parts—the Senate and the House of Representatives.

The Capitol, where Congress meets ▶

THE HOUSE OF REPRESENTATIVES

The number of members of the House of Representatives for each state depends on its population according to a recent census. But each state has at least one representative, no matter how small its population. A term lasts two years.

The first House of Representatives in 1789 had 65 members. As the country's population grew, the number of representatives increased. Since the 1910 census, however, the total membership has been kept at 435. After the results of Census 2000 were added up, 7 states gained seats and 9 states lost seats.

THE SENATE

The Senate has 100 members, two from each state. The Constitution says that the Senate will have equal representation (the same number of representatives) from each state. Thus, small states have the same number of senators as large states. Senators are elected for six-year terms. There is no limit on the number of terms a senator can serve.

The Senate also has the responsibility of approving people the president appoints for certain jobs: for example, cabinet members and Supreme Court justices. The Senate must approve all treaties by at least a two-thirds vote. It also has the responsibility under the Constitution of putting on trial high-ranking federal officials who have been impeached (see next page) by the House of Representatives.

You can reach the Senate and the House on-line at:

WEB SITE http://www.senate.gov
http://www.house.gov

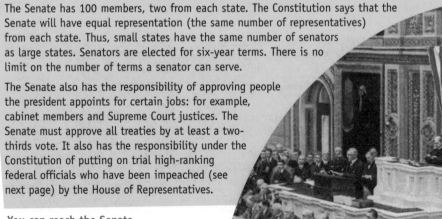

THE HOUSE OF REPRESENTATIVES, BY STATE

Here are the numbers of representatives each state will have by 2003, compared with 10 years earlier and 30 years earlier:

	2003	1993	1973		2003	1993	1973
Alabama	7	7	7	Montana	1	1	2
Alaska	1	1	1	Nebraska	3	3	3
Arizona	8	6	4	Nevada	3	2	1
Arkansas	4	4	4	New Hampshire	2	2	2
California	53	52	43	New Jersey	13	13	15
Colorado	7	6	5	New Mexico	3	3	2
Connecticut	5	6	6	New York	29	31	39
Delaware	1	1	1	North Carolina	13	12	11
Florida	25	23	15	North Dakota	1	1	1
Georgia	13	11	10	Ohio	18	19	23
Hawaii	2	2	2	Oklahoma	5	6	6
Idaho	2	2	2	Oregon	5	5	4
Illinois	19	20	24	Pennsylvania	19	21	25
Indiana	9	10	11	Rhode Island	2	2	2
Iowa	5	5	6	South Carolina	6	6	6
Kansas	4	4	5	South Dakota	1	1	2
Kentucky	6	6	7	Tennessee	9	9	9
Louisiana	7	7	8	Texas	32	30	24
Maine	2	2	2	Utah	3	3	2
Maryland	8	8	8	Vermont	1	1	1
Massachusetts	10	10	12	Virginia	11	11	10
Michigan	15	16	19	Washington	9	9	7
Minnesota	8	8	8	West Virginia	3	3	4
Mississippi	4	5	5	Wisconsin	8	9	9
Missouri	9	9	10	Wyoming	1	1	1

Washington, D.C., Puerto Rico, American Samoa, Guam, and the Virgin Islands each have one nonvoting member of the House of Representatives.

WHAT IMPEACHMENT MEANS

"Impeachment" means charging a high-ranking U.S. government official (such as a president or federal judge) with serious crimes — "high crimes and misdemeanors" — in order to possibly remove the person from office. Only the House of Representatives can vote to impeach officials. Once it does, there is a trial in the Senate.

The chief justice of the Supreme Court presides. A two-thirds vote is needed to remove the person from office.

In 1868, President Andrew Johnson (above) was impeached. He was found not guilty in a Senate trial. In 1974, a House committee recommended the impeachment of President Richard Nixon, but he resigned before the whole House could vote. On December 19, 1998, the House voted to impeach President Bill Clinton (left) for perjury and obstructing justice. On February 12, 1999, after a Senate trial, he was found not guilty of perjury, 55-45, and of obstructing justice, by a 50-50 vote.

THE JUDICIAL BRANCH
The SUPREME COURT

The highest court in the United States is the Supreme Court. It has nine justices who are appointed for life by the president with the approval of the Senate. Eight of the nine members are called associate justices. The ninth is the chief justice, who presides over the Court's meetings.

What Does the Supreme Court Do?
The Supreme Court's major responsibilities are to judge cases that involve reviewing federal laws, actions of the president, treaties of the United States, and laws passed by state governments to be sure they do not conflict with the U.S. Constitution. If the Supreme Court finds that a law or action violates the Constitution, the law is struck down.

The Supreme Court's Decision Is Final.
Most cases must go through other state courts or federal courts before they reach the Supreme Court. The Supreme Court is the final court for a case, and the justices decide which cases they will review. After the Supreme Court hears a case, it may agree or disagree with the decision by a lower court. When the Supreme Court makes a ruling, its decision is final, and all people involved in the case must abide by it. In December 2000, the Supreme Court made a decision that meant George W. Bush was the winner of the November election for president.

Who Is on the Supreme Court?
Below are the nine justices who were on the Supreme Court at the beginning of its 2000-2001 session.

Back row (from left to right): Ruth Bader Ginsburg, David H. Souter, Clarence Thomas, Stephen Breyer. **Front row** (from left to right): Antonin Scalia, John Paul Stevens, Chief Justice William H. Rehnquist, Sandra Day O'Connor, Anthony M. Kennedy.

SUPREME COURT PATH BREAKERS • The first Catholic to be named to the Supreme Court was Roger B. Taney, in 1836. In 1916, Louis D. Brandeis became the first Jewish justice. The first African American was Thurgood Marshall, in 1967. The first woman was Sandra Day O'Connor, in 1981.

HOW A BILL BECOMES A LAW

STEP 1 Senators and Representatives Propose Bill.

A proposed law is called a **bill**. Any member of Congress may propose (introduce) a bill. A bill is introduced in each house of Congress. The House of Representatives and the Senate consider a bill separately. A member of Congress who introduces a bill is known as the bill's **sponsor**. Bills to raise money always begin in the House of Representatives.

STEP 2 House and Senate Committees Consider the Bill.

The bill is then sent to appropriate committees for consideration. A bill relating to agriculture, for example, would be sent to the agriculture committees in the House and in the Senate. A committee is made up of a small number of members of the House or Senate. Whichever party has a majority in the House or Senate has a majority on each committee. When committees are considering a bill, they hold **hearings** at which people can speak for or against it.

STEP 3 Committees Vote on the Bill.

The committees can change the bill as they see fit. Then they vote on it.

STEP 4 The Bill is Debated in the House and Senate.

If the committees vote in favor of the bill, it goes to the full House and Senate, where it is debated and may be changed further. The House and Senate can then vote on it.

STEP 5 From the House and Senate to Conference Committee.

If the House and the Senate pass different versions of the same bill, the bill must go to a **conference committee,** where differences between the two versions must be worked out. A conference committee is a special committee made up of both Senate and House members.

STEP 6 Final Vote in the House and Senate.

The House and the Senate then vote on the conference committee version. In order for this version to become a law, it must be approved by a majority of members of both houses of Congress and signed by the president.

STEP 7 The President Signs the Bill into Law.

If the bill passes both houses of Congress, it goes to the president for his signature. Once the president signs a bill, it becomes law.

STEP 8 What if the President Doesn't Sign the Bill?

Sometimes the president does not approve of a bill and decides not to sign it. This is called **vetoing** it. A bill that has been vetoed goes back to Congress, where the members can vote again. If the House and the Senate pass the bill with a two-thirds majority vote, it becomes law. This is called **overriding** the veto.

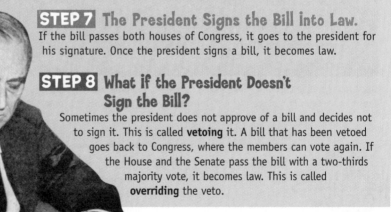

◄ *President Franklin D. Roosevelt, signing a bill*

TIME LINE

THE FIRST PEOPLE IN NORTH AMERICA: BEFORE 1492

14,000 B.C.–11,000 B.C.
Paleo-Indians use stone points attached to spears to hunt big mammoths in northern parts of North America.

11,000 B.C.
Big mammoths disappear and Paleo-Indians begin to gather plants for food.

AFTER A.D. 500
Anasazi peoples in the Southwestern United States live in homes on cliffs, called cliff dwellings. Anasazi pottery and dishes are well known for their beautiful patterns.

AFTER A.D. 700
Mississippian Indian people in Southeastern United States develop farms and build burial mounds.

40,000 B.C.

40,000 B.C.–11,000 B.C.
First people (called Paleo-Indians) cross from Siberia to Alaska and begin to move into North America.

9500 B.C.–1000 B.C.
North American Indians begin using stone to grind food and to hunt bison and smaller animals.

1000 B.C.–A.D. 500
Woodland Indians, who lived east of the Mississippi River, bury their dead under large mounds of earth (which can still be seen today).

700–1492
Many different Indian cultures develop throughout North America.

COLONIAL AMERICA AND THE AMERICAN REVOLUTION: 1492-1783

1492

1492
Christopher Columbus sails across the Atlantic Ocean and reaches an island in the Bahamas in the Caribbean Sea.

1513
Juan Ponce de León explores the Florida coast.

1524
Giovanni da Verrazano explores the coast from Carolina north to Nova Scotia, enters New York harbor.

1540
Francisco Vásquez de Coronado explores the Southwest.

1565
St. Augustine, Florida, the first town established by Europeans in the United States, is founded by the Spanish. Later burned by the English in 1586.

BENJAMIN FRANKLIN (1706-1790)

was a great American leader, printer, scientist, and writer. In 1732, he began publishing a magazine called *Poor Richard's Almanack*. Poor Richard was a make-believe person who gave advice about common sense and honesty. Many of Poor Richard's sayings are still known today. Among the most famous are "God helps them that help themselves" and "Early to bed, early to rise, makes a man healthy, wealthy, and wise."

1634

1634
Maryland is founded as a Catholic colony, with religious freedom for all granted in 1649.

1664
The English seize New Amsterdam from the Dutch. The city is renamed New York.

1699
French settlers move into Mississippi and Louisiana.

1732
Benjamin Franklin begins publishing *Poor Richard's Almanack*.

1754-1763
French and Indian War between England and France. The French are defeated and lose their lands in Canada and the American Midwest.

1764-1766
England places taxes on sugar that comes from their North American colonies. England also requires colonists to buy stamps to help pay for royal troops. Colonists protest, and the Stamp Act is repealed in 1766.

1607
Jamestown, Virginia, the first English settlement in North America, is founded by Captain John Smith.

1609
Henry Hudson sails into New York Harbor, explores Hudson River. Spaniards settle Santa Fe, New Mexico.

1619
The first African slaves are brought to Jamestown. (Slavery is made legal in 1650.)

1620
Pilgrims from England arrive at Plymouth, Massachusetts, on the *Mayflower*.

1626
Peter Minuit buys Manhattan island for the Dutch from Man-a-hat-a Indians for goods worth $24. The island is renamed New Amsterdam.

1630
Boston is founded by Massachusetts colonists led by John Winthrop.

FAMOUS WORDS FROM THE DECLARATION OF INDEPENDENCE, JULY 4, 1776

"We hold these truths to be self-evident, that all men are created equal, that they are endowed by their Creator with certain unalienable rights, that among these are life, liberty, and the pursuit of happiness."

1770
Boston Massacre: English troops fire on a group of people protesting English taxes.

1773
Boston Tea Party: English tea is thrown into the harbor to protest a tax on tea.

1775
Fighting at Lexington and Concord, Massachusetts, marks the beginning of the American Revolution.

1776
The Declaration of Independence is approved July 4 by the Continental Congress (made up of representatives from the American colonies).

1781
British General Cornwallis surrenders to the Americans at Yorktown, Virginia, ending the fighting in the Revolutionary War.

THE NEW NATION: 1783-1900

WHO ATTENDED THE CONVENTION?

The Constitutional Convention met in Philadelphia in the hot summer of 1787. Most of the great founders of America attended. Among those present were George Washington, James Madison, and John Adams. They met to form a new government that would be strong and, at the same time, protect the liberties that were fought for in the American Revolution. The Constitution they created is still the law of the United States.

THE LOUISIANA PURCHASE (1803)

1784

1784
The first successful daily newspaper, the *Pennsylvania Packet & General Advertiser*, is published.

1787
The Constitutional Convention meets to write a Constitution for the U.S.

1789
The new Constitution is approved by the states. George Washington is chosen as the first president.

1800
The federal government moves to a new capital, Washington, D.C.

1803
The U.S. makes the Louisiana Purchase from France. The Purchase doubles the area of the U.S.

The Trail of Tears

"THE TRAIL OF TEARS"

The Cherokee Indians living in Georgia were forced, by the state government of Georgia, to leave in 1838. They were sent to Oklahoma. On the long march, thousands died because of disease and the cold weather.

UNCLE TOM'S CABIN

Harriet Beecher Stowe's novel about the suffering of slaves was an instant bestseller in the North and banned in most of the South. When President Abraham Lincoln met Stowe, he called her "the little lady who started this war" (the Civil War).

1836

1836
Texans fighting for independence from Mexico are defeated at the Alamo.

1838
Cherokee Indians are forced to move to Oklahoma, along "The Trail of Tears."

1844
The first telegraph line connects Washington and Baltimore.

1846–1848
U.S. war with Mexico: Mexico is defeated, and the United States takes control of the Republic of Texas and of Mexican territories in the West.

1848
The discovery of gold in California leads to a "rush" of 80,000 people to the West in search of gold.

1852
Uncle Tom's Cabin is published.

1804

Lewis and Clark, with their guide Sacagawea, explore what is now the northwestern United States.

1812–1814

War of 1812 with Great Britain: British forces burn the Capitol and White House. Francis Scott Key writes the words to "The Star-Spangled Banner."

1820

The Missouri Compromise bans slavery west of the Mississippi River and north of 36°30′ latitude, except in Missouri.

1823

The Monroe Doctrine warns European countries not to interfere in the Americas.

1825

The Erie Canal opens linking New York City with the Great Lakes.

1831

The Liberator, a newspaper opposing slavery, is published in Boston.

CIVIL WAR DEAD AND WOUNDED

The U.S. Civil War between the North and South lasted four years (1861-1865) and resulted in the death or wounding of more than 600,000 people. Little was known at the time about the spread of diseases. As a result, many casualties were also the result of illnesses such as influenza, measles, and infections from battle wounds.

1898

Spanish-American War: The U.S. defeats Spain, gains control of the Philippines, Puerto Rico, and Guam.

1858

Abraham Lincoln and Stephen Douglas debate about slavery during their Senate campaign in Illinois.

1860

Abraham Lincoln is elected president.

1861

The Civil War begins.

1863

President Lincoln issues the Emancipation Proclamation, freeing most slaves.

1865

The Civil War ends as the South surrenders. President Lincoln is assassinated.

1869

The first railroad connecting the East and West coasts is completed.

1890

Battle of Wounded Knee is fought in South Dakota—the last major battle between Indians and U.S. troops.

263

UNITED STATES IN THE 20TH CENTURY

WORLD WAR I

In World War I the United States fought with Great Britain, France, and Russia (the Allies) against Germany and Austria-Hungary. The Allies won the war in 1918.

1900

1903
The United States begins digging the Panama Canal. The canal opens in 1914, connecting the Atlantic and Pacific oceans.

1908
Henry Ford introduces the Model T car, priced at $850.

1916
Jeannette Rankin of Montana becomes the first woman elected to Congress.

1917–1918
The United States joins World War I on the side of the Allies against Germany.

1927
Charles A. Lindbergh becomes the first person to fly alone nonstop across the Atlantic Ocean.

SCHOOL SEGREGATION

The U.S. Supreme Court ruled that separate schools for black students and white students were not equal. The Court said such schools were against the U.S. Constitution. The ruling also applied to other forms of segregation—separation of the races supported by some states.

1954

1954
The U.S. Supreme Court forbids racial segregation in public schools.

1963
President John Kennedy is assassinated.

1964
Congress passes the Civil Rights Act, which outlaws discrimination in voting and jobs.

1965
The United States sends large numbers of soldiers to fight in the Vietnam War.

1968
Civil rights leader Martin Luther King Jr. is assassinated in Memphis. Senator Robert F. Kennedy is assassinated in Los Angeles.

1969
U.S. Astronaut Neil Armstrong becomes the first person to walk on the moon.

1973
U.S. participation in the Vietnam War ends.

THE GREAT DEPRESSION

The stock market crash of October 1929 led to a period of severe hardship for the American people—the Great Depression. As many as 25 percent of all workers could not find jobs. The Depression lasted until the early 1940s. The Depression also led to a great change in politics. In 1932, Franklin D. Roosevelt, a Democrat, was elected president. He served as president for 12 years, longer than any other president.

1929
A stock market crash marks the beginning of the Great Depression.

1933
President Franklin D. Roosevelt's New Deal increases government help to people hurt by the Depression.

1941
Japan attacks Pearl Harbor, Hawaii. The United States enters World War II.

1945
Germany and Japan surrender, ending World War II. Japan surrenders after the U.S. drops atomic bombs on Hiroshima and Nagasaki.

1947
Jackie Robinson becomes the first black baseball player in the major leagues when he joins the Brooklyn Dodgers.

1950-1953
U.S. armed forces fight in the Korean War.

WATERGATE

In June 1972, five men were arrested in the Watergate building in Washington, D.C., for trying to bug telephones in the offices of the Democratic National Committee. Some of those arrested worked for the committee to reelect President Richard Nixon. Later it was discovered that Nixon was helping to hide information about the break-in.

1985
U.S. President Ronald Reagan and Soviet leader Mikhail Gorbachev begin working together to improve relations between their countries.

1991
The Persian Gulf War: The United States and its allies defeat Iraq.

1998
The federal government announces that, for the first time in many years, it will begin receiving more money than it spends.

1999
After an impeachment trial, the Senate finds President Clinton not guilty.

1974
President Richard Nixon resigns because of the Watergate scandal.

1979
U.S. hostages are taken in Iran, beginning a 444-day crisis that ends with their release in 1981.

1981
Sandra Day O'Connor becomes the first woman on the U.S. Supreme Court.

1992
Bill Clinton, a Democrat, is elected president, defeating George Bush.

1994
The Republican Party wins majorities in both houses of Congress for the first time in 40 years.

2000
George W. Bush narrowly defeats Al Gore in a hotly fought battle for the presidency. The race is finally settled by the U.S. Supreme Court in December.

Thurgood Marshall, the first black on the Supreme Court ▶

AFRICAN AMERICANS WORK FOR CHANGE

Would you like to learn more about the history of African Americans from the era of slavery to the present? These events and personalities can be a starting point. Can you add some more?

1619—⬤	First African Americans are brought to Virginia as slaves.
1831—⬤	Nat Turner starts a slave revolt in Virginia that is promptly put down.
1856-57—⬤	Dred Scott, a slave, sues to be freed because he had left slave territory, but the Supreme Court denies his claim.
1861-65—⬤	The North defeats the South in the brutal Civil War; the 13th Amendment ends nearly 250 years of slavery. The Ku Klux Klan is founded.
1865-77—⬤	Southern blacks play leadership roles in government under Reconstruction; 15th Amendment (1870) gives black men the right to vote.
1896—⬤	Supreme Court rules in a case called *Plessy versus Ferguson* that segregation is legal when facilities are "separate but equal." Discrimination and violence against blacks are increasing.
1910—⬤	W. E. B. Du Bois (1868-1963) founds National Association for the Advancement of Colored People, fighting for equality for blacks.
1920s—⬤	African American culture (jazz music, dance, literature) flourishes during the "Harlem Renaissance."
1954—⬤	Supreme Court rules in a case called *Brown versus Board of Education of Topeka* that school segregation is unconstitutional.
1957—⬤	Black students, backed by federal troops, enter segregated Little Rock Central High School.
1955-65—⬤	Malcolm X (1925-65) emerges as key spokesman for black nationalism.
1963—⬤	Rev. Dr. Martin Luther King Jr. (1929-68) gives his "I Have a Dream" speech at a peaceful March on Washington.
1964—⬤	Sweeping civil rights bill banning racial discrimination is signed by President Lyndon Johnson.
1965—⬤	King leads protest march in Selma, Alabama; blacks riot in Watts section of Los Angeles.
1967—⬤	Gary, Indiana, and Cleveland, Ohio, are first major U.S. cities to elect black mayors; Thurgood Marshall (1908-93) becomes first black on the Supreme Court.
1995—⬤	Hundreds of thousands of black men in take part in "Million Man March" rally in Washington, D.C., urging responsibility for families and communities.
2001—⬤	Retired Gen. Colin Powell becomes first African American secretary of state, filling the top foreign policy position in the president's cabinet.

THEY MADE HISTORY

The people below fought racial barriers in order to achieve their goals.

LOUIS ARMSTRONG
(1901-1971), jazz trumpet player and singer from New Orleans, Louisiana. His improvisational style brought him fame beginning in the late 1920s. Armstrong's music continues to influence musicians in and out of jazz to this day.

W. E. B. Du BOIS
(1868-1963) was the first black person to earn a doctorate, in sociology, from Harvard University. He helped found the National Association for the Advancement of Colored People (NAACP), and organized "Pan African" meetings that brought together American blacks and Africans. In books like *The Souls of Black Folks*, Du Bois urged people to see "Beauty in Black."

ALTHEA GIBSON
(born 1927) was the first African-American tennis player to compete at the U.S. championship (in 1950) and at Wimbledon (1951). In 1957 and 1958 she won both tournaments.

JOHN H. JOHNSON
(born 1918) is the head of Johnson Publishing Company, the largest black-owned publishing company in the world. In 1942, he published *Negro Digest*, the first successful magazine geared toward black readers. He started *Ebony* magazine in 1945 and *Jet* in 1951. Both were immediately popular and are highly successful today.

REVEREND MARTIN LUTHER KING JR.
(1929-1968) used his powerful speaking style, forceful personality, and belief in nonviolence to help change U.S. history. From the mid-1950s to his assassination in 1968, he was the most influential leader of the U.S. civil rights movement.

MALCOLM X
(1925-1965) was a militant Black Muslim leader who spoke against injustices toward blacks and called for blacks to keep separate from whites. He was assassinated by rivals in 1965, but his life story, *The Autobiography of Malcolm X*, became a best-seller and helped make him a hero to many in the black community.

Louis Armstrong

THURGOOD MARSHALL
(1908-1993) became the first African-American justice on the U.S. Supreme Court in 1967. In 1954, he won a historic case, *Brown v. Board of Education of Topeka*, before the Supreme Court. The Court ruled that separate schools for black and white students were not equal or legal.

COLIN POWELL
(born 1937) became the first African-American U.S. secretary of state in 2001. In 1991, while serving as the first black chairman of the Joint Chiefs of Staff, he oversaw Operation Desert Storm in the Persian Gulf War.

JACKIE ROBINSON
(1919-1972) was the first black player in the history of Major League Baseball. He joined the Dodgers, then in Brooklyn, in 1947. In 1949, he won the National League's MVP award and in 1962 was elected to the Baseball Hall of Fame.

HARRIET TUBMAN
(1821-1913) escaped slavery when she was in her twenties. Before the Civil War, she repeatedly risked her life to lead hundreds of slaves to freedom by way of a network of homes and churches called the "Underground Railroad."

NEIL DE GRASSE TYSON
(born 1959) became an astrophysicist, a scientist who studies the sky, and is now the director of the Hayden Planetarium in New York City. An author and teacher, he makes complicated ideas understandable and fun for people who are not scientists.

OPRAH WINFREY
(born 1954) has won many awards as a talk show host, actress, writer, publisher, and film producer. Through Oprah's Angel Network, she has collected millions of dollars to help people in need.

Jackie Robinson ▶

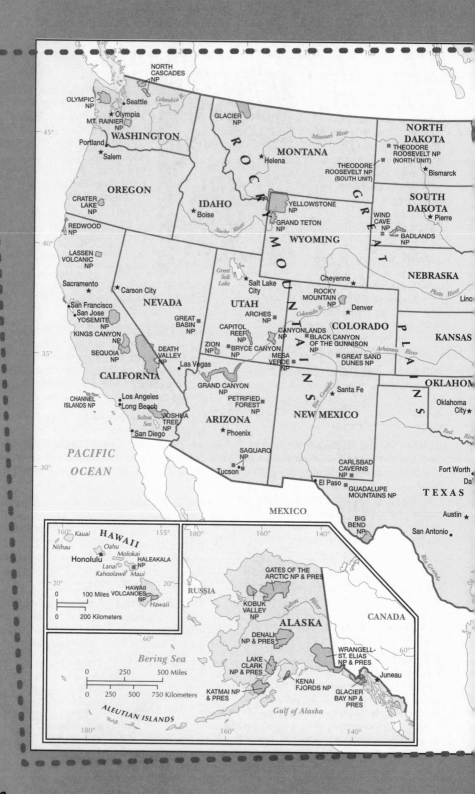

NORTH CASCADES NP

OLYMPIC NP
Seattle
Olympia
MT. RAINIER NP
Portland
Salem
WASHINGTON

Columbia R.

GLACIER NP

MONTANA
Helena

Missouri River

NORTH DAKOTA
THEODORE ROOSEVELT NP (NORTH UNIT)
Bismarck

OREGON

IDAHO
Boise

THEODORE ROOSEVELT NP (SOUTH UNIT)

ROCKY

YELLOWSTONE NP
GRAND TETON NP
WYOMING

SOUTH DAKOTA
Pierre
WIND CAVE NP
BADLANDS NP

CRATER LAKE NP

REDWOOD NP

Snake River

LASSEN VOLCANIC NP

Great Salt Lake
Salt Lake City

Cheyenne

NEBRASKA

Platte River

Linco

Sacramento
Carson City
NEVADA

San Francisco
San Jose
YOSEMITE NP
KINGS CANYON NP

GREAT BASIN NP

UTAH
CAPITOL REEF NP
ZION NP
ARCHES NP
BRYCE CANYON NP

MOUNTAINS

ROCKY MOUNTAIN NP
Denver

Colorado R.

CANYONLANDS NP
BLACK CANYON OF THE GUNNISON NP
MESA VERDE NP

COLORADO

GREAT SAND DUNES NP

KANSAS

Arkansas River

SEQUOIA NP
DEATH VALLEY NP
Las Vegas

CALIFORNIA

CHANNEL ISLANDS NP

Los Angeles
Long Beach

Salton Sea

JOSHUA TREE NP
San Diego

GRAND CANYON NP
PETRIFIED FOREST NP
ARIZONA
Phoenix

SAGUARO NP
Tucson

Santa Fe

NEW MEXICO

OKLAHOM

Oklahoma City

Rio Grande

CARLSBAD CAVERNS NP

El Paso
GUADALUPE MOUNTAINS NP

Red River

TEXAS

Fort Worth
Da

Austin
San Antonio

PACIFIC OCEAN

MEXICO

BIG BEND NP

Rio Grande

HAWAII

Kauai
Niihau
Oahu
Honolulu
Molokai
Lanai
Kahoolawe
Maui
HALEAKALA NP
HAWAII VOLCANOES NP
Hawaii

0   100 Miles
0   200 Kilometers

RUSSIA

Bering Sea

0   250   500 Miles
0   250   500   750 Kilometers

ALEUTIAN ISLANDS

GATES OF THE ARCTIC NP & PRES

KOBUK VALLEY NP

Yukon River

ALASKA

DENALI NP & PRES

LAKE CLARK NP & PRES

KATMAI NP & PRES

KENAI FJORDS NP

WRANGELL-ST. ELIAS NP & PRES

CANADA

Juneau

GLACIER BAY NP & PRES

Gulf of Alaska

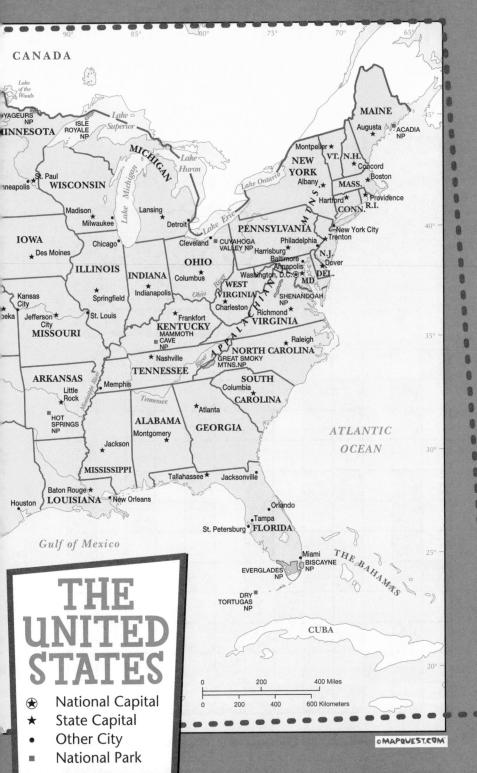

THE UNITED STATES

- ⊛ National Capital
- ★ State Capital
- • Other City
- ■ National Park

CANADA

Lake of the Woods

VOYAGEURS NP

MINNESOTA

ISLE ROYALE NP

Lake Superior

MICHIGAN

Lake Huron

WISCONSIN

Lake Michigan

St. Paul ★

Minneapolis •

Madison ★

Milwaukee •

Lansing ★

Detroit •

IOWA

Des Moines ★

Chicago •

ILLINOIS

INDIANA

Springfield ★

Indianapolis ★

Kansas City •

Topeka ★

Jefferson City ★

St. Louis •

MISSOURI

MAINE

Augusta ★

ACADIA NP

Montpelier ★

VT.

N.H.

Concord ★

NEW YORK

Albany ★

Boston ★

MASS.

Hartford ★

Providence ★

R.I.

CONN.

New York City •

Trenton ★

PENNSYLVANIA

Cleveland •

CUYAHOGA VALLEY NP

Harrisburg ★

Philadelphia •

N.J.

Dover ★

DEL.

OHIO

Columbus ★

Baltimore •

Annapolis ★

Washington, D.C. ⊛

MD

WEST VIRGINIA

Charleston ★

SHENANDOAH NP

Richmond ★

VIRGINIA

Frankfort ★

KENTUCKY

MAMMOTH CAVE NP

Raleigh ★

Nashville ★

NORTH CAROLINA

GREAT SMOKY MTNS. NP

TENNESSEE

Columbia ★

SOUTH CAROLINA

ARKANSAS

Little Rock ★

Memphis •

HOT SPRINGS NP

Atlanta ★

ALABAMA

GEORGIA

Jackson ★

Montgomery ★

MISSISSIPPI

Tallahassee ★

Jacksonville •

Baton Rouge ★

LOUISIANA

New Orleans •

Houston •

Orlando •

Tampa •

St. Petersburg •

FLORIDA

Miami •

BISCAYNE NP

EVERGLADES NP

DRY TORTUGAS NP

ATLANTIC OCEAN

Gulf of Mexico

THE BAHAMAS

CUBA

APPALACHIAN MTNS.

Ohio River

Mississippi River

Tennessee River

Lake Erie

Lake Ontario

90° 85° 80° 75° 70° 65°

45°

40°

35°

30°

25°

20°

0 200 400 Miles

0 200 400 600 Kilometers

©MAPQUEST.COM

269

◁ FILL IN THE FRAME ▷

Look at the words in the Word Box. Fill them in where they fit best in this framework puzzle. We've done one to get you started.

WORD BOX

12 LETTERS	11 LETTERS	10 LETTERS	8 LETTERS
Constitution	olive branch	amendments	majority

6 LETTERS
anthem
Arctic
rights
united

5 LETTERS
ideas
table
votes

4 LETTERS
hear   term
myth   veto

3 LETTERS
one

I D E A S

FACTS ABOUT THE STATES

After every state name is the postal abbreviation. The Area includes both land and water; it is given in square miles (sq. mi.) and square kilometers (sq. km.). Population figures come from the 2000 U.S. census. Numbers in parentheses after Population, Area, and Entered Union show the state's rank compared with other states.

ALABAMA (AL) *Heart of Dixie, Camellia State*

POPULATION (2000): 4,447,100 (23rd)
AREA: 52,237 sq. mi. (30th) (135,294 sq. km.)
ENTERED UNION: December 14, 1819 (22nd)
FLOWER: Camellia **BIRD:** Yellowhammer
TREE: Southern longleaf pine **SONG:** "Alabama"
CAPITAL: Montgomery **LARGEST CITIES (WITH POP.):** Birmingham, 242,820; Montgomery, 201,568; Mobile, 198,915; Huntsville, 158,216
IMPORTANT PRODUCTS: clothing and textiles, metal products, transportation equipment, paper, industrial machinery, food products, lumber, coal, oil, natural gas, livestock, peanuts, cotton
PLACES TO VISIT: Alabama Space and Rocket Center, Huntsville; Carver Museum, Tuskegee

WEB SITE *http://alaweb.asc.edu • http://www.touralabama.org*

DID YOU KNOW? *This is the birthplace of Helen Keller. Despite becoming deaf and blind when she was a baby, she became a world-renowned writer and speaker.*

ALASKA (AK) *The Last Frontier*

POPULATION (2000): 626,932 (48th)
AREA: 615,230 sq. mi. (1st) (1,593,444 sq. km.)
ENTERED UNION: January 3, 1959 (49th)
FLOWER: Forget-me-not **BIRD:** Willow ptarmigan
TREE: Sitka spruce **SONG:** "Alaska's Flag"
CAPITAL: Juneau (population, 30,711) **LARGEST CITIES (WITH POP.):** Anchorage, 260,283; Fairbanks, 30,224 **IMPORTANT PRODUCTS:** oil, natural gas, fish, food products, lumber and wood products, fur
PLACES TO VISIT: Glacier Bay and Denali national parks, Mendenhall Glacier, Mount McKinley

WEB SITE *http://www.state.ak.us • http://www.dced.state.ak.us/tourism/*

DID YOU KNOW? *Alaska was called "Seward's Folly" in 1867 when U.S. Secretary of State William Seward bought it from Russia for $7.2 million. Alaskans had the last laugh, though—in 1896, gold was discovered here.*

ARIZONA (AZ) *Grand Canyon State*

POPULATION (2000): 5,130,632 (20th)
AREA: 114,006 sq. mi. (6th) (295,276 sq. km.)
ENTERED UNION: February 14, 1912 (48th)
FLOWER: Blossom of the Saguaro cactus
BIRD: Cactus wren **TREE:** Paloverde **SONG:** "Arizona"
CAPITAL AND LARGEST CITY: Phoenix (population, 1,321,045)
OTHER LARGE CITIES (WITH POP.): Tucson, 486,699; Mesa, 396,375; Glendale, 218,812, Scottsdale, 202,705, Chandler, 176,581
IMPORTANT PRODUCTS: electronic equipment, transportation and industrial equipment, instruments, printing and publishing, copper and other metals
PLACES TO VISIT: Grand Canyon, Painted Desert, Petrified Forest, Navajo National Monument

WEB SITE *http://www.state.az.us • http://www.arizonaguide.com*

DID YOU KNOW? *Oraibi, which is part of the Hopi reservation, claims to be the oldest continually inhabited place in America.*

ARKANSAS (AR) *Natural State, Razorback State*

POPULATION (2000): 2,673,400 (33rd)
AREA: 53,182 sq. mi. (28th) (137,741 sq. km.)
FLOWER: Apple blossom **BIRD:** Mockingbird
TREE: Pine **SONG:** "Arkansas"
ENTERED UNION: June 15, 1836 (25th)
CAPITAL AND LARGEST CITY: Little Rock (population, 183,133)
OTHER LARGE CITIES (WITH POP.): Fort Smith, 80,268, North Little Rock, 60,433;
IMPORTANT PRODUCTS: food products, paper, electronic equipment, industrial machinery, metal products, lumber and wood products, livestock, soybeans, rice, cotton, natural gas
PLACES TO VISIT: Hot Springs National Park; Ozark Folk Center, near Mountain View.

WEB SITE http://www.state.ar.us • http://www.arkansas.com

DID YOU KNOW? *The fiddle is the official musical instrument of Arkansas.*

CALIFORNIA (CA) *Golden State*

POPULATION (2000): 33,871,648 (1st)
AREA: 158,869 sq. mi. (3rd) (411,471 sq. km.)
FLOWER: Golden poppy **BIRD:** California valley quail
TREE: California redwood **SONG:** "I Love You, California"
ENTERED UNION: September 9, 1850 (31st)
CAPITAL: Sacramento (population, 407,018) **LARGEST CITIES (WITH POP.):**
Los Angeles, 3,694,820; San Diego, 1,22,400; San Jose, 894,943; San Francisco, 776,733; **IMPORTANT PRODUCTS:** transportation and industrial equipment, electronic equipment, oil, natural gas, motion pictures, milk, cattle, fruit, vegetables
PLACES TO VISIT: Yosemite Valley, Lake Tahoe, Palomar Observatory, Disneyland, San Diego Zoo, Hollywood, Sequoia National Park

WEB SITE http://www.state.ca.us • http://www.gocalif.ca.gov

DID YOU KNOW? *After gold was discovered here in 1849, thousands of people traveled to California. These "49ers" found many ways to deal with the hardships along their journey. One woman baked bread daily to feed to her horses and keep them alive.*

COLORADO (CO) *Centennial State*

POPULATION (2000): 4,301,261 (24th)
AREA: 104,100 sq. mi. (8th) (269,619 sq. km.)
FLOWER: Rocky Mountain columbine
BIRD: Lark bunting **TREE:** Colorado blue spruce
SONG: "Where the Columbines Grow"
ENTERED UNION: August 1, 1876 (38th)
CAPITAL AND LARGEST CITY: Denver (population, 554,636)
OTHER LARGE CITIES (WITH POP.): Colorado Springs, 360,890; Aurora, 276,393; Lakewood, 144,126
IMPORTANT PRODUCTS: instruments and industrial machinery, food products, printing and publishing, metal products, electronic equipment, oil, coal, cattle
PLACES TO VISIT: Rocky Mountain National Park, Mesa Verde National Park, Dinosaur National Monument, old mining towns

WEB SITE http://www.state.co.us • http://www.colorado.com

DID YOU KNOW? *Several top national institutions make their home here: the U.S. Air Force Academy, the U.S. Mint, the North American Aerospace Defense Command, and the National Oceanic and Atmospheric Administration.*

CONNECTICUT (CT) *Constitution State, Nutmeg State*

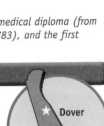
★ Hartford

POPULATION (2000): 3,406,565 (29th)
AREA: 5,544 sq. mi. (48th) (14,359 sq. km.)
FLOWER: Mountain laurel **BIRD:** American robin
TREE: White oak **SONG:** "Yankee Doodle"
ENTERED UNION: January 9, 1788 (5th)
CAPITAL: Hartford **LARGEST CITIES (WITH POP.):** Bridgeport, 139,529; New Haven, 123,626; Hartford, 121,578; Stamford, 117,083; Waterbury, 107,271
IMPORTANT PRODUCTS: aircraft parts, helicopters, industrial machinery, metals and metal products, electronic equipment, printing and publishing, medical instruments, chemicals, dairy products, stone
PLACES TO VISIT: Mystic Seaport and Marine Life Aquarium, in Mystic; P. T. Barnum Circus Museum, Bridgeport; Peabody Museum, New Haven

WEB SITE *http://www.state.ct.us • http://www.tourism.state.ct.us*

DID YOU KNOW? *Connecticut boasts a number of firsts for the U.S.: the first medical diploma (from Yale University in 1729), the first published dictionary (by Noah Webster in 1783), and the first hamburger (served at Louie's Lunch in 1895).*

DELAWARE (DE) *First State, Diamond State*

★ Dover

POPULATION (2000): 783,600 (45th)
AREA: 2,396 sq. mi. (49th) (6,206 sq. km.)
FLOWER: Peach blossom **BIRD:** Blue hen chicken
TREE: American holly **SONG:** "Our Delaware"
ENTERED UNION: December 7, 1787 (1st)
CAPITAL: Dover **LARGEST CITIES (WITH POP.):** Wilmington, 72,664; Dover, 32,135; Newark, 28,547 **IMPORTANT PRODUCTS:** chemicals, transportation equipment, food products, chickens
PLACES TO VISIT: Rehoboth Beach, Henry Francis du Pont Winterthur Museum near Wilmington

WEB SITE *http://www.state.de.us • http://www.visitdelaware.net*

DID YOU KNOW? *Wilmington was the site of a final Underground Railroad station for slaves escaping from the South to freedom. The station was the home of Thomas Garrett, who became an abolitionist in 1820 and helped more than 2,000 slaves escape.*

FLORIDA (FL) *Sunshine State*

★
Tallahassee

POPULATION (2000): 15,982,378 (4th)
AREA: 59,928 sq. mi. (23rd) (155,213 sq. km.)
FLOWER: Orange blossom **BIRD:** Mockingbird
TREE: Sabal palmetto palm **SONG:** "Old Folks at Home"
ENTERED UNION: March 3, 1845 (27th)
CAPITAL: Tallahassee (population, 150,624) **LARGEST CITIES (WITH POP.):** Jacksonville, 735,617; Miami, 362,470; Tampa, 303,447; St. Petersburg, 248,232
IMPORTANT PRODUCTS: electronic and transportation equipment, industrial machinery, printing and publishing, food products, citrus fruits, vegetables, livestock, phosphates, fish
PLACES TO VISIT: Walt Disney World and Universal Studios, near Orlando; Sea World, Orlando; Busch Gardens, Tampa; Spaceport USA, at Kennedy Space Center, Cape Canaveral; Everglades National Park

WEB SITE *http://www.state.fl.us • http://www.flausa.com*

DID YOU KNOW? *This state is proud of Marjorie Kinnan Rawlings, who lived in a tiny village named Cross Creek. She won a Pulitzer Prize for writing* The Yearling, *about a boy and his pet deer.*

GEORGIA (GA) *Empire State of the South, Peach State*

POPULATION (2000): 8,186,453 (10th)
AREA: 58,977 sq. mi. (24th) (152,750 sq. km.)
FLOWER: Cherokee rose **BIRD:** Brown thrasher
TREE: Live oak **SONG:** "Georgia on My Mind"
ENTERED UNION: January 2, 1788 (4th)
CAPITAL AND LARGEST CITY: Atlanta (population, 416,474)
OTHER LARGE CITIES (WITH POP.): Augusta, 199,775, Columbus, 186,291;
Savannah, 131,510
IMPORTANT PRODUCTS: clothing and textiles, transportation equipment, food products, paper,
chickens, peanuts, peaches, clay
PLACES TO VISIT: Stone Mountain Park; Six Flags Over Georgia; Martin Luther King, Jr., Natl.
Historic Site, Atlanta

WEB SITE http://www.state.ga.us • http://www.georgia.org

DID YOU KNOW? *The S.S. Savannah, named for its home port, was the first steamboat to sail across the Atlantic Ocean.*

HAWAII (HI) *Aloha State*

POPULATION (2000): 1,211,537 (42nd)
AREA: 6,459 sq. mi. (47th) (16,728 sq. km.)
FLOWER: Yellow hibiscus **BIRD:** Hawaiian goose
TREE: Kukui **SONG:** "Hawaii Ponoi"
ENTERED UNION: August 21, 1959 (50th)
CAPITAL AND LARGEST CITY: Honolulu (population, 371,657)
OTHER LARGE CITIES (WITH POP.): Hilo, 40,759; Kailua, 36,513;
Kaneohe, 34,970
IMPORTANT PRODUCTS: food products, pineapples, sugar, printing and publishing, fish, flowers
PLACES TO VISIT: Hawaii Volcanoes National Park; Haleakala National Park, Maui; U.S.S. *Arizona*
Memorial, Pearl Harbor; Polynesian Cultural Center, Laie

WEB SITE http://www.state.hi.us • http://www.gohawaii.com

DID YOU KNOW? *Around 1800, King Kamehameha the Great united the many Hawaiian islands. Hawaii's last queen, Liluokalani, lost her throne in 1893. Hawaii also has a state fish called the humuhumunukunukupuaa.*

IDAHO (ID) *Gem State*

POPULATION (2000): 1,293,953 (39th)
AREA: 83,574 sq. mi. (14th) (216,456 sq. km.)
FLOWER: Syringa **BIRD:** Mountain bluebird
TREE: White pine **SONG:** "Here We Have Idaho"
ENTERED UNION: July 3, 1890 (43rd)
CAPITAL AND LARGEST CITY: Boise (population, 185,787)
OTHER LARGE CITIES (WITH POP.): Nampa, 51,867; Pocatello, 51,466
IMPORTANT PRODUCTS: potatoes, hay, wheat, cattle, milk, lumber and wood products, food products
PLACES TO VISIT: Sun Valley; Hells Canyon; Craters of the Moon, near Arco; World Center for Birds of
Prey, Boise; ghost towns

WEB SITE http://www.visitid.com

DID YOU KNOW? *Idaho didn't get its first TV station until 1953. So it's ironic that Philo Farnsworth, who was born here, invented one of the first television cameras (in 1922 when he was still in high school).*

ILLINOIS (IL) *Prairie State*

Springfield ★

POPULATION (2000): 12,419,293 (5th)
AREA: 57,918 sq. mi. (25th) (150,007 sq. km.)
FLOWER: Native violet **BIRD:** Cardinal
TREE: White oak **SONG:** "Illinois"
ENTERED UNION: December 3, 1818 (21st)
CAPITAL: Springfield (population, 111,454) **LARGEST CITIES (WITH POP.):**
Chicago, 2,896,016; Rockford, 150,115; Aurora, 142,990; Naperville, 128,358;
Peoria, 112,936;
IMPORTANT PRODUCTS: industrial machinery, metals and metal products, printing and
publishing, electronic equipment, food products, corn, soybeans, hogs **PLACES TO VISIT:** Lincoln Park
Zoo, Adler Planetarium, Field Museum of Natural History, and Museum of Science and Industry, all in
Chicago; Abraham Lincoln's home and burial site, Springfield; New Salem Village

WEB SITE *http://www.state.il.us • http://www.enjoyillinois.com*

DID YOU KNOW? *How you've grown! When it became a state in 1818, Illinois had 34,620 people.
Today it has more than 12 million. Only four states have more people.*

INDIANA (IN) *Hoosier State*

Indianapolis ★

POPULATION (2000): 6,080,485 (14th)
AREA: 36,420 sq. mi. (38th) (94,328 sq. km.)
FLOWER: Peony **BIRD:** Cardinal
TREE: Tulip poplar **SONG:** "On the Banks of the
Wabash, Far Away"
ENTERED UNION: December 11, 1816 (19th)
CAPITAL AND LARGEST CITY: Indianapolis (population, 791,926)
OTHER LARGE CITIES (WITH POP.): Fort Wayne, 205,727; Evansville, 121,582; South
Bend, 107,789; Gary, 102,746; **IMPORTANT PRODUCTS:** transportation equipment, electronic
equipment, industrial machinery, iron and steel, metal products, corn, soybeans, livestock, coal
PLACES TO VISIT: Children's Museum, Indianapolis; Conner Prairie Pioneer Settlement, Noblesville;
Lincoln Boyhood Memorial, Lincoln City; Wyandotte Cave

WEB SITE *http://www.state.in.us*

DID YOU KNOW? *People in Indiana are called "hoosiers." Among the many famous hoosiers are actor
James Dean, TV hosts David Letterman and Jane Pauley, composer Cole Porter, writer Kurt Vonnegut,
and a U.S. president, Benjamin Harrison.*

IOWA (IA) *Hawkeye State*

Des Moines ★

POPULATION (2000): 2,926,324 (30th)
AREA: 56,276 sq. mi. (26th) (145,754 sq. km.)
FLOWER: Wild rose **BIRD:** Eastern goldfinch
TREE: Oak **SONG:** "The Song of Iowa"
ENTERED UNION: December 28, 1846 (29th)
CAPITAL AND LARGEST CITY: Des Moines (population, 198,682)
OTHER LARGE CITIES (WITH POP.): Cedar Rapids, 120,758; Davenport, 98,359;
Sioux City, 85,013
IMPORTANT PRODUCTS: corn, soybeans, hogs, cattle, industrial machinery, food products
PLACES TO VISIT: Effigy Mounds National Monument, Marquette; Herbert Hoover Birthplace,
West Branch; Living History Farms, Des Moines; Adventureland; the Amana Colonies; Fort Dodge
Historical Museum

WEB SITE *http://www.traveliowa.com*

DID YOU KNOW? *This state was part of the 1803 Louisiana Purchase. After the Black Hawk War in
1832, Native Americans here were forced to give up their land and move to the Kansas Territory.*

KANSAS (KS) *Sunflower State*

POPULATION (2000): 2,688,418 (32nd)
AREA: 82,282 sq. mi. (15th) (213,110 sq. km.)
FLOWER: Native sunflower
BIRD: Western meadowlark
TREE: Cottonwood **SONG:** "Home on the Range"
ENTERED UNION: January 29, 1861 (34th)
CAPITAL: Topeka **LARGEST CITIES (WITH POP.):** Wichita, 344,284; Overland Park, 149,080; Kansas City, 146,866; Topeka, 122,377
IMPORTANT PRODUCTS: cattle, aircraft and other transportation equipment, industrial machinery, food products, wheat, corn, hay, oil, natural gas
PLACES TO VISIT: Dodge City; Fort Scott and Fort Larned national historical sites; Eisenhower Center, Abilene; Kansas Cosmosphere and Space Discovery Center, Hutchinson

WEB SITE http:// www.accesskansas.org • http://www.kansas.commerce.com

DID YOU KNOW? *The only survivor from the cavalry at the Battle of Little Bighorn was a horse named Comanche. He was preserved after death and is on display at the University of Kansas.*

KENTUCKY (KY) *Bluegrass State*

POPULATION (2000): 4,041,769 (25th)
AREA: 40,411 sq. mi. (37th) (104,665 sq. km.)
FLOWER: Goldenrod **BIRD:** Cardinal
TREE: Tulip poplar **SONG:** "My Old Kentucky Home"
ENTERED UNION: June 1, 1792 (15th)
CAPITAL: Frankfort (population, 27,741)
LARGEST CITIES (WITH POP.): Lexington 260,512; Louisville, 256,231
IMPORTANT PRODUCTS: coal, industrial machinery, electronic equipment, transportation equipment, metals, tobacco, cattle
PLACES TO VISIT: Mammoth Cave National Park; Lincoln's Birthplace, Hodgenville; Cumberland Gap National Historical Park, Middlesboro

WEB SITE http:// www.stateky.us • http://www.kentuckytourism.com

DID YOU KNOW? *Daniel Boone blazed the Wilderness Trail through the Cumberland Gap, enabling Kentucky to become the first area west of the Alleghenies settled by pioneers.*

LOUISIANA (LA) *Pelican State*

POPULATION (2000): 4,468,976 (22nd)
AREA: 49,651 sq. mi. (31st) (128,596 sq. km.)
FLOWER: Magnolia **BIRD:** Eastern brown pelican
TREE: Cypress **SONG:** "Give Me Louisiana"
ENTERED UNION: April 30, 1812 (18th)
CAPITAL: Baton Rouge
LARGEST CITIES (WITH POP.): New Orleans, 484,674; Baton Rouge, 227,818; Shreveport, 200,145
IMPORTANT PRODUCTS: natural gas, oil, chemicals, transportation equipment, paper, food products, cotton, fish
PLACES TO VISIT: Aquarium of the Americas, Audubon Zoo and Gardens, both New Orleans

WEB SITE http://www.state.la.us • http://www.louisianatravel.com

DID YOU KNOW? *This state has been governed under 10 different flags, including those of France, Spain, and Great Britain.*

MAINE (ME) *Pine Tree State*

POPULATION (2000): 1,274,923 (40th)
AREA: 33,741 sq. mi. (39th) (87,389 sq. km.)
FLOWER: White pine cone and tassel **BIRD:**
Chickadee **TREE:** Eastern white pine **SONG:** "State
of Maine Song"
ENTERED UNION: March 15, 1820 (23rd) **CAPITAL:** Augusta (population,
18,560) **LARGEST CITIES (WITH POP.):** Portland, 64,249; Lewiston, 35,690;
Bangor, 31,473 **IMPORTANT PRODUCTS:** paper, transportation equipment, wood and
wood products, electronic equipment, footwear, clothing, potatoes, milk, eggs, fish, and seafood
PLACES TO VISIT: Acadia National Park, Bar Harbor; Booth Bay Railway Museum; Portland Headlight
Lighthouse, near Portland

WEB SITE *http://www.state.me.us • http://www.visitmaine.com*

DID YOU KNOW? *Covered bridges are few and far between these days, but you can still see 10 of them here. There used to be 120, but fires, floods, and ice destroyed many of them.*

MARYLAND (MD) *Old Line State, Free State*

POPULATION (2000): 5,296,486 (19th)
AREA: 12,297 sq. mi. (42nd) (31,849 sq. km.)
FLOWER: Black-eyed susan **BIRD:** Baltimore oriole
TREE: White oak **SONG:** "Maryland, My Maryland"
ENTERED UNION: April 28, 1788 (7th)
CAPITAL: Annapolis (population, 35,838)
LARGEST CITIES (WITH POP.): Baltimore, 651,154; Frederick, 52,767;
Gaithersburg, 52,613; Bowie, 50,269
IMPORTANT PRODUCTS: printing and publishing, food products, transportation equipment,
electronic equipment, chickens, soybeans, corn, stone
PLACES TO VISIT: Antietam National Battlefield; Fort McHenry National Monument, in Baltimore
Harbor; U.S. Naval Academy in Annapolis

WEB SITE *http://www.state.md.us • http://www.mdisfun.org*

DID YOU KNOW? *Two prominent black Americans were born here: Thurgood Marshall, the first African American appointed to the U.S. Supreme Court, and Harriet Tubman, an escaped slave who helped others as a leader of the Underground Railroad.*

MASSACHUSETTS (MA) *Bay State, Old Colony*

POPULATION (2000): 6,349,097 (13th)
AREA: 9,241 sq. mi. (45th) (23,934 sq. km.)
FLOWER: Mayflower **BIRD:** Chickadee
TREE: American elm **SONG:** "All Hail to
Massachusetts"
ENTERED UNION: February 6, 1788 (6th) **CAPITAL AND LARGEST CITY:**
Boston (population: 589,141) **OTHER LARGE CITIES (WITH POP.):** Worcester,
172,648; Springfield, 152,082; Lowell, 105,167
IMPORTANT PRODUCTS: industrial machinery, electronic equipment, instruments, printing and
publishing, metal products, fish, flowers and shrubs, cranberries
PLACES TO VISIT: Plymouth Rock; Minute Man National Historical Park; Children's Museum, Boston;
Basketball Hall of Fame, Springfield; Old Sturbridge Village; Martha's Vineyard; Cape Cod; historical
sites in Boston

WEB SITE *http://www.state.ma.us*

DID YOU KNOW? *The Pilgrims didn't mean to come here. They were aiming for Virginia Colony, but a storm blew their ship, the Mayflower, off course.*

MICHIGAN (MI) *Great Lakes State, Wolverine State*

POPULATION (2000): 9,938,444 (8th)
AREA: 96,705 sq. mi. (11th) (250,465 sq. km.)
FLOWER: Apple blossom **BIRD:** Robin
TREE: White pine **SONG:** "Michigan, My Michigan"
ENTERED UNION: January 26, 1837 (26th)
CAPITAL: Lansing (population, 127,825)
LARGEST CITIES (WITH POP.): Detroit, 951,270; Grand Rapids, 197,800; Warren, 138,247; Flint, 124,943
IMPORTANT PRODUCTS: automobiles, industrial machinery, metal products, office furniture, plastic products, chemicals, food products, milk, corn, natural gas, iron ore, blueberries
PLACES TO VISIT: Greenfield Village and Henry Ford Museum, Dearborn; Mackinac Island; Kalamazoo Aviation History Museum; Motown Historical Museum, Detroit

WEB SITE *http://www.migov.state.mi.us*

DID YOU KNOW? *This state has more than 11,000 lakes. People here say you're probably from Michigan if you learned to drive a boat before you learned to ride a bike.*

MINNESOTA (MN) *North Star State, Gopher State*

POPULATION (2000): 4,919,479 (21st)
AREA: 86,943 sq. mi. (12th) (225,182 sq. km.)
FLOWER: Pink and white lady's-slipper
BIRD: Common loon
TREE: Red pine **SONG:** "Hail! Minnesota"
ENTERED UNION: May 11, 1858 (32nd) **CAPITAL:** St. Paul
LARGEST CITIES (WITH POP.): Minneapolis, 382,618; St. Paul, 287,151
IMPORTANT PRODUCTS: industrial machinery, printing and publishing, computers, food products, scientific and medical instruments, milk, hogs, cattle, corn, soybeans, iron ore
PLACES TO VISIT: Voyageurs National Park; Minnesota State Fair, Fort Snelling; U.S. Hockey Hall of Fame, Eveleth; Walker Art Center, Minneapolis

WEB SITE *http://www.state.mn.us • http://www.exploreminnesota.com*

DID YOU KNOW? *The Mississippi River begins in Minnesota. Its source is Lake Itaska, one of the state's many lakes. (It's not called "land of 10,000 lakes" for nothing!)*

MISSISSIPPI (MS) *Magnolia State*

POPULATION (2000): 2,844,658 (31st)
AREA: 48,286 sq. mi. (32nd) (125,061 sq. km.)
FLOWER: Magnolia **BIRD:** Mockingbird
TREE: Magnolia **SONG:** "Go, Mississippi!"
ENTERED UNION: December 10, 1817 (20th)
CAPITAL AND LARGEST CITY: Jackson (population, 184,256)
OTHER LARGE CITIES (WITH POP.): Gulfport, 71,127; Biloxi, 50,644;
IMPORTANT PRODUCTS: transportation equipment, furniture, electrical machinery, lumber and wood products, cotton, rice, chickens, cattle
PLACES TO VISIT: Vicksburg National Military Park; Natchez Trace Parkway; Old Capitol, Jackson; Old Spanish Fort and Museum, Pascagoula

WEB SITE *http://www.mississippi.org*

DID YOU KNOW? *Author Mark Twain said the mighty Mississippi River was "a wonderful book [with] a new story to tell every day." The river system made up of the Mississippi and the Missouri is the 3rd-largest in the world, after the Nile and the Amazon.*

MISSOURI (MO) *Show Me State*

Jefferson City

POPULATION (2000): 5,595,211 (17th)
AREA: 69,709 sq. mi. (21st) (180,546 sq. km.)
FLOWER: Hawthorn **BIRD:** Bluebird
TREE: Dogwood **SONG:** "Missouri Waltz"
ENTERED UNION: August 10, 1821 (24th)
CAPITAL: Jefferson City (population, 39,636)
LARGEST CITIES (WITH POP.): Kansas City, 441,545; St. Louis, 348,189;
Springfield, 151,580; Independence, 113,288
IMPORTANT PRODUCTS: transportation equipment, electrical and electronic equipment, printing and publishing, food products, cattle, hogs, milk, soybeans, corn, hay, lead
PLACES TO VISIT: Gateway Arch, St. Louis; Mark Twain Area, Hannibal; Harry S. Truman Museum, Independence; George Washington Carver Birthplace, Diamond; Pony Express Museum, St. Joseph

WEB SITE http://www.missouritourism.org

DID YOU KNOW? *Pioneers heading West often began their journeys in St. Louis. Today, the starting point is marked by the majestic Gateway Arch.*

MONTANA (MT) *Treasure State*

★ Helena

POPULATION (2000): 902,195 (44th)
AREA: 147,046 sq. mi. (4th) (380,850 sq. km.)
FLOWER: Bitterroot **BIRD:** Western meadowlark
TREE: Ponderosa pine **SONG:** "Montana"
ENTERED UNION: November 8, 1889 (41st)
CAPITAL: Helena (population, 25,780)
LARGEST CITIES (WITH POP.): Billings, 89,847; Missoula, 57,053; Great Falls, 56,690; Butte, 34,606
IMPORTANT PRODUCTS: cattle, copper, gold, wheat, barley, wood and paper products
PLACES TO VISIT: Yellowstone and Glacier national parks; Little Bighorn Battlefield National Monument; Museum of the Rockies (in Bozeman); Museum of the Plains Indian, Blackfeet Reservation (near Browning)

WEB SITE http://www.state.mt.us

DID YOU KNOW? *Montanan Jeanette Rankin was the first woman elected to the U.S. House of Representatives. She was the only member of Congress to vote against the U.S. taking part in both World War I and World War II.*

NEBRASKA (NE) *Cornhusker State*

Lincoln
★

POPULATION (2000): 1,711,263 (38th)
AREA: 77,358 sq. mi. (16th) (200,358 sq. km.)
FLOWER: Goldenrod **BIRD:** Western meadowlark
TREE: Cottonwood **SONG:** "Beautiful Nebraska"
ENTERED UNION: March 1, 1867 (37th)
CAPITAL: Lincoln
LARGEST CITIES (WITH POP.): Omaha, 390,007; Lincoln, 225,581
IMPORTANT PRODUCTS: cattle, hogs, milk, corn, soybeans, hay, wheat, sorghum, food products, industrial machinery
PLACES TO VISIT: Oregon Trail landmarks; Stuhr Museum of the Prairie Pioneer, Grand Island; Agate Fossil Beds National Monument; Boys Town, near Omaha

WEB SITE http://www.state.ne.us • http://www.visitnebraska.org

DID YOU KNOW? *J. Sterling Morton, a U.S. Secretary of Agriculture, loved trees so much that he started Arbor Day in 1885. That year, people in his state planted one million trees. Now, 100 years after his death, more than 200 different kinds of trees stand at his former home.*

NEVADA (NV) *Sagebrush State, Battle Born State, Silver State*

POPULATION (2000): 1,998,257 (35th)
AREA: 110,567 sq. mi. (7th) (286,368 sq. km.)
FLOWER: Sagebrush **BIRD:** Mountain bluebird
TREES: Single-leaf piñon, bristlecone pine
SONG: "Home Means Nevada"
ENTERED UNION: October 31, 1864 (36th)
CAPITAL: Carson City (population, 52,457)
LARGEST CITIES (WITH POP.): Las Vegas, 478,434; Reno, 180,480;
Henderson, 175,381
IMPORTANT PRODUCTS: gold, silver, cattle, hay, food products, plastics, chemicals
PLACES TO VISIT: Great Basin National Park, including Lehman Caves; Nevada State
Museum, Carson City; Hoover Dam, Lake Tahoe, Pony Express Territory.

Carson City

WEB SITE *http://www.state.nv.us • http://www.travelnevada.com*

DID YOU KNOW? *Nevada's state reptile is the desert tortoise, and its state animal is the desert bighorn sheep. Unlike many of the state's human inhabitants, these animals don't work in the tourist industry.*

NEW HAMPSHIRE (NH) *Granite State*

POPULATION (2000): 1,235,786 (41st)
AREA: 9,283 sq. mi. (44th) (24,043 sq. km.)
FLOWER: Purple lilac **BIRD:** Purple finch
TREE: White birch **SONG:** "Old New Hampshire"
ENTERED UNION: June 21, 1788 (9th)
CAPITAL: Concord **LARGEST CITIES (WITH POP.):** Manchester, 107,006;
Nashua, 86,605; Concord, 40,687 **IMPORTANT PRODUCTS:** industrial machinery,
electric and electronic equipment, metal products, plastic products, dairy products, maple syrup
and maple sugar
PLACES TO VISIT: White Mountain National Forest; Mount Washington; Old Man in the Mountain,
Franconia Notch; Canterbury Shaker Village; Flume gorge and aerial tramway

Concord

WEB SITE *http://www.state.nh.us • http://www.visitnh.gov*

DID YOU KNOW? *This state is called "the mother of all rivers" because five of New England's great rivers—the Connecticut, Pemigewasset, Merrimack, Piscataqua, and Winnipesaukee—start here.*

NEW JERSEY (NJ) *Garden State*

POPULATION (2000): 8,414,350 (9th)
AREA: 8,215 sq. mi. (46th) (21,277 sq. km.)
FLOWER: Purple violet **BIRD:** Eastern goldfinch
TREE: Red oak **SONG:** none
ENTERED UNION: December 18, 1787 (3rd)
CAPITAL: Trenton (population, 85,403)
LARGEST CITIES (WITH POP.): Newark, 273,546; Jersey City, 240,055; Paterson,
149,222; Elizabeth, 120,568
IMPORTANT PRODUCTS: chemicals, pharmaceuticals/drugs, electronic equipment, nursery and
greenhouse products, food products, tomatoes, blueberries and peaches
PLACES TO VISIT: ocean beaches; Edison National Historical Site, West Orange; Liberty State Park;
Pine Barrens wilderness area; Revolutionary War sites

Trenton

WEB SITE *http://www.state.nj.us*

DID YOU KNOW? *If you are among the growing numbers of bird-watchers, fly over to Cape May County at the southern tip of this state. It is one of the top bird-watching spots in North America.*

NEW MEXICO (NM) *Land of Enchantment*

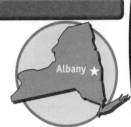
★ Santa Fe

POPULATION (2000): 1,819,046 (36th)
AREA: 121,598 sq. mi. (5th) (314,939 sq. km.)
FLOWER: Yucca **BIRD:** Roadrunner
TREE: Piñon **SONG:** "O, Fair New Mexico"
ENTERED UNION: January 6, 1912 (47th)
CAPITAL: Santa Fe **LARGEST CITIES (WITH POP.):** Albuquerque, 448,607;
Las Cruces, 74,267; Santa Fe, 62,203 **IMPORTANT PRODUCTS:** electronic
equipment, foods, machinery, clothing, lumber, transportation equipment, hay, onions, chiles
PLACES TO VISIT: Carlsbad Caverns National Park; Palace of the Governors and Mission of San
Miguel, Santa Fe; Chaco Culture Natl. Historical Park; cliff dwellings

WEBSITE *http://www.state.nm.us • http://www.newmexico.org*

DID YOU KNOW? *Santa Fe is the highest capital city in the United States. It is 7,000 feet above sea level. The Palace of the Governors there was built in 1610, making it the oldest government building in the U.S.*

NEW YORK (NY) *Empire State*

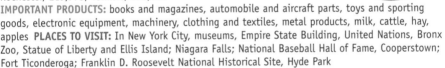
Albany ★

POPULATION (2000): 18,976,457 (3rd)
AREA: 53,989 sq. mi. (27th) (139,831 sq. km.)
FLOWER: Rose **BIRD:** Bluebird
TREE: Sugar maple **SONG:** "I Love New York"
ENTERED UNION: July 26, 1788 (11th)
CAPITAL: Albany (population, 95,658)
LARGEST CITIES (WITH POP.): New York, 8,008,278; Buffalo, 292,648;
Rochester, 219,773; Yonkers, 196,086
IMPORTANT PRODUCTS: books and magazines, automobile and aircraft parts, toys and sporting
goods, electronic equipment, machinery, clothing and textiles, metal products, milk, cattle, hay,
apples **PLACES TO VISIT:** In New York City, museums, Empire State Building, United Nations, Bronx
Zoo, Statue of Liberty and Ellis Island; Niagara Falls; National Baseball Hall of Fame, Cooperstown;
Fort Ticonderoga; Franklin D. Roosevelt National Historical Site, Hyde Park

WEBSITE *http://www.state.ny.us • http://www.iloveny.state.ny.us*

DID YOU KNOW? *This state has many connections to early American history. Almost one out of every three Revolutionary War battles was fought here, New York City was the new nation's first capital, and George Washington was inaugurated here on April 30, 1789.*

NORTH CAROLINA (NC) *Tar Heel State, Old North State*

Raleigh ★

POPULATION (2000): 8,049,313 (11th)
AREA: 52,672 sq. mi. (29th) (136,420 sq. km.)
FLOWER: Dogwood **BIRD:** Cardinal
TREE: Pine **SONG:** "The Old North State"
ENTERED UNION: November 21, 1789 (12th)
CAPITAL: Raleigh **LARGEST CITIES (WITH POP.):** Charlotte, 540,828;
Raleigh, 276,093; Greensboro, 223,891; Durham, 187,035; Winston-Salem,
185,776; **IMPORTANT PRODUCTS:** clothing and textiles, tobacco and tobacco
products, industrial machinery, electronic equipment, furniture, cotton, soybeans, peanuts
PLACES TO VISIT: Great Smoky Mountains National Park; Cape Hatteras National Seashore; Wright
Brothers National Memorial, Kitty Hawk

WEBSITE *http://www.state.nc.us • http://www.visitnc.com*

DID YOU KNOW? *One story about how the state got its nickname as the Tar Heel state: In the 1700s, turpentine from pine trees was turned into tar and pitch. Workers often got the tar stuck to their heels.*

NORTH DAKOTA (ND) *Peace Garden State*

POPULATION (2000): 642,200 (47th)
AREA: 70,704 sq. mi. (18th) (183,123 sq. km.)
FLOWER: Wild prairie rose
BIRD: Western meadowlark
TREE: American elm **SONG:** "North Dakota Hymn"
ENTERED UNION: November 2, 1889 (39th) **CAPITAL:** Bismarck
LARGEST CITIES (WITH POP.): Fargo, 90,599; Bismarck, 55,532; Grand Forks, 49,321; Minot, 36,567
IMPORTANT PRODUCTS: wheat, barley, hay, sunflowers, sugar beets, cattle, sand and gravel, food products, farm equipment, high-tech electronics
PLACES TO VISIT: Theodore Roosevelt National Park; Bonanzaville, near Fargo; Dakota Dinosaur Museum, Dickinson; International Peace Garden

WEB SITE *http://www.state.nd.us • http://www.discovernd.com*

DID YOU KNOW? *North Dakota's lowest recorded temperature was –60° F on Feb. 15, 1936.*

OHIO (OH) *Buckeye State*

POPULATION (2000): 11,353,140 (7th)
AREA: 44,828 sq. mi. (34th) (116,103 sq. km.)
FLOWER: Scarlet carnation **BIRD:** Cardinal
TREE: Buckeye **SONG:** "Beautiful Ohio"
ENTERED UNION: March 1, 1803 (17th)
CAPITAL AND LARGEST CITY: Columbus (population, 711,470)
OTHER LARGE CITIES (WITH POP.): Cleveland, 478,403; Cincinnati, 331,285; Toledo, 313,619; Akron, 217,074; Dayton, 166,179
IMPORTANT PRODUCTS: metal and metal products, transportation equipment, industrial machinery, rubber and plastic products, electronic equipment, printing and publishing, chemicals, food products, corn, soybeans, livestock, milk
PLACES TO VISIT: Mound City Group National Monuments, Indian burial mounds; Neil Armstrong Air and Space Museum; homes of and memorials to 8 U.S. presidents who lived here

WEB SITE *http://www.ohiotourism.com*

DID YOU KNOW? *Ohio must be out-of-this-world. It's the birthplace of 24 astronauts, more than any other state can claim.*

OKLAHOMA (OK) *Sooner State*

POPULATION (2000): 3,450,654 (27th)
AREA: 69,903 sq. mi. (20th) (181,049 sq. km.)
FLOWER: Mistletoe **BIRD:** Scissor-tailed flycatcher
TREE: Redbud **SONG:** "Oklahoma!"
ENTERED UNION: November 16, 1907 (46th)
CAPITAL AND LARGEST CITY: Oklahoma City (population, 506,132)
OTHER LARGE CITIES (WITH POP.): Tulsa, 393,049; Norman, 95,694; Lawton, 92,757
IMPORTANT PRODUCTS: natural gas, oil, cattle, nonelectrical machinery, transportation equipment, metal products, wheat, hay
PLACES TO VISIT: Indian City U.S.A., near Anadarko; Fort Gibson Stockade; National Cowboy Hall of Fame; White Water Bay and Frontier City theme parks; Cherokee Heritage Center

WEB SITE *http://www.state.ok.us*

DID YOU KNOW? *Well-known Native Americans Sequoyah, Jim Thorpe, and Maria Tallchief were born here. So were cowboys Tom Mix, Gene Autry, and Will Rogers (who was both a cowboy and an Indian).*

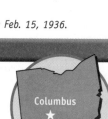

OREGON (OR) *Beaver State*

POPULATION (2000): 3,421,399 (28th)
AREA: 97,132 sq. mi. (10th) (251,572 sq. km.)
FLOWER: Oregon grape **BIRD:** Western meadowlark
TREE: Douglas fir **SONG:** "Oregon, My Oregon"
ENTERED UNION: February 14, 1859 (33rd)

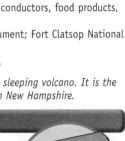

CAPITAL: Salem **LARGEST CITIES (WITH POP.):** Portland, 529,121;
Eugene, 137,893; Salem, 136,924
IMPORTANT PRODUCTS: lumber and wood products, electronics and semiconductors, food products, paper, cattle, hay, vegetables, Christmas trees
PLACES TO VISIT: Crater Lake National Park; Oregon Caves National Monument; Fort Clatsop National Memorial; Oregon Museum of Science and Industry, Portland

WEBSITE *http://www.state.or.us • http://www.traveloregon.com*

DID YOU KNOW? *Mt. Hood, the highest mountain in Oregon, is actually a sleeping volcano. It is the second-most-climbed mountain in the world, after Grand Mt. Monadnock in New Hampshire.*

PENNSYLVANIA (PA) *Keystone State*

POPULATION (2000): 12,281,054 (6th)
AREA: 46,058 sq. mi. (33rd) (119,290 sq. km.)
FLOWER: Mountain laurel **BIRD:** Ruffed grouse
TREE: Hemlock **SONG:** "Pennsylvania"
ENTERED UNION: December 12, 1787 (2nd)

CAPITAL: Harrisburg (population, 48,950)
LARGEST CITIES (WITH POP.): Philadelphia, 1,517,550; Pittsburgh, 334,563;
Allentown, 106,632; Erie, 103,717;
IMPORTANT PRODUCTS: iron and steel, coal, industrial machinery, printing and publishing, food products, electronic equipment, transportation equipment, stone, clay and glass products
PLACES TO VISIT: Independence Hall and other historic sites in Philadelphia; Franklin Institute Science Museum, Philadelphia; Valley Forge; Gettysburg; Hershey; Pennsylvania Dutch country, Lancaster County

WEBSITE *http://www.state.pa.us*

DID YOU KNOW? *Two of the most important documents of U.S. history had their roots in Pennsylvania: the U.S. Constitution, written in Philadelphia, and the Gettysburg Address, delivered by Abraham Lincoln on a Civil War battlefield.*

RHODE ISLAND (RI) *Little Rhody, Ocean State*

POPULATION (2000): 1,048,319 (43rd)
AREA: 1,231 sq. mi. (50th) (3,188 sq. km.)
FLOWER: Violet **BIRD:** Rhode Island red
TREE: Red maple **SONG:** "Rhode Island"
ENTERED UNION: May 29, 1790 (13th)

CAPITAL AND LARGEST CITY: Providence (population, 173,618)
OTHER LARGE CITIES (WITH POP.): Warwick, 85,808; Cranston, 79,269;
Pawtucket, 72,958
IMPORTANT PRODUCTS: costume jewelry, toys, textiles, machinery, electronic equipment, fish
PLACES TO VISIT: Block Island; mansions, old buildings, and harbor in Newport; International Tennis Hall of Fame, Newport

WEBSITE *http://www.state.ri.us • http://www.visitrhodeisland.com*

DID YOU KNOW? *Although Rhode Island was the first American colony to renounce the British king, it was the last colony to ratify the Constitution (in 1790).*

SOUTH CAROLINA (SC) *Palmetto State*

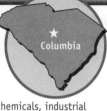

POPULATION (2000): 4,012,012 (26th)
AREA: 31,189 sq. mi. (40th) (80,779 sq. km.)
FLOWER: Yellow jessamine **BIRD:** Carolina wren
TREE: Palmetto **SONG:** "Carolina"
ENTERED UNION: May 23, 1788 (8th)
CAPITAL AND LARGEST CITY: Columbia (population, 116,278)
OTHER LARGE CITIES (WITH POP.): Charleston, 96,650; North Charleston, 79,641; Greenville, 56,002 **IMPORTANT PRODUCTS:** clothing and textiles, chemicals, industrial machinery, metal products, livestock, tobacco, Portland cement
PLACES TO VISIT: Grand Strand and Hilton Head Island beaches; Revolutionary War battlefields; historic sites in Charleston; Fort Sumter; Charleston Museum

WEB SITE *http://www.state.sc.us*

DID YOU KNOW? *In 1860, South Carolina became the first state to secede from the Union.*

SOUTH DAKOTA (SD) *Mt. Rushmore State, Coyote State*

POPULATION (2000): 754,844 (46th)
AREA: 77,121 sq. mi. (17th) (199,743 sq. km.)
FLOWER: Pasqueflower
BIRD: Chinese ring-necked pheasant
TREE: Black Hills spruce **SONG:** "Hail, South Dakota"
ENTERED UNION: November 2, 1889 (40th)
CAPITAL: Pierre (population, 13,876)
LARGEST CITIES (WITH POP.): Sioux Falls, 123,975; Rapid City, 59,607
IMPORTANT PRODUCTS: food and food products, machinery, electric and electronic equipment, corn, soybeans
PLACES TO VISIT: Mount Rushmore National Memorial; Crazy Horse Memorial; Jewel Cave; Badlands and Wind Caves national parks; Wounded Knee battlefield; Homestake Gold Mine

WEB SITE *http://www.state.sd.us*

DID YOU KNOW? *Buffalo, which once numbered in the thousands, are making a comeback on the Great Plains. You can see herds at the Lower Brule and Crow Creek Indian reservations and at the Triple U Buffalo Ranch near Fort Pierre.*

TENNESSEE (TN) *Volunteer State*

POPULATION (2000): 5,689,283 (16th)
AREA: 42,146 sq. mi. (36th) (109,158 sq. km.)
FLOWER: Iris **BIRD:** Mockingbird
TREE: Tulip poplar **SONG:** "The Tennessee Waltz"
ENTERED UNION: June 1, 1796 (16th)
CAPITAL: Nashville **LARGEST CITIES (WITH POP.):** Memphis, 650,100; Nashville, 569,891; Knoxville, 173,890; Chattanooga, 155,554
IMPORTANT PRODUCTS: chemicals, machinery, vehicles, food products, metal products, publishing, electronic equipment, paper products, rubber and plastic products, tobacco
PLACES TO VISIT: Great Smoky Mountains National Park; the Hermitage, home of President Andrew Jackson, near Nashville; Civil War battle sites; Grand Old Opry and Opryland, USA theme park, Nashville; Graceland, home of Elvis Presley, in Memphis

WEB SITE *http://www.state.tn.us • http://www.state.tn.us/tourdev*

DID YOU KNOW? *Three U.S. presidents came from this state: Andrew Jackson, James Polk, and Andrew Johnson. Tennessee was the last state to secede from the Union and the first readmitted after the Civil War.*

TEXAS (TX) *Lone Star State*

POPULATION (2000): 20,851,820 (2nd)
AREA: 267,277 sq. mi. (2nd) (692,247 sq. km.)
FLOWER: Bluebonnet **BIRD:** Mockingbird
TREE: Pecan **SONG:** "Texas, Our Texas"
ENTERED UNION: December 29, 1845 (28th)

Austin ★

CAPITAL: Austin **LARGEST CITIES (WITH POP.):** Houston, 1,953,631;
Dallas, 1,188,580; San Antonio, 1,144,646; Austin, 656,562; El Paso, 563,662;
Fort Worth, 534,694
IMPORTANT PRODUCTS: oil, natural gas, cattle, milk, eggs, transportation
equipment, chemicals, clothing, industrial machinery, electrical and electronic
equipment, cotton, grains
PLACES TO VISIT: Guadalupe Mountains and Big Bend national parks; the Alamo, in San Antonio;
Lyndon Johnson National Historic Site, near Johnson City; George Bush Presidential Library,
College Station

WEB SITE *http://www.state.tx.us • http://texasalmanac.com*

DID YOU KNOW? *El Paso claims the first Thanksgiving in North America. It was held in 1598 when Juan de Onate, a Spanish explorer, reached the Rio Grande River from Mexico.*

UTAH (UT) *Beehive State*

POPULATION (2000): 2,233,169 (34th)
AREA: 84,904 sq. mi. (13th) (219,902 sq. km.)
FLOWER: Sego lily **BIRD:** Seagull
TREE: Blue spruce **SONG:** "Utah, We Love Thee"
ENTERED UNION: January 4, 1896 (45th)

★ Salt Lake City

CAPITAL AND LARGEST CITY: Salt Lake City (population, 181,743)
OTHER LARGE CITIES (WITH POP.): West Valley City, 108,896; Provo, 105,166
IMPORTANT PRODUCTS: transportation equipment, medical instruments, electronic parts, food
products, steel, copper, cattle, corn, hay, wheat, barley
PLACES TO VISIT: Arches, Canyonlands, Bryce Canyon, Zion, and Capitol Reef national parks; Great
Salt Lake; Temple Square (Mormon Church headquarters) in Salt Lake City; Indian cliff dwellings

WEB SITE *http://www.state.ut.us • http://www.utah.org*

DID YOU KNOW? *In 1985, Senator Jake Garn of Utah became the first U.S. senator in space, aboard the space shuttle Discovery.*

VERMONT (VT) *Green Mountain State*

POPULATION (2000): 608,827 (49th)
AREA: 9,615 sq. mi. (43rd) (24,903 sq. km.)
FLOWER: Red clover **BIRD:** Hermit thrush
TREE: Sugar maple **SONG:** "These Green Mountains"
ENTERED UNION: March 4, 1791 (14th)

Montpelier ★

CAPITAL: Montpelier (population, 8,035)
LARGEST CITIES (WITH POP.): Burlington, 38,889; Essex, 18,626
IMPORTANT PRODUCTS: machine tools, furniture, scales, books, computer parts,
foods, dairy products, apples, maple syrup
PLACES TO VISIT: Green Mountain National Forest; Maple Grove Maple Museum, St. Johnsbury

WEB SITE *http://www.state.vt.us*

DID YOU KNOW? *Vermont became the first state admitted to the Union after the U.S. Constitution was ratified, and the 14th state overall. The state was birthplace to two U.S. presidents: Calvin Coolidge and Chester A. Arthur.*

VIRGINIA (VA) *Old Dominion*

POPULATION (2000): 7,078,515 (12th)
AREA: 42,326 sq. mi. (35th) (109,391 sq. km.)
FLOWER: Dogwood **BIRD:** Cardinal
TREE: Dogwood
SONG: "Carry Me Back to Old Virginia"

★ Richmond

ENTERED UNION: June 25, 1788 (10th) **CAPITAL:** Richmond
LARGEST CITIES (WITH POP.): Virginia Beach, 425,257; Norfolk, 234,403;
Chesapeake, 199,184; Richmond, 197,790; Newport News, 180,150
IMPORTANT PRODUCTS: transportation equipment, textiles, chemicals, printing, machinery,
electronic equipment, food products, coal, livestock, tobacco, wood products, furniture
PLACES TO VISIT: Colonial Williamsburg; Arlington National Cemetery; Mount Vernon (George
Washington's home); Monticello (Thomas Jefferson's home); Shenandoah National Park

WEB SITE http://www.state.va.us • http://www.virginia.org

DID YOU KNOW? *In 1919, Nancy Langhorne Astor became the first woman ever to serve in the British
House of Commons, but she was born and raised in Virginia.*

WASHINGTON (WA) *Evergreen State*

POPULATION (2000): 5,894,121 (15th)
AREA: 70,637 sq. mi. (19th) (182,950 sq. km.)
FLOWER: Western rhododendron
BIRD: Willow goldfinch
TREE: Western hemlock **SONG:** "Washington, My Home"
ENTERED UNION: November 11, 1889 (42nd)

★ Olympia

CAPITAL: Olympia (population, 42,514)
LARGEST CITIES (WITH POP.): Seattle, 563,374; Spokane, 195,629; Tacoma, 193,556
IMPORTANT PRODUCTS: aircraft, lumber and plywood, pulp and paper, machinery, electronics,
computer software, aluminum, processed fruits and vegetables
PLACES TO VISIT: Mount Rainier, Olympic, and North Cascades national parks; Mount St. Helens;
Seattle Center, with Space Needle and monorail

WEB SITE http://www.access.wa.gov

DID YOU KNOW? *This state is home to many kinds of wildlife, including bear, elk, mountain lions,
wildcats, mountain goats, and mule deer. Wild salmon make the Columbia River their spawning ground.*

WEST VIRGINIA (WV) *Mountain State*

POPULATION (2000): 1,808,344 (37th)
AREA: 24,231 sq. mi. (41st) (62,759 sq. km.)
FLOWER: Big rhododendron **BIRD:** Cardinal
TREE: Sugar maple **SONGS:** "The West Virginia
Hills"; "This Is My West Virginia"; "West Virginia,
My Home Sweet Home"

Charleston
★

ENTERED UNION: June 20, 1863 (35th)
CAPITAL AND LARGEST CITY: Charleston (population, 53,421)
OTHER LARGE CITIES (WITH POP.): Huntington, 51,475; Wheeling, 33,099
IMPORTANT PRODUCTS: coal, natural gas, fabricated metal products, chemicals, automobile parts,
aluminum, steel, machinery, cattle, hay, apples, peaches, tobacco
PLACES TO VISIT: Harpers Ferry National Historic Park; Exhibition Coal Mine, Beckley; Monongahela
National Forest

WEB SITE http://www.state.wv.us

DID YOU KNOW? *George Washington explored West Virginia in 1753, when he was a young man.*

WISCONSIN (WI) *Badger State*

POPULATION (2000): 5,363,675 (18th)
AREA: 65,499 sq. mi. (22nd) (169,642 sq. km.)
FLOWER: Wood violet **BIRD:** Robin
TREE: Sugar maple **SONG:** "On, Wisconsin!"
ENTERED UNION: May 29, 1848 (30th)

Madison ★

CAPITAL: Madison **LARGEST CITIES (WITH POP.):** Milwaukee, 596,974;
Madison, 208,054; Green Bay, 102,313; Kenosha, 90,352; Racine, 81,855
IMPORTANT PRODUCTS: paper products, printing, milk, butter, cheese, foods, food products, motor
vehicles and equipment, medical instruments and supplies, plastics, corn, hay, vegetables
PLACES TO VISIT: Wisconsin Dells; Cave of the Mounds, near Blue Mounds; Milwaukee Public
Museum; Circus World Museum, Baraboo; National Railroad Museum, Green Bay

WEB SITE *http://www.wisconsin.gov*

DID YOU KNOW? *The first ice cream sundaes were served in 1851 in the towns of Manitowoc and Two Rivers. The Ringling Brothers held their first circus in their hometown of Baraboo in 1884.*

WYOMING (WY) *Cowboy State*

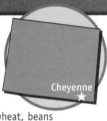

POPULATION (2000): 493,782 (50th)
AREA: 97,818 sq. mi. (9th) (253,349 sq. km.)
FLOWER: Indian paintbrush **BIRD:** Western
meadowlark **TREE:** Plains cottonwood **SONG:**
"Wyoming" **ENTERED UNION:** July 10, 1890 (44th)

Cheyenne ★

CAPITAL AND LARGEST CITY: Cheyenne (population, 53,011)
OTHER LARGE CITIES (WITH POP.): Casper, 49,644; Laramie, 27,204
IMPORTANT PRODUCTS: oil, natural gas, petroleum (oil) products, cattle, wheat, beans
PLACES TO VISIT: Yellowstone and Grand Teton national parks; Fort Laramie; Buffalo Bill Historical
Center, Cody; pioneer trails

WEB SITE *http://www.state.wy.us*

DID YOU KNOW? *This was the first state to grant women the right to vote, in 1869. It was also the home of Nellie Tayloe Ross, Wyoming's governor from 1925 to 1927. Later, she was the first woman to head the U.S. Mint.*

COMMONWEALTH OF PUERTO RICO (PR)

HISTORY: Christopher Columbus landed in Puerto Rico in
1493. Puerto Rico was a Spanish colony for centuries,
then was ceded (given) to the United States in 1898
after the Spanish-American War. In 1952, still
associated with the United States, Puerto Rico
became a commonwealth with its own constitution.

★ San Juan

POPULATION (2000): 3,808,610 **AREA:** 3,508 sq. mi. (9,086 sq. km.)
FLOWER: Maga **BIRD:** Reinita **TREE:** Ceiba **NATIONAL ANTHEM:** "La
Borinqueña" **CAPITAL AND LARGEST CITY:** San Juan (population, 421,958)
OTHER LARGE CITIES (WITH POP.): Bayamón, 203,499; Carolina, 168,164; Ponce, 155,038
IMPORTANT PRODUCTS: chemicals, food products, electronic equipment, clothing and textiles,
industrial machinery, coffee, sugarcane, fruit, hogs
PLACES TO VISIT: San Juan National Historic Site; beaches and resorts

WEB SITE *http://www.fortaleza.govpr.org • http://www.discoverpuertorico.com*

DID YOU KNOW? *Famous Puerto Ricans include entertainers Ricky Martin, Raul Julia, and Rita Moreno, and baseball player Roberto Clemente.*

HOW THE STATES

ALABAMA comes from an Indian word for "tribal town."

ALASKA comes from *alakshak*, the Aleutian (Eskimo) word meaning "peninsula" or "land that is not an island."

ARIZONA comes from a Pima Indian word meaning "little spring place," or the Aztec word *arizuma*, meaning "silver-bearing."

Arizona

ARKANSAS is a variation of *Quapaw*, the name of an Indian tribe. *Quapaw* means "south wind."

CALIFORNIA is the name of an imaginary island in a Spanish story. It was named by Spanish explorers of Baja California, a part of Mexico.

COLORADO comes from a Spanish word meaning "red." It was first given to the Colorado River because of its reddish color.

CONNECTICUT comes from an Algonquin Indian word meaning "long river place."

DELAWARE is named after Lord De La Warr, the English governor of Virginia in colonial times.

FLORIDA, which means "flowery" in Spanish, was named by the explorer Ponce de Leon, who landed there during Easter.

GEORGIA was named after King George II of England, who granted the right to create a colony there in 1732.

HAWAII probably comes from *Hawaiki*, or *Owhyhee*, the native Polynesian word for "homeland."

IDAHO's name is of uncertain origin, but it may come from a Kiowa Apache name for the Comanche Indians.

ILLINOIS is the French version of *Illini*, an Algonquin Indian word meaning "men" or "warriors."

INDIANA means "land of the Indians."

IOWA comes from the name of an American Indian tribe that lived on the land that is now the state.

KANSAS comes from a Sioux Indian word that possibly meant "people of the south wind."

KENTUCKY comes from an Iroquois Indian word, possibly meaning "meadowland."

LOUISIANA, which was first settled by French explorers, was named after King Louis XIV of France.

MAINE means "the mainland." English explorers called it that to distinguish it from islands nearby.

MARYLAND was named after Queen Henrietta Maria, wife of King Charles I of England, who granted the right to establish an English colony there.

MASSACHUSETTS comes from an Indian word meaning "large hill place."

MICHIGAN comes from the Chippewa Indian words *mici gama*, meaning "great water" (referring to Lake Michigan).

Michigan

MINNESOTA got its name from a Dakota Sioux Indian word meaning "cloudy water" or "sky-tinted water."

MISSISSIPPI is probably from Chippewa Indian words meaning "great river" or "gathering of all the waters," or from an Algonquin word, *messipi*.

MISSOURI comes from an Algonquin Indian term meaning "river of the big canoes."

MONTANA comes from a Latin or Spanish word meaning "mountainous."

Montana

GOT THEIR NAMES

NEBRASKA comes from "flat river" or "broad water," an Omaha or Otos Indian name for the Platte River.

NEVADA means "snow-clad" in Spanish. Spanish explorers gave the name to the Sierra Nevada Mountains.

Nevada

NEW HAMPSHIRE was named by an early settler after his home county of Hampshire, in England.

NEW JERSEY was named for the English Channel island of Jersey.

NEW MEXICO was given its name by 16th-century Spaniards in Mexico.

NEW YORK, first called New Netherland, was renamed for the Duke of York and Albany after the English took it from Dutch settlers.

NORTH CAROLINA, the northern part of the English colony of Carolana, was named for King Charles I.

NORTH DAKOTA comes from a Sioux Indian word meaning "friend" or "ally."

OHIO is the Iroquois Indian word for "fine or good river."

OKLAHOMA comes from a Choctaw Indian word meaning "red man."

OREGON may have come from *Ouaricon-sint,* a name on an old French map that was once given to what is now called the Columbia River. That river runs between Oregon and Washington.

Oregon

PENNSYLVANIA meaning "Penn's woods," was the name given to the colony founded by William Penn.

RHODE ISLAND may have come from the Dutch "Roode Eylandt" (red island) or may have been named after the Greek island of Rhodes.

SOUTH CAROLINA, the southern part of the English colony of Carolana, was named for King Charles I.

SOUTH DAKOTA comes from a Sioux Indian word meaning "friend" or "ally."

TENNESSEE comes from "Tanasi," the name of Cherokee Indian villages on what is now the Little Tennessee River.

TEXAS comes from a word meaning "friends" or "allies," used by the Spanish to describe some of the American Indians living there.

UTAH comes from a Navajo word meaning "upper" or "higher up."

Utah

VERMONT comes from two French words, *vert* meaning "green" and *mont* "mountain."

VIRGINIA was named in honor of Queen Elizabeth I of England, who was known as the Virgin Queen because she was never married.

WASHINGTON was named after George Washington, the first president of the United States. It is the only state named after a president.

WEST VIRGINIA got its name from the people of western Virginia, who formed their own government during the Civil War.

WISCONSIN comes from a Chippewa name that is believed to mean "grassy place." It was once spelled *Ouisconsin* and *Mesconsing*.

WYOMING comes from Algonquin Indian words that are said to mean "at the big plains," "large prairie place," or "on the great plain."

WASHINGTON, D.C.
The Capital of the United States

Land Area: 61 square miles
Population: 572,059
Flower: American beauty rose
Bird: Wood thrush

WEBSITE http://www.washington.org

HISTORY Washington, D.C., became the capital of the United States in 1800, when the federal government moved there from Philadelphia. The city of Washington was designed and built to be the capital. It was named after George Washington. Many of its major sights are on the Mall, an open grassy area that runs from the Capitol to the Potomac River.

Capitol, which houses the U.S. Congress, is at the east end of the Mall, on Capitol Hill. Its dome can be seen from far away.

Franklin Delano Roosevelt Memorial, honoring the 32nd president of the United States, and his wife, Eleanor, was dedicated in 1997. In a parklike setting, it has sculptures showing events during the president's years of service.

Jefferson Memorial, a circular marble building located near the Potomac River. Its design is partly based on one by Thomas Jefferson for the University of Virginia.

Korean War Veterans Memorial, dedicated in 1995, is at the west end of the Mall. It shows troops ready for combat.

Lincoln Memorial, at the west end of the Mall, is built of white marble and styled like a Greek temple. Inside is a large, seated statue of Abraham Lincoln. His Gettysburg Address is carved on a nearby wall.

National Archives, on Constitution Avenue, holds the Declaration of Independence, Constitution, and Bill of Rights.

National Gallery of Art, on the Mall, is one of the world's great art museums.

National World War II Memorial, to be located between the Lincoln Memorial and the Washington Monument at the Mall, will honor all 16 million Americans who served during the war. Ground was broken in November 2000.

Smithsonian Institution has 14 museums, including the National Air and Space Museum and the Museum of Natural History. The National Zoo is part of the Smithsonian.

U.S. Holocaust Memorial Museum presents the history of the Nazis' murder of more than six million Jews and millions of other people from 1933 to 1945. The exhibit *Daniel's Story* tells the story of the Holocaust from a child's point of view.

Vietnam Veterans Memorial has a black-granite wall shaped like a V. Names of the Americans killed or missing in the Vietnam War are inscribed on the wall.

Washington Monument, a white marble pillar, or obelisk, standing on the Mall and rising to over 555 feet. From the top, there are wonderful views of the city.

White House, at 1600 Pennsylvania Avenue, has been the home of every U.S. president except George Washington.

Women in Military Service for America Memorial, near the entrance to Arlington National Cemetery. It honors the 1.8 million women who have served in the U.S. armed forces.

NATIONAL PARKS

The world's first national park was Yellowstone, established in 1872. Since then, the U.S. government has set aside 54 other national parks. The 53 parks in the U.S. are listed below. The other 2 are outside the United States—one in the Virgin Islands and one in American Samoa. You can find out more about national parks by writing to the National Park Service, Department of the Interior, 1849 C Street NW, Washington, D.C. 20240. For information on-line, go to **WEBSITE** *http://www.nps.gov/parks.html*

ACADIA (Maine) **47,738 acres; established 1929.** Rugged coast and granite cliffs; seals, whales, and porpoises; highest land along the East Coast of the U.S.

ARCHES (Utah) **73,379 acres; established 1971.** Giant natural sandstone arches, including Landscape Arch, over 100 feet high and 291 feet long

BADLANDS (South Dakota) **242,756 acres; established 1978.** A prairie where, over centuries, the land has been formed into many odd shapes with a variety of colors

BIG BEND (Texas) **801,163 acres; established 1935.** Desert land and rugged mountains, on the Rio Grande River; dinosaur fossils

BISCAYNE (Florida) **172,924 acres; established 1980.** A water-park on a chain of islands in the Atlantic Ocean, south of Miami, with beautiful coral reefs

BLACK CANYON OF THE GUNNISON (Colorado) **30,300 acres; established 1999.** Newest national park, features the dramatic Black Canyon carved out by the Gunnison River

BRYCE CANYON (Utah) **35,835 acres; established 1928.** Odd and very colorful rock formations carved by centuries of erosion

CANYONLANDS (Utah) **337,598 acres; established 1964.** Sandstone cliffs above the Colorado River; rock carvings from an ancient American Indian civilization

CAPITOL REEF (Utah) **241,904 acres; established 1971.** Sandstone cliffs cut into by gorges with high walls; old American Indian storage huts

CARLSBAD CAVERNS (New Mexico) **46,766 acres; established 1930.** A huge cave system, with the world's largest underground chamber, "the Big Room"

Carlsbad Caverns

CHANNEL ISLANDS (California) **249,354 acres; established 1980.** Islands off the California coast, with sea lions, seals, and sea birds

CRATER LAKE (Oregon) **183,224 acres; established 1902.** The deepest in the U.S., this lake was formed by the collapse of an ancient volcano; lava walls up to 2,000 feet high

DEATH VALLEY (California, Nevada) **3,367,628 acres; established 1994.** Largest national park outside Alaska; vast hot desert, rocky slopes and gorges, huge sand dunes; lowest point (–282 ft.) in western hemisphere

Death Valley

Did You KNOW?

NATIONAL PARKS *are among the many kinds of places set aside by the federal government for recreation, conservation, or historical reasons. When he was president, Bill Clinton ordered many areas to be protected as "national monuments." Among them was a 150-mile stretch of the Missouri River, in Montana, along the trail followed by the explorers Lewis and Clark.*

DENALI (Alaska) 4,740,907 acres; **established 1980.** Huge park, containing America's tallest mountain, plus caribou, moose, sheep

DRY TORTUGAS (Florida) 64,700 acres; **established 1992.** Colorful birds and fish; a 19th-century fort, Fort Jefferson

EVERGLADES (Florida) 1,508,607 acres; **established 1934.** The largest subtropical wilderness within the U.S.; swamps with mangrove trees, rare birds, alligators

GATES OF THE ARCTIC (Alaska) 7,224,813 acres; **established 1984.** One of the largest national parks; huge tundra wilderness, with rugged peaks and steep valleys

GLACIER (Montana) 1,013,572 acres; **established 1910.** Rugged mountains, with glaciers, lakes, sheep, bears, and bald eagles

GLACIER BAY (Alaska) 3,224,794 acres; **established 1986.** Glaciers moving down mountainsides to the sea; seals, whales, bears, eagles

GRAND CANYON (Arizona) 1,217,403 acres; **established 1919.** Mile-deep expanse of multicolored layered rock, a national wonder

GRAND TETON (Wyoming) 309,993 acres; **established 1929.** Set in the Teton Mountains; a winter feeding ground for elks

GREAT BASIN (Nevada) 77,180 acres; **established 1986.** From deserts to meadows to tundra; caves; ancient pine trees

GREAT SMOKY MOUNTAINS (North Carolina, Tennessee) 521,621 acres; **established 1934.** Forests with deer, fox, and black bears; streams with trout and bass

Grand Teton

GUADALUPE MOUNTAINS (Texas) 86,416 acres; **established 1966.** Remains of a fossil reef formed 225 million years ago

HALEAKALA (Hawaii) 28,350 acres; **established 1960.** The largest crater of any inactive volcano in the world

HAWAII VOLCANOES (Hawaii) 209,695 acres; **established 1961.** Home of two large volcanoes, Mauna Loa and Kilauea, along with a desert and a tree fern forest

HOT SPRINGS (Arkansas) 5,549 acres; **established 1921.** 47 hot springs that provide warm waters for drinking and bathing

ISLE ROYALE (Michigan) 571,790 acres; **established 1931.** On an island in Lake Superior; woods, lakes, many kinds of animals—and no roads

JOSHUA TREE (California) 1,022,976 acres; **established 1994.** Large desert with rock formations and unusual desert plants, including many Joshua trees; fossils from prehistoric times; wildlife, including desert bighorn

Joshua

KATMAI (Alaska) 3,674,530 acres; **established 1980.** Contains the Valley of Ten Thousand Smokes, which was filled with ash when Katmai Volcano erupted in 1912

KENAI FJORDS (Alaska) 669,983 acres; **established 1980.** Fjords, rain forests, the Harding Icefield; sea otters, seals; a breeding place for many birds

KINGS CANYON (California) 461,901 acres; **established 1940.** Mountains and woods; the highest canyon wall in the U.S.

KOBUK VALLEY (Alaska) 1,750,698 acres; **established 1980.** Located north of the Arctic Circle, with caribou and black bears; archeological sites indicate humans have lived there for over 10,000 years

LAKE CLARK (Alaska) 2,619,859 acres; established 1980. Lakes, waterfalls, glaciers, volcanoes, fish and wildlife

LASSEN VOLCANIC (California) 106,372 acres; established 1916. Contains Lassen Peak, a volcano that began erupting in 1914, after being dormant for 400 years

MAMMOTH CAVE (Kentucky) 52,830 acres; established 1941. The world's longest known cave network, with 144 miles of mapped underground passages

MESA VERDE (Colorado) 52,122 acres; established 1906. A plateau covered by woods and canyons; the best preserved ancient cliff dwellings in the U.S.

Mesa Verde

MOUNT RAINIER (Washington) 235,613 acres; established 1899. Home of the Mount Rainier volcano; thick forests, glaciers

NORTH CASCADES (Washington) 504,781 acres; established 1968. Rugged mountains and valleys, with deep canyons, lakes and glaciers

OLYMPIC (Washington) 922,651 acres; established 1938. Rain forest, with woods and mountains, glaciers, and rare elk

PETRIFIED FOREST (Arizona) 93,533 acres; established 1962. A large area of woods which have petrified, or turned into stone; American Indian pueblos and rock carvings

REDWOOD (California) 112,430 acres; established 1968. Groves of ancient redwood trees, and the world's tallest trees

ROCKY MOUNTAIN (Colorado) 265,723 acres; established 1915. Located in the Rockies, with gorges, alpine lakes, and mountain peaks

SAGUARO (Arizona) 91,444 acres; established 1994. Forests of saguaro cacti, some 50 feet tall and 200 years old

SEQUOIA (California) 402,510 acres; established 1890. Groves of giant sequoia trees; Mount Whitney (14,494 feet)

SHENANDOAH (Virginia) 198,182 acres; established 1926. Located in the Blue Ridge Mountains, overlooking the Shenandoah Valley

THEODORE ROOSEVELT (North Dakota) 70,447 acres; established 1978. Scenic badlands and a part of the old Elkhorn Ranch that belonged to Theodore Roosevelt

VOYAGEURS (Minnesota) 218,200 acres; established 1971. Forests with wildlife and many scenic lakes for canoeing and boating

WIND CAVE (South Dakota) 28,295 acres; established 1903. Limestone caverns in the Black Hills; bison herds

WRANGELL-SAINT ELIAS (Alaska) 8,323,618 acres; established 1980. The biggest national park, with mountain peaks over 16,000 feet high

YELLOWSTONE (Idaho, Montana, Wyoming) 2,219,791 acres; established 1872. The first national park and world's greatest geysers; bears and moose

Yellowstone

YOSEMITE (California) 761,266 acres; established 1890. Yosemite Valley; highest waterfall in North America; mountain scenery

ZION (Utah) 146,592 acres; established 1919. Deep, narrow Zion Canyon and other canyons in different colors; Indian cliff dwellings over 1,000 years old

WEATHER

What causes twisters?
You can find the answer on page 295.

WEATHER WORDS

humidity Amount of water vapor (water in the form of a gas) in the air.

barometer an instrument that measures atmospheric pressure. A falling barometer means stormy weather, while a rising barometer means the weather is likely to be calm.

jet stream Long band of winds moving rapidly from west to east 20,000 to 40,000 feet above Earth.

El Niño Condition characterized by unusually warm temperatures in the Pacific Ocean near South America.

degree-day a measurement used in figuring out how much heat or fuel is needed in winter. Every degree below room temperature (65°F) on a certain day counts as one degree-day. So if the average temperature that day is 37°F, the number of degree-days is 28. Chilly New York City piles up 5,300 degree-days during the heating season, as opposed to only 1,200 for balmy New Orleans.

wind chill How much colder it feels when there is a wind. When it is 35°F and the wind is 15 miles an hour, it will feel like 16°F.

front Boundary between two air masses.

HOW WATER FALLS

precipitation Water that falls from clouds as rain, snow, hail, or sleet.

rain Water falling in drops.

freezing rain Water that freezes as it hits the ground.

sleet Drops of water that freeze in cold air and reach the ground as ice pellets or a mixture of snow and rain.

hail Frozen raindrops. Water keeps freezing on the hailstone until it is so heavy that it falls to the ground.

snow Ice crystals that form in clouds and fall.

STORMY WORDS

blizzard A heavy snowstorm with strong winds.

cyclone A storm with winds spinning around a center. Also the name for a hurricane in the Indian Ocean.

hurricane Big tropical cyclone with winds more than 73 mph; called a typhoon in the western Pacific Ocean.

monsoon A system of winds that changes direction between seasons; often brings heavy rains in summer.

tornado Violent winds of more than 200 mph that form a dark funnel.

CLOUDS

Clouds come from moisture in the atmosphere that cools and forms into tiny water droplets or ice crystals. There are more than 100 types of clouds. Here are a few you might recognize:

altostratus clouds form a smooth gray or bluish sheet high over the sky. The sun or moon can usually be seen faintly.

nimbostratus clouds form a shapeless dark layer across the sky blocking out the sun and moon. They often bring a long period of rain or snow.

cumulus clouds are puffy white vertical clouds that get biggest during mid-afternoon. They form many different shapes.

cumulonimbus clouds, also known as storm clouds, are darkish and ominous-looking. They can bring heavy storms, often with thunder and lightning.

WILD WINDS

For many years, hurricanes and other violent storms have been given names. Until the 20th century, people named storms after saints. In 1953, the U.S. government began to use women's names for hurricanes. Men's names came in 1978.

WHAT IS A HURRICANE?

Hurricanes are the largest storms. They form over warm, usually tropical, oceans. As the warm seawater evaporates into the air, the pressure drops and winds begin to circulate, creating a huge wall of clouds and rain, wrapped around a calm center. As warm, moist air continues to feed the storm, it gets stronger and can spread out to an area 300 miles wide. Winds up to 250 miles an hour can rip trees out by their roots and tear roofs off buildings. Torrential rains and giant waves caused by the fierce wind can cause flooding and massive damage before the storm finally moves out over land and dies down. This usually takes between three days and two weeks.

Hurricane Names in the North Atlantic

2001: Allison, Barry, Chantal, Dean, Erin, Felix, Gabrielle, Humberto, Iris, Jerry, Karen, Lorenzo, Michelle, Noel, Olga, Pablo, Rebekah, Sebastien, Tanya, Van, Wendy

2002: Arthur, Bertha, Cristobal, Dolly, Edouard, Fay, Gustav, Hanna, Isidore, Josephine, Kyle, Lili, Marco, Nana, Omar, Paloma, Rene, Sally, Teddy, Vicky, Wilfred

TORNADOES

Tornadoes, also called "twisters," are violent winds that spin in the shape of a funnel at speeds up to 250 miles per hour or more. A tornado can suck up and destroy anything in its path! The flying debris causes many deaths and injuries. Tornadoes form when winds change direction, speed up, and spin around before a thunderstorm. When this happens, the National Weather Service issues a tornado watch. A tornado warning is announced when a tornado has actually been seen in the area.

You can read more about tornadoes at
WEB SITE http://www.noaa.gov/tornadoes.html

TAKING TEMPERATURES

How to Measure Temperature Two systems for measuring temperature are used in weather forecasting. One is Fahrenheit (abbreviated F). The other is Celsius (abbreviated C). Another word for Celsius is Centigrade. Zero degrees (0°) Celsius is equal to 32 degrees (32°) Fahrenheit.

To Convert Fahrenheit Temperatures to Celsius:

❶ Subtract 32 from the Fahrenheit temperature value.
❷ Then multiply by 5.
❸ Then divide the result by 9. **Example:**
To convert 68 degrees Fahrenheit to Celsius,
68 − 32 = 36; 36 x 5 = 180; 180 ÷ 9 = 20

To Convert Celsius Temperatures to Fahrenheit:

❶ Multiply the Celsius temperature by 9.
❷ Then divide by 5.
❸ Then add 32 to the result.
Example: To convert
20 degrees Celsius to Fahrenheit,
20 x 9 = 180; 180 ÷ 5 = 36; 36 + 32 = 68

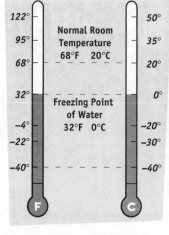

The HOTTEST and COLDEST Places in the World

CONTINENT	HIGHEST TEMPERATURE	LOWEST TEMPERATURE
Africa	El Azizia, Libya, 136°F (58°C)	Ifrane, Morocco, −11°F (−24°C)
Antarctica	Vanda Station, 59°F (15°C)	Vostok, −129°F (−89°C)
Asia	Tirat Tsvi, Israel, 129°F (54°C)	Verkhoyansk, Russia, and Oimekon, Russia, −90°F (−68°C)
Australia	Cloncurry, Queensland, 128°F (53°C)	Charlotte Pass, New South Wales, −9°F (−23°C)
Europe	Seville, Spain, 122°F (50°C)	Ust'Shchugor, Russia, −67°F (−55°C)
North America	Death Valley, California, 134°F (57°C)	Snag, Yukon Territory, −81°F (−63°C)
South America	Rivadavia, Argentina, 120°F (49°C)	Sarmiento, Argentina, −27°F (−33°C)

HOTTEST PLACES IN THE U.S.

State	Temperature	Year
California	134°F	1913
Arizona	128°F	1994*
Nevada	125°F	1994*

Tied with a record set earlier

COLDEST PLACES IN THE U.S.

State	Temperature	Year
Alaska	−80°F	1971
Montana	−70°F	1954
Utah	−69°F	1985

To read more about the weather try the Weather Channel at
WEBSITE http://www.weather.com

◀ WEATHER PUZZLES ▶

UPS & DOWNS

Fill in the right weather word on the blank lines below. Rearrange the words to fit in the puzzle. Write the correct word on each line of the puzzle. The letters in the diagonal "staircase" need to spell out "weather."

WORD BOX

twister   measure   winds   watch
Celsius   degrees   hottest

(Puzzle grid spelling W-E-A-T-H-E-R diagonally)

1 In 1913, California had the _____ temperatures ever recorded in the U.S.

2 A tornado is sometimes called a _____ .

3 A hurricane has _____ over 73 mph.

4 Fahrenheit is a _____ of temperature.

5 The National Weather Service may issue a tornado _____ .

6 Another word for _____ is Centigrade.

7 The freezing point of water is 32 _____ Fahrenheit.

WORDS WITHIN WORDS

How many words of four or more letters can you find in the word

temperature?

CHOICES

Circle the letter of the best phrase.

1 **Precipitation** is
   A. what the doctor gives the pharmacist
   B. what happens when you're very warm
   C. water that falls from clouds

2 A **monsoon** is
   A. a system of winds that change direction between seasons
   B. a violent wind system that forms a dark funnel
   C. another word for a cyclone

3 Puffy white clouds are called
   A. cumulonimbus
   B. cumulus
   C. calculus

ANSWERS ON PAGES 317-320. FOR MORE PUZZLES GO TO WWW.WORLDALMANACFORKIDS.COM

WEIGHTS & MEASURES

Which takes up more space, a cubic foot of popcorn or a cubic foot of rock?
You can find the answer on page 299.

THE EARLIEST MEASUREMENTS

We use weights and measures all the time—you can measure how tall you are, or how much gasoline a car needs. People who lived in ancient times—more than 1,000 years ago—developed measurements to describe the amounts or sizes of things. The first measurements were based on the human body and on everyday activities.

Ancient measure			
	1 FOOT = length of a person's foot	**1 YARD =** from nose to fingertip	**1 ACRE =** land an ox could plow in a day
Modern measure	12 inches	3 feet or 36 inches	43,560 square feet or 4,840 square yards

MEASUREMENTS WE USE TODAY

The system of measurement used in the United States is called the U.S. customary system. Most other countries use the metric system. A few metric measurements are also used in the United States, such as for soda, which comes in 1-liter and 2-liter bottles. In the tables below, abbreviations are given in parentheses the first time they are used.

LENGTH, HEIGHT, AND DISTANCE

The basic unit of **length** in the U.S. system is the **inch.** Length, width, depth, thickness, and the distance between two points all use the inch or larger related units.

1 foot (ft.) = 12 inches (in.)

1 yard (yd.) = 3 feet or 36 inches

1 rod (rd.) = 5½ yards

1 furlong (fur.) = 40 rods or 220 yards or 660 feet

1 mile (mi.) (also called statute mile) = 8 furlongs or 1,760 yards or 5,280 feet

1 league = 3 miles

AREA

Area is used to measure a section of a flat surface like the floor or the ground. Most area measurements are given in **square units**. Land is measured in **acres**.

1 square foot (sq. ft.) = 144 square inches (sq. in.)

1 square yard (sq. yd.) = 9 square feet or 1,296 square inches

1 square rod (sq. rd.) = 30¼ square yards

1 acre = 160 square rods or 4,840 square yards or 43,560 square feet

1 square mile (sq. mi.) = 640 acres

CAPACITY

Units of **capacity** are used to measure how much of something will fit into a container. **Liquid measure** is used to measure liquids, such as water or gasoline. **Dry measure** is used with large amounts of solid materials, like grain or fruit.

Dry Measure. Although both liquid and dry measures use the terms "pint" and "quart," they mean different amounts and should not be confused. Look at the lists below for examples.

1 quart (qt.) = 2 pints (pt.)

1 peck (pk.) = 8 quarts

1 bushel (bu.) = 4 pecks

Liquid Measure. Although the basic unit in liquid measure is the **gill** (4 fluid ounces), you are more likely to find liquids measured in pints or larger units.

1 gill = 4 fluid ounces

1 pint (pt.) = 4 gills or 16 ounces

1 quart (qt.) = 2 pints or 32 ounces

1 gallon (gal.) = 4 quarts = 128 ounces

For measuring most U.S. liquids,
   1 barrel (bbl.) = 31½ gallons

For measuring oil,
   1 barrel (bbl.) = 42 gallons

Cooking measurements. Cooking measure is used to measure amounts of solid and liquid foods used in cooking. The measurements used in cooking are based on the **fluid ounce**.

1 teaspoon (tsp.) = ⅙ fluid ounce (fl. oz.)

1 tablespoon (tbsp.) = 3 teaspoons or
                                ½ fluid ounce

1 cup = 16 tablespoons or 8 fluid ounces

1 pint = 2 cups

1 quart = 2 pints

1 gallon = 4 quarts

VOLUME

The amount of space taken up by an object (or the amount of space available within an object) is measured in **volume**. Volume is usually expressed in **cubic units**. If you wanted to buy a room air conditioner and needed to know how much space there was to be cooled, you could measure the room in cubic feet.

1 cubic foot (cu. ft.) = 1,728 cubic inches
                                  (cu. in.)

1 cubic yard (cu. yd.) = 27 cubic feet

DEPTH

Some measurements of length are used to measure ocean depth and distance.

1 fathom = 6 feet

1 cable = 120 fathoms or 720 feet

1 nautical mile = 6,076.1 feet or
                           1.15 statute miles

WEIGHT

Although 1 cubic foot of popcorn and 1 cubic foot of rock take up the same amount of space, they wouldn't feel the same if you tried to lift them. We measure heaviness as **weight**. Most objects are measured in **avoirdupois weight** (pronounced a-ver-de-POIZ), although precious metals and medicines use different systems.

1 dram (dr.) = 27.344 grains (gr.)

1 ounce (oz.) = 16 drams or 437.5 grains

1 pound (lb.) = 16 ounces

1 hundredweight (cwt.) = 100 pounds

1 ton = 2,000 pounds
   (also called short ton)

THE METRIC SYSTEM

Do you ever wonder how much soda you are getting when you buy a bottle that holds 1 liter? Or do you wonder how long a 50-meter swimming pool is? Or how far away from Montreal, Canada, you would be when a map says "8 kilometers"?

Every system of measurement uses a basic unit for measuring. In the U.S. customary system, the basic unit for length is the inch. In the metric system, the basic unit for length is the **meter**. The metric system also uses **liter** as a basic unit of volume or capacity and the **gram** as a basic unit of mass. The related units are made by adding a prefix to the basic unit. The prefixes and their meanings are:

MILLI- = 1/1,000	**DECI- = 1/10**	**HECTO- = 100**
CENTI- = 1/100	**DEKA- = 10**	**KILO- = 1,000**

FOR EXAMPLE:

millimeter (mm) = 1/1,000 of a meter	milligram (mg)	=	1/1,000 of a gram
centimeter (cm) = 1/10 of a meter	centigram (cg)	=	1/100 of a gram
decimeter (dm) = 1/10 of a meter	decigram (dg)	=	1/10 of a gram
dekameter (dm) = 10 meters	dekagram (dg)	=	10 grams
hectometer (hm) = 100 meters	hectogram (hg)	=	100 grams
kilometer (km) = 1,000 meters	kilogram (kg)	=	1,000 grams

To get a rough idea of what measurements equal in the metric system, it helps to know that a liter is a little more than a quart. A meter is a little over a yard. And a kilometer is less than a mile.

If you were 2 meters tall, you would be a little over 6 feet, 6 inches in height.

A 5-kilometer race is about 3 miles long.

A 100-kilogram man weighs more than 220 pounds.

METRIC BRAIN TEASERS

Use the information in this section to solve these puzzles.

1 Mike's American car can go 25 miles on 1 gallon of gas. Toby, in England, has a car that can run 100 kilometers on 3 liters of gas. Which car is more fuel-efficient, or covers more distance for each unit of fuel?

2 Two schools—one from Canada and one from the United States—are holding a sports contest. They have a 5-mile bike race, a 1,000-meter swimming race, a 1,500-yard relay race, and a 2-kilometer run. Organize these events from shortest to longest.

Answers are on pages 317-320.

How to Convert Measurements

Do you want to convert feet to meters or miles to kilometers? You first need to know how many meters are in one foot or how many kilometers are in one mile. The tables below show how to convert units in the U.S. customary system to units in the metric system and how to convert metric units to U.S. customary units.

If you want to convert numbers from one system to the other, a calculator would be helpful for doing the multiplication.

CONVERTING U.S. CUSTOMARY UNITS TO METRIC UNITS

If you know the number of	Multiply by	To get the number of
inches	2.5400	centimeters
inches	.0254	meters
feet	30.4800	centimeters
feet	.3048	meters
yards	.9144	meters
miles	1.6093	kilometers
square inches	6.4516	square centimeters
square feet	.0929	square meters
square yards	.8361	square meters
acres	.4047	hectares
cubic inches	16.3871	cubic centimeters
cubic feet	.0283	cubic meters
cubic yards	.7646	cubic meters
quarts (liquid)	.9464	liters
ounces	28.3495	grams
pounds	.4536	kilograms

CONVERTING METRIC UNITS TO U.S. CUSTOMARY UNITS

If you know the number of	Multiply by	To get the number of
centimeters	.3937	inches
centimeters	.0328	feet
meters	39.3701	inches
meters	3.2808	feet
meters	1.0936	yards
kilometers	.621	miles
square centimeters	.1550	square inches
square meters	10.7639	square feet
square meters	1.1960	square yards
hectares	2.4710	acres
cubic centimeters	.0610	cubic inches
cubic meters	35.3147	cubic feet
cubic meters	1.3080	cubic yards
liters	1.0567	quarts (liquid)
grams	.0353	ounces
kilograms	2.2046	pounds

WORLD HISTORY

What was so "Great" about Alexander?
You can find the answer on page 310.

HIGHLIGHTS OF WORLD HISTORY

The section on World History is divided into five sections. Each part covers a major region of the world: the Middle East, Africa, Asia, Europe, and the Americas. Major events from ancient times to the present are described under the headings for each region.

THE ANCIENT MIDDLE EAST 4000 B.C.–1 B.C.

4000–3000 B.C.
- The world's first cities are built by the Sumerian peoples in Mesopotamia, now southern Iraq.
- Sumerians develop a kind of writing called cuneiform.
- Egyptians develop a kind of writing called hieroglyphics.

2700 B.C. Egyptians begin building the great pyramids in the desert. The pharaohs' (kings') bodies are buried in them.

1792 B.C. Some of the first written laws are created in Babylonia. They are called the Code of Hammurabi.

ACHIEVEMENTS OF THE ANCIENT MIDDLE EAST
Early peoples of the Middle East:
1. Studied the stars (astronomy).
2. Invented the wheel.
3. Created written language from picture drawings (hieroglyphics and cuneiform). ▶

4. Established the 24-hour day.
5. Studied medicine and mathematics.

▼ *The pyramids and sphinx at Giza*

1200 B.C. Hebrew people settle in Canaan in Palestine after escaping from slavery in Egypt. They are led by the prophet Moses.

THE TEN COMMANDMENTS

Unlike most early peoples in the Middle East, the Hebrews believed in only one God (monotheism). They believed that God gave Moses the Ten Commandments on Mount Sinai when they fled Egypt.

1000 B.C. King David unites the Hebrews in one strong kingdom.

ANCIENT PALESTINE
Palestine was invaded by many different peoples after 1000 B.C., including the Babylonians, the Egyptians, the Persians, and the Romans. It came under Arab Muslim control in the 600s and remained mainly under Muslim control until the 1900s.

336 B.C. Alexander the Great, King of Macedonia, builds an empire from Egypt to India.

63 B.C. Romans conquer Palestine and make it part of their empire.

AROUND 4 B.C. Jesus Christ, the founder of the Christian religion, is born in Bethlehem. He is crucified about A.D. 29.

All About... MUMMIES OF EGYPT

The pyramids of Egypt, built beginning around 2700 B.C., were tombs of the pharaohs who ruled ancient Egypt. The remains of about 70 pyramids still exist.

Egyptians believed that the pharaohs would need their bodies in the next life. They developed advanced techniques for embalming and drying out bodies so that they could last for thousands of years. The Egyptian art of embalming peaked around 1600 to 1100 B.C. and came to an end around the A.D. 300s. At that time, many Egyptians were becoming Christians, and preserving bodies after death became less important. (A form of embalming is widely practiced today, but it is not long-lasting.)

Mask of King Tutankhamen

Perhaps the most famous mummy belongs to an Egyptian boy pharaoh named Tutankhamen. King Tut, as he's often called, ruled for less than 10 years, in the late 1300s B.C. He died of unknown causes when he was 16 years old. His tomb, discovered in 1922, was filled with rich treasures.

GODS AND GODDESSES

The ancient Greeks worshipped gods who they believed lived on Mount Olympus. The Romans had similar gods, with different names. For more information on ancient Greece and Rome, see pages 310-311.

GREEK NAME	ROMAN NAME	KNOWN AS
Zeus	Jupiter	All-powerful king of the gods. Used a lightning bolt to strike down wrongdoers.
Hera	Juno	Zeus's wife and sister. Angered Zeus by playing favorites with mortals.
Poseidon	Neptune	Zeus's brother and god of the sea. He could unleash storms. Sailors prayed to him for a safe voyage.
Hades	Pluto	Zeus's brother, god of the underworld, where the dead lived as ghostly shadows.
Athena	Minerva	Zeus's daughter, goddess of wisdom. Scholars, soldiers, and craftsmen prayed to her for sharp wits.
Aphrodite	Venus	Goddess of love. She could make people fall in love. Using this skill against other gods made her powerful.
Hephaestus	Vulcan	Son of Zeus and Hera, god of craftsmen and blacksmiths. Ugly and lame, he could work magic with a hammer and anvil.
Apollo	none	Zeus's son and god of the sun, medicine, poetry, and music. Every day, Apollo drove his golden chariot (the Sun) across the sky. He was handsome, coolheaded, and fierce in battle.
Artemis	Diana	Apollo's twin sister, goddess of the moon and the hunt. She punished those who killed animals unnecessarily.

THE MIDDLE EAST A.D. 1-1940s

ISLAM: A RELIGION GROWS IN THE MIDDLE EAST 570-632

Muhammad is born in Mecca in Arabia. Around 610, as a prophet, he starts to proclaim and teach Islam, a religion which spreads from Arabia to all the neighboring regions in the Middle East and North Africa. His followers are called Muslims.

THE KORAN

The holy book of Islam is the Koran. It was related by Muhammad beginning in 611. The Koran gives Muslims a program they must follow. For example, it gives rules about how one should treat one's parents and neighbors.

632 Muhammad dies. By now, Islam is accepted in Arabia as a religion.

641 Arab Muslims conquer the Persians.

LATE 600s Islam begins to spread to the west into Africa and Spain.

711-732 Umayyads invade Europe but are defeated by Frankish leader Charles Martel in France. This defeat halts the spread of Islam into Western Europe.

1071 Muslim Turks conquer Jerusalem.

1095-1291 Europeans try to take back Jerusalem and other parts of the Middle East for Christians during the Crusades.

THE SPREAD OF ISLAM

The Arab armies that went across North Africa brought great change:
1. The people who lived there were converted to Islam.
2. The Arabic language replaced many local languages as an official language. North Africa is still an Arabic-speaking region today, and Islam is the major faith.

Dome of the Rock and the Western Wall, Jerusalem ▼

ACHIEVEMENTS OF THE UMAYYAD AND ABBASID DYNASTIES

The Umayyads (661-750) and the Abbasids (750-1256) were the first two Muslim-led dynasties. Both empires stretched across northern Africa across the Middle East and into Asia. Both were known for great achievements. They:
1. Studied math and medicine.
2. Translated the works of other peoples, including Greeks and Persians.
3. Spread news of Chinese inventions like paper and gunpowder.
4. Wrote great works on religion and philosophy.

1300-1900s The Ottoman Turks, who are Muslims, create a huge empire, covering the Middle East, North Africa, and part of Eastern Europe. The Ottoman Empire falls apart gradually, and European countries take over portions of it beginning in the 1800s.

1914-1918 World War I begins in 1914. The Ottoman Empire has now broken apart. Most of the Middle East falls under British or French control.

1921 Two new Arab kingdoms are created: Transjordan and Iraq. The French take control of Syria and Lebanon.

1922 Egypt becomes independent from Britain.

JEWS MIGRATE TO PALESTINE

Jewish settlers from Europe began migrating to Palestine in the 1880s. They wanted to return to the historic homeland of the Hebrew people. In 1945, after World War II, many Jews who survived the Holocaust migrated to Palestine. Arabs living in the region opposed the Jewish immigration. In 1948, after the British left, war broke out between the Jews and the Arabs.

THE MIDDLE EAST 1940s-2000s

1948 The state of Israel is created.

THE ARAB-ISRAELI WARS Arab countries near Israel (Egypt, Iraq, Jordan, Lebanon, and Syria) attack the new country in 1948 but fail to destroy it. Israel and its neighbors fight wars again in 1956, 1967, and 1973. Israel wins each war. In the 1967 war, Israel captures the Sinai Desert from Egypt, the Golan Heights from Syria, and the area known as the West Bank from Jordan.

1979 Egypt and Israel sign a peace treaty, providing for Israel to return the Sinai to Egypt.

THE MIDDLE EAST AND OIL
Much of the oil we use to drive our cars, heat our homes, and run our machines comes from the Arabian peninsula in the Middle East. For a brief time in 1973-1974, Arab nations would not let their oil be sold to the United States because of its support of Israel. The United States relies less heavily on oil imports from the region today.

THE 1990s AND 2000s

► In 1991, the United States and its allies go to war with Iraq after Iraq invades neighboring Kuwait. The conflict, known as the Persian Gulf War, results in the defeat of Iraq's army. Iraq signs a peace agreement but is accused by the United States and others of violating the peace terms, especially of making weapons for chemical and germ warfare.

► Israel and the Palestine Liberation Organization (PLO) agree to work toward peace (1993). In 1995, Prime Minister Yitzhak Rabin of Israel is assassinated. The next two prime ministers fail to secure a peace deal. In 2001, Ariel Sharon is elected prime minister as violence in the Middle East continues.

Oil fire in Kuwait during the Persian Gulf War

ANCIENT AFRICA 3500 B.C.-A.D. 900

ANCIENT AFRICA In ancient times, northern Africa was dominated, for the most part, by the Egyptians, Greeks, and Romans. However, we know very little about the lives of ancient people in Africa south of the Sahara Desert (sub-Saharan Africa). The people of Africa south of the Sahara did not have written languages in ancient times. What we learn about them comes from such things as weapons, tools, and other items from their civilization that have been found in the earth.

2000 B.C. The Kingdom of Kush arises just south of Egypt. It becomes a major center of art, learning, and trade. Kush dies out around A.D. 350.

500 B.C. The Nok culture becomes strong in Nigeria, in West Africa. The Nok use iron for tools and weapons. They are also known for their fine terra-cotta sculptures of heads. ►

AROUND A.D. 1 Bantu-speaking peoples in West Africa begin to move into eastern and southern Africa.

50 The Kingdom of Axum in northern Ethiopia, founded by traders from Arabia, becomes a wealthy trading center for ivory.

300S Ghana, the first known African state south of the Sahara Desert, takes power in the upper Senegal and Niger river region. It controls the trade in gold that is being sent from the southern parts of Africa north to the Mediterranean Sea.

660s-900 The Islamic religion spreads across North Africa and into Spain.

Niger River, Mali ►

AFRICA 900s-2000s

900 Arab Muslims begin to settle along the coast of East Africa. Their contact with Bantu people produces the Swahili language, which is still spoken today.

1050 The Almoravid Kingdom in Morocco, North Africa, is powerful from Ghana to as far north as Spain.

1230 The Mali Kingdom begins in North Africa. Timbuktu, a center for trade and learning, is its main city.

1464 The Songhay Empire becomes strong in West Africa. By around 1500, it has destroyed Mali. The Songhay are remembered for their bronze sculptures.

1505-1575 Portuguese settlement begins in Africa. Portuguese people settle in Angola, Mozambique, and other areas.

THE AFRICAN SLAVE TRADE

Once Europeans began settling in the New World, they needed people to harvest their sugar. The first African slaves were taken to the Caribbean. Later, slaves were taken to South America and the United States. The slaves were crowded onto ships and many died during the long journey. Shipping of African slaves to the United States lasted until the early 1800s.

1652-1835

1. Dutch settlers arrive in southern Africa. They are known as the Boers.
2. Shaka the Great forms a Zulu Empire in eastern Africa. The Zulus are warriors.
3. The "Great Trek" (march) of the Boers north takes place. They defeat the Zulus at the Battle of Bloody River.

1899: BOER WAR The South African War between Great Britain and the Boers begins. It is also called the Boer War. The Boers accept British rule but are allowed a role in government.

1948 The white South African government creates the policy of apartheid, the total separation of blacks and whites. Blacks are banned from restaurants, theaters, schools, and jobs considered "white." Apartheid sparked protests, many of which ended in bloodshed.

1983 Droughts (water shortages) lead to starvation over much of Africa.

THE 1990s

▼ Nelson Mandela

Apartheid ends in South Africa. Nelson Mandela becomes South Africa's first black president in 1994. Also in 1994, civil war in Rwanda leads to the massacre of 500,000 civilians. Meanwhile, the disease AIDS kills thousands each year. Africa accounts for 70 percent of AIDS cases worldwide. In Zimbabwe, for example, one out of every four adults has HIV/AIDS.

COLONIES WIN THEIR FREEDOM

Most of the countries on the African continent and nearby islands were once colonies of a European nation such as Britain, France, or Portugal, but later became independent. Here are some major African countries that achieved independence in the 1900s.

Country	Became Independent	From
Egypt	1952	Britain
Morocco	1956	France
Sudan	1956	Britain
Ghana	1957	Britain
Burkina Faso	1960	France
Cameroon	1960	France
Congo, Dem. Rep. of	1960	Belgium
Côte d'Ivoire	1960	France
Mali	1960	France
Niger	1960	France
Nigeria	1960	Britain
Zimbabwe	1960	Britain
South Africa	1961	Britain
Tanzania	1961	Britain
Algeria	1962	France
Uganda	1962	Britain
Kenya	1963	Britain
Malawi	1964	Britain
Angola	1975	Portugal
Mozambique	1975	Portugal

ANCIENT ASIA 3500 B.C.–1 B.C.

3500 B.C. Communities of people settle in the Indus River Valley of India and Pakistan and the Yellow River Valley of China.

2500 B.C. Cities of Mohenjo-Daro and Harappa in Pakistan become centers of trade and farming.

AROUND 1523 B.C. Shang peoples in China build walled towns and use a kind of writing based on pictures. This writing develops into the writing Chinese people use today.

1500 B.C. The Hindu religion (Hinduism) begins to spread throughout India.

AROUND 1050 B.C. Chou peoples in China overthrow the Shang and control large territories.

700 B.C. In China, a 500-year period begins in which many warring states fight one another.

563 B.C. Siddhartha Gautama is born in India. He becomes known as the Buddha—which means the "Enlightened One"—and is the founder of the Buddhist religion (Buddhism).

551 B.C. The Chinese philosopher Confucius is born. His teachings—especially the rules about how people should treat each other—spread throughout China and are still followed today. ▶

TWO IMPORTANT ASIAN RELIGIONS

Many of the world's religions began in Asia. Two of the most important were:

1. **Hinduism.** Hinduism began in India and has spread to other parts of southern Asia and to parts of the Pacific region.
2. **Buddhism.** Buddhism also began in India and spread to China, Japan, and Southeast Asia. Today, both religions have millions of followers all over the world.

320–232 B.C.: INDIA

1. Northern India is united under the emperor Chandragupta Maurya.
2. Asoka, emperor of India, sends Buddhist missionaries throughout southern Asia to spread the Buddhist religion.

221 B.C. The Chinese ruler Shih Huang Ti makes the Chinese language the same throughout the country. Around the same time, the Chinese begin building the Great Wall of China. Its main section is more than 2,000 miles long and is meant to keep invading peoples from the north out of China.

202 B.C. The Han people of China win control of all of China.

ACHIEVEMENTS OF THE ANCIENT CHINESE

1. Invented paper.
2. Invented gunpowder.
3. Studied astronomy.
4. Studied engineering.
5. Invented acupuncture to treat illnesses.

▼ *The Great Wall of China*

ASIA A.D. 1-1700s

320 The Gupta Empire controls northern India. The Guptas are Hindus. They drive the Buddhist religion out of India. The Guptas are well known for their many advances in the study of mathematics and medicine.

618 The Tang dynasty begins in China. The Tang Dynasty is well known for music, poetry, and painting. They export silk and porcelains as far away as Africa.

THE SILK ROAD ▶

Around 100 B.C., only the Chinese knew how to make silk. Europeans were willing to pay high prices for the light, comfortable material. To get it, they sent fortunes in glass, gold, jade, and other items to China. The exchanges between Europeans and Chinese created one of the greatest trading routes in history—the Silk Road. Chinese inventions such as paper and gunpowder were also spread over the Silk Road. Europeans found out how to make silk around A.D. 500, but trade continued until about 1400.

960 The Northern Sung dynasty in China makes advances in banking and paper money. China's population of 50 million doubles over 200 years, thanks to improved ways of farming that lead to greater food production.

▼ *Statues from Angkor Wat temple, Cambodia*

1000 The Samurai, a warrior people, become powerful in Japan. They live by a code of honor known as Bushido. ▶

1180 The Khmer Empire based in Angkor is powerful in Cambodia. The empire became widely known for its beautiful temples.

1206 The Mongol people of Asia are united under the ruler Genghis Khan. He builds a huge army and creates an empire that stretches all the way from China to India, Russia, and Eastern Europe.

1264 Kublai Khan, the grandson of Genghis Khan, rules China as emperor from his new capital at Beijing.

1368 The Ming Dynasty comes to power in China. The Ming drive the Mongols out of the country.

1467-1603 WAR AND PEACE IN JAPAN
1. Civil war breaks out in Japan. The conflicts last more than 100 years.
2. Peace comes to Japan under the military leader Hideyoshi.
3. The Shogun period reaches its peak in Japan (it lasts until 1868). Europeans are driven out of the country and Christians are persecuted.

1526 THE MUGHALS IN INDIA
1. The Mughal Empire in India begins under Babur. The Mughals are Muslims who invade and conquer India.
2. Akbar, the grandson of Babur, becomes Mughal emperor of India. He attempts to unite Hindus and Muslims but does not succeed.

1644 The Ming dynasty in China is overthrown by the Manchu peoples. They allow more Europeans to trade in China.

1739 Nadir Shah, a Persian warrior, conquers parts of western India and captures the city of Delhi.

MODERN ASIA 1800s-2000s

1839 The Opium War takes place in China between the Chinese and the British. The British and other Western powers want to control trade in Asia. The Chinese want the British to stop selling opium to the Chinese. Britain wins the war in 1842.

1858 The French begin to take control of Indochina (Southeast Asia).

1868 The Shogunate dynasty ends in Japan. The new ruler is Emperor Meiji. Western ideas begin to influence the Japanese.

THE JAPANESE IN ASIA Japan became a powerful country during the early 20th century. It was a small country with few raw materials of its own. For example, Japan had to buy oil from other countries. The Japanese army and navy took control of the government during the 1930s. Japan soon began to invade some of its neighbors. In 1941, the United States and Japan went to war after Japan attacked the U.S. Navy at Pearl Harbor, Hawaii.

1945 Japan is defeated in World War II after the U.S. drops atomic bombs on the Japanese cities of Hiroshima and Nagasaki.

1947 India and Pakistan become independent from Great Britain, which had ruled them as colonies since the mid-1800s.

1949 China comes under the rule of the Communists led by Mao Zedong. ▶

CHINA UNDER THE COMMUNISTS The Communists brought great changes to China. Private property was abolished, and the government took over all businesses and farms. Religions were persecuted. China became more isolated from other countries.

1950-1953 THE KOREAN WAR North Korea, a Communist country, invades South Korea. The U.S. and other nations join to fight the invasion. China joins North Korea. The Korean War ends in 1953. Neither side wins.

1954-1975 THE VIETNAM WAR The French are defeated in Indochina in 1954 by the Vietminh. The Vietminh are Vietnamese fighters under the leadership of the Communists headed by Ho Chi Minh. The U.S. sends troops to fight in the Vietnam War in 1965 on the side of South Vietnam against Ho Chi Minh and Communist North Vietnam. The U.S. withdraws from the war in 1973. In 1975, South Vietnam is defeated and taken over by North Vietnam.

1972 President Richard Nixon visits Communist China. Relations between China and the United States improve.

1989 Chinese students protest for democracy, but the protests are brutally crushed by the army in Beijing's Tiananmen Square.

THE 1990s The economies of Japan, South Korea, Taiwan, and some other Asian countries show great strength in the early 1990s. But during the late 1990s, several Asian nations have serious financial trouble. The British return Hong Kong to China in 1997. Macao becomes part of China in 1999. China builds its economy, but is accused of violating human rights.

Tokyo, Japan ▼

ANCIENT EUROPE 4000 B.C.–300s B.C.

4000 B.C. People in many parts of Europe start building monuments out of large stones called megaliths. Examples can still be seen today, including Stonehenge in England.

2500 B.C.–1200 B.C.
THE MINOANS AND THE MYCENAEANS

1. People on the island of Crete (Minoans) in the Mediterranean Sea built great palaces and became sailors and traders.
2. People in the city of Mycenae in Greece built stone walls and a great palace.
3. Mycenaean people invaded Crete and destroyed the power of the Minoans.

Treasury of Atreus at Mycenae

THE TROJAN WAR The Trojan War was a conflict between invading Greeks and the people of Troas (Troy) in Southwestern Turkey around 1200 B.C. Although little is known today about the real war, it has become a part of Greek poetry and mythology. According to a famous legend, a group of Greek soldiers hid inside a huge wooden horse. The horse was pulled into the city of Troy. Then the soldiers jumped out of the horse and conquered Troy.

900–600 B.C. Celtic peoples in Northern Europe settle on farms and in villages and learn to mine for iron ore.

600 B.C. Etruscan peoples take over most of Italy. They build many cities and become traders.

SOME ACHIEVEMENTS OF THE GREEKS The early Greeks were responsible for:

1. The first governments that were elected by people. Greeks invented democratic government.
2. Great poets such as Homer, who composed the *Iliad,* a long poem about the Trojan War, and the *Odyssey,* an epic poem about the travels of Odysseus.
3. Great thinkers such as Socrates, Plato, and Aristotle.
4. Great architecture, like the Parthenon and the Propylaea on the Acropolis in Athens (*see below*).

431 B.C. The Peloponnesian Wars begin between the Greek cities of Athens and Sparta. The wars end in 404 B.C. when Sparta wins.

338 B.C. King Philip II of Macedonia in northern Greece conquers all the cities of Greece.

336 B.C. Philip's son Alexander becomes king. He conquers lands and makes an empire from the Mediterranean Sea to India. He is known as Alexander the Great. For the next 300 years, Greek culture dominates this vast area.

The Propylaea ▶

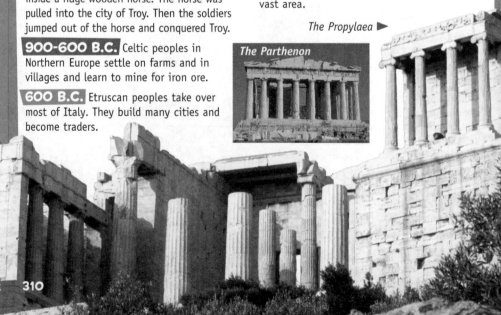

The Parthenon

EUROPE 300 B.C.–A.D. 800s

264 B.C.–A.D. 476
ROMAN EMPIRE The city of Rome in Italy begins to expand and captures surrounding lands. The Romans gradually build a great empire and control all of the Mediterranean region. At its height, the Roman Empire includes Western Europe, Greece, Egypt, and much of the Middle East. The Roman Empire lasts until A.D. 476.

ROMAN ACHIEVEMENTS

1. Roman law. Many of our laws are based on Roman law.
2. Great roads to connect their huge empire. The Appian Way, south of Rome, is a Roman road that is still in use today.
3. Aqueducts to bring water to the people in large cities.
4. Great sculpture. Roman statues can still be seen in Europe.
5. Great architecture. The Colosseum, which still stands in Rome today, is an example of great Roman architecture.
6. Great writers, such as the poet Vergil, who wrote the *Aeneid*.

49 B.C. A civil war breaks out that destroys Rome's republican form of government.

45 B.C. Julius Caesar becomes the sole ruler of Rome but is murdered one year later by rivals in the Roman army. ▶

27 B.C. Octavian becomes the first emperor of Rome. He takes the name Augustus. A peaceful period of almost 200 years begins.

THE CHRISTIAN FAITH Christians believe that Jesus Christ is the Son of God. The history and beliefs of Christianity are found in the New Testament of the Bible. Christianity spread slowly throughout the Roman Empire. The Romans tried to stop the new religion and persecuted the Christians. They were forced to hold their services in hiding, and some were crucified. Eventually, more and more Romans became Christian.

337 The Roman Emperor Constantine becomes a Christian. He is the first Roman emperor to be a Christian.

410 The Visigoths and other barbarian tribes from northern Europe invade the Roman Empire and begin to take over its lands.

476 The last Roman emperor is overthrown.

THE BYZANTINE EMPIRE, centered in modern-day Turkey, was made up of the eastern half of the old Roman Empire. Byzantine rulers extended their power into western Europe. The great Byzantine Emperor Justinian ruled parts of Spain, North Africa, and Italy. The city of Constantinople (now Istanbul, Turkey) became the capital of the Byzantine Empire in 330.

768 Charlemagne becomes king of the Franks in northern Europe. He rules a kingdom that includes parts of France, Germany and northern Italy.

800 Feudalism becomes important in Europe. Feudalism means that poor farmers are allowed to farm a lord's land in return for certain services to the lord.

▼ *The Colosseum, Rome*

The Temple of Saturn, Rome

EUROPE 800s-1500s

896 Magyar peoples from lands east of Russia found Hungary.

800s–900s Viking warriors and traders from Scandinavia begin to move into the British Isles, France, and parts of the Mediterranean.

Viking helmet ▼

989 The Russian state of Kiev becomes Christian.

1066 William of Normandy, a Frenchman, successfully invades England and makes himself king. He is known as William the Conqueror.

1096–1291 THE CRUSADES In 1096, Christian European kings and nobles sent a series of armies to the Middle East to try to capture the city of Jerusalem from the Muslims. Between 1096 and 1291 there were about ten Crusades. During the Crusades the Europeans briefly captured Jerusalem. But in the end, the Crusades did not succeed in their aim.

One of the most important results of the Crusades had nothing to do with religion: trade increased greatly between the Middle East and Europe.

1215 THE MAGNA CARTA The Magna Carta was a document agreed to by King John of England and the English nobility. The English king agreed that he did not have absolute power and had to obey the laws of the land. The Magna Carta was an important step toward democracy.

1290 The Ottoman Empire begins. It is controlled by Turkish Muslims who conquer lands in the eastern Mediterranean and the Middle East.

Ottoman Palace of Ciragan, Istanbul ▶

1337–1453 WAR AND PLAGUE IN EUROPE

❶ The Hundred Years' War (1337) begins in Europe between France and England. The war lasts until 1453 when France wins.

❷ The bubonic plague begins in Europe (1348). The plague, also called the Black Death, is a deadly disease caused by the bite of infected fleas. Perhaps as much as one third of the whole population of Europe dies from the plague.

1453 The Ottoman Turks capture the city of Constantinople and rename it Istanbul.

1517 THE REFORMATION The Reformation led to the breakup of the Christian church into Protestant and Roman Catholic branches in Europe. It started when the German priest Martin Luther opposed some teachings of the Church. He broke away from the pope (the leader of the Catholic church) and had many followers.

1534 King Henry VIII of England breaks away from the Roman Catholic church. He names himself head of the English (Anglican) church.

▲ *Queen Elizabeth I*

1558 The reign of King Henry's daughter Elizabeth I begins in England. During her long rule, England's power grows.

1588 The Spanish Armada (fleet of warships) is defeated by the English navy as Spain tries to invade England.

MODERN EUROPE 1600s-2000s

1600s The Ottoman Turks expand their empire through most of eastern and central Europe.

1618 The Thirty Years' War begins in Europe. The war is fought over religious issues. Much of Europe is destroyed in the conflict, which ends in 1648.

1642 The English civil war begins. King Charles I fights against the forces of the Parliament (legislature). The king's forces are defeated, and he is executed in 1649. But his son, Charles II, eventually returns as king in 1660.

Vladimir Lenin

1762 Catherine the Great becomes the Empress of Russia. She allows some religious freedom and extends the Russian Empire.

1789 THE FRENCH REVOLUTION
The French Revolution ended the rule of kings in France and led to democracy there. At first, however, there were wars, much bloodshed, and times when dictators took control. Many people were executed. King Louis XVI and Queen Marie Antoinette were overthrown in the Revolution, and both were executed in 1793.

1799 Napoleon Bonaparte, an army officer, becomes dictator of France. Under his rule, France conquers most of Europe by 1812.

1815 Napoleon's forces are defeated by the British and German armies at Waterloo (in Belgium). Napoleon is exiled to a remote island and dies there in 1821.

1848 Revolutions break out in countries of Europe. People force their rulers to make more democratic changes.

Napoleon Bonaparte ▶

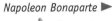

1914–1918 WORLD WAR I IN EUROPE At the start of World War I in Europe, Germany, Austria-Hungary and the Ottoman Empire opposed England, France, and Russia (the Allies). The United States joined the war in 1917 on the side of the Allies. The Allies won in 1918.

1917 The Russian Revolution takes place. The czar (emperor) is overthrown. The Bolsheviks (Communists) under Vladimir Lenin take control of the government. The country is renamed the Soviet Union. Huge numbers of people are jailed or killed under dictator Joseph Stalin (1929-1953).

THE RISE OF HITLER Adolf Hitler became dictator of Germany in 1933. He joined forces with rulers in Italy and Japan to form the Axis powers. By 1939, the Axis had started World War II. They fought against the Allies—Great Britain, the Soviet Union, and the U.S. By 1945, Hitler and the Axis powers were defeated. During his 12-year reign, Hitler killed millions of Jews (the Holocaust). He also persecuted and killed many political opponents, Gypsies, and others.

1945 The Cold War begins. It is a long period of tension between the United States and the Soviet Union. Both countries build up their armies and make nuclear weapons but do not go to war against each other.

THE 1990s Communist governments in Eastern Europe are replaced by democratic ones. Divided Germany becomes one nation. The Soviet Union breaks up. The European Union (EU), made up of 15 countries, takes steps toward European unity. The North Atlantic Treaty Organization (NATO) bombs Yugoslavia in an effort to protect Albanians driven out of the Kosovo region.

THE AMERICAS 10,000 B.C.–A.D. 1600s

10,000–8000 B.C.
People in North and South America gather plants for food and hunt animals using stone-pointed spears.

AROUND 3000 B.C.
People in Central America begin farming, growing corn and beans for food.

▲ *The landing of Columbus*

1500 B.C. Mayan people in Central America begin to live in small villages.

500 B.C. People in North America begin to hunt buffalo to use for meat and for clothing.

100 B.C. The city of Teotihuacán is founded in Mexico. It becomes the center of a huge empire extending from central Mexico to Guatemala. Teotihuacán contains many large pyramids and temples.

A.D. 150 Mayan people in Guatemala build many centers for religious ceremonies. They create a calendar and learn mathematics and astronomy.

900 Toltec warriors in Mexico begin to invade lands of Mayan people. Mayans leave their old cities and move to the Yucatan Peninsula of Mexico.

1000 Native Americans in the southwestern United States begin to live in settlements called pueblos. They learn to farm.

1325 Mexican Indians known as Aztecs create huge city of Tenochtitlán and rule a large empire in Mexico. They are warriors who practice human sacrifice.

Mayan pyramid, Yucatan Peninsula, Mexico ▶

1492 Christopher Columbus sails from Europe across the Atlantic Ocean and lands in the Bahamas, in the Caribbean Sea. This marked the first step toward the founding of European settlements in the Americas.

1500 Portuguese explorers reach Brazil and claim it for Portugal.

1519 Spanish conqueror Hernán Cortés travels into the Aztec Empire in search of gold. The Aztecs are defeated in 1521 by Cortés. The Spanish take control of Mexico.

WHY DID THE SPANISH WIN? How did the Spanish defeat the powerful Aztec Empire in such a short time? One reason is that the Spanish had better weapons. Another is that the Aztecs became sick and died from diseases brought to the New World by the Spanish. The Aztecs had never had these illnesses before and, as a result, did not have immunity to them. Also, many neighboring Indians hated the Aztecs as conquerors. Those Indians helped the Spanish to defeat them.

1534 Jacques Cartier of France explores Canada.

1583 The first English colony in Canada is set up in Newfoundland.

1607 English colonists led by Captain John Smith settle in Jamestown, Virginia. Virginia was the oldest of the Thirteen Colonies that turned into the United States.

1619 First African slaves arrive in English-controlled America.

1682 The French explorer Robert Cavelier, sieur de la Salle, sails down the Mississippi River. The area is named Louisiana after the French King Louis XIV.

THE AMERICAS 1700s–2000s

EUROPEAN COLONIES By 1700, most of the Americas are under the control of Europeans:

Spain: Florida, southwestern United States, Mexico, Central America, western South America.

Portugal: eastern South America.

France: central United States, parts of Canada.

England: eastern U.S., parts of Canada.

Holland: eastern U.S., West Indies, eastern South America.

1700 European colonies in North and South America begin to grow in population and wealth.

1775-1783 AMERICAN REVOLUTION The American Revolution begins in 1775 when the first shot is fired in Lexington, Massachusetts. The thirteen original British colonies in North America become independent under the Treaty of Paris, signed in 1783.

SIMÓN BOLÍVAR: LIBERATOR OF SOUTH AMERICA

In 1810, Simón Bolívar began a revolt against Spain. He fought for more than 10 years against the Spanish and became president of the independent country of Greater Colombia in 1824. As a result of his leadership, ten South American countries had become independent from Spain by 1830. However, Bolívar himself was criticized as being a dictator.

1810-1910 MEXICO'S REVOLUTION In 1846, Mexico and the United States go to war. Mexico loses parts of the Southwest and California to the United States. A revolution in 1910 overthrows Porfirio Díaz.

1867 The Canadian provinces are united as the Dominion of Canada.

1898 THE SPANISH-AMERICAN WAR Spain and the United States fight a brief war in 1898. Spain loses its Caribbean colonies Cuba and Puerto Rico, and the Philippines in the Pacific.

U.S. POWER IN THE 1900s During the 1900s the United States influenced affairs in Central America and the Caribbean. The United States sent troops to Mexico (1914; 1916–1917), Nicaragua (1912–1933), Haiti (1915–1934; 1994–1995), Dominican Republic (1965), Grenada (1983), and Panama (1989). In 1962, the United States went on alert when the Soviet Union put missiles on Cuba, only 90 miles from Florida.

THE 1990s In 1994, the North American Free Trade Agreement (NAFTA) is signed to increase trade between the United States, Canada, and Mexico. Relations between the United States and Cuba remain hostile.

SOUTH AMERICAN INDEPENDENCE

Mexico and most countries of South America became independent of Spain in the early 1800s. Here are the dates each country became independent of European control:

COUNTRY	YEAR OF INDEPENDENCE
Argentina	1816
Bolivia	1825
Brazil[1]	1822
Chile	1818
Colombia	1819
Ecuador	1822
Guyana[2]	1966
Mexico	1821
Paraguay	1811
Peru	1824
Suriname[3]	1975
Uruguay	1825
Venezuela	1821

[1] Brazil was governed by Portugal.
[2] Guyana was a British colony.
[3] Suriname was a Dutch colony.

315

Find all the words in the Word Box. They go across, up, down, backward, and diagonally. Some letters are used more than once. Seven are not used. And four letters form two words: one goes forward and one goes backward.

```
G   N   I   M   R   A   F   H   S
H   A   N   C   I   E   N   T   I
N   O   D   I   E   S   O   P   Y
S   U   E   Z   E   N   O   A   C
N   O   P   A   E   W   S   M   A
I   T   E   Y   E   O   O   R   R
G   R   N   R   R   D   R   O   C
E   E   D   R   E   A   E   M   O
R   M   E   R   I   P   M   E   M
I   O   N   A   P   A   J   I   E
A   H   T   W   O   R   G   Y   D
```

WORD BOX

ancient	Homer	ore	Suez
democracy	independent	Poseidon	weapon
empire	Japan	power	zen
farming	map	pyramid	Zeus
growth	modern	Rome	
han	Nigeria	stone	

◀ PUZZLE ANSWERS ▶

ANIMALS, Page 42: WHO LIVES WHERE?

Camel–Desert; Dog–House; Dolphin–Ocean; Lion–Plains; Parrot–Tree; Polar bear–Ice floe

BOOKS, Page 51: FIND THAT NAME

```
T  (T  T  I  B  B  A  (B)  (E)  (H)    O
L  (J  K  R  O  W  (L  I)  N   G    (I
(B  A  U  M) K  I  (E  S)  I   R     B
(Y  R  W  O  L) E  (W  H)  V   E     B
(G  V  (K  C  E  P) I  O)  E   B     O
(N  I  T  R  A  M) S  P)  L)  D     T
(S) T  G  E  O  R  G  E)   N     S
(W  O  O  D  S  O  N) L  N)  I     O
(D  I  C  A  M  I  L) L  O)  L)    N
```

The leftover letters spell **TOLKIEN.**

COMPUTERS

Page 61: FAQ: WHAT'S A BL?
1. a; 2. b; 3. a; 4. a; 5. b; 6. a; 7. a; 8. b.

Page 63: KEY IN THE WORDS *(see right)*

Page 63: ON SITE 1. c; 2. d; 3. e; 4. b; 5. a.

```
M O N I T O R
    K E Y B O A R D
V I R U S
      M O U S E
      I N T E R N E T
P R I N T E R
    H A R D    C O P Y
D O W N L O A D
    D I S K
```

HEALTH, Page 95: BODY MAZE

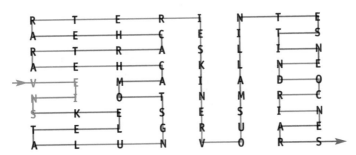

PUZZLE ANSWERS

INVENTIONS, Page 103: MIND-BOGGLING

1. D; 2. E; 3. G; 4. H; 5. C; 6. J; 7. A; 8. B; 9. F; 10. I

LANGUAGE

Page 106: PICTURE THIS
1. a skeleton in the closet; 2. shake a leg; 3. let the cat out of the bag

Page 110: PICTURE THESE
2. innocent bystander; 3. 6 o'clock on the dot; 4. Great Dane; 5. tied game; 6. Batman; 7. stepfather; 8. X ray; 9. play in the big leagues; 10. strawberry shortcake; 11. double chin; 12. check mate; 13. spiral staircase

NATIONS

Page 152: NATIONS CROSSWORD

¹T	H	A	I	L	²A	N	³D		
A					R		E		
⁴L	A	T	⁵V	I	A		N		⁶E
A			I		B		M		G
			E		⁷I	T	A	L	Y
⁸C			T		C		R		P
⁹F	R	A	N	C			K		T
A			A						
			¹⁰M	A	L	T	A		

NUMBERS

Page 169: ROMAN NUMERALS CDIV

Page 172: EVEN VS ODD
If you always choose an even number (2 or 4), the answer will always be even.

Page 172: FROM LETTERS TO NUMBERS
1. 2,313; 2. 2,656; 3. 562

Page 172: CENTS AND SHAPES

PUZZLE 1
2 pennies in 2 moves

PUZZLE 2
2 pennies in 5 moves

Page 172: WHAT AM I? 11

POPULATION, Page 182: A CITIZENSHIP TEST

1. 50; 2. there is one star for each state; 3. George Washington; 4. nine;
5. the president, with the approval of the Senate; 6. the executive, judicial, and
legislative branches; 7. 100; 8. for six-year terms; 9. "The Star-Spangled Banner";
10. the Speaker of the House of Representatives

SIGNS & SYMBOLS, Page 203

TAKE A SECOND LOOK I'LL SEE YOU AT 3 AFTER SCHOOL

THE HORSE CORRAL CODE A. THE SNOW FALLS; B. SEND ME A MESSAGE

TRANSPORTATION, Page 233

TRANSPORTATION PUZZLE

1. THE FIRST WHEELS WERE MADE OF WOOD.
2. THE FIRST MASS-PRODUCED CAR WAS THE MODEL T.
3. THE FIRST MASS-TRANSIT SYSTEM USED HORSE-DRAWN STAGECOACHES.

UNITED STATES, Page 270: FILL IN THE FRAME

	M	A	J	O	R	I	T	Y			
A		M						O			
R		E		R				L		A	
C	O	N	S	T	I	T	U	T	I	O	N
T		D		G		N		V			T
I		M	Y	T	H		I		E		H
C		E		T			T	A	B	L	E
		N		S			E		R		M
V	O	T	E	S		I	D	E	A	S	
E		S						N			
T				T	E	R	M		C		
O	N	E						H	E	A	R

◀ PUZZLE ANSWERS ▶

WEATHER, Page 297

UPS & DOWNS

3.	W	I	N	D	S	
6.	C	E	L	S	I	U	S
4.	M	E	A	S	U	R	E
1.	H	O	T	T	E	S	T
5.	W	A	T	C	H	
7.	D	E	G	R	E	E	S
2.	T	W	I	S	T	E	R

CHOICES

1. c; 2. a; 3. b

WORDS WITHIN WORDS

Here are some words that can be formed from TEMPERATURE. How many of them did you find? Did you find any others?

4 letters: epee, mare, mart, mate, meat, meet, mere, mute, mutt, pare, part, pate, pear, peat, peer, perm, pert, pram, puma, pure, putt, ramp, rapt, rare, rate, ream, reap, rear, rump, tame, tape, tarp, tart, taut, team, tear, teem, temp, term, tram, trap, tree, true

5 letters: eater, erupt, matte, meter, peter, prate, rupee, puree, purer, taper, tempt, tepee, tramp, treat, truer, trump, utter

6 letters: ampere, matter, mature, mutate, mutter, patter, putter, reaper, repeat, repute, tamper, teeter, temper, turret

7 letters: amputee, rapture, retreat, tempera, tempura

8 letters: permeate

9 letters: premature, temperate

WEIGHTS & MEASURES, Page 300

METRIC BRAIN TEASERS

1. Toby's car, which runs the equivalent of about 40 miles per gallon, is the more fuel-efficient car. 2. swimming race, relay, run, and bike race.

WORLD HISTORY, Page 316: HISTORY SEARCH

G	N	I	M	R	A	F	H	S
H	A	N	C	I	E	N	T	I
N	O	D	I	E	S	O	P	Y
S	U	E	Z	E	N	O	A	C
N	O	P	A	E	W	S	M	A
I	T	E	Y	E	O	O	R	R
G	R	N	R	R	D	R	O	C
E	E	D	R	E	A	E	M	O
R	M	E	R	I	P	M	E	M
I	O	N	A	P	A	J	I	E
A	H	T	W	O	R	G	Y	D

A

B

C

M

Illustration and Photo Credits

This product/publication includes images from Artville, Comstock, Corbis, Corel, Map Art, PhotoDisc, and the ArtToday web site, which are protected by the copyright laws of the U.S., Canada, and elsewhere. Used under license.

ILLUSTRATION: Teresa Anderko: **59, 65, 91, 92, 106, 198, 270**; Dolores Bego: **73, 82, 86, 88, 89, 175, 204**; Olivia McElroy: **94**; Chris Reed: **53**.

PHOTOGRAPHY: 9: Britney Spears, © AP/Wide World Photos; Tiger Woods, © AP/Wide World Photos; Steve Irwin, © AP/Wide World Photos; Julia Roberts & Benjamin Bratt, © AP/Wide World Photos. **10:** Drew Barrymore & Tom Green, © Reuters NewMedia Inc./Corbis. **11:** Sarah Michelle Gellar & Freddie Prinze Jr., © AP/Wide World Photos; Julia Roberts & Benjamin Bratt, © AP/Wide World Photos. **12:** Destiny's Child, © AP/Wide World Photos. **13:** O-Town, © AP/Wide World Photos; Britney Spears, © AP/Wide World Photos. **14:** Steve Irwin, © AP/Wide World Photos. **15:** Amanda Bynes, © Reuters NewMedia Inc./Corbis; Carson Daly, © Reuters NewMedia Inc./Corbis. **16:** Mary-Kate & Ashley Olsen, © AP/Wide World Photos. **17:** Frankie Muniz, © Reuters NewMedia Inc./Corbis; Billy Gilman, © AP/Wide World Photos. **18:** Tiger Woods, © AP/Wide World Photos. **19:** Derek Jeter & Alex Rodriguez, © AP/Wide World Photos; Venus & Serena Williams, © AP/Wide World Photos. **20:** Ichiro Suzuki, Robert Laberge/Allsport; Mia Hamm & Julie Foudy, © AP/Wide World Photos. **21:** Marshall Faulk, © AP/Wide World Photos; Tony Hawk, © AP/Wide World Photos. **22:** Bush inauguration, © AP/Wide World Photos; Hillary Rodham Clinton, © AP/Wide World Photos. **23:** Dale Earnhardt, © AP/Wide World Photos/Fort Pierce News Tribune; Petty Officer Josef Edmunds, © Reuters NewMedia Inc./Corbis. **24:** George Thampy, © AP/Wide World Photos; The Beatles, © AP/Wide World Photos. **27:** Venus Williams, © Clive Brunskill/AllSport. **33:** Licker the Dachshund, © Jeff Rutzky. **43:** Cassatt painting, Copyright ©2001 National Gallery of Art, Washington D.C. **45:** Rock and Roll Hall of Fame, © Jay Jaffe; Cézanne painting, Copyright ©2001 National Gallery of Art, Washington D.C.; **46:** *A Year Down Yonder* by Richard Peck, Dial Books for Young Readers. **48:** *Miracle's Boys* by Jacqueline Woodson, G.P. Putnam's Sons. **52:** Burj al Arab hotel, Courtesy of Jumeirah International. **80:** Addie Joss baseball card, Courtesy of Library of Congress Prints and Photographs Division; AIBO, Courtesy of Sony Electronics, Inc. **101:** Titanium Power Book, © Jeff Rutzky. **113:** Quarters, Sacagawea, Courtesy of the U.S. Mint. **120:** *Shrek*, © AP/Wide World Photos/Film Magic. **121:** *Chicken Run*, © AP/Wide World Photos/Dreamworks Pictures. **123:** Julia Stiles, © AP/Wide World Photos; Daniel Radcliffe, © AP/Wide World Photos. **125:** Museum exhibit, Courtesy of Troy State Univ. Montgomery Rosa Parks Library & Museum. **126:** Barbie, © Ken Botto & Gazelle Technologies, Inc.; Willamette meteorite, © AP/Wide World Photos. **128:** 'N Sync, © AP/Wide World Photos. **185:** Macy Gray, © AP/Wide World Photos. **197:** COSI exhibit, Photo by Brad Feinknopf © COSI, 1999. **207:** Surface of Mars, Courtesy of NASA/JPL/Caltech. **208:** Hale-Bopp, Courtesy of NASA/JPL/Caltech. **210:** Meteor, Courtesy of NASA/MSF. **213:** Space Station, Courtesy of NASA/HSF. **214:** Kazuhiro Sasaki, © AP/Wide World Photos. **215:** Willie Mays and Roy Campanella, Courtesy of Library of Congress Prints and Photographs Division. **216:** Bill Russell & Michael Jordan, © AP/Wide World Photos. **217:** Cynthia Cooper, © AP/Wide World Photos. **218:** Jackie Stiles, © AP/Wide World Photos/Springfield News-Leader. **219:** Peyton Manning, © AP/Wide World Photos. **221:** Chris Weinke, © AP/Wide World Photos. **222:** Annika Sorenstam, © AP/Wide World Photos. **223:** Mario Lemieux, © AP/Wide World Photos. **226:** Michelle Kwan, © AP/Wide World Photos. **229:** Gustavo Kuerten, © AP/Wide World Photos. **232:** Submarine, © AP/Wide World Photos. **233:** Boeing 777, Courtesy of The Boeing Company. **237:** Roller coaster (bottom), © AP/Wide World Photos. **246:** George W. & Laura Bush, © AP/Wide World Photos. **248–253:** U.S. Presidents 1–36, © 1967 by Dover Publications. **253:** President Nixon, Courtesy of Richard Nixon Library; President Ford, Courtesy of Gerald R. Ford Museum; President Carter, Courtesy of Jimmy Carter Library; President Reagan, Courtesy of Ronald Reagan Library; President George Bush, Courtesy of Bush Presidential Material Project; President Clinton, Courtesy of the White House; President George W. Bush, Eric Draper—The White House. **254:** Laura Bush, Eric Draper—The White House. **256:** President Johnson, © 1967 by Dover Publications; President Clinton, Courtesy of the White House. **257:** Supreme Court, Courtesy of the Supreme Court Historical Society. **264:** Model T Ford, Courtesy of The Center for American History, The University of Texas at Austin. **265:** Jackie Robinson, Courtesy of Library of Congress Prints and Photographs Division; Bill Clinton, Courtesy of Library of Congress Prints and Photographs Division. **266:** Thurgood Marshall, Courtesy of Library of Congress Prints and Photographs Division. **267:** Louis Armstrong, Courtesy of Library of Congress Prints and Photographs Division; Jackie Robinson, Courtesy of Library of Congress Prints and Photographs Division. **295:** Hurricane, © AP/Wide World Photos; Tornado, © J. Pat Carter/AP/Wide World Photos. **302:** Egyptian hieroglyphs, © Edward A. Thomas.

FRONT COVER: Venus Williams, © Clive Brunskill/AllSport; X-33, Courtesy of NASA/HSF; Cybiko, Courtesy of Cybiko, Inc.

THE WORLD ALMANAC FOR KIDS
"KIDS SPEAK OUT!" Contest
TELL US WHO'S IMPORTANT

The World Almanac for Kids is proud to present its "Kids Speak Out!" Contest. One Grand Prize Winner and 2,000 Runners-Up will be chosen from among the entries received.

▶ The **Grand Prize Winner** will receive an all-expense-paid trip for four to Washington, D.C.

▶ **2,000 Runners-Up** will receive a limited edition *World Almanac for Kids* T-shirt.

The Grand Prize includes transportation to Washington, D.C., lodging for four nights, and three meals per day for four days. The winner will receive the opportunity to meet with a member of Congress, plus the chance to visit such noted national landmarks as the White House, the Capitol, the Washington Monument, the Lincoln Memorial, Ford's Theater, the Smithsonian National Air and Space Museum, and much more.

To enter, kids must write and explain who they think are the **three most important people** in the world today, and why. Entry is limited to kids aged 6-14, and all entries must be received by February 28, 2002. All entries must include the respondent's name, complete address, age, and daytime phone number. Entries should be sent via our Web site or via mail, fax, or e-mail to:

World Almanac for Kids
"Kids Speak Out!" Contest
512 Seventh Avenue, 22nd Floor
New York, NY 10018

Fax: (646) 312-6839

EMAIL info@waegroup.com

WEB SITE http://www.worldalmanacforkids.com

Frank Maguire, winner of The World Almanac for Kids *"2000 In 2000" Contest, with Senator Bill Nelson of Florida* ▶

The World Almanac for Kids "Kids Speak Out!" Contest Rules:
No purchase necessary. Contest open to all residents of the continental United States aged six to fourteen. Enter by explaining who you think are the three most important people in the world today, and why. Send your name, complete address, age, and daytime phone number to: World Almanac for Kids "Kids Speak Out!" Contest, 512 Seventh Avenue, 22nd Floor, New York, NY 10018. Entries may be received by February 28, 2002. Multiple entries in one submission are not permitted. Entries will be judged on originality of content and description. One winner will receive an all-expense-paid trip for four to Washington, D.C., including transportation, lodging for four nights, and three meals per day for four days; 2,000 runners-up will receive a specially designed *World Almanac for Kids* T-shirt. All taxes on prizes are the responsibility of the winners. Winners will be notified on or about March 15, 2002. Submission of entry constitutes entrant's consent (or that of their parent/legal guardian) to irrevocably assign to World Almanac Books any and all rights to entry, including, but not limited to, intellectual property rights. Acceptance of prize constitutes winners' permission to use their names, likenesses, cities, and states, and to be photographed for advertising and publicity purposes without additional compensation except where prohibited by law. Void where prohibited or restricted by law. All federal, state, and local laws and regulations apply. All entries are bound by the full Rules. To obtain full Rules, send a self-addressed, stamped envelope to World Almanac Books, World Almanac for Kids "Kids Speak Out!" Contest Rules, 512 Seventh Avenue, 22nd Floor, New York, NY 10018 or visit http://www.worldalmanacforkids.com.